ISSUES IN AMERICAN PROTESTANTISM

ROBERT L. FERM is John Knox McLean Professor of
Religion and Chairman of the Department of Reli-
gion at Pomona College in Claremont, California.
He holds degrees from the College of Wooster, the
Yale University Divinity School and the Yale Grad-
uate School. He has published one previous book,
Readings in the History of Christian Thought
(1964).

ISSUES IN AMERICAN PROTESTANTISM:

A DOCUMENTARY HISTORY
FROM THE PURITANS
TO THE PRESENT

•

Edited with
an Introduction and Notes
by ROBERT L. FERM

ANCHOR BOOKS
DOUBLEDAY & COMPANY, INC.
GARDEN CITY, NEW YORK

The Anchor Books edition is the first publication of *Issues in American Protestantism*.
Anchor Books edition: 1969

Grateful acknowledgment is made to the following for material included in this book:

ABINGDON PRESS "The Fatal Apostasy of the Modern Church," by Edwin Lewis. *Religion in Life*, Autumn, 1933. Reprinted by permission of the publisher and Faulkner Lewis; "The Post-Protestant-Concept and America's Two Religions," by Sidney E. Mead. *Religion in Life*, copyright © 1964 Abingdon Press. Reprinted by permission of the publisher and Dr. Sidney E. Mead.

THE CHRISTIAN CENTURY FOUNDATION "Beyond Modernism," by Harry Emerson Fosdick. Copyright 1935 Christian Century Foundation; "Reformation: Continuing Imperative," by H. Richard Niebuhr. Copyright © 1960 Christian Century Foundation; "Ten Years that Shook my World," by Reinhold Niebuhr. Copyright 1939 Christian Century Foundation. All reprinted by permission of the publisher.

HARPER & ROW, PUBLISHERS Excerpts from *Acres of Diamonds*, by Russell Conwell; excerpts from *The Evanston Report; The Second Assembly of the World Council of Churches*, 1954. Edited by W. A. Visster 'T Hooft. Copyright © 1955 Harper & Brothers, Publishers, Inc. Reprinted by permission of Harper & Row, Publishers and World Council of Churches.

DR. CARL MC INTIRE Excerpts from *Servants of Apostasy*. Reprinted by permission.

ROBERT E. MATHEWS "Modernism and the Bible," from *The Faith of Modernism*, by Shailer Mathews. Reprinted by permission.

PRINCETON THEOLOGICAL SEMINARY "The New Theological Situation," by Daniel Day Williams. *Theology Today*, January, 1968. Reprinted by permission of Princeton Theological Seminary and the author.

TO
Flournoy

CONTENTS

Contents

Introduction

Religion has been the basis of the most important American settlements; religion kept their little community together—religion assisted them in their revolutionary struggle; it was religion to which they appealed in defending their rights, and it was religion, in fine, which taught them to prize their liberties. It is with the solemnities of religion that the declaration of independence is yet annually read to the people from the pulpit, or that Americans celebrate the anniversaries of the most important events in their history. It is to religion they have recourse whenever they wish to impress the popular feeling with anything relative to their country; and it is religion which assists them in all their national undertakings. The Americans look upon religion as a promoter of civil and political liberty; and have, therefore, transferred to it a large portion of the affection which they cherish for the institutions of their country.[1]

This comment of the perceptive Czech observer of American life, Francis Grund, writing in 1837, could be applied to every period of American history. However, despite the pervasive religious sentiment in our national character we have not lacked theological and ecclesiastical conflict. American Protestantism has experienced many periods of rigorous and intense controversy, some engaging the attention of the entire population while others have been confined to small circles. This volume presents fundamental issues of debate, chosen to illustrate the major concerns of successive periods of Protestant history in the United States.

The first three sections deal with the development of Puritanism, from the founding of the New England colonies to the middle of the eighteenth century. Lately there has been great interest in the interpretation of the Puritan experiment in America and the complexity of this movement is gradually

[1] Francis Grund, *The Americans, in their Moral, Social and Political Relations* (Boston, 1837).

being recognized. The Puritans identified themselves with the Old Testament theme of God's chosen and covenanted people; to preserve their identity and unity in the new world, the structures of civil and ecclesiastical organization were clearly outlined. The church consisted only of the visible saints, though it was established and supported by all members of the state. Clarity of purpose and common presuppositions were possible within the original small group of settlers, but dissent soon appeared and it had to be dealt with and justification for its prevention and punishment stated. Section I presents the controversy between John Cotton and Roger Williams concerning the role of the state in matters of individual religious freedom.

By the 1650s the theological structure of the Puritan community was challenged. The "Holy Commonwealth" was comprised of the visible saints, and the full acts of grace were available only to those who publicly entered into covenant with God; only the children of regenerate members were baptised. The rationale and means to bind to the church the children of those members who as adults could not testify to their converted condition was stated in the Half Way Covenant of 1662 which permitted unregenerate members to present their children for baptism, though the Lord's Supper continued to be withheld. This led to the lengthy debate in the latter half of the seventeenth century concerning the place of the Lord's Supper in the life of the church. The issue between Solomon Stoddard and Increase Mather over the interpretation of the Lord's Supper caused a severe split within Congregationalism. [Section II] Though many came to adopt Stoddard's practice of allowing non-scandalous but unregenerate members to partake of the Eucharist, there were those who condemned this departure from the New England way. The issue recurred during and after the Great Awakening in the mid-eighteenth century.

There were sporadic revivals of religion in the later seventeenth and early eighteenth centuries, but the Great Awakening of the 1730s and 1740s, led by Jonathan Edwards, George Whitefield, and Gilbert Tennent, created vigorous controversy. Churches were divided and reorganized; ministers were ridi-

culed and dismissed; new evangelistic tools and tech-
niques were devised. Gilbert Tennent's support and Charles
Chauncy's criticism of revivalistic measures [Section III] illustrate the wide divergence of contemporary opinion.

Recent interpretations of the Great Awakening have noted
there the seeds of political change which were nurtured by
new theological currents in the latter half of the eighteenth
century, especially the rise of rational religion with its appeals
to natural law and reason and its emphasis on God's benevolence and man's freedom.[2] Domination of churches by foreign
authority ran counter to the spirit of the age. The attempt to
secure a colonial bishop for the Anglican churches in America
was viewed by many denominational leaders as a threat to
the developing desire for political independence. This issue,
which is an important part of the revolutionary period, is seen
in the controversy between Thomas Bradbury Chandler, the
Episcopalian, and Isaac Backus, a prominent Baptist leader.
[Section IV]

The nineteenth century was the formative period in the
shaping of American Protestantism. The first half of the century was marked by the effects of new issues in the New
England theological tradition, the influx of new immigrants,
the constitutional separation of church and state, westward
expansion, and the controversies which led to national tragedy
in the Civil War. The New Haven theology, so called because
of the work of Timothy Dwight and Nathaniel William Taylor, Professors at Yale College, became a major force in the
development of American Christianity. Taylor's role was to
steer a middle course between the rigidity of later Edwardsean Calvinism and the growth of Unitarianism, led by William Ellery Channing. Edwardsean theology or the New
Divinity tradition (developed by Jonathan Edwards, Joseph
Bellamy, and Samuel Hopkins) emphasized the sovereignty
of God, the depravity of man, and a strict view of church

[2] See Alan Heimert, *Religion and the American Mind: from
the Great Awakening to the Revolution* (Cambridge, Mass., 1966)
and Alan Heimert and Perry Miller, editors, *The Great Awakening*
(Indianapolis, 1967).

membership. It was a theology which did not fit the temper of the revolutionary era. The Unitarianism of Channing showed clearly the themes of enlightenment religion: the parental and benevolent character of God, the stress on human agency and freedom, and the need for conformity of doctrine to enlightened reason. Though Taylor assumed the role of a defender of the old against the innovation of Channing, his position was on middle ground between the New Divinity and Unitarian strains. Sydney Ahlstrom has perceptively described Taylor's influence. "The chief representative significance of (Timothy) Dwight, Taylor, and (Lyman) Beecher[3] consists in the impetus they gave to a broad New School tradition of Reformed theology and practice. As expounded by various Congregational, Presbyterian, Methodist, and Baptist theologians, 'New Schoolism' became, in effect, the ecumenical theology of nonsectarian revivalism, the Sunday School movement, foreign and domestic missions, and a wide array of organized reform activities, notably the temperance crusade. One can almost speak of it as the theology of American Evangelical Protestantism during its nineteenth century heyday. It was frankly Arminian in its modifications of predestinarian dogma, vigorous in its emphasis on conversion and personal holiness, immensely moralistic in its definition of the good life, strong in millennial fervor, determined to make a model of America's Protestant democracy, and belligerently suspicious of Roman Catholicism both as a rapidly growing church and as a possible influence on Christian belief and practice."[4] Section V includes selections from major essays of Taylor and Channing.

Revivalism permeated most denominations in the westward movement of the population. Charles Finney, probably the best-known revivalist of the period, shows affinity with Taylor's theology, though he moved beyond the Yale theologian into more pietistic modes of argument and activity. The fervor

[3] Lyman Beecher was a student of Timothy Dwight, close friend of N. W. Taylor, and a defender of the "New Haven" Theology.

[4] Sydney E. Ahlstrom, *Theology in America* (Indianapolis, 1967), pp. 44–45.

prompted by the numerous revivalists was strongly resisted by those seeking to retain a tie to the confessional patterns of continental Protestantism. The Mercersburg theology, led by John W. Nevin and Philip Schaff, attempted to preserve the denominational identity of the German Reformed Church in the face of the adoption of revivalistic measures. Section VI deals with the issue between Charles Finney and John W. Nevin.

Other issues brought denominational conflict. Opposing views over the institution of slavery can be directly related to the divisions within the Methodist, Baptist, and Presbyterian Churches in the 1830s and 1840s. Included in Section VII are selections from southern spokesmen indicating the character of the arguments pro and con. Though immigrant churches were not as involved in the issue of slavery, division occurred in these bodies as a result of controversy over the accommodation of the churches to developing patterns of American church life. The controversy within Lutheranism is the most illustrative; in that church opposing schools of thought were created, with one group, led by Samuel Simon Schmucker, emphasizing the similarities and possible lines of co-operation between Lutherans and other denominations, and those within Lutheranism who sought to retain an ecclesiastical and confessional distinctiveness. [Section VIII] The turn to denominational self-consciousness was not restricted to the Lutheran Church; similar issues occurred within the Presbyterian, Baptist, Methodist and Roman Catholic traditions.

After the Civil War the major issues in American Protestantism cut across denominational lines. The general trend is that described as the rise of liberalism, a product of changes in the intellectual and social realms. The liberals sought to interpret Christian faith in light of discoveries in the sciences and new needs produced by an increasingly urbanized and industrialized society. In Section IX selections illustrating two major issues of this period, the Social Gospel and Modernism, are included, beginning with Theodore T. Munger's essay on "The New Theology"; this irenic testimony of the pastor of the Congregational Church in New Haven, Connecticut, described the differences between the "old" and "new" theology.

The Social Gospel arose from liberal theological presuppositions. Those who claimed allegiance to this movement were concerned for the relevance of the Christian faith to the problems of human degradation and urban blight that accompanied the industrial expansion of the latter half of the nineteenth century. Walter Rauschenbusch and Washington Gladden stand out as the leading spokesmen of the movement. On the opposite side of the spectrum, Russell Conwell, an evangelist for the "Gospel of Wealth," defended the theme of "wealth to the man of morality" in his address, "Acres of Diamonds." Though there were similar theological presuppositions in Gladden and Conwell they saw the issue differently. As Winthrop Hudson has remarked, Gladden interpreted Christianity in ethical terms. "Being a Christian," Gladden wrote, "was not to be confused with submission to certain outward rites, nor with an acceptance of a body of dogma, nor with an emotional mystical experience. To be a Christian means simply to follow Christ . . . and the way to begin is just to begin. All disturbing questions of ability and inability, of election and condemnation, can be laid to one side."[5] If Gladden had what may be described as the practical interest of the churchman, it would be fair to describe Walter Rauschenbusch as the theological interpreter of the Social Gospel. He shared the marks of the "new" theology: the stress on the divine immanence, the theme of the Kingdom of God, the change from an individualistic to a social interpretation of traditional Christian themes, though he was not as sanguine about the possibilities of the redemption of the social order as were other leaders. H. Richard Niebuhr's description of his task is accurate: "Though his theory of the relation of God and man often seemed liberal he continued to speak the language of the prophets and St. Paul."[6]

After 1920 some theologians centered their attention on

[5] Winthrop Hudson, *The Great Tradition of the American Churches* (New York, 1963), p. 187.

[6] H. Richard Niebuhr, *The Kingdom of God in America* (New York, 1937, 1959), p. 194.

the relation between science and religion. These "modernists" were not pastors of churches, but theological professors, trained in the disciplines of philosophy and the social sciences. All questions were open for examination; confessional presuppositions came under close scrutiny. Shailer Mathews was a central spokesman for this movement, which may be described as the "left wing" branch of liberal theology. This more radical interpretation of the Christian faith brought forth vehement protests from conservative theologians. The accommodation of theology to scientific methodologies, historical studies which questioned the normative character of creedal and doctrinal expression, the criticism of the Bible which undercut, for some, the authority of the Biblical witness, could not go unchallenged. Defenders of the old appeared in most of the major denominations, causing intense debates and frequent heresy trials. The character of the issue may be seen in the selections from Mathews and a conservative theologian, J. Greshman Machen.

In recent years American Protestantism has seen the pendulum swing from a revival of classical Christian doctrine and theological argument, as witnessed in the "neo-orthodox" movement, to the wide public notice that has been given to the "radical" or "death of God" theology. The 1930s and 1940s brought a swift change to Protestant theology. The critiques of liberalism which had begun a generation earlier on the continent reached the United States in this period and the work of Soren Kierkegaard, Karl Barth, and Emil Brunner became the major diet of the theological curriculum. In Section X some issues of the period are posed in the selections from Edwin Lewis' early and vehement attack on the presuppositions of liberalism, the statement of a "chastened" liberal, Harry Emerson Fosdick, and autobiographical reflections of Reinhold Niebuhr. To paraphrase Niebuhr, these were ten years that shook the theological world.

In the neo-orthodox movement the classical themes of the sovereignty of God, the sinfulness of man, and the search for a theological basis for church unity were dominant. The ecumenical movement cannot be understood apart from the revival of these traditional affirmations of the church's faith.

Ecumenical activity brought strong reaction from conservative churchmen. They saw a dangerous involvement of the churches in social issues and the threat of the formation of an inclusive church without doctrinal distinctiveness. Dimensions of this issue are presented in Section XI, in selections from the Evanston Assembly of the World Council of Churches and from the testimony of Carl McIntire, perhaps the most outspoken critic of ecumenical activity.

In the past decade American Protestantism has been moving in widely divergent directions. We have gone beyond the heyday of neo-orthodoxy to a new form of liberalism, shaped by men who were trained by Richard and Reinhold Niebuhr, Karl Barth, and Paul Tillich. New forms of social action within the churches recall to mind some facets of the Social Gospel. Much attention is being given to the problems and possibilities of a religiously pluralistic culture and to tentative and probing searches for ways to state the Christian faith in new forms. Section XII presents an analysis of the religiosity of Americans and a critique of that analysis, from Will Herberg and Sidney Mead respectively. Included also are statements from two contemporary theologians, H. Richard Niebuhr and Daniel Day Williams, which indicate the breadth of theological interest in this decade.

*   *   *

The purpose of this volume is to serve as a catalyst to the student of Protestant history in the United States. It makes no pretense of being a comprehensive text. The guiding intent of the editor has been to illustrate major issues with documents of the period, some of which are chosen as direct confrontations between individuals, others as perspectives of contemporaries on issues of their period. Substantial selections from essays and documents are in the editor's judgment more valuable to the student than short pieces from many sources.

The only change in the documents has been the modernization of the spelling and correction of obvious typographical errors. Each section has an introductory preface to set a brief context for the selections included; in addition, a bibliographical note is placed at the end of each section to direct the student to pertinent interpretations of the period.

In recent years there have appeared several excellent surveys of American religious history. The student's attention should be called to four major studies. Winthrop Hudson's *Religion in America: An Historical account of the development of American Religious life* (New York: Charles Scribner's Sons, 1965) is the most comprehensive work presently available. Hudson's other volume, *American Protestantism* (Chicago: University of Chicago Press, 1961) is a broad sketch, though it tends to be marked by definite theological presuppositions which color his interpretations. Clifton E. Olmstead, *History of Religion in the United States* (Englewood Cliffs, N.J.: Prentice Hall, 1960) is a thorough, though unimaginative, encyclopedic tool. Edwin Gaustad, *A Religious History of America* (New York: Harper & Row, 1966) is useful and contains excerpts from documents placed within the text of the book. The forthcoming work of Sydney E. Ahlstrom, to be published by the Yale University Press, should be the most thorough study of American religious history.

I refer the reader also to five volumes which do not attempt a comprehensive survey but offer suggestive interpretations of American religion: Will Herberg, *Protestant Catholic Jew* (Garden City, N.Y.: Doubleday, Anchor Books, 1955, revised edition, 1960); Sidney E. Mead, *The Lively Experiment: The Shaping of Christianity in America* (New York: Harper & Row, 1963); Franklin Littell, *From State Church to Pluralism: A Protestant Interpretation of Religion in America* (Garden City, N.Y.: Doubleday, Anchor Books, 1962); H. Richard Niebuhr, *The Kingdom of God in America* (New York: Harper & Row, 1959) and William Clebsch, *From Sacred to Profane America* (New York: Harper & Row, 1967).

In addition the two volumes of H. Shelton Smith, Robert T. Handy, and Lefferts Loetscher, *American Christianity: An Historical Interpretation with Representative Documents* (New York: Charles Scribner's Sons, Volume I, 1960 and Volume II, 1963) are valuable for both source materials and introductory comments. Other documents are available in

Sydney E. Ahlstrom, editor, *Theology in America: The Major Protestant Voices from Puritanism to Neo-Orthodoxy* (Indianapolis: Bobbs-Merrill, 1967). Edwin Scott Gaustad's *Historical Atlas of Religion in America* (New York: Harper & Row, 1962) is an unusually helpful volume with maps and charts showing the growth and location of denominational groups.

ROBERT L. FERM

Pomona College
Claremont, California

I. LIBERTY OF CONSCIENCE

INTRODUCTION

In New England the issue of freedom of conscience in religious matters was present from the beginning. The first generation immigrants came to establish the "city on the hill," the "holy Commonwealth." In tightly knit communities It was possible to deal with dissent, but with new colonists who came for economic rather than religious reasons and the appearance of the second and third generation Puritans, challenges were made to the "New England Way."

In working out the covenant theme, the basis of Puritan theology, the New England Puritans devised a complicated relationship between church and state.[1] The Cambridge Platform of 1648 was the ecclesiastical articulation of Puritan theory.[2] Though the Platform states that civil government was not to intrude upon church government, or *vice versa*, the relation between the two realms in matters of ecclesiastical dissension became ambiguous. Though "it is unlawful for church officers to meddle with the sword of the Magistrate, so it is unlawful for the Magistrate to meddle with the work proper to church officers." It is, however, "the duty of the Magistrate, to take care of matters of religion, and to improve his civil authority, for the observing of the duties commanded in the first, as well as for the duties commanded

[1] See Perry Miller, "The Marrow of Puritan Divinity," in *Errand into the Wilderness* (New York, 1964), p. 48 ff.

[2] The Cambridge Platform was adopted by a Synod in 1648 and received approval of the general Court of Massachusetts in 1651. The chapters of the Platform summarize the "Congregational Way" after two decades of Puritan experimentation and experience. The covenant was the basis of the local church; the autonomy of the church was affirmed, though mutual counsel among churches was encouraged. The full authority of Scripture in matters of doctrine and polity was recognized.

in the second table. They are called God's. The end of the
Magistrate's office, is not only the quiet and peaceable life of
the subject, in matters of righteousness and honesty, but
also in matters of godliness, yea of all godliness."[3]

John Winthrop (1588–1649) led a group of Puritans
within the Church of England to the New World in 1630. His
A Model of Christian Charity was composed aboard the
Arbella as the small group approached the shores of Massachusetts. Here was laid out the design of the Puritan
theocracy, based on the covenant idea.

The controversy between John Cotton (1584–1652) and
Roger Williams (1604–1684) must be seen against the structure of church-state relations and the theological presuppositions of New England Puritanism. Cotton, a graduate of
Trinity College, Cambridge, 1603, was the major spokesman
for the Congregational way. Williams, a graduate of Pem-
broke College, Cambridge, in 1627, sought the clear divorce
of the New England churches from the Anglican communion
and the separation of civil and ecclesiastical powers. In 1635
he was banished from the Massachusetts Bay Colony and
settled in Providence where he was instrumental in the
formation of the first Baptist Church in Rhode Island. The
pamphlet warfare between them lasted for several years;
the original treatise by Williams was entitled: *The Bloody
Tenent of Persecution for the cause of conscience discussed
in a conference between Truth and Peace;* Cotton replied
with *The Bloody Tenent washed white in the Blood of the
Lamb.* The New England church leaders sought to establish
a scriptural form of church government, with close relations
between the role of the magistrate and that of the clergy; the
will of God must prevail in both the secular and religious
domains. Heresy or dissent was viewed by Cotton as a threat
to the civil and religious peace and must be dealt with.

. . . the Church of Christ does not use the Arms of secular
power to compel men to the faith, or profession of the truth,

[3] Williston Walker, "The Cambridge Synod and Platform," in
The Creeds and Platforms of Congregationalism (New York, 1893),
p. 236.

for this is to be done by spiritual weapons, whereby Christians are to be exhorted, not compelled. But this hinders not that Christians sinning against light of faith and conscience, may justly be censured by the Church by excommunication, and by the civil sword also, in case they shall corrupt others to the perdition of their souls.[4]

This Williams could not accept. In the social realm the will of God must prevail, but the state may not enter into ecclesiastical disputes. The civil government may not interfere with the Church and the Church may not intrude upon the rights of the magistrates.

I hence observe, that there being in this Scripture held forth a two-fold state, a Civil state and a Spiritual, Civil officers and spiritual, civil weapons and spiritual weapons, civil vengeance and punishment, and a spiritual vengeance and punishment: although the Spirit speaks not here expressly of Civil Magistrates and their civil weapons, yet these States being of different Natures and Considerations, as far differing as Spirit from Flesh, I first observe, that Civil weapons are most improper and unfitting in matters of the Spiritual state and kingdom, though in the Civil state most proper and suitable . . .[5]

This was a challenge to the well being and orderliness of the "holy Commonwealth." Williams was a precursor of the idea of separation between church and state and had profound effect on later political theory.

[4] *The Controversy Concerning Liberty of Conscience in Matters of Religion, Truly Stated, and distinctly and plainly handled*, by Mr. John Cotton of Boston in New England (London, 1646), p. 13.

[5] Roger Williams, *The Bloody Tenet of Persecution for Cause of Conscience Discussed in a Conference Between Truth and Peace* (London, 1644), Ch. XLIV.

[1]

John Winthrop

A Model of Christian Charity*

God Almighty in his most holy and wise providence hath
so disposed of the Condition of mankind, as in all times some
must be rich some poor, some high and eminent in power
and dignity; others mean and in subjection.

THE REASON HEREOF:

1. *First,* to hold conformity with the rest of his works, being delighted to show forth the glory of his wisdom in the
variety and difference of the Creatures and the glory of his
power, in ordering all these differences for the preservation
and good of the whole, and the glory of his greatness that
as it is the glory of princes to have many officers, so this great
King will have many Stewards counting himself more honoured in dispensing his gifts to man by man, than if he did it
by his own immediate hand.

2. *Secondly,* That he might have the more occasion to
manifest the work of his Spirit: first, upon the wicked in
moderating and restraining them: so that the rich and mighty
should not eat up the poor, nor the poor, and despised rise
up against their superiors, and shake off their yoke; secondly
in the regenerate in exercising his graces in them, as in the
great ones, their love, mercy, gentleness, temperance etc., in
the poor and inferior sort, their faith patience, obedience etc:

3. *Thirdly,* That every man might have need of other,
and from hence they might be all knit more nearly together
in the Bond of brotherly affection: from hence it appears
plainly that no man is made more honorable than another

* From *Winthrop Papers,* Vol. II. The Massachusetts Historical
Society, 1931.

or more wealthy etc., out of any particular and singular respect to himself but for the glory of his Creator and the Common good of the Creature, Man; Therefore God still reserves the property of these gifts to himself, he there [Ezek. xvi, 17] calls wealth his gold and his silver etc. [Prov. iii, 9]. He claims their service as his due honor the Lord with thy riches etc. All men being thus (by divine providence) ranked into two sorts, rich and poor; under the first, are comprehended all such as are able to live comfortably by their own means duely improved; and all others are poor according to the former distribution. There are two rules whereby we are to walk one towards another: JUSTICE and MERCY. These are always distinguished in their Act and in their object, yet may they both concur in the same Subject in each respect; as sometimes there may be an occasion of showing mercy to a rich man, in some sudden danger of distress, and also doing of mere Justice to a poor man in regard of some particular contract etc. There is likewise a double Law by which we are regulated in our conversation one towards another: in both the former respects, the law of nature and the law of grace, or the moral law or the law of the gospel, to omit the rule of Justice as not properly belonging to this purpose otherwise then it may fall into consideration in some particular Cases: By the first of these laws man as he was enabled so withall [is] commanded to love his neighbor as himself upon this ground stands all the precepts of the moral law, which concerns our dealings with men. To apply this to the works of mercy this law requires two things first that every man afford his help to another in every want or distress; Secondly, That he perform this out of the same affection, which makes him careful of his own good according to that of our Savior, "Whatsoever ye would that men should do to you" [Matt. vii, 12]. This was practised by Abraham and Lot in entertaining the Angels and the old man of Gibea.

The Law of Grace or the Gospel hath some difference from the former as in these respects: first the law of nature was given to man in the estate of innocency; this of the gospel in the estate of regeneracy: secondly, the former propounds one man to another, as the same flesh and Image of God, this as a

brother in Christ also, and in the Communion of the same
spirit and so teacheth us to put a difference between Christians and others. Do good to all especially to the household
of faith; upon this ground the Israelites were to put a difference between the brethren of such as were strangers though
not of the Canaanites. Thirdly, The Law of nature could give
no rules for dealing with enemies for all are to be considered
as friends in the estate of innocency, but the Gospel commands love to an enemy. Proof! "If thine Enemy hunger feed
him; Love your Enemies, do good to them that hate you."
[Matt. v, 44.]

This Law of the Gospel propounds likewise a difference of
seasons and occasions. There is a time when a christian must
sell all and give to the poor as they did in the Apostles' times.
There is a time also when a christian (though they give not
all yet) must give beyond their ability, as they of Macedonia.
Likewise, community of perils calls for extraordinary liberality
and so doth Community in some special service for the
Church. Lastly, when there is no other means whereby our
Christian brother may be relieved in this distress, we must
help him beyond our ability, rather than tempt God, in putting
him upon help by miraculous or extraordinary means. . . .

The Apostle tells us that this love is the fulfilling of the
law, not that it is enough to love our brother and so no further, but in regard of the excellency of his parts giving any
motion to the other as the Soul to the body and the power it
hath to set all the faculties on work in the outward exercise
of this duty, as when we bid one make the clock strike he
doth not lay hand on the hammer which is the immediate
instrument of the sound but sets on work the first mover or
main wheel, knowing that will certainly produce the sound
which he intends; so the way to draw men to the works of
mercy is not by force of Argument from the goodness or
necessity of the work, for though this course may enforce a
rational mind to some present Act of mercy as is frequent in
experience, yet it cannot work such a habit in a Soul as shall
make it prompt upon all occasions to produce the same effect
but by framing these affections of love in the heart which

will as natively bring forth the other, as any cause doth produce the effect.

The definition which the scripture gives us of love is this Love is the bond of perfection. First, it is a bond, or ligament. Secondly, it makes the work perfect. There is no body but consists of parts and that which knits these parts together gives the body its perfection, because it makes each part so contiguous to others as thereby they do mutually participate with each other, both in strength and infirmity in pleasure and pain, to instance in the most perfect of all bodies, Christ and his church make one body: the several parts of this body considered apart before they were united were as disproportionate and as much disordering as so many contrary qualities or elements but when Christ comes and by his spirit and love knits all these parts to himself and each to other, it is become the most perfect and best proportioned body in the world. [Eph.: iv, 16.] "Christ by whom all the body being knit together by every joint for the furniture thereof according to the effectual power which is in the measure of every perfection of parts a glorious body without spot or wrinkle the ligaments hereof being Christ or his love for Christ is love." [I John: iv, 8.] So this definition is right Love is the bond of perfection.

From hence we may frame these Conclusions.

First, all true Christians are of one body in Christ. . . .

Secondly, The ligaments of this body which knit together are love.

Thirdly, No body can be perfect which wants its proper ligaments.

Fourthly, All the parts of this body being thus united are made so contiguous in a special relation as they must needs partake of each others strength and infirmity, joy, and sorrow, weal and woe. If one member suffers all suffer with it, if one be in honor, all rejoice with it.

Fifthly, This sensibleness and Sympathy of each others Conditions will necessarily infuse into each part a native desire and endeavour, to strengthen defend preserve and comfort the other. . . .

It rests now to make some application of this discourse by

the present design which gave the occasion of writing of it. Herein are 4 things to be propounded: first, the persons; secondly, the work; thirdly, the end; fourthly, the means.

First, for the persons, we are a Company professing ourselves fellow members of Christ, In which respect only though we were absent from each other many miles, and had our employments as far distant, yet we ought to account ourselves knit together by this bond of love, and live in the exercise of it, if we would have comfort of our being in Christ. . . .

Secondly, for the work we have in hand, it is by a mutual consent through a special overruling providence, and a more than an ordinary approbation of the Churches of Christ to seek out a place of Cohabitation and Consortship under a due form of Government both civil and ecclesiastical. In such cases as this the care of the public must oversway all private respects, by which not only conscience, but mere Civil policy doth bind us; for it is a true rule that particular estates cannot subsist in the ruin of the public.

Thirdly, the end is to improve our lives to do more service to the Lord the comfort and increase of the body of Christ whereof we are members, that ourselves and posterity may be the better preserved from the Common corruptions of this evil world to serve the Lord and work out our Salvation under the power and purity of his holy Ordinances.

Fourthly, for the means whereby this must be effected, they are twofold: a Conformity with the work and end we aim at; these we see are extraordinary, therefore we must not content ourselves with usual ordinary means. Whatsoever we did or ought to have done when we lived in England, the same must we do and more also where we go. That which the most in their Churches maintain as a truth in profession only, we must bring into familiar and constant practice; as in this duty of love we must love brotherly without dissimulation, we must love one another with a pure heart fervently, we must bear one another's burdens, we must not look only on our own things, but also on the things of our brethren. Neither must we think that the Lord will bear with such failings at our hands as he doth from those among whom we have lived, and that for three Reasons. I. In regard of the more near bond of marriage between him and us, wherein he hath taken us to be his after a most strict and peculiar manner which will make him the more Jealous of our love and obedience, so he tells the people of Israel: "you only have I known of all the families of the Earth therefore will I punish you for your Trangressions." II. Because the Lord will be sanctified in them that come near him. We know that there were many that corrupted the service of the Lord some setting up Altars before his own, others offering both strange fire and strange Sacrifices also; yet there came no fire from heaven, or other sudden Judgement upon them as did upon Nadab and Abihu, who yet we may think did not sin presumptuously. III. When God gives a special Commission he looks to have it strictly observed in every Article. When he gave Saul a Commission to destroy Amaleck, he indented with him upon certain Articles, and because he failed in one of the least, and that upon a fair pretence, it lost him the kingdom which should have been his reward, if he had observed his Commission. Thus stands the cause between God and us. We are entered into Covenant with him for this work, we have taken out a Commission, the Lord hath given us leave to draw our own Articles. We have professed to enterprise these Actions upon these and these ends, we have hereupon besought him of favor and blessing. Now if the Lord shall please to hear us, and bring us in peace to the place we desire, then hath he ratified this Covenant and sealed our Commission, [and] will expect a strict performance of the Articles contained in it; but if we shall neglect the observation of these Articles which are the ends we have propounded, and dissembling with our God, shall fall to embrace this present world and prosecute our carnal intentions, seeking great things for ourselves and our posterity, the Lord will surely break out in wrath against us, be revenged of such a perjured people, and make us know the price of the breach of such a Covenant.

Now the only way to avoid this shipwreck and to provide for our posterity is to follow the Counsel of Micah, to do Justly, to love mercy, to walk humbly with our God. For this end, we must be knit together in this work as one man; we must entertain each other in brotherly Affection; we must be willing to abridge ourselves of our superfluities, for the supply of others' necessities; we must uphold a familiar Commerce together in all meekness, gentleness, patience and liberality; we must delight in each other, make others' Conditions our own, rejoice together, mourn together, labor and suffer together, always having before our eyes our Commission and Community in the work, our Community as members of the same body. So shall we keep the unity of the spirit in the bond of peace. The Lord will be our God and delight to dwell among us, as his own people and will command a blessing upon us in all our ways, so that we shall see much more of his wisdom, power, goodness, and truth than formerly we have been acquainted with. We shall find that the God of Israel is among us, when ten of us shall be able to resist a thousand of our enemies, when he shall make us a praise and glory, that men shall say of succeeding plantations: the Lord make it like that of New England. For we must Consider that we shall be as a City upon a Hill, the eyes of all people are upon us. So that if we shall deal falsely with our God in this work we have undertaken and so cause him to withdraw his present help from us, we shall be made a story and a by-word through the world; we shall open the mouths of enemies to speak evil of the ways of God and all professors for God's sake; we shall shame the faces of many of God's worthy servants, and cause their prayers to be turned into Curses upon us till we be consumed out of the good land whither we are going. And to shut up this discourse with that exhortation of Moses, that faithful servant of the Lord, in his last farewell to Israel, [Deut. xxx]. . . . Beloved there is now set before us life and good, death and evil in that we are Commanded this day to love the Lord our God, and to love one another, to walk in his ways and to keep his Commandments and his Ordinance and his laws and the Articles of our Covenant with him, that we may live and be multiplied, and that the Lord our God may bless us in the land whither we go to possess it. But if our hearts shall turn away so that we will not obey, but shall be seduced and worship . . . other

gods, our pleasures, and profits, and serve them, it is propounded unto us this day, we shall surely perish out of the
good Land whither we pass over this vast Sea to possess it.

> Therefore, let us choose life,
> that we, and our Seed,
> may live; by obeying his
> voice, and cleaving to him,
> for he is our life, and
> our prosperity.

[2]

John Cotton
Liberty of Conscience*

The question which you put is, whether persecution for cause
of conscience be not against the doctrine of Jesus Christ,
the King of Kings.

Now by persecution for cause of conscience, I conceive you
mean either, for professing some point of doctrine; which you
believe in conscience to be a truth, or for practising some
work in conscience you believe to be a Religious duty.

Now in points of Doctrine, some are fundamental, without
right beliefs whereof a man cannot be saved; others are cir-
cumstantial or less principal, wherein men may differ in judgment without prejudice of salvation on either part. In like
sort, is points of practice, some concern the weightier duties
of the Law, as, what God we worship, and with what kind
of worship; whether such, as if it be right, Fellowship with
God is held; if corrupt, Fellowship with him is lost.

* John Cotton, *The Controversy Concerning Liberty of Conscience in Matters of Religion, Truly Stated, and Distinctly and
Plainly Handled* (London, 1646), pp. 7–14. This article of John
Cotton was in response to a statement from an English Baptist held
prisoner in Newgate.

Again, in points of Doctrine and Worship less principal, either they are held forth is a meek and peaceable way, though the King be erroneous or unlawful, or they are held forth with such arrogance and impetuousness, as tends and reaches (even of itself) to the disturbance of civil peace.

Finally, let me add this one distinction more; when we are persecuted for conscience sake, it is either for conscience rightly informed, or for erroneous and blind conscience. These things premised, I would lay down my answer to the question in certain conclusions.

First, it is not lawful to persecute any for conscience sake rightly informed, for in persecuting such, Christ himself is persecuted in them. *Acts* 9.4.

Secondly, for an erroneous and blind conscience, (even in fundamental and weighty points) it is not lawful to persecute any, until after admonition once or twice, and so the Apostle directs, *Titus* 3.10 and gives the reason, that in fundamental and principal points of Doctrine, or Worship, the Word of God is so clear, that he cannot but be convinced in conscience of the dangerous error of his way, after once and twice admonition wisely and faithfully dispensed. And then if any one persist it is not out of conscience, but against his conscience, as the Apostle says *Ver.* 11. he is subverted and sins, being condemned of himself, *viz.* of his own conscience: So that if such man after such admonition, shall still persist in the error of his ways, and be therefore punished, he is not persecuted for cause of conscience, but for sinning against his own conscience.

Thirdly, in things of lesser moment, whether points of Doctrine or Worship, if a man hold them forth in a spirit of Christian meekness and love (though with zeal and constancy) he is not to be persecuted, but tolerated, till God may be pleased to manifest his truth to him, *Phil.* 3.17. *Rom.* 14. 1, 2, 3, 4.

Fourthly, but if a man hold forth, or profess any error, or false way, with a boisterous and arrogant spirit, to the disturbance of civil peace, he may justly be punished according to the quality and measure of his disturbance caused by him.

Now let us consider your reasons or objections to the contrary.

1. *Object.* Your first head of Objections is taken from the Scripture, because Christ commands *to let alone the tares and wheat to grow together till the harvest. Mat.* 13.30. &c.

Answ. Tares are not briars and thorns, but partly hypocrites, like unto the godly, but indeed carnal, as the tares are like the wheat, but are not wheat: or partly such corrupt doctrine or practises as are indeed unfound, but yet such as come very near the truth, (as tares do to the wheat) and so near that good men may be taken with them, and so the persons in whom they grow, cannot be rooted out, but good will be rooted up with them. And in such a case Christ calls for toleration, not for penal prosecution, according to the third conclusion.

2. *Object.* In *Mat.* 15.14. Christ commands his Disciples *to let the blind alone till they fall into the ditch,* therefore he would have their punishment deferred till their final destruction.

Answ. He there speaks not to public Officers, whether in Church or Commonwealth, but to his private Disciples, concerning the Pharisees, over whom they had no power: And the command he gives to let them alone, is spoken in regard of themselves, or regarding the offence which they took at the wholesome Doctrine of the Gospel; as who should say, *though they be offended at this saying of mine, yet do not you fear their fear, nor be troubled at their offence which they take at my Doctrine, not out of sound judgment but, out of their blindness.* But this makes nothing to the matter in hand.

3. *Object.* In *Luk.* 9.54. Christ reproves his Disciples, who would have had fire come down from heaven, to consume the Samaritans, who refused to receive him.

And *Paul* teaching *Timothy,* not to strive, but to be gentle towards all men, suffering evil patiently.

Answ. Both these are directions to Ministers of the Gospel, how to deal (not with obstinate offenders in the Church that sin against conscience, but) either with men without, as the Samaritans were, and many unconverted Christians in Crete, whom *Titus* (as an Evangelist) was to seek to convert, or at best with some Jews or Gentiles in the Church, who though carnal, yet were not convinced of the error of their way: And it is true, it became not the spirit of the Gospel to convert Aliens, to the faith of Christ (such as the Samaritans were) by fire and brimstone, not to deal harshly in public Ministry, or private conference with all such contrary-minded men, as either had not entered into Church-fellowship, or if they had yet did hitherto sin of ignorance, not against conscience; But neither of both these do hinder the Ministers of the Gospel to proceed in a Church-way against Church-Members, when they become scandalous offenders, either in life or doctrine, much less do they speak at all of the civil Magistrates.

4. *Object.* From the prediction of the Prophets who foretold, that *carnal weapons should cease in the days of the Gospel, Esa.* 2.4. & 11.9. *Micah* 4.3.4. And the Apostle professes, *the weapons of our warfare are not carnal, 2., Cor.* 10.4. and Christ is so far from persecuting those that would not be of his Religion, that he charges his Disciples when they are persecuted themselves they should pray, when they are cursed they should bless: the reason whereof, seemed to be that they who are now persecutors, and wicked persecutors, may become true Disciples and converts.

Answ. Those predictions in the Prophets do only show, first with what kind of weapons he will subdue the Nations, to the obedience of the faith of the Gospel, not by fire and sword, and weapons of war, but by the power of the Word and Spirit, which no man doubts. Secondly, those predictions of the Prophets, show what the meek and peaceable temper will be of all the true converts to Christianity, not Lions, or Leopards, &c. not cruel oppressors, nor malignant opposers, or biters of one another: but do not forbid to drive ravenous wolves from the sheepfold, and to restrain them from devouring the sheep of Christ.

And when *Paul* says, *the weapons of our warfare are not carnal, but spiritual,* he denies not civil weapons of Justice to the civil Magistrate, but only to Church-Officers; and yet the weapons of such Officers he acknowledges to be such as though they be spiritual, yet are ready to take Vengeance of all disobedience, 2 *Cor.* 10.6. which have reference (amongst other Ordinances) to the censure of the Church against scandalous offenders.

When Christ commands his Disciples to bless them that curse them, and persecute them, he gives not a rule to Public Officers either in Church or Commonwealth, to suffer notorious sinners either in life or doctrine, to pass away with a blessing, but to private Christians to suffer persecution patiently, yes and to pray for their persecutors.

Again, Christ, it is true, would have his Disciples to be far from persecuting (for that is a sinful oppression of men) for righteousness sake, but that hinders not, but that he would have them execute upon all disobedience the judgment and vengeance required in the Word, 2 *Cor.* 10.6. *Rom.* 13.4. Fourthly, though it be true that wicked persons now may by the grace of God, become true Disciples, and Converts, yet may we not do evil, that good may come thereof, and evil it would be to tolerate notorious evil doers, whether seducing, teachers, or scandalous livers. Christ had something against the Angel of the Church of *Pergamus,* for tolerating them that held the Doctrine of *Balaam,* and against the Church of *Thiarira,* for tolerating *Jezabell* to teach and seduce, *Rev.* 2.14.20.

Your second head of reasons is taken from the professional and practice of famous Princes, King *James, Stephen* of *Poland,* King of *Bohemia.* Whereunto a treble Answer may briefly be returned.

1. We willingly acknowledge that none is to be persecuted at all, no more than they may be oppressed for righteousness sake.

Again, we acknowledge that none is to be punished for his conscience, though mis-informed, as has been said, unless his error be fundamental, or seditiously and turbulently promoted, and that after due conviction of conscience, that it may appear he is not punished for his conscience, but for sinning against his conscience.

Furthermore, we acknowledge none to be constrained to believe or profess the true Religion till he be convinced in judgment of the truth of it; but yet restrained he may from blaspheming the truth, and from seducing any unto pernicious errors.

2. We answer, what Princes profess and practice, is not a rule of conscience, they many times tolerate that in point of State policy, which cannot be justly tolerated in point of true Christianity.

Again, Princes many times tolerate offenders out of very necessity, when the offenders are too many or too mighty for them to punish; in which respect *David* tolerated *Joab* and his murderers but against his will.

3. We answer, that for those three Princes, named by you, who tolerated Religion, we can name you more and greater, who have not tolerated Heretics and Schismatics, not withstanding their pretense of conscience: For example, *Constantine* the great, at the request of the general Council of Nicea, banished *Arius* with some of his fellows, *Sozom. lib. 1 Eccles. Hist. cap.* 29.20. The same *Constantine* made a severe law against the Donatists, and the like proceedings were used against them by *Valentinian, Gratian* and *Theodosious,* as Augustine reports in *Epist.* 166 only *Julian* the Apostle granted liberty to Heretics, as well as unto Pagans, that he might by tolerating all weeds to grow, choke the vitals of Christianity, which was also the practice and sin of *Valens* the *Arius.*

Queen *Elizabeth* as famous for Government as any of the former, it is well known what Laws she made, and executed against Papists: yes and King *James* (one of your own witnesses) though he was slow in proceeding against Papists (as you say) for conscience sake, yet you are not ignorant how severely and sharply he punished those whom the malignant word calls Puritans, men of more conscience and better faith, than he tolerated.

I come now to your third and last argument taken from the judgment of ancient writers, yes even of Papists themselves, who have condemned persecution for conscience sake.

You begin with Hilary, whose testimony we might admit without any prejudice to the truth; for it is true the Christian Church does not persecute, but is persecuted, but to excommunicate a Heretic is not to persecute, that is not to punish an innocent, but a culpable and damnable person, and that not for conscience, but for persisting in error against light of conscience whereof it has been convinced.

It is true also what he says, that the Apostles did, neither may we propagate Christian Religion by the Sword, but if Pagans cannot be won by the Word, they are not to be compelled by the Sword: Nevertheless this hinders not, but that if they or any other should blaspheme the true God and his true Religion, they ought not to be severely punished, and no less do they deserve, who seduce from the truth to damnable Heresy or Idolatry.

Your next writer, (which is *Tertullian*) speaks to the same purpose in the place alleged by you, his intent was only to restrain *Scapula* the Romane Governor of *Africa* from the persecution of Christians, for not offering sacrifice to their Gods; and for that end fetches an Argument from natural equity not to compel any to say Religion, but to permit them either to believe willingly, or not to believe at all; which we acknowledge, and accordingly permit the Indians to continue in their unbeliefs: Nevertheless it will not therefore be lawful openly to tolerate the Worship of Devils or Idols; or the seduction of any from the truth.

When *Tertullian* faith, another man's Religion neither hurts nor profits any: It must be understood of private worship, and Religion professed in private, otherwise a false Religion professed by the Members of a Church, or by such as have given their names to Christ, will be the ruin and desolation of the Church, as appears by the threats of Christ to the Churches of *Asia, Rev. 2.*

Your next Author *Jerome* crosses not the truth, nor advantages not your cause, for we grant what he says, that heresy must be cut off with the sword of the spirit: But this hinders not but that being so cut down, if the Heretic will still persist in his heresies to the seducing of others, he may be cut off by the civil sword, to prevent the perdition of others. And that to be *Jerome's* meaning appears by his note upon that of the Apostle (a little leaven leavens the whole lump) therefore, says he, a spark as soon as it appears, is to be extinguished, and the leaven to be removed from the rest of the dough, rotten pieces of flesh are to be cut off, and a scabbed beast is to be driven from the sheepfold, least the whole house, mass of dough, body and flock, be set on fire with the spark, be sowed with the leaven, be putrified with the rotten flesh, perish with the scabbed beast.

Brentius (whom you quote next) speaks not to your cause, we willingly grant him and you, that man has no power to make Laws to bind the conscience; but this hinders not, but that men may see the Laws of God observed, which do bind conscience.

The like answer may be returned to *Luther*, whom you next allege.

First, the government of the civil Magistrate reaches no further than over the bodies and goods of their subjects, not over their souls, and therefore they may not undertake to give laws to the souls and consciences of men.

Secondly, that the Church of Christ does not use the Arms of secular power to compel men to the faith, or profession of the truth, for this is to be done by spiritual weapons, whereby Christians are to be exhorted, not compelled. But this hinders not that Christians sinning against the light of faith and conscience, may justly be censored by the Church by excommunication, and by the civil sword also, in case they shall corrupt others to the perdition of their souls.

As for the testimony of the Popish book, we weigh it not, as knowing (whatsoever they speak for toleration of Religion, where themselves are under the hatches) when they came to sit at Stern, they judge and practice quite the contrary, as both their writing and judicial proceedings have testified to the world these many years.

To shut up this Argument from testimony of Writers; It is well known, that *Augustine* retracted this opinion of yours, which in his younger times he had held, but after in riper age reversed and refuted, as appears in his second book of retractions, *cap.* 5. and in his *Epistles* 48.50. and in his first book against *Parmenianus, cap.* 17. he shows that if the Donatists were punished with death, they were justly punished, and in his 1 Tractate upon *John,* they murder, says he, souls, and themselves are afflicted in body, they put men to everlasting death, and yet they complain when themselves are put to suffer temporal death.

Optatus in his third book, justified *Macharius*, who had put some Heretics to death, that he had done no more herein, than what Moses, Phineas, and Elias had done before him.

Bernard in his 66. Sermon in *Cantica*, out of doubt (says he) it is better they should be restrained by the sword of him who bears not the sword in vain, than that they should be suffered to draw many others into their error, for he is the Minister of God for wrath to every evil doer.

Calvins judgment is well known, who procured the death *Michael Servetus* for pertinacy in heresy, and defended his fact by a book written of that Argument.

Beza also wrote a book *de Hereticis morte plectendis*, that Heretics are to be punished with death, Arelius likewise took the like course about the death of *Valentius Gentilis*, and justified the Magistrates proceeding against him, in a history written of that Argument.

Finally, you come to answer an objection, that it is no prejudice to the Commonwealth if liberty of conscience were suffered to such as fear God indeed, which you prove by the example of the Patriarchs and others.

But we readily grant you, liberty of conscience is to be granted to men that fear God indeed, as knowing they will not persist in heresy, or turbulent schism, when they are convinced in conscience of the sinfulness thereof.

But the question is whether a Heretic after once or twice admonition (and so after conviction) or any other scandalous or heinous, offender, may be tolerated either in the Church without excommunication, or in the Commonwealth, without such punishment as may preserve others, from dangerous and damnable infection.

This much I thought needful to be spoken, for avoiding the grounds of your Error.

I forbear adding reasons to justify the contrary, because you may find that done to your hand, in a Treatise sent to some of the brethren late of *Salem*, who doubted as you do.

The Lord Jesus lead you by a spirit of truth in all trials.

[3]

Roger Williams
The Bloody Tenet of Persecution*

[INTRODUCTION]

First, that the blood of so many hundred thousand souls of Protestants and Papists, spilt in the Wars of present and former Ages, for their respective Consciences, is not required nor accepted by Jesus Christ the Prince of Peace.

Secondly, Pregnant Scriptures and Arguments are throughout the Work proposed against the Doctrine of persecution for cause of Conscience.

Thirdly, Satisfactory Answers are given to Scriptures, and objections produced by Mr. Calvin, Beza, Mr. Cotton, and the Ministers of the New English Churches and others former and later, tending to prove the Doctrine of persecution for cause of Conscience.

Fourthly, The Doctrine of persecution for cause of Conscience, is proved guilty of all the blood of the Souls crying for vengeance under the Altar.

Fifthly, All Civil States with their Officers of justice in their respective constitutions and administrations are proved essentially Civil, and therefore not Judges, Governors or Defenders of the Spiritual or Christian State and Worship.

Sixthly, It is the will and command of God, that (since the coming of his Son the Lord Jesus) a permission of the most

---

* From Roger Williams, *The Bloody Tenet, of Persecution, for cause of Conscience, discussed, in A Conference between Truth and Peace* (1644), reprinted in *Publications of the Narragansett Club*, first series, Vol. III (Providence, 1867). The text is taken from Chapters III, VI, XVI, XXIX, XXXVII, XLIV, LXXI, LXXII, LXXVIII, LXXIX, LXXXIII, CII, CV, CXV, CXXI, CXXXII, CXXXVII. The spelling has been modernized.

Paganish, Jewish, Turkish, or Antichristian consciences and worships, be granted to all men in all Nations and Countries: and they are only to be fought against with that Sword which is only (in Soul matters) able to conquer, to wit, the Sword of God's Spirit, the Word of God.

Seventhly, The state of the Land of Israel, the Kings and people thereof in Peace and War, is proved figurative and ceremonial, and no pattern nor precedent for any Kingdom or civil state in the world to follow.

Eighthly, God requireth not an uniformity of Religion to be inacted and inforced in any civil state; which inforced uniformity (sooner or later) is the greatest occasion of civil War, ravishing of conscience, persecution of Christ Jesus in his servants, and of the hypocrisy and destruction of millions of souls.

Ninthly, In holding an inforced uniformity of Religion in a civil state, we must necessarily disclaim our desires and hopes of the Jews' conversion to Christ.

Tenthly, An inforced uniformity of Religion throughout a Nation or civil state, confounds the Civil and Religious, denies the principles of Christianity and civility, and that Jesus Christ is come in the Flesh.

Eleventhly, The permission of other consciences and worships than a state professeth, only can (according to God) procure a firm and lasting peace, (good assurance being taken according to the wisdom of the civil state for uniformity of civil obedience from all sorts).

Twelfthly, lastly, true civility and Christianity may both flourish in a state or Kingdom, notwithstanding the permission of divers and contrary consciences, either of Jew or Gentile. . . .

[TO EVERY COURTEOUS READER]

While I plead the Cause of Truth and Innocence against the bloody Doctrine of Persecution for cause of conscience, I judge it not unfit to give alarm to my self, and all men to prepare to be persecuted or hunted for cause of conscience.

Whether thou standest charged with 10 or but 2 Talents, if thou hunts any for cause of conscience, how canst thou say thou follows the Lamb of God who so abhorred that practice? . . .

Who can now but expect that after so many scores of years preaching and professing of more Truth, and among so many great contentions among the very best of Protestants, a fiery furnace should be heat, and who sees not now the fires kindling?

I confess I have little hopes till those flames are over, that this Discourse against the doctrine of persecution for cause of conscience should pass current (say not among the Wolves and Lions, but even among the Sheep of Christ themselves) yet *liberavi animam meam,* I have not hid within my breast my souls belief: And although sleeping on the bed either or the pleasures or profits of sin thou think they conscience bound to smite at him that dares to waken thee? Yet in the midst of all these civil and spiritual Wars (I hope we shall agree in these particulars.)

First, how ever the proud (upon the advantage of an higher earth or ground) overlook the poor and cry out Schismatics, Heretics, etc. shall blasphemers and seducers escape unpunished? etc. Yet there is a sorer punishment in the Gospel for despising of Christ than Moses, even when the despiser of Moses was put to death without mercy, Heb. 10. 28, 29. He that believes not shall be damned, Mark 10. 16.

Secondly, whatever Worship, Ministry, Ministration, the best and purest are practiced without faith and true persuasion that they are the true institutions of God, they are sin, sinful worships, Ministries, etc. And however in Civil things we may be servants unto men, yet in Divine and Spiritual things the poorest peasant must disdain the service of the highest Prince: Be yet not the servants of men, I Cor. 14 (vii: 23).

Thirdly, without search and trial no man attains this faith and right persuasion, I Thes. 5. Try all things.

In vain have English Parliaments permitted English Bibles in the poorest English houses, and the simplest man or woman to search the Scriptures, if yet against their souls persuasion from the Scripture, they should be forced (as if they lived in Spain or Rome itself without the sight of a Bible) to believe as the Church believes.

Fourthly, having tried, we must hold fast, I Thes. 5. upon the loss of a Crown, Revel. 13. we must not let go for all the flea bitings of the present afflictions, etc. having bought Truth dear, we must not sell it cheap, not the least grain of it for the whole World, no not for the saving of Souls, though our own most precious; least of all for the bitter sweetning of a little vanishing pleasure.

For a little puff of credit and reputation from the changeable breath of uncertain sons of men.

For the broken bags of Riches on Eagles wings: For a dream of these, any or all of these which on our death-bed vanish and leave tormenting stings behind them: Oh how much better is it from the love of Truth, from the love of the Father of lights, from whence it comes, from the love of the Son of God, who is the way and the Truth, to say as he, John 18. 37. For this end was I born, and for this end came I into the World that I might bear witness to the Truth. . . .

[THE TEXT]

Truth. I acknowledge that to molest any person, Jew or Gentile, for either professing doctrine, or practising worship merely religious or spiritual, it is to persecute him, and such a person (what ever his doctrine or practice be true or false) suffereth persecution for conscience.

But withal I desire it may be well observed, that this distinction is not full and complete: for beside this that a man may be persecuted because he holdeth or practiseth what he believes in conscience to be a Truth, (as Daniel did, for which he was cast into the Lions' den, Dan. 6.) and many thousands of Christians, because they durst not cease to preach and practise what they believed was by God commanded, as the Apostles answered (Acts 4. & 5.) I say besides this a man may also be persecuted, because he dares to be constrained to yield obedience to such doctrines and worships as are by men invented and appointed. So the three famous Jews were cast into the fiery furnace for refusing to fall down (in a nonconformity to the whole conforming world) before the golden Image, Dan. 3. 21. So thousands of Christ's witnesses (and of late in those bloody

Marian days) have rather chose to yield their bodies to all sorts of torments, than to subscribe to doctrines, or practise worships, unto which the States and Times (as Nabuchadnezzar to his golden Image) have compelled and urged them. . . .

The Church or company of worshippers (whether true or false) is like unto a Body or College of Physicians in a City; like unto a Corporation, Society, or Company of East-Indie or Turkie-Merchants, or any other Society or Company in London: which Companies may hold their Courts, keep their Records, hold disputations; and in matters concerning their Society, may dissent, divide, break into Schisms and Factions, sue and implead each other at the Law, yea, wholly break up and dissolve into pieces and nothing, and yet the peace of the City not be in the least measure impaired or disturbed; because the essence or being of the City, and so the wellbeing and peace thereof is essentially distinct from those particular Societies; the City Courts, City Laws, City punishments distinct from theirs. The City was before them, and stands absolute and entire, when such a Corporation or Society is taken down. For instance further, the City or Civil state of Ephesus was essentially distinct from the worship of Diana in the City, or of the whole city. Again, the Church of Christ in Ephesus (which were God's people, converted and called out from the worship of that City unto Christianity or worship of God in Christ) was distinct from both.

Now suppose that God remove the Candlestick from Ephesus, yea though the whole Worship of the City of Ephesus should be altered: yet (if men be true and honestly ingenuous to City-covenants, Combinations and Principles) all this might be without the least impeachment or infringement of the Peace of the City of Ephesus.

Thus in the City of Smirna was the City itself or Civil estate one thing, the Spiritual or Religious state of Smirna, another; the Church of Christ in Smirna, distinct from them both; and the Synagogue of the Jews, whether literally Jews (as some thing) or mystically, false Christians (as others) called the Synagogue of Sathan, Revel. 2. distinct from all these. And notwithstanding these spiritual oppositions in point of Worship and Religion, yet hear we not the least noise (nor need we, if Men keep but the Bond of Civility) of any Civil breach, or breach of Civil peace amongst them: and to persecute God's people there for Religion, that only was a breach of Civility itself. . . .

But as the Lily is amongst the Thorns, so is Christ's Love among the Daughters; and as the Apple tree among the Trees of the Forest, so is her Beloved among the Sons: so great a difference is there between the Church in a City or Country, and the Civil state, City or Country in which it is.

No less then (as David in another case, Psal. 103. as far as the Heavens are from the Earth) are they that are truly Christ's (that is, anointed truly with the Spirit of Christ) [different] from many thousands who love not the Lord Jesus Christ, and yet are and must be permitted in the World or Civil State, although they have no right to enter into the gates of Jerusalem the Church of God.

And this is the more carefully to be minded, because whenever a toleration of others' Religion and Conscience is pleaded for, such as are (I hope in truth) zealous for God, readily produce plenty of Scriptures written to the Church, both before and since Christ's coming, all commanding and pressing the putting forth of the unclean, the cutting off the obstinate, the purging out the Leaven, rejecting of Heretics. As if because briars, thorns, and thistles may not be in the Garden of the Church, therefore they must all be plucked up out of the Wilderness: whereas he that is a Briar, that is, a Jew, a Turk, a Pagan, an Antichristian today, may be (when the Word of the Lord runs freely) a member of Jesus Christ tomorrow cut out of the wild Olive, and planted into the true. . . .

Peace. The second Scripture brought against such persecution for cause of Conscience, is Matth. 15. 14. where the Disciples being troubled at the Pharisees carriage toward the Lord Jesus and his doctrines, and relating how they were offended at him, the Lord Jesus commandeth his Disciples to let them alone, and gives this reason, that the blind lead the blind, and both should fall into the ditch.

Unto which, answer is made, "That it makes nothing to the

Cause, because it was spoken to his private Disciples, and not to public Officers in Church or State: and also, because it was spoken in regard of not troubling themselves, or regarding the offence which the Pharisees took."

Truth. I answer, (to pass by his assertion of the privacy of the Apostles) in that the Lord Jesus commanding to let them alone, that is, not only not be offended themselves, but not to meddle with them; it appears it was no ordinance of God nor Christ for the Disciples to have gone further, and have complained to, and excited the Civil Magistrate to his duty: which if it had been an Ordinance of God and Christ, either for the vindicating of Christ's doctrine, or the recovering of the Pharisees, or the preserving of others from infection, the Lord Jesus would never have commanded them to omit that which should have tended to these holy ends. . . .

I observe that he implies that beside the censure of the Lord Jesus, in the hands of his spiritual governors, for any spiritual evil in life or doctrine, the Civil Magistrate is also to inflict corporal punishment upon the contrary minded: whereas

First, if the Civil Magistrate be a Christian, a Disciple or follower of the meek Lamb of God, he is bound to be far from destroying the bodies of men, for refusing to receive the Lord Jesus Christ, for otherwise he should not know (according to this speech of the Lord Jesus) what spirit he was of, yea and to be ignorant of the sweet end of the coming of the Son of Man, which was not to destroy the bodies of Men, but to save both bodies and souls, vers. 55. 56.

Secondly, if the Civil Magistrate, being a Christian, gifted, prophesy in the Church, I Cor. 1. 14. although the Lord Jesus Christ, whom they in their own persons hold forth, shall be refused, yet they are here forbidden to call for fire from heaven, that is, to procure or inflict any corporal judgment upon such offenders, remembering the end of the Lord Jesus his coming, not to destroy men's lives, but to save them.

Lastly, this also concerns the conscience of the Civil Magistrate, as he is bound to preserve the civil peace and quiet of the place and people under him, he is bound to suffer no man to break the Civil Peace, by laying hands of violence upon any, though as vile as the Samaritans for not receiving of the Lord Jesus Christ. . . .

I hence observe, that there being in this Scripture held forth a two-fold state, a Civil state and a Spiritual, Civil officers and spiritual, civil weapons and spiritual weapons, civil vengeance and punishment, and a spiritual vengeance and punishment: although the Spirit speaks not here expressly of Civil Magistrates and their civil weapons, yet these States being of different Natures and Considerations, as far differing as Spirit from Flesh, I first observe, that Civil weapons are most improper and unfitting in matters of the Spiritual state and kingdom, though in the Civil state most proper and suitable. . . .

It is no Argument to prove that Tertullian meant a civil sword, by alleging I Cor. 5. or Gal. 5. which properly and only approve a cutting off by the sword of the Spirit in the Church, and the purging out of the leaven in the Church in the Cities of Corinth and Galatia.

And if Tertullian should so mean as himself doth, yet

First, that grant of his, that Heresy must be cut off with the sword of the Spirit, implies an absolute sufficiency in the sword of the Spirit to cut it down, according to that mighty operation of Spiritual weapons, (II Cor. 10. 4.) powerfully sufficient either to convert the Heretic to God, and subdue his very thoughts into subjection to Christ, or else spiritually to slay and execute him.

Secondly, it is clear to be the meaning of the Apostle, and of the Spirit of God, not there to speak to the Church in Corinth or Galatia, or any other Church, concerning any other dough, or house, or body, or flock, but the dough, the body, the house, the flock of Christ his Church: Out of which such sparks, such leaven, such rotten flesh and scabbed sheep are to be avoided.

Nor could the eye of this worthy Answerer ever be so obscured, as to run to a Smith's shop for a Sword of iron and steel to help the Sword of the Spirit, if the Sun of Righteousness had once been pleased to show him, that a National Church (which elsewhere he professeth against) a state Church (whether explicit, as in Old England, or implicit, as in New) is not the Institution of the Lord Jesus Christ. . . .

Peace. Brentius (whom you next quote, saith he) speaketh not to your cause. We willingly grant you, that man hath no power to make Laws to bind conscience, but this hinders not, but men may see the Laws of God observed which do bind conscience.

Truth. I answer, In granting with Brentius that man hath not power to make Laws to bind conscience, he overthrows such his tenent and practice as restrain men from their Worship, according to their Conscience and belief, and constrain them to such worships (though it be out of a pretence that they are convinced) which their own souls tell them they have no satisfaction nor faith in.

Secondly, whereas he affirmeth that men may make Laws to see the Laws of God observed.

I answer, as God needeth not the help of a material sword of steel to assist the sword of the Spirit in the affairs of conscience, so those men, those Magistrates, yea, that Commonwealth which makes such Magistrates, must needs have power and authority from Christ Jesus to fit Judge and to determine in all the great controversies concerning doctrine, discipline, government, etc.

And then I ask, whether upon this ground it must not evidently follow, that

Either there is no lawful Commonwealth nor civil State of men in the world, which is not qualified with this spiritual discerning: (and then also that the very Commonweal hath more light concerning the Church of Christ, than the Church itself.)

Or, that the Commonweal and Magistrates thereof must judge and punish as they are persuaded in their own belief and conscience, (be their conscience Paganish, Turkish, or Antichristian) what is this but to confound Heaven and Earth together, and not only to take away the being of Christianity out of the World, but to take away all civility, and the world out of this world, and to lay all upon heaps of confusion? . . .

Since there is so much controversy in the World, where the name of Christ is taken up, concerning the true Church, the Ministry and Worship, and who are those that truly fear God;

I ask who shall judge in this case, who be they that fear God?

It must needs be granted, that such as have the power of suffering or not suffering, such Consciences, must judge: and then must it follow (as before I intimated) that the Civil State must judge of the truth of the Spiritual; and then Magistrates fearing or not fearing God, must judge of the fear of God: also that their judgement or sentence must be according to their conscience, of what Religion soever: Or that there is no lawful Magistrate, who is not able to judge in such cases. And lastly, that since the Sovereign power of all Civil Authority is founded in the consent of the People, that every Common-weal hath radically and fundamentally in it a power of true discerning the true fear of God, which they transfer to their Magistrates and Officers: Or else that there are no lawful Kingdoms, Cities, or Towns in the World, in which a man may live, and unto whose Civil Government he may submit: and then (as I said before) there must be no World, nor is it lawful to live in it, because it hath not a true discerning Spirit to judge them that fear or not fear God. . . .

Truth. Alas, who knows not what lamentable differences have been between the same Ministers of the Church of England, some conforming, others leaving their livings, friends, country, life, rather than conform; when others again (of whose personal godliness it is not questioned) have succeeded by conformity into such forsaken (so called) Livings? How great the present differences even amongst them that fear of God, concerning Faith, Justification, and the evidence of it? concerning Repentance and godly sorrow, as also and mainly concerning the Church, the Matter, Form, Administrations and Government of it?

Let none now think that the passage to New England by Sea, or the nature of the Country can do what only the Key of David can do, to wit, open and shut the Consciences of men.

Beside, how can this be a faithful and upright acknowledgement of their weakness and imperfection, when they preach, print, and practise such violence to the souls and bodies of others, and by their Rules and Grounds ought to proceed even to the killing of those whom they judge so dear unto them, and in respect of godliness far above themselves? . . .

Truth. From this confession, that the Church or Kingdom of Christ may be set up without prejudice of the Commonweal, according to John 18. 36. My Kingdom is not of this World, etc. I observe that although the Kingdom of Christ, the Church and the Civil Kingdom or Government be not inconsistent, but that both may stand together; yet that they are independent according to that Scripture, and that therefore there may be (as formerly I have proved) flourishing Commonweals and Societies of men where no Church of Christ abideth; and secondly, the Commonweal may be in perfect peace and quiet, notwithstanding the Church, the Commonweal of Christ be in distractions, and spiritual oppositions both against their Religions, and sometimes amongst themselves, as the Church of Christ in Corinth troubled with divisions, contentions, etc.

Secondly, I observe it is true the Church helpeth forward the prosperity of the Commonweal by spiritual means, Jer. 29. 7. The prayers of God's people procure the peace of the City, where they abide, yet that Christ's Ordinances and administrations of Worship are appointed and given by Christ to any Civil State, Town or City as is implied by the instance of Geneva, that I confidently deny.

The Ordinances and Discipline of Christ Jesus, though wrongfully and profanely applied to natural and unregenerate men may cast a blush of civility and morality upon them as in Geneva and other places (for the shining brightness of the very shadow of Christ's Ordinances casts a shame upon barbarism and incivility) yet withal I affirm that the misapplication of Ordinances to unregenerate and unrepentant persons hardens up their souls in a dreadful sleep and dream of their own blessed estate, and sends millions of souls to hell in a secure expectation of a false salvation. . . .

However they affirm that persons are not to be compelled to be members of Churches, nor the Church compelled to receive any: Yet if persons be compelled to forsake their Religion which their hearts cleave to, and to come to Church, to the worship of the Word, Prayers, Psalms, and Contributions, and this all their days: I ask whether this be not this people's Religion, unto which submitting, they shall be quiet all their days, without the inforcing them to the practice of any other Religion? And if this be not so, then I ask, Will it not inevitably follow, that they (not only permit, but) enforce people to be of no Religion at all, all their days?

This toleration of Religion, or rather irreligious compulsion, is above all tolerations, monstrous, to wit, to compel men to be of no Religion all their days. I desire all men and these worthy Authors of this Model, to lay their hands upon their heart, and to consider whether this compulsion of men to hear the Word, (as they say) whether it carries men, to wit, to be of no Religion all their days, worse than the very Indians, who dare not live without Religion according as they are persuaded.

Lastly, I add, from the Ordinances of the Lord Jesus, and practice of the Apostles (Acts 2. 42.) where the Word and Prayer is joined with the exercise of their fellowship, and breaking of Bread; in which Exercises the Church continued constantly: that it is apparent that a Civil State may as lawfully compel men by the civil sword to the breaking of bread, or Lord's Supper, as to the Word or Prayer, or Fellowship.

For first, they are all of the same nature, Ordinances in the Church (I speak of the feeding Ministry in the Church, unto which persons are compelled) and Church Worship. Secondly, every conscience in the World is fearful, at least shy of the Priests and Ministers of other Gods and Worships, and of holding Spiritual fellowship in any of their Services. Which is the case of many a Soul, viz. to question the Ministers themselves, as well as the Supper itself. . . .

It is reasonable to expect and demand of such as live within the State a Civil maintenance of their civil officers, and to force it where it is denied. It is reasonable for a Schoolmaster to demand his recompence for his labor in his School: but it is not reasonable to expect or force it from strangers, enemies, rebels to that City, from such as come not within, or else would not be received into the School.

What is the Church of Christ Jesus, but the City, the School, and Family of Christ? the Officers of this City, School, Family, may reasonable expect maintenance from such [as] they minister unto, but not from strangers, enemies, etc. . . .

Peace. By these weights we may try the weight of that commonly received and not questioned opinion, viz. That the civil state and the spiritual, the Church and Commonweal, they are like Hippocrates' twins, they are born together, grow up together, laugh together, weep together, sicken and die together.

Truth. A witty, yet a most dangerous Fiction of the Father of Lies, who hardened in Rebellion against God, persuades God's people to drink down such a deadly poison, though he knows the truth of these five particulars, which I shall remind you of.

First, many flourishing States in the World have been and are at this day, which hear not of Jesus Christ, and therefore have not the presence and concurrence of a Church of Christ with them.

Secondly, there have been many thousands of God's people, who in their personal estate and life of grace were awake to God, but in respect of Church estate they knew no other than a Church of dead stones, the Parish Church; or though some light be of late come in through some cranny, yet they seek not after, or least of all are joined to any true Church of God, consisting of living and believing stones.

So that by these New English Ministers' principles, not only is the door of calling to Magistracy shut against natural and unregenerate men (though excellently fitted for civil offices) but also against the best and ablest servants of God, except they be entered into Church estate; so that thousands of God's own people (excellently qualified) not knowing, or not entering into such a Church estate, shall not be accounted fit for civil services.

Thirdly, admit that a civil Magistrate be neither a member of a true Church of Christ (if any be in his dominions) nor in his person fear God, yet may he (possibly) give free permission without molestation, yea, and sometimes encouragement and assistance to the service and Church of God.

Thus we find Abraham permitted to build and set up an Altar to his God wheresoever he came amongst the idolatrous Nations in the Land of Canaan. Thus Cyrus proclaims liberty to all the people of God in his Dominions, freely to go up and build the Temple of God at Jerusalem, and Artaxerxes after him confirmed it.

Thus the Roman Emperors and Governors under him permitted the Church of God, the Jews in the Lord Christ's time, their Temple and Worship, although in Civil things they were subject to the Romans.

Fourthly, the Scriptures of Truth and the Records of Time concur in this, that the first Churches of Christ Jesus, the lights, patterns, and precedents to all succeeding Ages, were gathered and governed without the aid, assistance, or countenance of any Civil Authority, from which they suffered great persecutions for the name of the Lord Jesus professed amongst them.

The Nations, Rulers, and Kings of the Earth tumultuously rage against the Lord and his Anointed, Psal. 2. 1.2. Yet vers. 6. it hath pleased the Father to set the Lord Jesus King upon his holy Hill of Zion.

Christ Jesus would not be pleased to make use of the Civil Magistrate to assist him in his Spiritual Kingdom; nor would he yet be daunted or discouraged in his Servants by all their threats and terrors: for Love is strong as death, and the coals thereof give a most vehement flame, and are not quenched by all the waters and floods of mightiest opposition, Cant. 8.

Christ's Church is like a chaste and loving wife, in whose heart is fixed her Husband's love, who hath found the tenderness of his love towards her, and hath been made fruitful by him, and therefore seeks she not the smiles, nor fears the frowns of all the Emperors in the World to bring her Christ unto her, or keep him from her.

Lastly, we find in the tyrannical usurpations of the Romish Antichrist, the 10 horns (which some of good note conceive to be the 10 Kingdoms, into which the Roman Empire was quartered and divided) are expressly said Revel. 17. 13. to have one mind to give their power and strength unto the Beast, yea (ver. 17.) their Kingdom unto the Beast, until the Words of God shall be fulfilled: whence it follows, that all those Nations that are guilded over with the name of Christ, have under that mask or vizard (as some Executioners and Tormentors in the Inquisition use to torment) persecuted the Lord Jesus Christ, either with a more open, gross and bloody, or with a more subtle, secret and gentle violence.

Let us cast our eyes about, turn over the Records and examine the experience of past and present Generations, and see if all particular observations amount not to this sum, viz. that the great whore hath committed fornication with the Kings of the Earth, and made drunk thereof Nations with the cup of the wine of her fornications: In which drunkedness and whoredom (as whores use to practice) she hath robbed the Kings and Nations of their power and strength, and (Jezebel-like) having procured the King's names and seals, she drinks drunk, Revel. 17. with the blood of Naboth, who (because he dares not part with his rightful inheritance in the land of Canaan, the blessed land of promise and salvation in Christ) as a Traitor to the civil State, and Blasphemer against God, she (under the color of a day of humiliation in Prayer and Fasting) stones to death. . . .

But (to wind up all) as it is most true that Magistracy in general is of God (Rom. 13.) for the preservation of Mankind in civil order and peace, (the World otherwise would be like the Sea, wherein Men, like Fishes would hunt and devour each other, and the greater devour the less:) so also it is true, that Magistracy in special for the several kinds of it is of Man, I Pet. 2. 13. Now what kind of Magistrate soever the people shall agree to set up, whether he receive Christianity before he be set in office, or whether he receive Christianity after, he receives no more power of Magistracy, than a Magistrate that hath received no Christianity. For neither of them both can receive more, than the Commonweal, the Body of People and civil State, as men, communicate unto them, and betrust with them.

All lawful Magistrates in the World, both before the coming of Christ Jesus, and since, (excepting those unparalleled typical Magistrates of the Church of Israel) are but Derivatives and Agents immediately derived and employed as eyes

and hands, serving for the good of the whole: Hence they
have and can have no more Power, than fundamentally lies
in the Bodies or Fountains themselves, which Power, Might,
or Authority, is not Religious, Christian, etc. but natural, humane and civil.

And hence it is true, that a Christian Captain, Christian
Merchant, Physician, Lawyer, Pilot, Father, Master, and (so
consequently) Magistrate, etc. is no more a Captain, Merchant, Physician, Lawyer, Pilot, Father, Master, Magistrate,
etc. than a Captain, Merchant, etc. of any other Conscience
or Religion.

'Tis true, Christianity teacheth all these to act in their several callings, to an higher ultimate end, from higher principles in a more heavenly and spiritual manner, etc. . . .

Truth. In his season God will glorify himself in all his
Truths: but to gratify thy desire, thus: A Pagan or Antichristian Pilot may be as skilful to carry the Ship to its desired Port, as any Christian Mariner or Pilot in the World, and
may perform that work with as much safety and speed: yet
have they not command over the souls and consciences of
their passengers or mariners under them, although they may
justly see to the labor of the one, and the civil behavior of
all in the ship: A Christian Pilot he performs the same work,
(as likewise doth the Metaphorical Pilot in the ship of the
Commonweal) from a principle of knowledge and experience: but more than this, he acts from a root of the fear of
God and love to mankind, in his whole course. Secondly, his
aim is more to glorify God than to gain his pay, or make his
voyage. Thirdly, he walks heavenly with Men, and God, in a
constant observation of God's hand in storms, calms, etc. so
that the thread of Navigation being equally spun by a believing or unbelieving Pilot, yet is it drawn over with the gold of
Godliness and Christianity by a Christian Pilot, while he is
holy in all manner of Christianity, I Pet. 1. 15. But lastly, the
Christian Pilot's power over the Souls and consciences of his
Sailors and Passengers is not greater than that of the Antichristian, otherwise than he can subdue the souls of any by
the two-edged sword of the Spirit, the Word of God, and by
his holy demeanor in his place, etc. . . .

Peace. Dear Truth, We are now arrived at their last Head: the Title is this, viz.

Their power in the Liberties and Privileges of these Churches.

First, all Magistrates ought to be chosen out of Church members, Exod. 18. 21. Deut. 17. 15. Prov. 29. 2. When the Righteous rule, the people rejoice. Secondly, that all free men elected, be only Church members.

1. Because if none but Church members should rule, then others should not choose, because they may elect others beside Church members.

2. From the pattern of Israel, where none had power to choose but only Israel, or such as were joined to the people of God.

3. If it shall fall out, that in the Court consisting of Magistrates and Deputies, there be a dissent between them which may hinder the common good, that they now return for ending the same, to their first principles, which are the Free men, and let them be consulted with.

Truth. In this Head are 2 branches: First concerning the choice of Magistrates, that such ought to be chosen as are Church members: for which is quoted, Exod. 18. 21. Deut. 17. 15. Prov. 19. 29.

Unto which I answer: It were to be wished, that since the point is so weighty, as concerning the Pilots and Steersmen of Kingdoms and Nations, etc., on whose ability, care and faithfulness depends most commonly the peace and safety of the commonweals they sail in: I say it were to be wished that they had more fully explained what they intend by this Affirmative, viz. Magistrates ought to be chosen out of Church members.

For if they intend by this (ought to be chosen) necessity of convenience, viz. that for the greater advancement of common utility and rejoicing of the people, according to the place quoted (Prov. 29. 2.) it were to be desired, prayed for, and peaceably endeavored, then I readily assent unto them.

But if by this (Ought) they intend such a necessity as those Scriptures quoted imply, viz. that people shall sin by choosing such for Magistrates as are not members of

Churches; as the Israelites should have sinned, if they had not (according to Jethro's counsel, Exod. 18. and according to the command of God. Deut. 18.) chosen their Judges and Kings within themselves in Israel: then I propose these necessary Queries.

First, whether those are not lawful Civil combinations, societies, and communions of men, in Towns, Cities, States or Kingdoms, where no Church of Christ is resident, yea, where his name was never yet heard of: I add to this, that Men of no small note, skilful in the state of the World, acknowledge, that the World divided into 30 parts, 25 of that 30 have never yet heard of the name of Christ: If their Civil polities and combinations be not lawful, (because they are not Churches, and their Magistrates Church members) then disorder, confusion, and all unrighteousness is lawful, and pleasing to God.

Secondly, whether in such States or Commonweals, where a Church or Churches of Christ are resident, such persons may not lawfully succeed to the Crown or Government, in whom the fear of God (according to Jethro's counsel) cannot be discerned, nor are brethren of the Church, (according to Deut. 17.) but only are fitted with Civil and Moral abilities, to manage the Civil affairs of the Civil State.

Thirdly, since not many Wise and Noble are called, but the poor receive the Gospel, as God hath chosen the poor of the World to be rich in Faith, I Cor. 1. Jam. 2. Whether it may not ordinarily come to pass, that there may not be found in a true Church of Christ (which sometimes consisteth but of few persons) persons fit to be either Kings or Governors, etc., whose civil office is no less difficult than the office of a Doctor of Physic, a Master or Pilot of a Ship, or a Captain or Commander of a Band or Army of men: for which services, the children of God may be no ways qualified, though otherwise excellent for the fear of God, and the knowledge and Grace of the Lord Jesus.

Fourthly, if Magistrates ought (that is, ought only) to be chosen out of the Church, I demand if they ought not also to be dethroned and deposed, when they cease to be of the Church, either by voluntary departure from it, or by excommunication out of it, according to the bloody tenents and practice of some Papists, with whom the Protestants (according to their principles) although they seem to abhor it, do absolutely agree?

Fifthly, therefore, lastly, I ask if this be not to turn the World upside down, to turn the World out of the World, to pluck up the roots and foundations of all common society in the World? to turn the Garden and Paradise of the Church and Saints into the Field of the Civil State of the World, and to reduce the World to the first chaos or confusion.

BIBLIOGRAPHICAL NOTE

Two essays of Perry Miller are highly instructive for this period in New England Puritanism: *Orthodoxy in Massachusetts* (Cambridge, 1933) and "The Marrow of Puritan Divinity," in *Errand into the Wilderness* (New York, 1965, paperback edition); this reprint contains a useful introduction to the essay which was originally published in 1935. Alan Simpson, *Puritanism in Old and New England* (Chicago, 1955) is a helpful study of the broad Puritan movement. Eminently readable is Herbert Schneider, *The Puritan Mind* (Ann Arbor, 1958), which covers the period to the Revolution. Perry Miller and Thomas H. Johnson have collected source materials in *The Puritans: Sourcebook of their Writings*, Two Volumes, (New York, 1963), a paperback edition of the work published in 1938. Williston Walker's *The Creeds and Platforms of Congregationalism* (New York, 1893) is an indispensable source. A fresh discussion of the period from 1629–1650 is David Kobrin, "The Expansion of the Visible Church in New England: 1629–1650, *Church History*, xxxvi, June, 1967, p. 189 ff.

For John Winthrop I refer the reader to the excellent biography of Edmund Morgan, *The Puritan Dilemma: The Story of John Winthrop* (Boston, 1958). The recent biography by Lazar Ziff, *The Career of John Cotton: Puritanism and The American Experience* (Princeton, 1962) is the most adequate treatment of John Cotton. For Roger Williams see: Perry Miller, *Roger Williams His Contribution to the American Tradition* (Indianapolis, 1953) and Leroy Moore, Religious Liberty: "Roger Williams and the Revolutionary Era," *Church History*, xxxiv, March, 1965, p. 57 ff.

II. THE LORD'S SUPPER

INTRODUCTION

The debate over the Lord's Supper between Solomon Stoddard (1643–1729) and Increase Mather (1639–1723) was lengthy and severe: Mather, the defender of the "New England Way," and Stoddard, the innovator.

Their controversy must be seen in relation to earlier Puritan theory. The Cambridge Platform of 1648 defined the "Saints" of the Visible Church as: "1) Such as have not only attained the knowledge of the Principles of Religion, and are free from gross and open Scandals, but also do together with the Profession of their Faith and Repentance, walk in blameless Obedience to the Word, so as that in charitable Discretion, they may be accounted Saints by calling . . . 2) The Children of such, who are also holy."[1] Orthodox belief, a non-scandalous life, and profession of faith and repentance were the marks of the "Saint." These requirements for full church membership could not always be fulfilled by the children and grandchildren of the early colonists. In 1662 a Synod was called to consider the status of those who could not make a profession of faith and repentance. The decision reached permitted full members of the church to present their children for baptism, even though they had not met all the stipulations of the Cambridge Platform, but they could not partake of the Lord's Supper—thus, "Half-way covenanters."[2]

Solomon Stoddard became the pastor of the church in Northampton, Massachusetts, in 1672. The religious make-up of the village consisted of three groups: the professing Saints, the "Half-way covenanters," and those outside the church. In 1677 Stoddard altered further the "New England Way" by his willingness to baptise children of parents who were not church members and to open the Lord's Supper to all.

[1] Williston Walker, *The Creeds and Platforms of Congregationalism* (New York, 1893), pp. 205–206.
[2] *Ibid.*, p. 328.

Perry Miller has remarked that Stoddard, by this action, "identified the visible church no longer with the communion of the saints, but with the town meeting . . ."[3] Stoddard's theological justification was based on Calvinistic premises: "Because the covenant is dispensed by an arbitrary and unpredictable divinity, because it definitely is not reasonable, it is open to all and no man can tell who is really a saint."[4] The Lord's Supper was viewed as a "converting ordinance," not just a means of strengthening the faith of the believers. This was a radical change.

Increase Mather, though he had originally opposed the Half Way Covenant, became one of its supporters by the late 1670s. He was not willing, however, to follow Stoddard's new departure and engaged during the next thirty years in a pamphlet warfare with the pastor of the Northampton church. The following selections, published in 1708, indicate some of the issues of debate.

[4]

Solomon Stoddard

The Inexcusableness of Neglecting the
Worship of God*

No scandalous person may be admitted to Baptism, neither may any Scandalous person be admitted to the Lord's Sup-

[3] Perry Miller, "Solomon Stoddard, 1643–1729," *Harvard Theological Review*, xxxiv (1941), p. 298.

[4] Solomon Stoddard, *The Safety of Appearing at the Day of Judgement* (Boston, 1729), p. 275. This work was originally published in 1687.

* From Solomon Stoddard, *The Inexcusableness of Neglecting the Worship under a Pretence of being in an Unconverted Condition, Showed in a Sermon Preached at Northampton, the 17th Decemb. 1707, being the time of the Sitting Inferior Court.* (Boston, 1708), pp. 11–15; 17–20; 20–24; 27–28.

per; but those that are not scandalous may partake of it,
though they are not Regenerate. Such persons as might lawfully come to the Passover, may also if they have Knowledge
to discern the Lord's body, lawfully come to the Lord's Supper, for they are alike figures; the Passover was a type of
Christ to die; the Lord's Supper is a representation of Christ
who had died: It is lawful for Unregenerate men to celebrate the Memory of the death of Christ, which is a great
encouragement and comfort unto them; and so they do in
this Ordinance: It is lawful for Unregenerate men to give
Solemn Testimony to the virtues of the death of Christ, and
show it forth; and so they do in this Ordinance, I Cor. II, 26.
To show forth the Lord's Death till he come. That which
God teaches us in this Ordinance, is very needful for Unregenerate men to learn; namely the insufficiency of all other things
besides the death of Christ for Salvation, and the all-
sufficiency of Christ for Salvation: that which we profess in
this Ordinance is very fit for Unregenerate men to profess;
namely the need of Christ and saving virtue of his blood:
as it may be of great advantage to natural men to hear God's
Promise in the Covenant of Grace. So to see God setting his
seal to the Covenant of Grace. If it be lawful for all the
Adult Members of the Church to partake of the Lord's Supper, then, it is lawful for some Unregenerate men to do it:
but it is lawful for all the Adult Members of the Church to
do it: this was the practice in the primitive Church, I Cor.
10. 17. *We are all partakers of that one bread:* if it be lawful for the Church to require Unregenerate persons to come
to the Lord's Supper, then it is lawful for them to come; but
it is lawful for the Church to require all its Adult Members
to keep the Covenant with God: If it be lawful for an Unregenerate man to be in Covenant with God, it is lawful for
them to come to the Lord's Supper, for if it be lawful for
them to be in Covenant, it is lawful for them to keep the
Covenant: if Sanctification were a necessary qualification to
partaking in the Lord's Supper, then it would be a very Sinful
thing for any unsanctified person to come, though he hoped
he was Godly, though he was confident of his Godliness.
When Christ Instituted this Ordinance, He commanded his

Disciples to attend it, Luke 22. 19. Therefore, it is an Ordinance to be attended by the whole Church, by all the Disciples of Christ, that have Knowledge. If Sanctification were a necessary qualification, in order to partake, then the Church should let no others come, and then God would have given them a certain Rule in attending of which, they might keep all others away. Men had need have good arguments to make the World believe, that coming to the Lord's Table is a privilege equally confined with Justification, Adoption and eternal Glory; and that none may venture to the Lord's Table, but those that shall be admitted into the Kingdom of Heaven.

. . . If a man do know himself to be Unregenerate, yet it is lawful for him to administer Baptism and the Lord's Supper. The blessing of this Ordinance does not depend upon the Piety of him that doth administer it. Christ knew Judas to be Unregenerate, yet he let him as well as the rest of the Disciples to administer Baptism: John 4. 2. *Jesus baptised not but his Disciples.* If men be destitute of Regenerating Grace, yet they may administer God's Ordinances in such a manner as may be for the glory of God, and the Edification of his People. It is most desirable upon all accounts that they who Officiate in the work of the Ministry, be holy and gracious men: but men that are destitute of Grace are not prohibited in the word of God, to administer the Ordinances of God, if such may Preach, surely they may administer Sacraments. Paul speaks of Preaching as a greater work than administering Baptism, I. Cor. 1. 17. And we may argue that it is greater than administering the Lord's Supper.

The Reasons of the Doctrine are:

There is no certain knowledge who have Sanctifying Grace. If we should be limited by God, in that we might admit none to Church fellowship, but such as have Sanctifying Grace, we should be under extreme difficulties and great scruples of Conscience: for it we make the most exact search, we should often be very much mistaken, and in danger to accept some that were not sincere, and to reject some that were sincere. There is no certain rule given in the Scripture to the guides of the Church, whereby they can distinguish Saints from Hypocrites; neither do many Persons know what to make of themselves: Some that are Godly have many fears whether their hearts be right in the sight of God: which is implied in that Precept, II Peter 1. 10. *Give a diligence to make your Calling and your Election sure.* And many Hypocrites have a great confidence that they are Saints, John 9. 40. *Are we blind also?* It is not to be imagined that God would give a Rule to his People that is impracticable: If that were the Rule that only Godly men, were to be admitted to communion in the Church, there is not knowledge enough upon Earth in order to the practice of it: the Church through their ignorance must wholly forbear acting: for their knowledge of other men's Piety is but a supposition, I Peter 5. 12. *By Silvanus, a faithful brother as I suppose.* And particular Persons, would never be able to attend that Rule for want of the knowledge of themselves; some would exclude themselves, and others would obtrude themselves contrary to it, so that the Rule would come to nothing. God's Rules are such that no man has any just cause to object against them: but if this were the Rule that Godly men only might enjoy Ordinances: the Church might object, that it is God's prerogative to know the hearts of men, and we are utterly incapable to attend that Rule.

It is needful that others should attend duties of Worship, that the Worship of God be carried on . . .

The Attending of these duties are part of the External Covenant: The Covenant People of God are bound to attend Covenant duties. If any part of the External Covenant be neglected, the Covenant is broken . . .

The Use of this Doctrine of Warning; That you be not afraid to attend duties of Worship, because destitute of Sanctifying Grace. Men that are destitute of Sanctifying Grace can perform no duty in an acceptable manner; but yet you must not give way to a spirit of fear, so as to neglect your duty. Men must be afraid to neglect it and not afraid to attend it: You must make haste to get Sanctifying Grace, but you must not deny God any part of his Worship, till that is done. It is a poor thing for men to be scared into Religion, but it is sad indeed for men to be feared out of Religion, and to neglect God's Worship out of fear of God . . .

*Many that judge that Persons should be Converted before
they come to the Sacrament, do run into a great fault, viz.*
they persuade Persons that they are Converted before they
are: they are zealous against men's coming to the Lord's
Supper in an Unconverted condition, yet advise and encourage such persons to come under a notion that they are Converted: if persons do but carry civilly and religiously, they
think they are Converted, and urge them to join the Church;
hereby abundance of wrong is done; men are greatly hardened in a natural Estate: and they are laid under great
Temptation to flatter themselves, as if the bitterness of death
were past: this is a means to prevent many men's Conversion:
if men are made to believe that they are Godly before they
be, that is like to prove a mighty impediment unto their Conversion, they don't lie open to the threatenings of the Word,
they think others spoken to, and they pity them; but they
are not sensible of their own danger: John 9. 41. *Because
you say, you see, therefore your sin remaineth.*

*If none that are destitute of Sanctifying Grace may come,
then two sorts of Persons that do come should stay away.*
First, such persons as are in a natural condition, yet have
got a confidence that they are Converted: there are many
such. Proverbs 30. 12. *There is a Generation that are pure
in their own eyes, yet are not cleansed from their selfishness:* But since there is no way to keep them from it, the
church can't keep them from it, because they are visible
Saints; and their own Consciences will not forbid them, because they are confident that they are Converted. And Secondly, there is another sort that should forbear, viz. Such
Godly men as do not know that they are Converted. If a
man be Godly, yet how can he with a good Conscience
come to an Ordinance, peculiar to Godly men, when he don't
know himself to be Godly: if only Saints are allowed to come,
he must know himself to be a Saint, before he can know that
he is allowed of God to come. As if a man has power to Sell
nothing but what is his own, then he must know a thing to
be his own before he can sell it with a good Conscience. Or
if a Church have power to censure only Scandalous persons,
then they must know a man to be Scandalous before they

can with a good Conscience censure him. So in this case, if the Sacrament be only for Godly men, they don't know that they have any right to it, until they know that they are Godly.

It is from the misunderstanding of one Scripture principally, that these are afraid to come to the Lord's Supper: viz. I Cor. 11. There are two expressions in that Chapter that they are terrifyed with, One that *He that eateth and drinketh unworthily, is guilty of the body and blood of the Lord:* that is of prophaning the Ordinance. And they are said *to eat and drink damnation or judgment to themselves:* but this unworthy eating is doing of it in a rude manner, as v. 21. *For in eating every one taketh before others his own Supper, and one is hungry and another is drunken.* And he explains himself, v. 29. *Not discerning the Lord's body;* that is, not discerning that bread from common bread. Another expression is, *Let a man examine himself and so let him eat,* v. 28. But it is not said, Let him examine himself whether he should eat or forbear, but *let him Examine himself, and so let him eat.* The meaning is, that he must come solemnly to that Ordinance, Examining what need he has of it.

The Church is bound to receive men if they be externally qualified, whether they be Godly or no. If men make a profession and are not Scandalous in their Conversation, the Church cannot refuse them. The Apostle still received those that made a profession of the Gospel, Acts 2. 41 and 6. 7. Those that are Saints by calling are to be accepted of the Church, whether they be Converted or not. The matter of the Church are visible Saints: if the Church were only to receive those that are Converted, God would have given them a certain rule, in attending of which Unconverted Persons should be excluded, but there is no such Rule given: Neither is there any external sign, that does certainly distinguish Converted men from Unconverted; the Church is not concerned to see that they be all real Saints, their work is to see they be visible Saints, if they reject such they are to blame.

It cannot be an unlawful thing for men to keep the External Covenant. As the visible People of God have a natural power, so they have a lawful power to keep the External

Covenant: if they keep the External Covenant they are accepted as a righteous People, Deuteronomy 6. 25. *It shall be our righteousness if we observe to do all those Commandments:* If they neglect to do any part of the Covenant, they lay themselves open to the judgments of God. God brings War to avenge the quarrel of his Covenant; and this is one part of God's Covenant, Genesis 17. 10. Circumcision is called the Covenant. It is required in the second Command, That we worship God in that way which he has appointed: and this is the appointment of God, that his whole visible Church do celebrate the Memorial of the Death of Christ, I Cor. 10. 17. *We being many do all partake of that one bread.* And indeed it is the duty of the Church to require all its Adult orderly Members to come to the Lord's Supper, and it would be very strange that it should be the duty of the Church to require them to come, and censure them for not coming, and yet be their duty to stay away because Unconverted . . .

The neglect of this Ordinance is one great cause of God's judgments. We are under sorrowful dispensation, and have reason to conclude this neglect to be one especial cause of them. There be indeed abundance of Moral Evils in the Land, that do provoke God to anger: but generally when God brought judgments on Israel, it was mainly for corruptions in Worship. As we may not introduce Ceremonies of men's Invention, so we must not neglect Ordinances that are of Divine Institution. Neglects of Worship bring destroying Judgments: Exodus 5. 3. *Let us Sacrifice to the Lord our God, lest he fall upon us with Pestilence or with Sword.* Let men have what pretences they will, yet these pretences will not excuse them in the neglect of God's Ordinances. God don't allow men to be feared out of his Worship. But I do judge that the generality that do neglect it, do it out of a careless and profane Spirit, and then it is no wonder, if it brings down the Wrath of God.

It is Objected by some against this Doctrine, *That is the Lord's Supper be a Converting Ordinance, then not only such as are Civil and Religious may be admitted to it, but profane and vicious Persons for they likewise need Conversion, and it is a pity but they should have all helps to Conversion?*

A. 1. *That Baptism is a Converting Ordinance, but yet is not to be administered to Adult Persons that are profane:* For Baptism is only a Converting Ordinance to the Members of the Church, who are Unconverted. The Hearing of the Word only is the appointed means for the Conversion of others.

2. *The Lord's Supper is an Ordinance for the strengthening and exercising of Grace:* yet it doth not follow that it is to be administered to Godly men, who are guilty of Scandal, the need that they have to have their Grace strengthened, is no argument, that the Lord's Supper should in that case be administered to them.

3. *Though the Lord's Supper is a Converting Ordinance, yet it is not to be administered to any profane and vicious men:* for it is a Converting Ordinance only to those that it is appointed to be administered unto; viz. Members of the Church, walking orderly. When Church Members carry Scandalous, there are other Ordinances appointed for their Conversion, in case they be Unconverted.

It is also Objected, *That those who were Unclean were not to partake of the Passover, Numbers 9. 7. which seems to hold forth to us, That those that are spiritually Unclean in the days of the Gospel, may not partake of the Lord's Supper.*

A. 1. *If those that were spiritually Unclean might come to the Passover, no reason can be assigned why they may not also come to the Lord's Supper:* For the Passover was an holy Ordinance as well as the Lord's Supper; and the Passover ought to be attended in an holy manner, as well as the Supper.

2. *The Ordinance of the Old Testament were not Types of the Ordinances of the New Testament.* If the reason why the Unclean might not come to the Lord's Supper: of what Edification would that Institution be to the Jews. They did not understand any such meaning, and if they had, it would have done them no good. But the Ordinances of the Old Testament did signify Evangelical Doctrines, which were of

great use to the Jews, so this appointment, that Unclean Persons might not come to the Passover did signify, that those who were spiritually Unclean, should not have communion with God in the highest Heaven, but be Excluded out of the Kingdom of God.

Finis.

[5]

Increase Mather
The Strange Doctrine*

In Mr. Stoddard's Sermon on Exodus xii. 47, 48. lately published, there are many Passages which have given Offence to the Churches in *New England*, as being contrary to the Doctrine which they have learned from the Scriptures, and from those blessed Servants of the Lord, who were the Instruments in the hand of Christ in building Sanctuaries for His Name, in this part of the Earth. But there are Especially two Heterodox Assertions therein; One is, *That Sanctification is not a necessary qualification to Partaking in the Lord's Supper.* The other is, *That the Lord's Supper is a Converting Ordinance;* Consequently, That Persons who know themselves to be in an Unregenerate Estate, may & ought to approach unto the Holy Table of the Lord, whilest they remain in their Sins. For the right Stating of the controversy, we must remember that the Question is not (as some of Mr. S. [in] his Arguings do insinuate) Whether the Church must certainly know that those whom they admit to their Communion are Sincere in their Profession of Faith and Repentance; for God

* From Increase Mather, *A Dissertation, Wherein The Strange Doctrine Lately Published in a Sermon, The Tendency of which, is to Encourage Unsanctified Persons (while such) to Approach the Holy Table of the Lord, is Examined and Confuted.* (Boston, 1708), pp. 1–7; 20–22; 25; 27–30; 33–36; 80–84; 89–90.

only knows the hearts of all men. Nor is the Question, Whether a Christian must have Assurance of his being in a good Estate before his Partaking; for that Ordinance is appointed for true tho' weak Believers, that so their Faith may be Strengthened. And there are many weak but true Believers, who have not Assurance, and for them with due Preparation to attend upon the Lord in this holy Institution, is the way to obtain Assurance. Nor is the Question, Whether Persons Orthodox in Judgment, and not Scandalous in their Conversation, are not to be Esteemed as true Believers: To Affirm that would not be an Error comparable to Mr. S. [in] his Positions. I conceive more than that, or then a meer Negative Righteousness, is requisite as a sufficient ground for Rational Charity, to conclude that there is a Work of Saving Grace wrought in the Soul: The Scripture acknowledgeth none to be Righteous, but such as *Positively* do Righteousness, I John 3. 7. And Mr. S. himself complains of those who judge men to be *Converted because they carry themselves Civilly & Religiously.* But the Question is, *Whether God requires Unsanctified Persons while such, to come to his Table;* and Consequently, *Whether the Church may admit into their Holy Communion in Special Ordinances, such as are not in the judgment of rational Charity, true Believers?* This being the Question, I maintain the Negative.

My *first* Argument shall be that which being Cleared, may be *Instar Omnium;* it is this, *Assertions which are contrary to many Scriptures, ought not to be received by the Churches.* But the impleaded Assertions are contrary to many Scriptures. I begin with a Scripture, which is like a flaming Sword to keep all Unregenerate Persons from daring to approach unto the Holy Table of the Lord: It is in, Mat. 22. 11, 12. *And when the King came in to see the Guests, he saw there a man which had not on a Wedding Garment; and he saith unto him, Friend, how camest thou in hither not having a Wedding Garment? And he was speechless.* When it is said, *How camest thou in hither?* It is as much to say, Thou art a bold Intruder, thou oughtest not to be here. It is then Evident, that they who come to the Lord's Table without a Wedding Garment, are Guests more bold than welcome. The Church is the House where the Marriage Feast is kept: 'Tis true, that the Servants were commanded to *Invite all;* but (as our Great Cotton observes) they were not commanded, *to bring all into the House;* but such as in *Obedience* to the *Invitation* put on the Wedding Garment. Otherwise the Servants themselves would displease the Lord by bringing in such unmeet Guests to his Holy Table. As he was offended with the Guest that presumed to come without the Wedding Garment, so he must needs be offended with the Servants for affronting him with such a Guest, had not they who are not able to discern as their Lord can, thought him to be adorned with that Garment. Could the Guest have said, The Servants found me in my Rags, and commanded me in their Lord's Name to come; if they had not also required him to put on the Wedding Garment in order to his coming to their Lord's Table, he would not have been speechless. For he might have said, I was commanded to come; and therefore why am I taxed for coming? The scope of the Parable is . . . to show, that he who Invited them to come, did intend that they should come with that Preparation as is suitable to the Nature, & for the Honour of the Master of the Feast: otherwise they would be obnoxious to a greater Punishment than those that never came. Now by the Wedding Garment, Faith in the Righteousness of Christ, and Inherent Sanctification also, is doubtless intended. To *Come in hither,* is to come into the Church. It remains then, that the Lord will Condemn those men who come into his Church, and so to his Holy Table without true Faith and Holiness. . . . Another Scripture, (and a terrible one it is) which is very contrary to Mr. S. his impleaded Assertions, is that, I Cor. 11. 27, 29. *Whosoever shall Eat this Bread, & Drink this Cup of the Lord unworthily, shall be guilty of the Body & Blood of the Lord. He that Eats & Drinks unworthily, Eats & Drinks Damnation* (or Judgment) *to himself.* . . . if the unworthiness of a particular Act in respect of the manner of doing it, may make a man Guilty, and expose him to Judgment, how much more the unworthiness of his Person? He that in respect of his state is an unworthy person will not eat & drink worthily, or with a due meetness & preparedness for such an Ordinance: But this is true of every Unregenerate man. He that is yet in his Sins without true Repentance for them, and that has not an interest in Christ by Faith is unworthy, and therefore will Eat and Drink unworthily at the Lord's Table, if he shall presume to come thither. A particular act of Ungodliness may render a man unworthy; that is to say, unmeet to partake at the Lord's Table. A Church-Member falling into a scandalous Sin is justly kept from the Sacrament, until he has manifested sincere Repentance: Then surely they that are in a state of Ungodliness, and that never Repented of any sin, are not worthy or meet Communicants. If impenitence for a particular sin makes a man unfit for the Lord's Supper, certainly impenitence under a state or course of sin does so much more . . .

I then in the second Place argue thus, *They that are not duly Qualified to be Members of Particular Gospel Churches, are not fit to be admitted to the Lord's Supper*. This will be readily yielded, so that it is needless to spend time in the Proof of it. I will not deny but that persons may be admitted to Baptism on the account of their being of the Visible Church, which many are, tho' not in Fellowship with any Particular Church. . . . Certain it is, that the Apostles Baptised many who were not joyned to any particular Church, as I have elsewhere many years ago fully declared. But the Lord's Supper may not be Administred to any, who are not Members of some particular Instituted Church: Nor indeed to them, except in a Church Assembly, I. Cor. 11. 20. . . . I proceed to *Assume, Unsanctified Persons are not fit to be Admitted Members in Particular Churches*. None but such as are (so far as men exercising a due Charity are able to judge) Sincere Converts, or True Believers on Christ, ought to be received into the Churches. Rough Stones were not laid in Solomon's Temple, but such as were hewen and prepared, I. King 6. 7. Surely then Unconverted, Unprepared Sinners ought not to be laid in Christ's Temple . . . But Mr. S. has the strangest Notion that ever was heard of in the World. For his assertion is, *The Saints by calling are to be accepted of the Church, whether they be Converted or no*. But did you ever hear of *Unconverted Saints by calling* before? Had he said, Visible Saints, and Seemingly Called, but not Really and Inwardly such in the sight of God, may be accepted by the Church, he would have affirmed, that which no body will contradict; but as he expresseth it, his Notion is *Contradictio in adjecto*, a notorious Contradiction of itself. Certainly, so far as men are *Sanctified*, they are *Converted*. If they are called to be Saints, they are called out of their Worldly, and so out of their Natural Unconverted Estate, John 15. 19. . . . .

We have done with the Second Argument, which refutes Mr. S. his Assertions, and proveth the contrary. We proceed to a third Argument, which is this;

If men meddle with that which they are no right until, they have not a Divine Allowance for their doing so. We cannot suppose that the Presumption of men in laying a claim unto that which they have no right unto, has a Divine Approbation. But Unsanctified persons have no true right to the Lord's Supper. They that have a right to the outward Sign, have also a right to the inward Grace signified thereby. The Lord has joyned the Exhibiting Sign, and the Grace Exhibited thereby, together. But Unregenerate persons have no right to the Grace signified in the Lord's Supper. It does Seal to the worthy partaker, all the Blessings promised in the New Covenant, and in particular the Remission of Sins. When our Saviour instituted this Holy Supper, he said to his Disciples, *This is my Blood of the New Testament, which is shed for many for the Remission of Sins*, Mat. 26. 28. The Sacrament ought not to be Administred unto those, to whom we cannot in charitable Judgment say, You are in Covenant with God, and the Blood of Christ has obtained for you, the Remission of your Sins. But an Unconverted Person has no real interest in the Covenant, Ephes. 2. 12. As long as he's to be Converted, he has nothing to do with God's Covenant, Psal. 50. 16, 17. He has no right to any of the saving Blessings promised in the Covenant. It is Faith in Christ which giveth a right thereunto. They then who are in a state of Unbelief, have no right to the Salvation of the Covenant; and consequently, no right to the Seal of that Salvation. The Question is not, (as in the stating of it has been declared) Whether some unregenerate men have not a visible right to the Sacrament

Coram Ecclesia, so as that the Churches charitably judging them to be Sanctified persons, cannot refuse them; but whether they have a right *Coram Deo;* or whether God bids them come to his Table, before they have repented and turned from their Sins? The Old Protestant Doctrine, was, That it is *only a Justifying Faith,* that gives right to the Sacrament in the sight of God: It is the Visibility of that Faith, which giveth a right before men. The reason why some Unregenerate persons have a right to Sacraments before men, is because they seem to be Regenerate, & to have that Faith, which giveth them a right unto the Grace Exhibited therein. Men look on the Outward appearance, but cannot look on the Heart, as the Lord does, I. Sam. 15. To give the Sacrament to those who are not so far as men can Judge, in a Regenerate Estate, is to set the Lord's Seal to a Blank: It is to Seal a Pardon to those whom the Lord has not Pardoned, and whom we are not by any rule of Charity bound to believe that he has Pardoned . . .

Another argument which is a clear Confutation of what Mr. S. affirms, is this, *If the Lord's Supper is a Converting Ordinance, then Profane Persons ought to be admitted to partake of it.* For we may not withold from the Profanest Person in the World that which is appointed to be the means of his Conversion. Nay, the more Wicked any are, the greater reason there is that the means of Conversion should be applied unto them. Therefore it is that the Gospel is to be Preached unto the worst of Sinners, yes, to Publicans the worst of men, and to Harlots the worst of Women, because that is an Ordinance appointed for Conversion, Mat. 21. 31. But such are not to be admitted to the Lord's Supper. Mr. S. himself confesseth that. But then how do's he Answer this Unanswerable Argument? He has Excogitated a new notion and an odd one; viz. *That the Sacrament is a Converting Ordinance for Church Members only, & not for other men.* I think the honour of this Invention belongs to himself alone. For in my small reading, I have not met with it in any other Author. His alledging that it is an Ordinance appointed for the Conversion of Non-Scandalous Church Members and none others, that which *Logicians* call *Petitio Principii,* or a begging of the Question. I should rather think as Learned Gillespy does, whose Words are these: *If the Sacrament is a Converting Ordinance for known Impenitent Scandalous Profane Persons within the Church,* (to make it a Converting Ordinance for Non-Scandalous Persons only, is a Phansy peculiar to Mr. S.) *What reason is there imaginable why it is not also a Converting Ordinance for Heathen, Pagans, Turks, Jews, or have we the least hint in the Scripture that an Ordinance which may convert the Profanest Un-excommunicated Person within the Church, cannot Convert both Heathen and Excommunicated Christians?* What rational reply Mr. S. can make to this I know not, unless he will Pretend that a Church-censure, and why not a Sacrament, is an Ordinance appointed for the Conversion of one within the Church; but not for any other: But then *Disputat ex non concessis,* he takes it for granted that the Person under censure is Unconverted; whenas that Ordinance is appointed for the Recovery of a fallen converted Brother, II Thes. 3. 15. . . . It remains that the new devised Distinction, of the Lord's Supper being appointed to be a Converting Ordinance for Church-Members; but not a Converting Ordinance for Non-Members, is not Solid nor Scriptural . . .

It is reasonable that all Mr. S. reasons for his new Tenent, should be weighed in the balance of the Sanctuary. He objects *That there is no certain Knowledge who has Sanctifying Grace; and that if only Godly men were to be admitted to Communion, there is not Knowledge enough on the Earth in order to the Practice of it. If the Church were only to receive those that are Converted, God would have given a certain Rule, whereby Converted Men might be discovered from those that are Unconverted:* To this purpose he speaks. . . . A Solution to this Objection may be given by Proposing another Objection for himself to answer. He maintains, That none but such as have a Dogmatical and Historical Faith, may come to the Sacrament. Heterodox or Heretical Persons erring in any Fundamental Article of the Christian Religion, may not come. Then according to his Notion, there must be a certain Rule whereby it may be discerned what men's inward Sentiments, and the belief of their Hearts is, Whether they do not speak falsely, when they say, That they believe such Articles of the Christian Faith, as they pretend to believe. Julian before his open Apostasy Professed, that he believed all the Doctrines of Christianity, because he thought he should not obtain the Empire without such a Profession. But afterwards he declared, That he never believed any of them. Arius Pretended, and by an Oath made others think, that he believed the Deity of our Saviour, that so he might have Communion with the Churches. And yet all was a deceit, he believed it not. If then only Orthodox Christians must be admitted to the Lord's Supper, *There is not* (as Mr. S. speaks) *Knowledge enough on Earth to order our Practice in this matter.* Let him answer this, and he will answer his own Objection concerning our Ignorance, of the Spiritual Estate of men, whether they have true Saving Grace or no. No doubt he will say, If men are Knowing, and Profess they believe the Principles of true Religion, and do not Profess any Error that is inconsistent therewith; the Rule requires that Churches who cannot Know the hearts, and inward Persuasions of men, should accept of their outward Profession. And why then should we not believe, That men that give us an account of their Conversion, & whose Conversations are outwardly blameless and holy, are really according to what they seem to be? If Mr. S. Argument is put into form, it will run thus, *If it is true that None but Regenerate Persons have in the sight of God a right to the Sacrament, then it is necessary that the Church before they admit them into their Communion, should infallibly know that they are Regenerate:* But it is not necessary that the Church should before they admit them into their Communion, infallibly know that they are Regenerate; therefore it is not true, That none but Regenerate Persons have in the sight of God a right unto the Sacrament. Now the consequence is denied. The Church may and ought to admit those into Communion, of whom they have no infallible knowledge, of their being in a Regenerative Estate. Because, as we have shewed they may have right before the Church, and yet not before God. The Hypocrisy of a man's Profession, is a sufficient bar in the sight of God, but it is not so in the sight of Men, if there is no evidence of it, Deut. 29. 29. Mr. S. has another objection. . . . viz. *That they who maintain that only Converted Persons, should come to the Sacrament, by that Doctrine harden Men in their Natural Estate, and hinder their Conversion, by making them believe that they are Converted already.* Whenas this Doctrine has no such tendency, but rather the contrary, that men should endeavour to make sure of their Conversion, that so they may Eat and Drink Salvation, and not Damnation to themselves, when they approach to the Holy Table. But the other Doctrine does rather tend to harden Unregenerate men in their Sins, by not only promising but Sealing Life unto them, and thereby hindring them from turning from their Evil way, Ezek. 13. 22. In the next page he objects, *That if only Saints are allowed to come to the Sacrament, then a man must know himself to be a Saint, before he can know that he is allowed to come.* Answ. Altho' it is true that if a man does know that he is not a Saint, but in a State of Sin, he ought not to come; it does not follow that a real Saint should neglect coming, because, he wants Assurance. There is a difference between a man's *knowing* that he is Unconverted, and having *some doubts* about it. If after serious Self-Examination, he cannot but hope that there is a Good Work begun in his Soul, he ought to come altho' his Hopes are not Assurance . . .

It is a sad Consideration that any of those who should set themselves to Promote a R*eformation,* in the *Collapsed Churches* in *New England,* by reducing them to their Primitive Purity, endeavour the contrary. I shall conclude with the Testimony of a whole Synod, the last General Synod that was in this Colony, and according to all appearing Probability, the last that ever will be. This Synod consisting of the Elders and Messengers of Churches, met in Boston in the year 1679. To consider of two Questions. 1. What are the Evils which have Provoked the Lord to bring his Judgments on New-England? 2. What is to be done that so these Evils may be Reformed? In Answer to the latter Question, there are these two Paragraphs. 1. *Inasmuch as the Present standing Gen-*

eration (both as to Leaders and People) is for the greater Part another Generation, than what was in New England Forty years ago, for us to declare our adherence to the Faith, and Order of the Gospel, according to what is from the Scripture expressed in the Platform of Church Discipline, may be a good means to recover those who have erred from the Truth, and to prevent Apostacy for the future. 2. It is requisite, that Persons be not admitted unto Communion in the Lord's Supper, without making a Personal and Publick Profession of their Faith, & Repentance, either orally, or in some other way, so as shall be to the Just Satisfaction of the Church, & that therefore both Elders, & Churches, be duely Watchful, & Circumspect in this matter, I Cor. 11. 28, 29. Act. 2. 41, 42. Ezek. 44. 7, 8, 9. Thus has Mr. Stoddard's Doctrine been Condemned, by a *whole* Synod of Elders, and Messengers of the Churches.

BIBLIOGRAPHICAL NOTE

For the most adequate discussion of the controversy consult, Perry Miller, "Solomon Stoddard, 1643–1729," *Harvard Theological Review*, xxxiv, 1941, pp. 277–320. Miller's other important essays are: "The Half-Way Covenant," *New England Quarterly*, vi, 1933, pp. 676–715; "The Marrow of Puritan Divinity," *Publications of the Colonial Society of Massachusetts*, xxxii, 1933–1937, pp. 247–300, also reprinted in his *Errand into the Wilderness*, Cambridge, Mass., 1956 and New York, 1964; and "Preparation for Salvation in Seventeenth Century New England," *Journal of the History of Ideas*, iv, 1943, pp. 253–286. A criticism of Miller's interpretation of the covenant theme is Everett H. Emerson, "Calvin and Covenant Theology," *Church History*, xxv, 1956, p. 136 ff. See also Kenneth B. Murdock, *Increase Mather: The Foremost American Puritan* (Cambridge, Mass., 1925).

Two standard sources are: Williston Walker, *The Creeds and Platforms of Congregationalism* (New York, 1893) and Henry M. Dexter, *Congregationalism of the Last Three Hundred Years as Seen in its Literature* (New York, 1880).

III. THE GREAT AWAKENING

INTRODUCTION

The arrival of settlers whose interest in the colonies was economic rather than religious, the increase of population, the loss of fervor which came with stability led to a decline in religious zeal in the first half of the eighteenth century. The Great Awakening in the 1730s and 1740s, led by Jonathan Edwards (1703–1758), George Whitefield (1714–1770), and Gilbert Tennent (1703–1764) was the effort to invigorate the personal religious life of the colonists with strong "measures" employed to prompt the conversion of the sinner. Itinerant revivalism, new forms of worship, altered styles of preaching were part of the "new measures" which elicited such great response. The enthusiasm led to division of congregations, challenges to the clergy, and theological debate. The emphasis on the immediacy of the believer's relation to God and increased stress on individual initiative brought a subtle change to the view of the Christian life. Leonard Trinterud's comment that the Great Awakening "gave to nearly four fifths of the [Presbyterian] Church a common understanding of the Christian life and the Christian faith"[1] may be extended to larger segments of American Protestantism.

Jonathan Edwards' sermon, "God Glorified in Man's Dependence," preached in Boston in 1731, while not directly related to the Great Awakening literature, shows the theological presuppositions upon which this major American writer worked. Though the essay was published very early in his career, it is, perhaps, the most generally representative of Edwards' thoughts. Educated at Yale (A.B. 1720), Edwards became pastor in 1729 of the church his grandfather, Solomon Stoddard, had ministered to at Northampton. Until his expul-

[1] Leonard Trinterud, *The Forming of an American Tradition: A Re-examination of Colonial Presbyterianism* (Philadelphia, 1949), p. 197.

sion in 1750 Edwards was the leading figure in New England
Congregationalism. After a period of approximately seven
years as a missionary in Stockbridge, Massachusetts, where
Edwards completed his major theological treatises, he became
President of the College of New Jersey (Princeton) only to
die three months later as a result of a smallpox inoculation.
Edwards was the "father" of the New Divinity party in New
England theology, the defenders of a "consistent" Calvinism.

Gilbert Tennent, a graduate of Yale in 1725, was strongly
influenced by the evangelistic zeal of the Dutch Reformed
revivalist, Theodore Frelinghuysen (1691–1746). During
Tennent's pastorate at New Brunswick, there was considerable
conflict within the Presbyterian Church over educational and
theological standards for the clergy, a controversy which made
clear the division between two national groups within the
church: the Scotch-Irish, seeking rigorous subscription to confessions of the church and the English, more willing to adopt
new measures for the enlivening of the religious life. Gilbert
Tennent, though Scotch-Irish in background, became aligned
with the English strain of Presbyterianism. His famous sermon, "The Danger of an Unconverted Ministry," was
preached on March 8, 1740, and was designed as a strong
attack upon those clergy who rejected the claim that a direct
call of God was required of them: "Is a dead Man fit to bring
others to life?", Tennent asked. Here was an issue which was
to continue to cause conflict in many churches.

Charles Chauncy (1704–1787), a graduate of Harvard in
1721, was pastor of the First Church in Boston. His *Season-
able Thoughts on the State of Religion in New England,*
published in 1743, attracted wide attention and made his
reputation as the main critic of the revivals. Chauncy's sober
and dispassionate character led him to challenge the extreme
measures of the revivalists and to deny that there is any one
form of Christian experience. During the course of his life, he
became increasingly involved in the theological conflicts
within Calvinism and served as a spokesman for the liberal,
"Arminian" party. Though it cannot be said with certainty
that the letter included as Selection 8 is from his pen, it is

likely that it is and certainly resembles his style and perspective.

[6]
Jonathan Edwards
God Glorified in Man's Dependence*

"God is glorified in the work of redemption in this, that there appears in it so absolute and universal a dependence of the redeemed on him."

Here I propose to show, 1st, That there is an absolute and universal dependence of the redeemed on God for all their good. And 2dly, That God hereby is exalted and glorified in the work of redemption.

I. There is an absolute and universal dependence of the redeemed on God. The nature and contrivance of our redemption is such, that the redeemed are in every thing directly, immediately, and entirely dependent on God: they are dependent on him for all, and are dependent on him every way.

The several ways wherein the dependence of one being may be upon another for its good, and wherein the redeemed of Jesus Christ depend on God for all their good, are these, viz., that they have all their good of him, and that they have all through him, and that they have all in him: that he is the cause and original whence all their good comes, therein it is *of* him; and that he is the medium by which it is obtained and conveyed, therein they have it *through* him; and that he is that good itself that is given and conveyed, therein it is *in* him.

Now those that are redeemed by Jesus Christ do, in all these respects, very directly and entirely depend on God for their all.

* From *The Works of President Edwards in Four Volumes,* iv (New York, 1844), pp. 170–177.

FIRST. The redeemed have all their good of God; God is the great author of it; he is the first cause of it, and not only so, but he is the only proper cause.

It is of God that we have our Redeemer: it is God that has provided a Saviour for us. Jesus Christ is not only of God in his person, as he is the only begotten Son of God, but he is from God, as we are concerned in him, and in his office of Mediator: he is the gift of God to us: God chose and anointed him, appointed him his work, and sent him into the world.

And as it is God that gives, so it is God that accepts the Saviour. As it is God that provides and gives the Redeemer to buy salvation for us, so it is of God that salvation is bought: he gives the purchaser, and he affords the thing purchased.

It is of God that Christ becomes ours, that we are brought to him, and are united to him: it is of God that we receive faith to close with him, that we may have an interest in him. Eph. ii, 8, "For by grace ye are saved, through faith; and that not of yourselves, it is the gift of God." It is of God that we actually do receive all the benefits that Christ has purchased. It is God that pardons and justifies, and delivers from going down to hell, and it is his favor that the redeemed are received into, and are made the objects of, when they are justified. So it is God that delivers from the dominion of sin, and cleanses us from our filthiness, and changes as from our deformity. It is of God that the redeemed do receive all their true excellency, wisdom, and holiness; and that two ways, viz., as the Holy Ghost, by whom these things are immediately wrought, is from God, proceeds from him, and is sent by him; and also as the Holy Ghost himself is God, by whose operation and indwelling, the knowledge of divine things, and a holy disposition, and all grace, are conferred and upheld.

And though means are made use of in conferring grace on men's souls, yet it is of God that we have these means of grace, and it is God that makes them effectual. It is of God that we have the holy Scriptures; they are the word of God. It is of God that we have ordinances, and their efficacy depends on the immediate influence of the Spirit of God. The ministers of the gospel are sent of God, and all their sufficiency is of him. 2 Cor. iv. 7, "We have this treasure in earthen vessels, that the excellency of the power may be of God, and not of us." Their success depends entirely and absolutely on the immediate blessing and influence of God. The redeemed have all,

1. Of the grace of God. It was of mere grace that God gave us his only begotten Son. The grace is great in proportion to the dignity and excellency of what is given: the gift was infinitely precious, because it was a person infinitely worthy, a person of infinite glory; and also because it was a person infinitely near and dear to God. The grace is great in proportion to the benefit we have given us in him: the benefit is doubly infinite, in that in him we have deliverance from an infinite, because an eternal misery; and do also receive eternal joy and glory. The grace in bestowing this gift is great in proportion to our unworthiness to whom it is given; instead of deserving such a gift, we merited infinitely ill of God's hands. The grace is great according to the manner of giving, or in proportion to the humiliation and expense of the method and means by which way is made for our having the gift. He gave him to us dwelling amongst us; he gave him to us incarnate, or in our nature; he gave him to us in our nature, in the like infirmities, in which we have it in our fallen state, and which in us do accompany, and are occasioned by the sinful corruption of our nature. He gave him to us in a low and afflicted state; and not only so, but he gave him to us slain, that he might be a feast for our souls.

The grace of God in bestowing this gift is most free. It was what God was under no obligation to bestow: he might have rejected fallen man, as he did the fallen angels. It was what we never did any thing to merit; it was given while we were yet enemies, and before we had so much as repented. It was from the love of God that saw no excellency in us to attract it; and it was without expectation of ever being requited for it.

And it is from mere grace that the benefits of Christ are applied to such and such particular persons. Those that are called and sanctified are to attribute it alone to the good pleasure of God's goodness, by which they are distinguished. He is sovereign, and hath mercy on whom he will have mercy, and whom he will, he hardens.

Man hath now a greater dependence on the grace of God than he had before the fall. He depends on the free goodness of God for much more than he did then: then he depended on God's goodness for conferring the reward of perfect obedience: for God was not obliged to promise and bestow that reward: but now we are dependent on the grace of God for much more: we stand in need of grace, not only to bestow glory upon us, but to deliver us from hell and eternal wrath. Under the first covenant we depended on God's goodness to give us the reward of righteousness; and so we do now. And not only so, but we stand in need of God's free and sovereign grace to give us that righteousness; and yet not only so, but we stand in need of his grace to pardon our sin, and release us from the guilt and infinite demerit of it.

And as we are dependent on the goodness of God for more now than under the first covenant, so we are dependent on a much greater, more free and wonderful goodness. We are now more dependent on God's arbitrary and sovereign good pleasure. We were in our first estate dependent on God for holiness: we had our original righteousness from him; but then holiness was not bestowed in such a way of sovereign good pleasure as it is now. Man was created holy, and it became God to create holy all the reasonable creatures he created: it would have been a disparagement to the holiness of God's nature, if he had made an intelligent creature unholy. But now when a man is made holy, it is from mere and arbitrary grace; God may forever deny holiness to the fallen creature if he pleases, without any disparagement to any of his perfections.

And we are not only indeed more dependent on the grace of God, but our dependence is much more conspicuous, because our own insufficiency and helplessness in ourselves is much more apparent in our fallen and undone state, than it was before we were either sinful or miserable. We are more apparently dependent on God for holiness, because we are first sinful, and utterly polluted, and afterwards holy: so the production of the effect is sensible, and its derivation from

God more obvious. If man was ever holy and always was so, it would not be so apparent, that he had not holiness necessarily, as an inseparable qualification of human nature. So we are more apparently dependent on free grace for the favor of God, for we are first justly the objects of his displeasure and afterwards are received into favor. We are more apparently dependent on God for happiness, being first miserable, and afterwards happy. It is more apparently free and without merit in us, because we are actually without any kind of excellency to merit, if there could be any such thing as merit in creature excellency. And we are not only without any true excellency, but are full of, and wholly defiled with, that which is infinitely odious. All our good is more apparently from God, because we are first naked and wholly without any good, and afterwards enriched with all good.

2. We receive all of the power of God. Man's redemption is often spoken of as a work of wonderful power as well as grace. The great power of God appears in bringing a sinner from his low state, from the depths of sin and misery, to such an exalted state of holiness and happiness. Eph. i. 19, "And what is the exceeding greatness of his power to usward who believe, according to the working of his mighty power."

We are dependent on God's power through every step of our redemption. We are dependent on the power of God to convert us, and give faith in Jesus Christ, and the new nature.

It is a work of creation: "If any man be in Christ, he is a new creature," 2 Cor. v. 17. "We are created in Christ Jesus," Eph. ii. 10. The fallen creature cannot attain to true holiness, but by being created again. Eph. iv. 24, "And that ye put on the new man, which after God is created in righteousness and true holiness." It is a raising from the dead. Col. ii. 12, 13, "Wherein ye also are risen with him, through the faith of the operation of God, who hath raised him from the dead." Yea, it is a more glorious work of power than mere creation, or raising a dead body to life, in that the effect attained is greater and more excellent. That holy and happy being, and spiritual life which is reached in the work of conversion, is a far greater and more glorious effect, than mere being and life. And the state from whence the change is made, of such a death in sin, and total corruption of nature, and depth of misery, is far more remote from the state attained, than mere death or nonentity.

It is by God's power also that we are preserved in a state of grace: 1 Pet. i. 5, "Who are kept by the power of God through faith unto salvation." As grace is at first from God, so it is continually from him, and is maintained by him, as much as light in the atmosphere is all day long from the sun, as well as at first dawning, or at sunrising.

Men are dependent on the power of God, for every exercise of grace, and for carrying on the work of grace in the heart, for the subduing of sin and corruption, and increasing holy principles, and enabling to bring forth fruit in good works, and at last bringing grace to its perfection, in making the soul completely amiable in Christ's glorious likeness, and filling of it with a satisfying joy and blessedness; and for the raising of the body to life, and to such a perfect state, that it shall be suitable for a habitation and organ for a soul so perfected and blessed. These are the most glorious effects of the power of God, that are seen in the series of God's acts with respect to the creatures.

Man was dependent on the power of God in his first estate, but he is more dependent on his power now; he needs God's power to do more things for him, and depends on the more wonderful exercise of his power. It was an effect of the power of God to make man holy at the first; but more remarkably so now, because there is a great deal of opposition and difficulty in the way. It is a more glorious effect of power to make that holy that was so depraved, and under the dominion of sin, than to confer holiness on that which before had nothing of the contrary. It is a more glorious work of power to rescue a soul out of the hands of the devil, and from the powers of darkness, and to bring it into a state of salvation, than to confer holiness where there was no prepossession or opposition. Luke xi. 21, 22, "When a strong man armed keepeth his palace, his goods are in peace; but when a stronger than he shall come upon him, and overcome him, he taketh from him all his armor wherein he trusted, and divideth his spoils." So it is a more glorious work of power to uphold a soul in a state of grace and holiness, and to carry it on till it is brought to glory, when there is so much sin remaining in the heart resisting, and Satan with all his might opposing, than it would have been to have kept man from falling at first, when Satan had nothing in man.

Thus we have shown how the redeemed are dependent on God for all their good, as they have all of him.

SECONDLY. They are also dependent on God for all, as they have all through him. It is God that is the medium of it, as well as the author and fountain of it. All that we have, wisdom, and the pardon of sin, deliverance from hell, acceptance in God's favor, grace and holiness, true comfort and happiness, eternal life and glory, we have from God by a Mediator; and this Mediator is God, which Mediator we have an absolute dependence upon as he through whom we receive all. So that here is another way wherein we have our dependence on God for all good. God not only gives us the Mediator, and accepts his mediation, and of his power and grace bestows the things purchased by the Mediator, but he is the Mediator.

Our blessings are what we have by purchase; and the purchase is made of God, the blessings are purchased of him, and God gives the purchaser; and not only so, but God is the purchaser. Yea, God is both the purchaser and the price; for Christ, who is God, purchased these blessings for us, by offering up himself as the price of our salvation. He purchased eternal life by the sacrifice of himself. Heb. vii. 27, "He offered up himself;" and ix. 26, "He hath appeared to take away sin by the sacrifice of himself." Indeed it was the human nature that was offered; but it was the same person with the divine, and therefore was an infinite price; it was looked upon as if God had been offered in sacrifice.

As we thus have our good through God, we have a dependence on God in a respect that man in his first estate had not. Man was to have eternal life then through his own righteousness; so that he had partly a dependence upon what was in himself; for we have a dependence upon that through which we have our good, as well as that from which we have it; and though man's righteousness that he then depended on was indeed from God, yet it was his own, it was inherent in himself; so that his dependence was not so immediately on God. But now the righteousness that we are dependent on is not in ourselves, but in God. We are saved through the righteousness of Christ: he *is made unto us righteousness;* and therefore is prophesied of, Jer. xxiii. 6, under that name, "the Lord our righteousness." In that the righteousness we are justified by is the righteousness of Christ, it is the righteousness of God: 2 Cor. v. 21, "That we might be made the righteousness of God in him."

Thus in redemption we have not only all things of God, but by and through him: 1 Cor. viii. 21, "But to us there is but one God, the Father, of whom are all things, and we in him; and one Lord Jesus Christ, by whom are all things, and we by him."

THIRDLY. The redeemed have all their good in God. We not only have it of him, and through him, but it consists in him; he is all our good.

The good of the redeemed is either objective or inherent. By their objective good, I mean that extrinsic object, in the possession and enjoyment of which they are happy. Their inherent good is that excellency or pleasure which is in the soul itself. With respect to both of which the redeemed have all their good in God, or, which is the same thing, God himself is all their good.

1. The redeemed have all their objective good in God. God himself is the great good which they are brought to the possession and enjoyment of by redemption. He is the highest good, and the sum of all that good which Christ purchased. God is the inheritance of the saints; he is the portion of their souls. God is their wealth and treasure, their food, their life, their dwelling place, their ornament and diadem, and their everlasting honor and glory. They have none in heaven but God; he is the great good which the redeemed are received to at death, and which they are to rise to at the end of the world. The Lord God, he is the light of the heavenly Jerusalem; and is the "river of the water of life," that runs, and "the tree of life that grows, in the midst of the paradise of God." The glorious excellencies and beauty of God will be what will for ever entertain the minds of the saints, and the

love of God will be their everlasting feast. The redeemed will indeed enjoy other things; they will enjoy the angels, and will enjoy one another; but that which they shall enjoy in the angels, or each other, or in any thing else whatsoever that will yield them delight and happiness, will be what will be seen of God in them.

2. The redeemed have all their inherent good in God. Inherent good is twofold; it is either excellency or pleasure. These the redeemed not only derive from God, as caused by him, but have them in him. They have spiritual excellency and joy by a kind of participation of God. They are made excellent by a communication of God's excellency: God puts his own beauty, i. e., his beautiful likeness, upon their souls: they are made partakers of the divine nature, or moral image of God, II Pet. i. 4. They are holy by being made partakers of God's holiness, Heb. xii. 10. The saints are beautiful and blessed by a communication of God's holiness and joy, as the moon and planets are bright by the sun's light. The saint hath spiritual joy and pleasure by a kind of effusion of God on the soul. In these things the redeemed have communion with God; that is, they partake with him and of him.

The saints have both their spiritual excellency and blessedness by the gift of the Holy Ghost, or Spirit of God, and his dwelling in them. They are not only caused by the Holy Ghost, but are in the Holy Ghost as their principle. The Holy Spirit becoming an inhabitant, is a vital principle in the soul: he, acting in, upon, and with the soul, becomes a fountain of true holiness and joy, as a spring is of water, by the exertion and diffusion of itself. John iv. 14, "But whosoever drinketh of the water that I shall give him, shall never thirst; but the water that I shall give him, shall be in him a well of water springing up into everlasting life." Compared with chap. vii. 38, 39, "He that believeth on me, as the Scripture hath said, out of his belly shall flow rivers of living water; but this spake he of the Spirit, which they that believe on him should receive." The sum of what Christ has purchased for us, is that spring of water spoken of in the former of those places, and those rivers of living water spoken of in the latter. And the sum of the blessings, which the redeemed shall receive in

heaven, is that river of water of life that proceeds from the
throne of God and the Lamb, Rev. xxii. 1. Which doubtless
signifies the same with those rivers of living water, explained,
John vii. 38, 39, which is elsewhere called the "river of God's
pleasures." Herein consists the fulness of good, which the
saints receive by Christ. It is by partaking of the Holy Spirit,
that they have communion with Christ in his fulness. God
hath given the Spirit, not by measure unto him, and they do
receive of his fulness, and grace for grace. This is the sum of
the saints' inheritance; and therefore that little of the Holy
Ghost which believers have in this world, is said to be the
earnest of their inheritance. II Cor. i. 22, "Who hath also
sealed us, and given us the Spirit in our hearts." And chap.
v. 5, "Now he that hath wrought us for the self-same thing,
is God, who also hath given unto us the earnest of the Spirit."
And Eph. i. 13, 14, "Ye were sealed with that Holy Spirit of
promise, which is the earnest of our inheritance, until the
redemption of the purchased possession."

The Holy Spirit and good things are spoken of in Scripture
as the same; as if the Spirit of God communicated to the
soul, comprised all good things: Matt. vii. 11, "How much
more shall your heavenly Father give good things to them
that ask him?" In Luke it is, chap. xi. 13, "How much
more shall your heavenly Father give the Holy Spirit to them that
ask him?" This is the sum of the blessings that Christ died
to procure, and that are the subject of gospel promises: Gal.
iii. 13, 14, "He was made a curse for us, that we might receive the promise of the Spirit through faith." The Spirit of
God is the great promise of the Father: Luke xxiv. 49, "Behold, I send the promise of my Father upon you." The Spirit
of God therefore is called "the Spirit of promise," Eph. i. 13.
This promised thing Christ received, and had given into his
hand, as soon as he had finished the work of our redemption,
to bestow on all that he had redeemed: Acts ii. 33, "Therefore, being by the right hand of God exalted, and having
received of the Father the promise of the Holy Ghost, he
hath shed forth this, which ye both see and hear." So that all
the holiness and happiness of the redeemed is in God. It is
in the communications, indwelling, and acting of the Spirit

of God. Holiness and happiness are in the fruit, here and hereafter, because God dwells in them, and they in God.

Thus it is God that has given us the Redeemer, and it is of him that our good is purchased: so it is God that is the Redeemer, and the price; and it is God also that is the good purchased. So that all that we have is of God,, and through him, and in him: Rom. xi. 36, "For of him, and through him, and to him, or in him, are all things." The same in the Greek that is here rendered *to him,* is rendered *in him,* 1 Cor. vii. 6.

II. God is glorified in the work of redemption by this means, viz., By there being so great and universal a dependence of the redeemed on him.

1. Man hath so much the greater occasion and obligation to take notice and acknowledge God's perfections and all-sufficiency. The greater the creature's dependence is on God's perfections, and the greater concern he has with them, so much the greater occasion has he to take notice of them. So much the greater concern any one has with, and dependence upon, the power and grace of God, so much the greater occasion has he to take notice of that power and grace. So much the greater and more immediate dependence there is on the divine holiness, so much the greater occasion to take notice of, and acknowledge that. So much the greater and more absolute dependence we have on the divine perfections, as belonging to the several persons of the Trinity, so much the greater occasion have we to observe and own the divine glory of each of them. That which we are most concerned with, is surely most in the way of our observation and notice; and this kind of concern with any thing, viz., dependence, does especially tend to command and oblige the attention and observation. Those things that we are not much dependent upon, it is easy to neglect; but we can scarce do any other than mind that which we have a great dependence on. By reason of our so great dependence on God, and his perfections, and in so many respects, he and his glory are the more directly set in our view, which way soever we turn our eyes.

We have the greater occasion to take notice of God's all-sufficiency, when all our sufficiency is thus every way of him. We have the more occasion to contemplate him as an infinite

good, and as the fountain of all good. Such a dependence
on God, demonstrates God's all-sufficiency. So much as the
dependence of the creature is on God, so much the greater
does the creature's emptiness in himself appear to be; and
so much the greater the creature's emptiness, so much the
greater must the fulness of the Being be who supplies him. Our having all of God shows the fulness of his
power and grace: our having all through him shows the fulness of his merit and worthiness; and our having all in him
demonstrates his fulness of beauty, love, and happiness.

And the redeemed, by reason of the greatness of their dependence on God, have not only so much the greater occasion, but obligation to contemplate and acknowledge the glory
and fulness of God. How unreasonable and ungrateful should
we be if we did not acknowledge that sufficiency and glory
that we do absolutely, immediately, and universally depend
upon!

2. Hereby is demonstrated how great God's glory is considered comparatively, or as compared with the creature's. By
the creature's being thus wholly and universally dependent
on God, it appears that the creature is nothing, and that God
is all. Hereby it appears that God is infinitely above us; that
God's strength, and wisdom, and holiness, are infinitely greater
than ours. However great and glorious the creature appre-
hends God to be, yet if he be not sensible of the difference
between God and him, so as to see that God's glory is great,
compared with his own, he will not be disposed to give God
the glory due to his name. If the creature, in any respect,
sets himself upon a level with God, or exalts himself to any
competition with him, however he may apprehend that great
honor and profound respect may belong to God from those
that are more inferior, and at a greater distance, he will not
be so sensible of its being due from him. So much the more
men exalt themselves, so much the less will they surely be
disposed to exalt God. It is certainly a thing that God aims
at in the disposition of things in the affair of redemption (if
we allow the Scriptures to be a revelation of God's mind),
that God should appear all, and man nothing. It is God's declared design that others should not "glory in his presence;"

which implies that it is his design to advance his own comparative glory. So much the more man "glories in God's presence," so much the less glory is ascribed to God.

3. By its being thus ordered, that the creature should have so absolute and universal a dependence on God, provision is made that God should have our whole souls, and should be the object of our undivided respect. If we had our dependence partly on God, and partly on something else, man's respect would be divided to those different things on which he had dependence. Thus it would be if we depended on God only for a part of our good, and on ourselves, or some other being for another part: or if we had our good only from God, and through another that was not God, and in something else distinct from both, our hearts would be divided between the good itself, and him from whom, and him through whom we received it. But now there is no occasion for this, God being not only he from or of whom we have all good, but also through whom and one that is that good itself, that we have from him and through him. So that whatsoever there is to attract our respect, the tendency is still directly towards God, all unites in him as the centre.

[7]

Gilbert Tennent

The Danger of An Unconverted Ministry[*]

"And Jesus, when he came out, saw much People and was moved with Compassion towards them, because they were as Sheep not having a Shepherd." [Mark 6. 34.]

As a faithful Ministry is a great Ornament, Blessing and Comfort, to the Church of GOD; even the Feet of such Messengers are beautiful: So on the contrary, an ungodly Ministry

[*] Gilbert Tennent, *The Danger of An Unconverted Ministry* (Boston, 1742), pp. 2–12; 16; 19–20.

is a great Curse and Judgment: These Caterpillars labour to
devour every green Thing.

There is nothing that may more justly call forth our saddest
Sorrows, and make all our Powers and Passions mourn, in
the most doleful Accents, the most incessant, insatiable, and
deploring Agonies; than the melancholy Case of such, who
have no faithful Ministry! This Truth is set before our Minds
in a strong Light, in the Words that I have chosen now to
insist upon! in which we have an Account of our LORD'S
Grief with the Causes of it.

We are informed, That our dear Redeemer was moved with
Compassion towards them. The Original Word signifies the
strongest and most vehement Pity, issuing from the innermost
Bowels.

But what was the Cause of this great and compassionate
Commotion in the Heart of Christ? It was because he saw
much People as Sheep, having no Shepherd. Why, had the
People then no Teachers? O yes! They had heaps of Pharisee-
Teachers, that came out, no doubt after they had been at
the Feet of Gamaliel the usual Time, and according to the
Acts, Cannons, and Traditions of the Jewish Church. But notwithstanding of the great Crowds of these Orthodox, Letter-
learned and regular Pharisees, our Lord laments the unhappy
Case of that great Number of People, who, in the Days of
his Flesh, had no better Guides: Because that those were as
good as none (in many Respects) in our Saviour's Judgment.
For all them, the People were as Sheep without a Shepherd.

From the Words of our Text, the following Proposition offers itself to our Consideration, viz.

That the Case of such is much to be pitied, who have no
other but Pharisee-Shepherds, or unconverted Teachers.

In discoursing upon this Subject, I would

I. Enquire into the Characters of the Old Pharisee-
Teachers.

II. Shew, why the Case of such People, who have no better, should be pitied. And

III. Shew, how Pity should be expressed upon this mournful Occasion! And

First I am to enquire into the Characters of the Old

Pharisee-Teachers. Now, I think, the most notorious Branches of their Character, were these, viz. Pride, Policy, Malice, Ignorance, Covetousness, and Bigotry to human Inventions in religious Matters.

The old Pharisees were very proud and conceity; they loved the uppermost Seats in the Synagogues, and to be called Rabbi, Rabbi; they were masterly and positive in their Assertions, as if forsooth Knowledge must die with them; they look'd upon others that differed from them, and the common People with an Air of Disdain; and especially any who had a Respect for JESUS and his Doctrine, and dislik'd them; they judged such accursed.

The old Pharisee-Shepherds were as crafty as Foxes; they tried by all Means to ensnare our Lord by their captious Questions, and to expose him to the Displeasure of the State; while in the mean Time, by sly and sneaking Methods, they tried to secure for themselves the Favour of the Grandees, and the People's Applause; and this they obtained to their Satisfaction. John 7. 48.

But while they exerted the Craft of Foxes, they did not forget to breathe forth the Cruelty of Wolves, in a malicious Aspersing the Person of Christ, and in a violent Opposing of the Truths, People and Power of his Religion. Yea, the most stern and strict of them were the Ring-leaders of the Party. Witness Saul's Journey to Damascus, with Letters from the Chief-Priest, to bring bound to Jerusalem all that he could find of that Way. It's true the Pharisees did not proceed to violent Measures with our Saviour and his Disciples just at first; but that was not owing to their good Nature, but their Policy; for they feared the People. They must keep the People in their Interests: Ay, that was the main Chance, the Compass that directed all their Proceedings: and therefore such sly cautious Methods must be pursued as might consist herewith. They wanted to root vital Religion out of the World; but they found it beyond their Thumb.

Although some of the old Pharisee-Shepherds had a very fair and strict Outside; yet were they ignorant of the New-Birth: Witness Rabbi Nicodemus, who talk'd like a Fool about it. Hear how our LORD cursed those plaister'd Hypocrites,

Mat. 23. 27, 28. Wo unto you, Scribes and Pharisees, Hypocrites; for ye are like whited Sepulchres, which indeed appear beautiful outward, but are within full of dead Bones, and of all Uncleanness, Even so ye also appear righteous unto Men, but within ye are full of Hypocrisy and Iniquity. Ay, if they had but a little of the Learning then in Fashion, and a fair Out-side, they were presently put into the Priest's Office, though they had no Experience of the New-Birth. O sad!

The old Pharisees, for all their long Prayers and other pious Pretences, had their Eyes, with Judas, fixed upon the Bag. Why, they came into the Priest's Office for a Piece of Bread; they took it up as a Trade, and therefore endeavoured to make the best Market of it they could. O Shame!

It may be further observed, That the Pharisee-Teachers in Christ's Time, were great Bigots to small Matters in Religion. . . .

Second General Head of Discourse, is to shew, Why such People, who have no better than the Old Pharisee-Teachers, are to be pitied? And

1. Natural Men have no Call of GOD to the Ministerial Work under the Gospel-Dispensation.

Isn't it a principal Part of the ordinary Call of GOD to the Ministerial Work, to aim at the Glory of GOD, and, in Subordination thereto, the Good of Souls, as their chief Marks in their Undertaking that Work? And can any natural Man on Earth do this? No! no! Every Skin of them has an evil Eye; for no Cause can produce Effects above its own Power. Are not wicked Men forbid to meddle in Things sacred? . . .

2. The Ministry of natural Men is uncomfortable to gracious souls. . . .

Natural Men, not having true Love to Christ and the Souls of their Fellow-Creatures, hence their Discourses are cold and sapless, and as it were freeze between their Lips. And not being sent of GOD, they want that divine Authority, with which the faithful Ambassadors of Christ are clothed, who herein resemble their blessed Master, of whom it is said, That He taught as one having Authority, and not as the Scribes. Mat. 7. 29.

And Pharisee-Teachers, having no Experience of a special

Work of the Holy Ghost, upon their own Souls, are therefore neither inclined to, nor fitted for, Discoursing, frequently, clearly, and pathetically, upon such important Subjects. The Application of their Discourses, is either short, or indistinct and general. They difference not the Precious from the Vile, and divide not to every Man his Portion, according to the Apostolical Direction to Timothy. No! they carelessly offer a common Mess to their People, and leave it to them, to divide it among themselves, as they see fit. This is indeed their general Practice, which is bad enough: But sometimes they do worse, by misapplying the Word, through Ignorance, or Anger. They often strengthen the Hands of the Wicked, by promising him Life. They comfort People, before they convince them; sow before they plow; and are busy in raising a Fabrick, before they lay a Foundation. These fooling Builders do but strengthen Men's carnal Security, by their soft, selfish, cowardly Discourses. They have not the Courage, or Honesty, to thrust the Nail of Terror into sleeping Souls; nay, sometimes they strive with all their Might, to fasten Terror into the Hearts of the Righteous, and so to make those sad, whom GOD would not have made sad! And this happens, when pious People begin to suspect their Hypocrisy, for which they have good Reason. I may add, That inasmuch as Pharisee-Teachers seek after Righteousness as it were by the Works of the Law themselves, they therefore do not distinguish, as they ought, between Law and Gospel in their Discourses to others. They keep Driving, Driving, to Duty, Duty, under this Notion, That it will recommend natural Men to the Favour of GOD, or entitle them to the Promises of Grace and Salvation: and thus those blind Guides fix a deluded World upon the false Foundation of their own Righteousness; and so exclude them from the dear Redeemer. All the Doings of unconverted Men, not proceeding from the Principles of Faith, Love, and a new Nature, nor being directed to the divine Glory as their highest End, but flowing from, and tending to Self, as their Principle and End; are doubtless damnably Wicked in their Manner of Performance, and do deserve the Wrath and Curse of a Sin-avenging GOD; neither can any other Encouragement be justly given them, but this, That in the Way of Duty, there is a Peradventure or Probability of obtaining Mercy.

And natural Men, wanting the Experience of those spiritual Difficulties, which pious Souls are exposed to, in this Vale of Tears; they know not how to speak a Word to the Weary in Season. Their Prayers are also cold; little childlike Love to God or Pity to poor perishing Souls, runs thro' their Veins. Their Conversation hath nothing of the Savour of Christ, neither is it perfum'd with the Spices of Heaven. They seem to make as little Distinction in their Practice as Preaching. They love those Unbelievers that are kind to them, better than many Christians, and chuse them for Companions . . . O! it is ready to break their very Hearts with Grief, to see how lukewarm those Pharisee-Teachers are in their publick Discourses, while Sinners are sinking into Damnation, in Multitudes! But

3. The Ministry of natural Men, is for the most part unprofitable; which is confirmed by a three-fold Evidence, viz. of Scripture, Reason, and Experience . . .

Is a blind Man fit to be a Guide in a very dangerous Way? Is a dead Man fit to bring others to Life? a mad Man fit to give Counsel in a Matter of Life and Death? Is a possessed Man fit to cast out Devils? a Rebel, an Enemy to GOD, fit to be sent on an Embassy of Peace, to bring Rebels into a State of Friendship with GOD? a Captive bound in the Massy Chains of Darkness and Guilt, a proper Person to set others at Liberty? a Leper, or one that has Plague-sores upon him, fit to be a good Physician? Is an ignorant Rustick, that has never been at Sea in his Life, fit to be a Pilot, to keep Vessels from being dashed to Pieces upon Rocks and Sand-banks? 'Isn't an unconverted Minister like a Man who would learn others to swim, before he has learn'd it himself, and so is drowned in the Act, and dies like a Fool?'

I may add, That sad Experience verifies what has been now observed, concerning the Unprofitableness of the Ministry of unconverted Men. Look into the Congregations of unconverted Ministers, and see what a sad Security reigns there; not a Soul convinced that can be heard of, for many Years together; and yet the Ministers are easy; for they say they do their Duty! Ay, a small Matter will satisfy us in the Want of that, which we have no great Desire after. . . .

What if some Instances could be shewn, of unconverted Ministers being Instrumental, in convincing Persons of their lost State? The Thing is very rare, and extraordinary. And for what I know, as many Instances may be given, of Satan's convincing Persons by his Temptations. Indeed it's a kind of Chance-medly, both in Respect of the Father, and his Children; when any such Event happens. And isn't this the Reason, why a Work of Conviction and Conversion has been so rarely heard of, for a long Time, in the Churches, till of late, viz. That the Bulk of her spiritual Guides, were stone-blind and stone-dead?

1. The Ministry of natural Men is dangerous, both in respect of the Doctrines, and Practice of Piety. The Doctrines of Original Sin, Justification by Faith alone, and the other Points of Calvinism, are very cross to the Grain of unrenew'd Nature. And tho' Men, by the Influence of a good Education, and Hopes of Preferment may have the Edge of their natural Enmity against them blunted; yet it's far from being broken or removed: It's only the saving Grace of GOD, that can give us a true Relish for those Nature-humbling Doctrines; and so effectually secure us from being infected by the contrary. Is not the Carnality of the Ministry, one great Cause of the general Spread of Arminianism, Socinianism, Arianism, and Deism, at this Day through the World? . . .

Third general Head was to shew, How Pity should be expressed upon this mournful Occasion?

My Brethren, we should mourn over those, that are destitute of faithful Ministers, and sympathize with them. Our Bowels should be moved with the most compassionate Tenderness, over those dear fainting Souls, that are as Sheep having no Shepherd; and that after the Example of our blessed LORD.

Dear Sirs! we should also most earnestly pray for them, that the compassionate Saviour may preserve them, by his mighty Power, thro' Faith unto Salvation; support their sinking Spirits, under the melancholy Uneasinesses of a dead Ministry; sanctify and sweeten to them the dry Morsels they

get under such blind Men, when they have none better to
repair to.

And more especially, my Brethren, we should pray to the
LORD of the Harvest, to send forth faithful Labourers into
his Harvest; seeing that the Harvest truly is plenteous, but
the Labourers are few. And O Sirs! how humble, believing,
and importunate should we be in this Petition! O! let us follow the LORD, Day and Night, with Cries, Tears, Pleadings
and Groanings upon this Account! For GOD knows there is
great Necessity of it. O! thou Fountain of Mercy, and Father
of Pity, pour forth upon thy poor Children a Spirit of Prayer,
for the Obtaining this important Mercy! Help, help, O
Eternal GOD and Father, for Christ's sake!

And indeed, my Brethren, we should join our Endeavours
to our Prayers. The most likely Method to stock the Church
with a faithful Ministry, in the present Situation of Things, the
publick Academies being so much corrupted and abused
generally, is, To encourage private Schools, or Seminaries of
Learning, which are under the Care of skilful and experienced
Christians; in which those only should be admitted, who upon
strict Examination, have in the Judgment of a reasonable
Charity, the plain Evidences of experimental Religion. Pious
and experienced Youths, who have a good natural Capacity,
and great Desires after the Ministerial Work, from good Motives, might be sought for, and found up and down in the
Country, and put to Private Schools of the Prophets; especially in such Places, where the Publick ones are not. This
Method, in my Opinion, has a noble Tendency, to build up
the Church of God. And those who have any Love to Christ,
or Desire after the Coming of his Kingdom, should be ready,
according to their Ability, to give somewhat, from time to
time, for the Support of such poor Youths, who have nothing
of their own. And truly, Brethren, this Charity to the Souls
of Men, is the most noble kind of Charity. O! if the Love of
God be in you, it will constrain you to do something, to promote so noble and necessary a Work. It looks Hypocrite-like
to go no further, when other Things are required, than cheap
Prayers. Don't think it much, if the Pharisees should be
offended at such a Proposal; these subtle selfish Hypocrites

are wont to be scar'd about their Credit, and their Kingdom; and truly they are both little worth, for all the Bustle they make about them. If they could help it, they wo'dn't let one faithful Man come into the Ministry; and therefore their Opposition is an encouraging Sign. Let all the Followers of the Lamb stand up and act for GOD against all Opposers: Who is upon GOD's Side? Who?

The Improvement of this Subject remains. And

1. If it be so, That the Case of those, who have no other, or no better than Pharisee-Teachers, is to be pitied: Then what a Scrole and Scene of Mourning, and Lamentation, and Wo, is opened! because of the Swarms of Locusts, the Crowds of Pharisees, that have as covetously as cruelly, crept into the Ministry, in this adulterous Generation! who as nearly resemble the Character given of the old Pharisees, in the Doctrinal Part of this Discourse, as one Crow's Egg does another. It is true some of the modern Pharisees have learned to prate a little more orthodoxly about the New Birth, than their Predecessor Nicodemus, who are, in the mean Time, as great Strangers to the feeling Experience of it, as he. They are blind who see not this to be the Case of the Body of the Clergy, of this Generation. And O! that our Heads were Waters, and our Eyes a Fountain of Tears, that we could Day and Night lament, with the utmost Bitterness, the doleful Case of the poor Church of God, upon this account.

2. From what has been said, we may learn, That such who are contented under a dead Ministry, have not in them the Temper of that Saviour they profess. It's an awful Sign, that they are as blind as Moles, and as dead as Stones, without any spiritual Taste and Relish. And alas! isn't this the Case of Multitudes? If they can get one, that has the Name of a Minister, with a Band, and a black Coat or Gown to carry on a Sabbath-days among them, although never so coldly, and insuccessfully; if he is free from gross Crimes in Practice, and takes good Care to keep at a due Distance from their Consciences, and is never troubled about his Insuccessfulness; O! think the poor Fools, that is a fine Man indeed; our Minister is a prudent charitable Man, he is not always harping upon Terror, and sounding Damnation in our Ears, like some

rash-headed Preachers, who by their uncharitable Methods, are ready to put poor People out of their Wits, or to run them into Despair; O! how terrible a Thing is that Dispair! Ay, our Minister, honest Man, gives us good Caution against it. Poor silly Souls! consider seriously these Passages, of the Prophet, Jeremiah 5. 30, 31.

3. We may learn, the Mercy and Duty of those that enjoy a faithful Ministry. Let such glorify GOD, for so distinguishing a Privilege, and labour to walk worthy of it, to all well-pleasing; lest for their Abuse thereof, they be exposed to a greater Damnation.

4. If the Ministry of natural Men be as it has been represented; Then it is both lawful and expedient to go from them to hear Godly Persons; yea, it's so far from being sinful to do this, that one who lives under a pious Minister of lesser Gifts, after having honestly endeavour'd to get Benefit by his Ministry, and yet gets little or none, but doth find real Benefit and more Benefit elsewhere; I say, he may lawfully go, and that frequently, where he gets most Good to his precious Soul, after regular Application to the Pastor where he lives, for his Consent, and proposing the Reasons thereof; when this is done in the spirit of Love and Meekness, without Contempt of any, as also without rash Anger or vain Curiosity. . . .

Is not the visible Church composed of Persons of the most contrary Characters? While some are sincere Servants of God, are not many Servants of Satan, under a religious Mask? and have not these a fixed Enmity against the other? How is it then possible, that a Harmony should subsist between such, till their Nature be changed? Can Light dwell with Darkness? . . .

And let those who live under the Ministry of dead Men, whether they have got the Form of Religion or not, repair to the Living, where they may be edified. Let who will, oppose it. . . . But tho' your Neighbours growl against you, and reproach you for doing your Duty, in seeking your Soul's Good; bear their unjust Censures with Christian Meekness, and persevere; as knowing that Suffering is the lot of Christ's

Followers, and that spiritual Benefits do infinitely overbalance all temporal Difficulties.

[8]

Charles Chauncy
A Letter Concerning the State of Religion in New England*

Reverend Sir,

I Perceive by a printed Letter from a Friend in *Edinburgh,* containing *Excerpts of Letters concerning the Success of the Gospel in these Parts,* that marvellous Accounts have been sent Abroad of a most glorious Work of Grace going on in *America,* as begun by Mr. *Whitefield,* and helped forward by those in his way of preaching and acting. I should be glad there had been more Truth in those Accounts. Some of the Things related are known Falsehoods, others strangely enlarged upon; and the Representations, in general, such, as exhibit a wrong Idea of the *religious* State of Affairs among us. I had Thoughts of sending you the needful Corrections of that *Pamphlet;* but my Circumstances being such, at present, as not to allow of this, must content myself with giving you the following *summary* Narration of things as they have appeared among us.

The Minds of People in this Part of the World, had been great prepossest in Favour of Mr. *Whitefield,* from the Accounts transmitted of him, from time to time, as a *Wonder of Piety, a Man of God,* so as *no one was like him:* Accordingly,

---

* From "A Letter from a Gentleman in Boston, to Mr. George Wishart, One of the Ministers of Edinburgh, Concerning the State of Religion in New England," in *The Clarendon Historical Society's Reprints,* Series I., 1882–1884 (Edinburgh, 1883), pp. 73–83. The author of the letter is not indicated, but it most probably is from Charles Chauncy.

when he came to *Town,* about two Years since, he was
received as though he had been an *Angel of God;* yea, *a God
come down in the likeness of Man.* He was strangely flocked
after by all Sorts of Persons, and much admired by the *Vul-
gar,* both *great* and *small.* The *Ministers* had him in Veneration, at least in Appearance, as much as the People; encouraged his Preaching, attended it themselves every Day in
the Week, and mostly *twice* a Day. The grand Subject of
Conversation was Mr. *Whitefield,* and the whole Business of
the Town to run, from Place to Place, to hear him preach:
And, as he preach'd under such uncommon Advantages,
being high in the Opinion of the People, and having the
Body of the Ministers hanging on his Lips, he soon insinuated
himself still further into the Affections of Multitudes, in so
much that it became dangerous to mention his Name, without saying something in commendation of him.

His Reception as he passed through *this* and the neighbouring Governments of *Connecticut* and *New York,* till he came
to *Philadelphia,* was after much the same Manner; save only,
that he met with no Admirers among the *Clergy,* unless here
and there one, any where but in *Boston:* And, whether the
Ministers here in general, really thought better of him than
they did elsewhere, I will not be too positive to affirm. 'Tis
possible, they might act as tho' they had a great Veneration
for him, and so as to lead People into such an Apprehension,
from *Cowardice, Affectation of Popularity,* or a *rigid Attachment to some Sentiments in Divinity,* they might imagine
there was now an Advantage to establish and propagate: And
I would not undertake to prove, that they might none of
them be under an undue Influence from some or other of
these Motives.

Much began to be now said of a *glorious Work of God*
going on in the Land. *Evening-lectures* were set up in one
Place and another; no less than six in this Town, *four* weekly,
and *two* monthly ones, tho' the Town does not consist of
above 5000 Families at the largest Computation. At some of
these Lectures, it was common to mention Mr. *Whitefield* by
Name, both in the *Prayers* and *Sermons;* giving God Thanks
for sending such an *extraordinary* Man among us, and making

him the Instrument of *such extraordinary Good* to so many souls. He was indeed spoken of, as *the Angel flying through Heaven with the Everlasting Gospel,* and such Honours sacrificed to him as were due to no meer Man: Nay, to such a Height did this Spirit rise, that all who did not express a very high Thought of Mr. *Whitefield,* were lookt upon with an evil Eye; and as to those who declared their Dislike of what they judged amiss of the Times, they were stigmatised as *Enemies of God and true Religion;* yea, they were openly represented, both from the *Pulpit* and the *Press,* as in danger of committing *the Sin against the Holy Ghost,* if not actually guilty even of this *unpardonable* Sin.

And here you will doubtless be disposed to enquire, what was the *great Good* this *Gentleman* was the Instrument of.

In answer whereto, I freely acknowledge, wherever he went he generally moved the *Passions,* especially of the *younger* People, and the *Females* among them; the Effect whereof was, a great Talk about Religion, together with a Disposition to be perpetually hearing Sermons, to neglect of all other Business; especially, as preach'd by those who were Sticklers for the *new Way,* as it was called. And in these things *chiefly* consisted the Goodness so much spoken of. I deny not, but there might be here and there a Person stopp'd from going on in a Course of Sin, and some might be made really better: But so far as I could judge upon the nicest Observation, the Town, in general, was not much mended in those things wherein a Reformation was greatly needed. I could not discern myself, nor many others whom I have talked with, and challenged on this Head, but that there was the same Pride and Vanity, the same Luxury and Intemperance, the same lying and tricking and cheating, as before this Gentleman came among us. There was certainly no *remarkable* Difference as to these things: And 'tis vain in any to pretend there was. This, I am sure of, there was raised such a Spirit of bitter, censorious, uncharitable judging, as was not known before; and is, wherever it reigns, a Scandal to all who call themselves Christians: Nor was it ever evident to me, but that the greatest Friends to Mr. *Whitefield* were as much puffed up with Conceit and Pride as any of their Neighbours;

and as to some of them, and the more eminent too, I verily believe they possess a *worse Spirit* than before they heard of his Name, and it had been as well for them if they had never seen his Face.

But I have only entered as yet upon that Scene of Things, which has made so much Noise in the Country. A Number of Ministers in one Place and another, were by this Time formed into Mr. *Whitefield's* Temper, and began to appear and go about preaching, with a Zeal more flaming, if possible, than his. One of the most famous among these was Mr. *Gilbert Tennent*, a Man of no great Parts or Learning; his preaching was in the *extemporaneous* Way, with much Noise and little Connection. If he had taken suitable Care to prepare his Sermons, and followed Nature in the Delivery of them, he might have acquitted himself as a *middling* Preacher; but as he preached, he was an *awkward Imitator* of Mr. *Whitefield*, and too often turned off his Hearers with *mere Stuff*, which he uttered with a Spirit more bitter and uncharitable than you can easily imagine; all were *Pharisees*, *Hypocrites*, *carnal unregenerate Wretches*, both Ministers and People, who did not think just as he did, particularly as to the Doctrines of *Calvinism;* and those who opposed him, and the Work of God he was sure he was carrying on, would have opposed *Christ Jesus himself* and *his Apostles*, had they lived in their Day. This Gentleman came from *New-Brunswick* in the *Jersies* to *Boston*, in the Middle of Winter, (a Journey of more than 300 Miles) to *water the good Seed sown by Mr.* Whitefield in this Place. It was indeed at Mr. *Whitefield's* Desire, and in consequence of a Day of *Fasting and Prayer*, kept on purpose to know the Mind of God as to this Matter, that he came among us; the *Ministers in the Town*, though *fourteen* in number, being thought insufficient to carry on the *good Work* he had begun here in the Hearts of People. And though the Design this Gentleman professedly came upon, was a bare-faced Affront to the *Body of the Ministers*, yet not only the People, (which is not to be wondred at) but some of the Ministers themselves admired and followed him, as much as they had done Mr. *Whitefield* before him; and here he was, by their Encouragement, a great Part of the Winter, preaching every Day in the Week, to the taking People off from their Callings, and the introducing a Neglect of all Business but that of hearing him preach. He went from *Boston* to the *eastward*, to visit the Places where Mr. *Whitefield* had been; and on his Return home passed through the Country, preaching every where as he went along, in the same Manner, and with the same Spirit he did here in *Boston.*

And now it was, that Mr. *Whitefield's* Doctrine of *inward Feelings* began to discover itself in Multitudes, whose *sensible Perceptions* arose to such a Height, as that they *cried out, fell down, swooned away,* and, to all Appearance, were like Persons in *Fits;* and this, when the Preaching (if it may be so called) had in it as little well digested and connected good Sense, as you can well suppose. Scores in a Congregation would be in such Circumstances at a Time; nay some hundreds in some Places, to the filling the Houses of Worship with Confusion not to be expressed in Words, nor indeed conceived of by the most lively Imagination, unless where Persons have been Eye and Ear witnesses to these Things. Though I may add here, that to a Person in possession of himself, and capable of Observation, this surprising Scene of Things may be accounted for: The *Speaker* delivers himself, with the *greatest Vehemence* both of *Voice* and *Gesture,* and in the most *frightful Language* his Genius will allow of. If this has its intended Effect upon *one* or *two weak Women,* the Shrieks catch from one to another, till a great Part of the Congregation is affected; and some are in the Thought, that it may be too common for those *zealous in the new Way to cry out themselves,* on purpose to move others, and bring forward a *general Scream. Visions* now became common, and *Trances* also, the Subjects of which were in their own Conceit transported from Earth to Heaven, where they saw and heard most glorious Things; conversed with *Christ* and *holy Angels;* had opened to them the *Book of Life,* and were permitted to read the names of persons there, and the like. And what is a singular Instance (so far as I remember) of the working of Enthusiasm, *laughing, loud hearty laughing,* was one of the Ways in which our *new Converts,* almost

every where, were wont to join together in expressing their
Joy at the Conversion of others.

'Tis scarce imaginable what Excesses and Extravagancies
People were running into, and even encouraged in; being told
such Things were Arguments of the *extraordinary Presence
of the Holy Ghost* with them. The same Houses of Worship
were scarce emptied Night nor Day for a Week together,
and unheard of Instances of supposed Religion were carried
on in them, some would be *praying*, some *exhorting*, some
singing, some *clapping their Hands*, some *laughing*, some *crying*, some *shrieking and roaring out;* and so invincibly set
were they in these Ways, especially when encouraged by
any Ministers, (as was too often the Case) that it was a
vain Thing to argue with them, to shew them the Indecency
of such Behaviour; and whoever indeed made an Attempt
this Way, might be sure aforehand of being called an *Op-
poser* of the *Spirit,* and a *Child of the Devil.*

At these Times there were among the People what we
call here EXHORTERS; these are such as are esteemed to be
Converts in the *new Way*. Sometimes they are *Children,
Boys* and *Girls,* sometimes *Women;* but most commonly *raw,
illiterate, weak* and *conceited young Men,* or *Lads.* They
pray with the People, call upon them to come to Christ, tell
them they are dropping into Hell, and take upon them what
they imagine is the Business of preaching. They are generally
much better thought of than any Ministers, except those in
the *new Way,* I mean by the Friends to the *Extraordinaries*
prevalent in the Land; and they are the greatest promoters
of them. 'Tis indeed at the *Exhortations* of these poor
ignorant Creatures, that there is ordinarily the most Noise
and Confusion: And what may be worth a particular Remark,
'tis *seldom* there are any great Effects wrought, till the
Gloominess of the Night comes on. It is in the *Evening,* or
more late in the *Night,* with only a *few Candles* in a *Meeting-
house,* that there is the *screaming* and *shrieking* to the greatest Degree; and the Persons thus affected are generally
Children, young People, and *Women.* Other Instances there
may have been, but they are more rare; these bear the chief
Part.

I shall here insert a Paragraph of a Letter sent me by a Friend living at *Newhaven,* the seat of one of our *Colleges,* a Gentleman of known Integrity and Veracity, giving an Account of the Managements of one of the Preachers of Mr. *Whitefield's* making, with the Appearance following thereupon. Says he, "After the Conclusion of the Exercises usual in our religious Assemblies, he came down from the *Pulpit* into the *Deacon's* Seat. His Exercises were, 1. *Short Prayers;* wherein he used very uncommon Expressions, and such as had no Tendency, at least in my Mind, to excite Devotion; which he delivered with a boisterous Voice, and in a Manner to me very disagreeable. 2. *Singing Psalms* and *Hymns;* which he himself repeated with an awful Tone and frightful Gestures. 3. *Exhorting,* as they called it: to which many *Laymen* were admitted as *Assistants.* In performing these Exercises they observed no stated Method, but proceeded as their present Thought or Fancy led them: And by this means the Meeting-house would be filled with what I could not but judge great Confusion and Disorder, for the whole House would many times seem to be in a perfect Hubbub, and People filled with Consternation. These Meetings they would continue till 10, 11, 12 o'Clock at Night; in the midst of them sometimes 10, 20, 30, and sometimes many more would *scream* and *cry out,* or send forth the most *lamentable Groans,* whilst others made great Manifestations of Joy, by *clapping their Hands,* uttering *extatick Expressions, singing Psalms,* and *inviting* and *exhorting* others. Some would *swoon away* under the Influence of distressing Fears, and others *swallowed up with insupportable Joy.* While some were *fainting,* others laboured under *convulsive Twitches of Body,* which they said were involuntary. But in vain shall I pretend to describe all the Proceedings at those Meetings. But what appeared to me most dangerous and hurtful was, that very much Stress was laid on these *Extraordinaries,* as tho' they were *sure Marks,* or, at least *sufficient Evidences* of a just Conviction of Sin on the one Hand; or, on the other, of that Joy which there is in Believing, and so of an Interest in the Favour of God."

You may be ready perhaps to think I have here given you

a romantick Representation of Things; but it is the real Truth
of the Case without a Figure; yea, this has been the Appearance in all Parts of the Land more or less, and so known
to have been so, that there is no room for Debate upon the
Matter: Nay, those who are Friends to the *new Way* were
once so far from being ashamed of these Things, that they
boasted of them, and entertained an ill Opinion of all who
did not speak of them as *Evidences* of the *wonderful Power
of the Spirit of God:* I say, they *at first* boasted of these
Things, and some of them do so still; though the Generality
have begun, for some time, to speak publickly of the *Subtility
of Satan,* to tell People he may appear as *an Angel of Light,*
and to warn them against being carried away by his Devices.
Nay Mr. *Tennent* himself, one of the main Instruments of
all our Disorders, has, in a couple of Letters to some of his
Friends,[1] expressed his Fears lest the Churches should be

[1] One Letter, with the Title prefixed to it in the *Boston Evening-
Post, July* 26, 1742, is as follows:

Extract of a Letter from the Rev. Mr. G. Tennent, *to the Rev. Mr.*
Dickinson *of the* Jerseys, *the Original of which is in the Hands
of the Rev. Mr.* Clap, *Rector of* Yale-College, *and was lately
given him by Mr.* Dickinson.

Dear Sir,
I have had many afflicting Thoughts about the Debates that have
subsisted for some time in our Synod: I would to God the Breach
were healed, if it was the Will of the Almighty.—As for my *own*
Part, wherein I have mismanaged in doing what I did;—I do look
upon it to be my Duty, and should be willing to acknowledge it
in the openest manner.—I cannot justify the *excessive Heat of
Temper* which has sometimes appeared in my Conduct.—I have
been of late (since I returned from *New-England*) visited with
much spiritual Desertions, Temptations, and Distresses of various
kinds, coming in a thick, and almost continual Succession, which
have given me a greater Discovery of myself than I think I ever
had before. These Things, with the Trials I have had of the *Moravians,* have given me a clear View of the Danger of everything
which tends to *Enthusiasm* and *Division* in the visible Church.—I
think that while the enthusiastical *Moravians* and *Long-beards,* or
Pickists, are uniting their Bodies, (no doubt to increase their

undone with a *Spirit of Enthusiasm,* and *these Exhorters* which have risen up everywhere in the Land. He seems indeed to have quite turned about: The Reason whereof may be this; the *Moravians* who came to *Philadelphia* with Count *Zinzendorf,* have been among his People, and managed with them as he did elsewhere, and brought the like Confusion

---

Strength, and render themselves more considerable) it is a shame that the Ministers (who are in the main of sound Principles of Religion) should be divided and quarrelling.—Alas for it! my Soul is sick of these things: I wish that some scriptural healing Methods could be fallen upon to put an End to these confusions. Sometimes since I felt a Disposition to fall upon my Knees, if I had Opportunity, to intreat them to be at Peace. I add no more at present, but humble and hearty Salutations, and remain with all due Honour and Respect,

Your poor worthless Brother
in the Gospel-Ministry,

G. TENNENT

New-Brunswick,
Feb. 12. 1741–2.

P. S. I break open the Letter myself to add my Thoughts about some extraordinary Things in Mr. *Davenport's* Conduct.— to his making his Judgment about the *internal* State of Persons, or their *Experience,* a Term of Church-fellowship, I believe it is *inscriptural,* and of awful Tendency to rend and tear the Church: It is bottomed upon a false Base, *viz.* That a certain and infallible Knowledge of the good Estate of Men, from their Experience, is attainable in this Life. The Practice is *schismatical,* in as much as it sets up a *new Term* of Communion which CHRIST has not fixed.

The late Method of setting up *separate Meetings,* upon the *supposed Unregeneracy* of Pastors of Places, is *enthusiastical, proud,* and *schismatical.* All that fear GOD ought to oppose it as a most dangerous Engine to bring the Churches into the most damnable Errors and Confusions. The Practice is built upon a twofold false Hypothesis, *viz.* Infallibility of knowledge; and that unconverted Ministers will be used as Instruments of no good to the Church.

The Practice of *openly exposing Ministers,* who are supposed to be unconverted in publick Discourse, by particular Application of such Times and Places, serves only to provoke them, (instead of doing them any good) and to declare our own Arrogance. It is an unprecedented, divisial, and pernicious Practice; it is a lording it over our Brethren, a Degree superior to what any Prelate has pretended since the coming of CHRIST, (so far as I know) the *Pope*

among them; and now he cries out of Danger, and expresses himself much as those did, whom before he had sent to the Devil by wholesale.

Various are the Sentiments of Persons about this *unusual Appearance* among us. Some think it to be a *most wonderful Work of God's Grace;* others a *most wonderful Spirit of Enthusiasm;* some think there is a *great deal of Religion,* with some *small Mixture* of Extravagance; others a *great deal of Extravagance* with some *small Mixture* of that which may be called *good;* some think the *Country* was never in such a *happy* State on a *religious* account, others that it was never in a *worse.*

For my self, I am among those who are clearly in the Opinion, that there never was such a *Spirit* of *Superstition* and *Enthusiasm* reigning in the Land before; never such *gross Disorders* and *barefaced Affronts* to *common Decency;* never such *scandalous Reproaches* on the *Blessed Spirit,* making him the Author of the greatest *Irregularities* and *Confusions:* Yet, I am of Opinion also, that the Appearances among us (so much out of the ordinary Way, and so unaccountable to persons not acquainted with the History of the World) have been the Means of awakening the Attention of many; and a

---

only excepted; though I really do not remember to have read that the *Pope* went on at this Rate.

The sending out of *unlearned Men* to *teach others,* upon the Supposition of their Piety, in ordinary Cases, seems to bring the Ministry into Contempt; to cherish *Enthusiasm,* and bring all into Confusion: Whatever fair Face it may have, it is a most perverse Practice.

The Practice of *singing in the Streets* is a Piece of *Weakness,* and *enthusiastical Ostentation.*

I wish you Success, *dear Sir,* in your Journey: My soul is grieved for such *enthusiastical Fooleries,* they portend much mischief to the poor Church of GOD, if they be not seasonably checked: May your Labours be blessed for that End.

I must also declare my Abhorence of all Pretence to *immediate Inspiration,* or following *immediate Impulses,* as an enthusiastical perillous *ignis fatuus.*

T. G.

good Number, I hope, have settled into a truly *Christian
Temper*: Tho' I must add, at the same time, that I am far
from thinking, that the Appearance, in *general*, is any other
than the Effect of *enthusiastick Heat*. The Goodness that has
been so much talked of, 'tis plain to me, is nothing more, in
general, than a *Commotion in the Passions*. I can't see that
Men have been made *better*, if hereby be meant, their being
formed to a nearer Resemblance to the *Divine Being* in *moral
Holiness*. 'Tis not evident to me, that Persons, generally, have
a better Understanding of Religion, a better Government of
their Passions, a more Christian Love to their Neighbour, or
that they are more decent and regular in their Devotions
towards God. I am clearly of the Mind, they are worse in all
these Regards. They place their Religion so much in the *Heat*
and *Fervour* of their *Passions*, that they too much neglect
their *Reason* and *Judgment*: And instead of being more kind
and gentle, more full of Mercy and good Fruits, they are
more bitter, fierce and implacable. And what is a *grand dis
criminating Mark of this Work*, where-ever it takes place, is,
that it makes Men *spiritually proud* and *conceited* beyond
Measure, infinitely *censorious* and *uncharitable*, to *Neighbours*, to *Relations*, even the nearest and dearest; to *Ministers*
in an especial Manner; yea, to all Mankind, who are not as
they are, and don't think and act as they do: And there are
few places where *this Work* has been in any *remarkable*
manner, but they have been filled with Faction and Contention; yea, in some, they have divided into Parties, and openly
and scandalously separated from one another.

Truly the Accounts sent Abroad, were sent too soon; too
soon, I am satisfied, to reflect Honour upon the Persons who
wrote them: And they bewray such a want of Judgment, as
I was really sorry to see them falling into. There are few
Persons now, perhaps none but such as are evidently over-
heated, but begin to see that Things have been carried too
far, and that the Hazard is great, unless God mercifully inter-
pose, lest we should be over-run with *Enthusiasm*. And to
speak the plain Truth, my Fear is, lest the End of these things
should be *Quakerism* and *Infidelity*: These we have now
chiefly to guard against.

A particular Account of one Mr. *James Davenport*, with his *strange Conduct* in *Town* and *elsewhere*, I doubt not would have been agreeable: But I have exceeded already. He is the *wildest Enthusiast* I ever saw, and acts in the wildest manner; and yet, he is vindicated by some in all his Extravagancies.

I now beg Pardon, Sir, for thus trespassing upon your Patience. As Mr. *Whitefield* has been in *Scotland*, and *human Nature* is the *same every where;* this Narration of the Effects he has been the Instrument of producing here, may excite your Zeal to guard the People in time against any such Extravagancies, if there should be Danger of them where you may be concerned. I am,

Reverend Sir,
With all due Regard, &c.

Boston, August 4.
    1742.

BIBLIOGRAPHICAL NOTE

There is no comprehensive study of the Great Awakening in the colonies, though there are three works dealing with particular areas: Edwin Scott Gaustad, *The Great Awakening in New England* (New York, 1957), Charles H. Maxson, *The Great Awakening in the Middle Colonies* (Chicago, 1920), and Wesley M. Gewehr, *The Great Awakening in Virginia, 1740–1790* (Durham, 1930). Other essays of particular importance are: Leonard J. Trinterud, *The Forming of an American Tradition* (Philadelphia, 1949), which deals with the Tennent family and developments in Presbyterianism; Conrad Wright, *The Beginnings of Unitarianism in America* (Boston, 1955) which discusses Charles Chauncy and the "liberal" reaction to the "awakenings;" and C. C. Goen, *Re-*

vivalism and Separatism in New England, 1740–1800 (New Haven, 1962), a thorough study of "Strict Congregationalists and Separate Baptists in the Great Awakening." John E. Smith has written an instructive introduction to Jonathan Edwards' *Religious Affections,* Vol. II of the *Works of Jonathan Edwards* (New Haven, 1959). Two biographies of Edwards complement each other's strengths: Ola Elizabeth Winslow, *Jonathan Edwards 1703–1758* (New York, 1941), a study of the life and times of the Northampton pastor and Perry Miller, *Jonathan Edwards* (New York, 1949), an intellectual biography.

Alan Heimert and Perry Miller have collected source materials of the revivals in *The Great Awakening* (Indianapolis, 1967).

IV. RELIGIOUS FREEDOM

INTRODUCTION

The advocates of religious freedom in the latter half of the eighteenth century came from a wide variety of backgrounds: Quaker, Baptist, Episcopalian, Congregationalist, Presbyterian, and Deist.

Thomas Bradbury Chandler (1726–1790), a graduate of Yale in 1745, argued that the Episcopal Church was the only denomination not granted full toleration by the colonies. In the 1760s and 1770s, he engaged in a protracted debate over a proposal for American bishops with Charles Chauncy, pastor of the First Church (Congregational) in Boston. In 1767 Chandler published *An Appeal to the Public, in Behalf of the Church of England in America*. This *Appeal* was carefully stated to insure that the plan would not be interpreted as seeking the "establishment" of the church; the Bishops were to have only "spiritual" authority.

. . . the Bishops to be sent to America, shall have no authority, but purely of a Spiritual and Ecclesiastical Nature, such as is derived altogether from the Church and not from the State—That this Authority shall operate only upon the Clergy of the Church, and not upon the Laity nor Dissenters of any Denomination—That the Bishops shall not interfere with the Property or Privileges, whether civil or religious, of Churchmen or Dissenters. . . . But, that they shall only exercise the original Powers of their Office as before stated, i.e. ordain and govern the Clergy, and administer Confirmation to those who shall desire it.[1]

Chandler's work, however, was seen by other religious bodies as a veiled desire for establishment, and it came at a time when the conflict with England was intensifying.

[1] Thomas Bradbury Chandler, *An Appeal to the Public, in Behalf of the Church of England in America* (New York, 1767), p. 79.

The Congregationalists and Presbyterians met in annual conventions from 1766 to 1775 to form a plan of union to prevent the establishment of an American episcopate and also to increase cooperation in their missionary efforts in the west. It became clear to the Presbyterians and Congregationalists that religious liberty was inescapably tied to civil liberty; Chandler remained a loyalist throughout the Revolution.

Within the Baptist tradition the name of Isaac Backus (1724–1806) stands out. Backus was converted during the Great Awakening and became a "Separatist" within Congregationalism. Later, in 1756, he organized a Baptist Church and became its pastor. Members of dissenting groups within New England were not treated equally in religious matters. Baptists were taxed for the support of the established churches (Congregational); though provision was made in the law for exemption from taxation, it was frequently not observed. Backus's tract, *"Government and Liberty Described and Ecclesiastical Tyranny Exposed"* (1778), outlines his arguments for religious liberty.

One further comment should be made. In all the appeals for religious freedom there was the common assumption that religious presuppositions were essential for the future of the United States. Sidney Mead, in an unusually illuminating essay, remarked:

Establishment rested upon two basic assumptions: that the existence and well-being of any society depends upon a body of commonly shared religious beliefs—the nature of man, his place in the cosmos, his destiny, and his conduct toward his fellow men—and that the only guarantee that these necessary beliefs will be sufficiently inculcated is to put the coercive power of the state behind the institution responsible for their definition, articulation, and inculcation. At least, it was supposed, there must be enough coercive power to compel attendance upon the teachings, and to suppress or cut off dangerous aberrations. . . .

Religious freedom did not mean giving up the first assumption, that is, the necessity for the commonly shared basic religious ideas. It meant only the rejection of the second assumption, namely, that the institution(s) responsible for their inculcation must have the coercive power of the state behind it (or them). The essence of the revolution was, then, the rejection of coercion in favor of persuasion.[2]

This assumption of "commonly shared basic religious ideas" was noted in James Madison's "A Memorial and Remonstrance on the Religious Rights of Man," (1784). This document was especially important in the formation of the First Amendment (1791) which states: "Congress shall make no law respecting an establishment of religion, or prohibiting the free exercise thereof . . ."—a statement which has caused considerable judicial argument in practical application of the establishment and free exercise clauses.

[9]

Thomas Bradbury Chandler

An Appeal to the Public,
in Behalf of the Church of
England in America[*]

The Plan on which alone American Bishops have been requested, fairly stated, with Expostulations on the Reasonableness thereof.

The Design of what has been offered in the foregoing Section, is to show—That the Propagation of the Gospel among those who are Strangers to it, is a Duty incumbent upon every Christian Nation, as they have Opportunity:—That the English Nation in particular has, at this Time, a much better Opportunity, for converting to the Christian Faith the Heathen Nations on the Borders of our Settlements, than has hereto-

[2] Sidney Mead, *The Lively Experiment: The Shaping of Christianity in America* (New York, 1963), Chapter IV, "Thomas Jefferson's 'Fair Experiment'—Religious Freedom," p. 63.

[*] Thomas Bradbury Chandler, *An Appeal to the Public, in Behalf of the Church of England in America* (New York, 1767), pp. 75–86.

fore offered, and that the Obligations of Gratitude to perform this Duty are stronger, and the Providence of God points it out more plainly, than ever:—That the commercial and political Advantages to be expected from such a Conversion, if it can be effected, are a strong Argument for attempting it, on the mere Principles of worldly Policy:—That the true Method to be taken for the Conversion of Savages, is by previously teaching them the Arts and Manners of civil Life, in order to which, proper Schools in different Parts of the Country are necessary:—That *the Society for the Propagation of the Gospel*, not waiting to see what the Nation will attempt, have, on these Principles, formed a general Plan for the Erection of Indian Schools, with a Design to put it in Execution, as soon, and as extensively, as possible:—And that in Order thereto, it is reasonable to think, that an American Episcopate will be most eminently useful, and indeed that the Work cannot be properly conducted without it. From these Considerations it evidently follows, that every Friend, not only to the Church of England, but to Christianity in general, ought most earnestly to desire the Settlement of Bishops in America, on *this Account*, and to use his Influence for obtaining it.

The Reasons which have been offered in Favour of an American Episcopate, appear to us to be of that real Weight and Importance as to deserve, and we humbly hope that they will obtain, the Attention of our Superiors; and if they are duly considered, we are unable to conceive that they can fail of producing the desired Effect, under so mild and equal a System of Government.

The Principles of Liberty, Justice and Benevolence, are the main Pillars that support the fair Fabric of the British Constitution. It is the Glory of British Subjects, that they enjoy as much Happiness and Freedom as is consistent with Government, and infinitely more than is consistent with the Want of Government—and that their Liberties are secured by Laws that have been made by, and cannot be suspended or repealed without the Consent of, those whom they have chosen to act as their Representatives. No undue Superiority over some can legally be claimed by others; and for every Act of

Injustice or Oppression, a sure Remedy is provided. Provision has been carefully made, that all may have the full Enjoyment both of civil and religious Liberty; and so free and equitable an Execution of the Powers of Government is established, that no Body of Subjects, not an Individual, can justly complain of any Suffering or Grievance, without Confidence of Redress. Such is the happy Tendency of our Constitution, and we trust that our present Rulers have a Disposition to act, in all Cases, agreeably to the Genius and Spirit of it.

Will not then the Complaints of near a Million of British Subjects in America, of unimpeached Loyalty and Fidelity, who are suffering under the most unprecedented Hardships with Regard to their Religion, an Interest dearer than Property and more invaluable than civil Liberty, be regarded, and procure the Redress of so intolerable a Grievance? When an impartial Tenderness and Care for the religious Rights of all, is the professed Principle of the Administration, as well as of our Legislature, is it not absurd and injurious, and ungrateful, to entertain any Suspicions, that so large a Number of Subjects will be treated with a cruel Partiality?—of such Subjects especially, as have ever been dutiful and faithful, and who stand in a peculiar Connection with, and Relation to, the national Body? Can it be imagined that so gross a Partiality against the national Religion, may ever be justly imputed to the British Nation, as no other Nation upon Earth was ever guilty of? For no "Nation has ever treated their Gods, which are no Gods," in such a Manner, as this Imputation would charge a Christian and Protestant Nation with treating the great Sovereign of the World.

As therefore we cannot but hope that the Voice of so many Petitioners will be heard, and that so reasonable a Request will be granted; so we cannot but flatter ourselves that it will be granted *speedily*, and that no unnecessary Delays will prevent its good Effect. The Reasons which have been assigned for granting us an Episcopate, are now in full Force, and stronger than ever; and if they require it at all, they require it *immediately*.

It is not apprehended that any Difficulties can attend the

Execution of this Plan at the present Time, which will not always continue; and some peculiar Motives and Advantages now concur to favour it, which probably no future Period will afford. If then our Application fails of Success now, we shall despair of it hereafter; and—we want Language to express the ill Consequences we fear from such a Disappointment.

What has been said implies not an Opinion, that there are at this Time *no* Difficulties in the Way, but only that there are no Difficulties but such as must be always expected. We are very sensible that a Work of this Nature will have many to oppose it. Some will oppose it from an Enmity to all Religion. Others will oppose it from an Enmity, either open or secret, to the *Protestant Religion;* of which the Church of England is confessedly the strongest Barrier against Popery. There are others again who heretofore have opposed it, from an Apprehension, that either the Property or religious Liberty of their Friends might be affected by it; as it was not so well known, with what Powers and with what Views it had been requested that Bishops might be sent to us. But this has been so often and explicitly mentioned of late, that it can hardly be supposed, that any Persons of Power and Influence can remain ignorant of our true Plan.

However, for the Sake of others, and of such as mistake It, it may be proper, in a Work of this Nature, to make the following Declaration to the Public, (and I appeal to every Reader, who is acquainted with the Matter, for the Truth of it) that is has been long settled by our Friends and Superiors at Home, and the Clergy of this Country have often signified their entire Approbation and Acquiescence therein— *That the Bishops to be sent to America, shall have no Authority, but purely of a Spiritual and Ecclesiastical Nature, such as is derived altogether from the Church and not from the State—That this Authority shall operate only upon the Clergy of the Church, and not upon the Laity nor Dissenters of any Denomination—That the Bishops shall not interfere with the Property or Privileges, whether civil or religious, of Churchmen or Dissenters—That, in particular, they shall have no Concern with the Probate of Wills, Letters of Guardianship and Administration, or Marriage-Licences, nor be Judges of any Cases relating thereto—But, that they shall only exercise the original Powers of their Office as before stated, i.e. ordain and govern the Clergy, and administer Confirmation to those who shall desire it.*

This, without any Reservation or Equivocation, is the exact Plan of an American Episcopate which has been settled at Home; and it is the only one, on which Bishops have been requested here, either in our general or more particular Addresses. And so far is it from being our Desire to molest the Dissenters, or any Denominations of Christians, in the Enjoyment of their present religious Privileges, that we have carefully consulted their Safety and Security, and studied not to injure, but oblige them.

Many may have received different Accounts of our Designs, and of our Conduct; but such as have not proceeded from Ignorance, must have been the Effect of Maliciousness. When Bishops were first proposed and mentioned under the Title of *Suffragans.* This is no ambiguous Term; it has a fixed and determinate Meaning in the Laws of England, and cannot be mistaken. Suffragan Bishops are the same with those that were called *Chorepiscopi,* or Bishops of the Country, in the primitive Church; and it is their Business to discharge all Offices *merely* Episcopal, in the remote Parts of the Diocese wherein they reside, according to the Direction of, and by Virtue of a Commission from, the Diocesan.[1] And since the Term has been omitted, such Explanations have attended our Petitions for American Bishops, that I know not of a single Instance, wherein Reason has been given to suspect, that a Departure from the same general Plan has been aimed at or desired. And of this I am *certain,* that all our Addresses from this and several of the neighbouring Colonies, for many years, have had one consistent and unvaried Tenor, agreeable to the preceding Explanation.

What Weight will be allowed to these Assertions, the Au-

---

[1] Richard Grey, *A System of English Ecclesiastical Law* (London, 1730). Grey (1694–1771), rector at Hinton, Northamptonshire for fifty years, was awarded a D.D. degree from Oxford for this book.

thor knows not; but the Authority of the following Declaration to the same Purpose, contained in *An Answer to Dr. Mayhew's Observations*,[2] cannot fairly be disputed; as the Author of it, supposed to be a very high Dignitary in the Church, manifestly discovers that he is perfectly acquainted with the Affairs of the *Society*, and of the Church in America. Speaking of the Members of the latter, he says: "It is desired, that Two or more Bishops may be appointed for them, to reside where his Majesty shall think most convenient; that they may have no Concern in the least with any Persons who do not profess themselves to be of the Church of England, but may ordain Ministers for such as do; may confirm their Children, when brought to them at a fit Age for that Purpose, and take such Oversight of the Episcopal Clergy, as the Bishop of *London's* Commissaries in those Parts have been empowered to take, and have taken, without Offence. But *it is not desired in the least* that they should hold Courts to try Matrimonial or Testamentary Causes, or be vested with any Authority now exercised, either by provincial Governors or subordinate Magistrates, or infringe or diminish any Privileges and Liberties enjoyed by any of the Laity, even of our own Communion. This is the real and the *only Scheme* that hath been planned for Bishops in *America;* and whoever hath heard of any other, hath been misinformed through Mistake or Design."[3]

Now what reasonable Objections can be offered against such a Plan as this, which is so universally harmless in every Respect, that none can be injured by it; and so useful withal, that near a Million of Persons will receive Benefit, and perhaps the Salvation of many Souls will be effected, by its being put in Execution? Can any Thing be promoted by it, but the Good of the Church? Can any Thing then be objected against it, but that this End will be promoted? But

[2] This anonymous tract was published in 1763 in answer to Jonathan Mayhew's *Observations on the charter and conduct of the Society for the propagation of the Gospel in foreign parts* which appeared in the same year.

[3] *Ibid.,* p. 59.

will any dare, in this Age of British Freedom and improved
Liberty, to avow the Objection? Would not such a barefaced
Attempt thus wantonly to oppress us, and to prevent our
Enjoyment of those invaluable Rights, to which we are
equally intitled with others—which there is no Pretence that
we have ever forfeited—and no Appearance of a Disposition
to abuse—rouse the Indignation and Resentment of all the
Friends of religious Liberty and Toleration, whether Churchmen or Dissenters?

Every Opposition to such a Plan, has the Nature of Persecution, and deserves the Name. For to punish us for our religious Principles, when no Reasons of State require it, is Persecution in its strictest and properest Sense. Will it be said,
that the Prevention of an Episcopate in America, is no
Punishment? It may as well be said, that keeping a Man out
of his Right is no Injustice. Whatever Evil is inflicted on us
on account of our Principles or Practices, is properly Punishment; and every Good we are deprived of, is equivalent to an
Evil inflicted. Wherever therefore an Evil is inflicted, or we
are deprived of a Good, on account of our Religion, unless it
be necessary for the Security of the Public, we suffer Persecution.

As such Treatment has the very Essence of Persecution,
so it can have its Source only in an intolerant persecuting
Disposition. And it is not to be doubted but a Disposition that
will produce thus much, if armed with Power, would be productive of more—and that they, who only endeavour now
to prevent our Enjoyment of those Advantages, to which we
are intitled by the Laws of God and the Constitution, would
bring us, if they could, to the Stake or Gibbet. But what an
Abomination is such a Disposition and Behavior, in the Eyes
of every true Englishman, of every true Protestant! What an
Indignity and Affront to the Nation, to desire it to countenance such Injustice and Cruelty!

It is hard to believe that any Protestants, especially that
any English Dissenters, who have generally, for a Century
past, been warm Advocates for religious Liberty, and who are
greatly indebted to a Toleration themselves, can be so inconsistent, as to wish this Harm to the Members of the national

Church. It would be a very ungrateful Return, for the most ample, compleat and generous Toleration, which is this Day to be found upon Earth. Many of the most sensible Men belonging to that Body, have expressed, on this Subject, Sentiments that are candid and liberal; and he who was lately considered in some Sense as their Head,[4] when our Plan was explained to him, and his Opinion thereupon was desired, did not hesitate to declare his free Consent to, and Approbation of, American Bishops, in the Manner that we request them.

The Principles of religious Liberty professed by the Dissenters, must not only restrain them from opposing an American Episcopate, as now settled and explained, but oblige them, if they would act consistently, even to *befriend* it. Some of them, I am fully persuaded, would freely join with us in our Applications for Bishops, if their Assistance was needed, as we should be ready to assist them, in Case of the like Grievances; and all of them will really have a much worse Opinion of the Church of England in general, or of those who belong to it, as probably their Reproaches on future Occasions will testify, if this Matter should not be brought to a speedy and happy Termination. For certainly nothing can more degrade our national Religion, in the Eyes of Dissenters and others, both Protestants and Papists, at Home and abroad, than to see that it is in so small Estimation, and its Interest so little regarded, by those who profess it.

For, wherever Men are indifferent towards the Religion they profess, one of these Conclusions will necessarily be made, and there is no preventing it—either that their Religion, upon a more intimate Acquaintance, appears to be unworthy of their Esteem and Affection—or, that its Professors are of an irreligious Character, and have no Regard for that which is the most invaluable of all Things. And in either Case, the Reputation of their Religion will greatly suffer.

At the Time of writing this, casting my Eyes upon the *Public Paper* of the Day, I was struck with the following Paragraph, said to be an Answer from the King of *Poland* to the Empress

[4] Dr. Samuel Chandler, an English Presbyterian.

of *Russia,* who had interposed with that Monarch, in Behalf of his Protestant Subjects. "I have not forgot the Obligations I am under to the Empress of Russia, among the Means which God Almighty made Use of to raise me to the Throne: but when I came to it, I promised the exact Observation of my Religion throughout my Kingdom. If I was weak enough to abandon it, my Life and my Throne would be exposed to the just Resentment of my Subjects. I am threatened with forcible Means to oblige me to do what is asked of me, which would reduce me to an Extremity equally unhappy. I perceive some Danger in whatever Resolution I may take; but I had rather be exposed to such as my *Duty and Honour* induce me to make Choice of; and from this Time I join with my Country in Defence of our holy Religion."

On the Supposition, that the Proposals, made by her Russian Majesty to the King of Poland, were believed to be inconsistent with the Safety of the national Religion, there is Something so sensible, spirited and open in this Declaration, that every candid and consistent Protestant must applaud it, at the same Time that he condems the established Religion of Poland. Popery is a gross Corruption of the Christian Religion, and it has been wrought up to its present State, by the Application and Policy of many Ages. It presents to us, not the amiable and undefiled Religion of the Gospel, but under the Name of it, an intolerant System, compounded of Superstition, Absurdity, and I know not what; and it manifestly appears to be the general Interest of Mankind, to endeavour, in the Use of all proper and fair Means, to reform it. But although this appears to be so evident to Protestants, there are undoubtedly others, to whom it does not appear at all, and who believe the contrary.

As the King of Poland has solemnly bound himself by Oath, to maintain and defend the Popish Religion, we must charitably suppose that he believes it to be true. And as he believes it to be true, and has sworn to maintain it, he cannot give it up, he cannot neglect it, without betraying his *Duty and Honour,* in the Opinion of all reasonable and unprejudiced Persons. If therefore the Dissenters and others, who are sensible of the Absurdities and Corruptions of the Popish Religion, cannot but commend this firm Adherence to it in his Polish Majesty, so long as he believes it to be the true Religion; surely they must at least equally commend the like Conduct, with Regard to the national Religion, in Protestant Princes—more especially, when the Security of the established Religion, and a Toleration of those who peaceably dissent from it, are allowed to be consistent.

In the same Public Paper we are told, that the Courts of *London, Berlin* and *Copenhagen,* have agreed to assist and co-operate with the Russian Empress, in Favour of the Protestants in Poland. It must give Pleasure to every considerate Protestant, to hear of so generous an Effort to be made, provided it be made properly, in Behalf of the reformed Religion; and we cannot but earnestly wish it Success. But could it be conceived, that those Powers who are thus active for the Protestant Interest in foreign Countries, would neglect to encourage it in their own proper Dominions, their Zeal for it abroad would be esteemed but little better than political Grimace. And on this Principle our English Dissenters would have a much better Opinion of England, and of our Superiors who are Members of it, if, while they warmly interest themselves in Favour of Protestantism in Poland, they do not inconsistently neglect, what they profess to esteem the purest Species of It, in our own Colonies. A true Regard for the Protestant Religion is not confined to particular Places: it will produce vigorous Endeavours to improve and secure it, and to render it as respectable as we can, in all Places; and especially in those Places, wherewith we are most closely connected, and wherein our Power and Influence are greatest.

[10]
Isaac Backus
Government and Liberty Described; and Ecclesiastical Tyranny Exposed*

TO THE PUBLIC

As the affairs of GOVERNMENT and LIBERTY, are the greatest points of controversy, now in the world, it certainly is of great importance, that our ideas be clear and just concerning them. Permit me therefore to offer a few thoughts, upon a familiar metaphor, which the holy Ghost has used to illustrate their true nature. In Amos, v. 24. he says, "Let judgment run down *as waters,* and righteousness as a *mighty stream.*" From whence we may observe,

First. That judgment and righteousness are essential to freedom. When we would represent any thing as quite free, we say, it is as free as water. And not only the flow of mercy and grace from God to men, but also its effects in them, in producing obedience unto him, are often compared thereto in the word of truth—John, iv. 14. and vii. 38. Titus, 2. 11, 12. and 3, 5–8. This is most certain, because,

Second. Freedom is not acting at random, but by reason and rule. Those who walk after their own lusts, are *clouds without water, carried about of winds;* or *raging waves of the sea foaming out their own shame;* while the true SONS OF LIBERTY are like *streams,* which *run down* in a clear and steady channel. David says, *I will run the way of thy commandments, when thou shalt enlarge my heart. I will walk at liberty, for I seek thy precepts.* Streams and rivers must have steady channels to run in; but they that *promise liberty* while they *despise government, are wells without water, clouds that are carried with a tempest.* II Pet. 2. 10–19.

* Isaac Backus, *Government and Liberty Described; and Ecclesiastical Tyranny Exposed* (Boston, 1778).

Third. Though tyranny and licentiousness often make a great noise, yet government and liberty are much stronger than they are. The former, like raging waves, dash themselves against the rocks, and die upon the shore; or like a tempest, after making sad waste and devastation, their strength is gone, and their force is over. While the latter, like a *mighty stream,* carry all before them, and never rest till they can get through, or over all obstacles, which are put in their way.

Fourth. Streams and rivers are of great use, and cause a constant flow of refreshment and blessings wherever they come; so does the exercise and administration of judgment and righteousness, among all people that enjoy them. Hence,

Fifth. The command of heaven is, *Let them run down,* put no obstruction in their way. No, rather be in earnest to remove every thing that hinders their free course.

Sixth. The context plainly shews, that a main obstruction to these great blessings, among the people then spoken to, was their assuming a power to govern religion, instead of being governed by it. True religion is a voluntary obedience unto God. And the great design of all ordinances and acts of worship towards him, is that thereby we may obtain pardon and cleansing, with direction and assistance to behave as we ought towards our fellow-men. But instead of this, those people added their own inventions to divine institutions, and substituted their acts of devotion towards God, in the place of a righteous practice towards men; or for a cover to their contrary conduct: And they would fain have been thought very religious, although they turned *judgment into wormwood, hated him that rebuked in the gate, and abhorred him that spoke uprightly.* These things were written for our admonition: and all things of that nature, if indulged, will prove as pernicious to us, as they did to the Jews. And since self-interest, and self-flattery have an amazing influence to blind men, concerning their own conduct in these affairs, great care ought to be taken to two late publications from the ruling party in this State, may be very serviceable in that respect.

Eleven years ago, the Episcopal clergy appeared very ear-

nest for having Bishops established in America; which caused
Dr. Chauncy of Boston, to write an answer the next year, to
what Dr. Chandler had published upon that subject.[1] And
as Chandler had declared, that all they wanted, was only to
have their church compleatly organized, without the least design of injuring others, the best reason that Chauncy could
give, why his request ought not to be granted, was this:
Says he,

"We are, in principle, against all civil establishments in
religion.—It does not appear to us that God has entrusted the
State with a right to make religious establishments. If the
state in England has this delegated authority, must it not be
owned, that the state in China, in Turkey, in Spain, has this
authority likewise? What should make the difference in the
eye of true reason? Hath the state of England been distinguished by heaven by any peculiar grant, beyond the state
in other countries? If it has let the grant be produced. If
it has not, all states have, in common, the same authority, in
establishments conformable to their own sentiments in religion: what can the consequence be, but infinite damage to
the cause of God and true religion! And such in fact has
been the consequence of these establishments in all ages,
and in all places. Should it be said we claim liberty of conscience, and fully enjoy it; and why would we confine this
privilege to our selves? Is it not as reasonable, episcopalians
should both claim and enjoy it? It is readily allowed; and
we are as willing they should possess and exercise religious
liberty in its full extent, as we desire to do it ourselves. But
then, let it be heedfully minded, we claim *no right* to desire
the interposition of the *state* to *establish* that mode of worship, government, or discipline, we apprehend is most agreeable to the mind of Christ. We desire no other liberty, than
to be left unrestrained in the exercise of our principles, in so
far as we are good members of society: And we are perfectly
willing episcopalians should enjoy this liberty to the full. If

[1] For Thomas Bradbury Chandler's essay see Selection 9,
p. 98 ff. Charles Chauncy's essay is *A Reply to Dr. Chandler*
(Boston, 1768).

they think Bishops, in their appropriated sense, were constituted by Christ or his apostles, we object not a word against
their having as many of them as they please, if they will be
content to have them with authority *altogether* derived from
Christ. But they both claim and desire a great deal more.
They want to be distinguished by having bishops upon the
footing of a *state*-establishment. The plain truth is, by the
gospel-charter, all professed christians are vested with precisely the same rights; nor has one denomination any more
a right to the interposition of the civil magistrate, in their
favour, than another; and where-ever this difference takes
place, it is beside the rule of *scripture*, and I may say also,
the genuine dictates of *uncorrupted reason*."[2] From whence
we may learn, that *corrupt reasonings*, have carried Dr.
Chauncy's denomination on in a way *beside scripture rule*,
for these hundred and forty years; for just so long have their
rulers interposed their authority, to support their religious
ministers by *assessment* and *distress*, to the unspeakable damage of other denominations, and contrary to the practice of
the first planters of the country, for eighteen years. And that
partiality was wholly an arbitrary usurpation of the ruling
party, without the least warrant for it, in either of our charters;
yet the majority of the convention last winter, voted to incorporate those ecclesiastical laws with others, into the new
constitution of government, which they were framing for us,
which, if it had been received by the people, would have
established them in another manner than ever they were before.—Upon hearing of which, the agent and committee of
our Baptist churches met at Boston, Feb. 21, and drew up a
protest, and petition to our next Assembly against it; wherein
they shew, that these laws are contrary to christian liberty,
exclude Christ from being the only lawgiver and head of
his church, are a breach of public faith, as they tax people
where they are not represented, and impower the majority
to judge for the rest about spiritual guides, which naturally
causes *envying and strife*, contrary to the wisdom that is from
above, which is *without partiality, and without hypocrisy.*

[2] *Ibid.,* pp. 152, 153, 179, 180.

And they close with saying, "Our earnest prayer is, that your honors may be the happy instruments of promoting such *impartial peace*, as to fix it as a fundamental principle of our constitution, that religious ministers shall be supported only by Christ's authority, and not at all by assessment and secular force: which impartial liberty has long been claimed and enjoyed by the town of Boston."

Great numbers, and of various denominations, subscribed this address to our Assembly; which alarmed a number of ministers; and Mr. Phillips Payson, who preached the Election sermon, at Boston, May 27th, commended the constitution that was framed for us last winter, and says, "It may justly be considered as a high evidence of the abilities of its compilers, and if it should not be complied with, it is very probable we never shall obtain a better." And he said to the Assembly,

"The importance of religion to civil society and government, is great indeed, as it keeps alive the best sense of moral obligation, a matter of such extensive utility, especially in respect to an oath, which is one of the principal instruments of government. The fear and reverence of God, and the terrors of eternity, are the most powerful restraints upon the minds of men. And hence it is of special importance in a free government, the spirit of which being always friendly to the sacred rights of conscience, it will hold up the gospel as the great rule of faith and practice. Established modes and usages in religion, more especially the stated public worship of God, so generally form the principles and manners of a people, that changes, or alterations in these, especially, when nearly conformed to the spirit and simplicity of the gospel, may well be esteemed very dangerous experiments in government. For this and other reasons, the thoughtful and wise among us trust that our civil fathers, from a regard to gospel worship, and the constitution of these churches, will carefully preserve them; and at all times, guard against every innovation, that might tend to overset the public worship of God, though such innovations may be urged from the most foaming zeal. Persons of a gloomy, ghostly and mystic cast, absorbed in visionary scenes, deserve but little notice in matters, either of religion or government. Let the restraints of religion, once be broken down, as they infallibly would be, by leaving the subject of public worship to the humors of the multitude; and we might well defy all human wisdom and power, to support and preserve order and government in the State."[3]

Perhaps many may think, that the two authors I have quoted upon religious establishments, are of opposite denominations, in religion. Could this thought be supported by evidence, it would readily be admitted; rather than to suppose them guilty, of such self-contradiction, as they most certainly are. For facts abundantly shew, that Dr. Chauncy has exerted himself, from time to time, to defend the establishment we complain of, much more than Mr. Payson has done. And to defend it against the bishops, the first of these gentlemen says, "It does not appear, to us, that God has entrusted the state with a right to make religious establishments." The other warns our civil rulers, against suffering any changes in their "established modes and usages in religion." The first declares, that such establishments have, in *fact, been of infinite damage to the cause of God and true religion, in all ages, and in all places.* The other says, "The thoughtful and wise among us, trust that our *civil fathers,* from a regard to gospel worship, and the *constitution of these churches,* will carefully *preserve them;* and at all times guard against every innovation, that might tend to overset the public *worship of God."*

The Jews at Thessalonica, when moved with envy, cried to their rulers, *These that have turned the world upside down, are come hither also.* But for a professed minister of Christ, to alarm our civil rulers of danger, that the *worship of God* would be *overset,* if they did not carefully *preserve these churches,* is much more surprising! He says, "Persons of a gloomy, ghostly and mystic cast, absorbed in visionary scenes, deserve but little notice in matters, either of religion

[3] Phillips Payson, *A Sermon Preached Before the Honorable Council, and the Honorable House of Representatives, of the State of Massachusetts Bay, May 27, 1778* (Boston, 1788), pp. viii, xviii–xx.

or government." And indeed I think so too; and to whom can these epithets belong so properly, as to those, who think that the church of Christ, and the worship of God, would be overset, if secular force was not used to support them? Are such churches built upon the ROCK, or upon the *sand?*

This gentleman says, "The language of just complaint, the voice of real grievance, in most cases, may easily be distinguished from the meer clamor of *selfish, turbulent* and *disappointed* men. The ear of a righteous government will always be open to the former; its hand, with wisdom and prudence will suppress the latter." ——This is an important truth. And since he warns our rulers against innovations, I think it my duty, plainly to mention some of them, which his party have been guilty of in our land. The learned tell us, that to innovate, is "to introduce, or practice new customs, opinions, or laws, after a sly, clandestine manner." And let the public judge, whether his party have not done so, in the following instances; although they have doubtless had many pious men among them.

The Massachusetts company came over to New England, ten years after Plymouth people had begun the settlement thereof. The charter, which constituted them a civil government, expressly limited them, not to make any laws contrary to the laws of England; and all the freemen, who were admitted to vote for their rulers, took an oath of allegiance to the government, wherein they solemnly engaged to submit to "all such laws, orders, sentences and decrees, as should be *lawfully* made and published by them." But when they set out to frame and enforce a new religious establishment, very contrary to that of England, they found that their oath stood in the way of it; therefore they passed an act, four years after they came to Boston, to absolve themselves, and all the freemen, from their oath to keep acts *lawfully* made, and framed another, of submission to all such laws as they called *wholesome.* Was not this an innovation of the worst kind?

The following year the court sent out to all their ministers and brethren, for advice and assistance, about *one uniform* order of discipline in their churches; and at the same time, passed an act, to compel every male within their jurisdiction, of sixteen years old and above, to take this new invented oath, or be punished at their discretion.

Mr. Roger Williams was then minister of Salem; and because he publicly warned his flock against taking that oath, he was soon convented before the rulers at Boston. But he boldly stood his ground, against them and their ministers too. The next time their assembly met, they took away a valuable tract of land from his church, till they should give the court satisfaction upon these matters. For this, Mr. Williams and his church, wrote letters of reproof to the churches where those rulers belonged; but instead of repenting of this iniquity, they banished him out of their colony. Whereupon he went and founded the first civil government, that ever established equal religious liberty, since the rise of Antichrist. And soon after gathered the first Baptist church in America. He also did the most to prevent the ruin of all these colonies by the Indians, of any one man in the country. Thus he overcame evil with good; while the advocates for the use of secular force in religion, have requited him, and his friends, evil for good ever since.

And they were so far from promoting peace among themselves by these means, that in less than a year after his banishment the two ministers of Boston, and the two chief rulers of the colony, who belonged to that church, got to open clashings in their meeting-house, on the Lord's day, and the flame spread through the land. This moved them to call a general synod upon it. And because a new house of representatives refused to join in punishing such as the synod had condemned, it was immediately dissolved, and another house called; and then several were banished, and seventy-six men were disarmed, of whom fifty-eight were of Boston. The year after they made their first law to support ministers by assessment and distress; which was followed with finings, imprisonings, whippings and hangings; and with the exertion of all their art and power, for forty years after, in various attempts to divide and conquer Rhode-Island colony. And all the disorders, which these and other means could produce therein,

have been used ever since, as a most prevailing argument
for an established religion by human laws.

And those violations of the rights of conscience, furnished
the British court with the most plausable plea they ever had,
for taking away our first charter; and in the second, for depriving us of the inestimable privilege of choosing our chief
rulers; which was evidently the root of all the gall and wormwood, blood and slaughter, which we now deplore. For the
crown being vested with an arbitrary power of appointing our
chief officers, the arbitrary requirement of our property to
support them, was the natural consequence. And it is well
known that contests about that matter kindled this bloody
war. So that the scheme of religious establishments by human
laws, is stained with the guilt of all this blood.

In my late history of New England, a great number of
proofs are produced to the above facts, and our opponents
are welcome to discover any mistakes therein if they can.
And I shall now close, with earnestly requesting the attention
of my dear countrymen to two points.

1. Consider what our civil liberties will be, if these men
can have their wills. I need not inform you that all America
are in arms against being taxed where they are not represented. But it is not more certain, that we are not represented
in the British parliament, than it is, that our *civil* rulers are
not our representatives in *religious* affairs: Yet ministers have
long prevailed with them, to impose religious taxes, entirely
out of their jurisdiction. And they have now been defied to
preserve order in the state, if they should drop that practice.
"That magistrates should thus suffer these incendiaries, and
disturbers of the public peace, might justly be wondered at
(says the great Mr. Locke) if it did not appear, that they have
been invited by them unto a participation of the spoil, and
have therefore thought fit to make use of their covetousness
and pride, as a means whereby to increase their own power."

2. How can liberty of conscience be rightly enjoyed, till
this iniquity is removed? The word of truth says, *why is my
liberty judged of another man's conscience? Let every man
be fully persuaded in his own mind.* But Mr. Payson says,
"Let the restraints of religion once be broken down, as they

INFALLIBLY would be, by leaving the subject of public worship to the humours of the multitude, and we might well defy all human wisdom and power to support and preserve order in the state." He tells of humours, but it is well known that no men are influenced more by distempered humours, than those who are fond of arbitrary power. And if he had not been deeply absorbed thereby in visionary scenes, how could he possibly have delivered this sentence as he did, directly in the face of glaring facts which then surrounded him, as well as against divine truth! By an express law of this government, the *multitude* of people in Boston, have been *left* entirely free, these eighty-five years, to choose what worship they would attend upon, and not to be compelled to pay a farthing to support any that they did not choose: And there are proofs enough to shew, that this liberty has greatly contributed to the welfare and not the injury of the town. And his great swelling word INFALLIBLY, is as contrary to the holy scriptures, as it is to experienced facts. That word says, *in vain do they worship me, teaching for doctrines the commandments of men. If we have sown unto you spiritual things, is it a great thing if we shall reap your carnal things? The Lord hath ordained, that they who preach the gospel should live of the gospel. Let him that is taught in the word, communicate with him that teacheth in all good things. Be not deceived, God is not mocked.* And Christ solemnly forbids the giving of any countenance or support to teachers who bring not HIS DOCTRINE; of which each rational soul has an equal right to judge for himself.—Mat. xv.—Rom. xiv. 4, 5.—I Cor. ix. 1, 14 and x. 15, 29.—Gal. i. 8, 9. and vi. 6, 7.— II John, x. 11. But the *commandments of men among us,* while they have allowed this liberty to Boston, have expressly denied the same to the country; where they have ordained, that they who preach the gospel, shall live of human laws; which laws are so opposite to these laws of Christ, that they empower the majority in each town or parish to judge for the rest; even so, that if the minority were ever so *fully persuaded,* that the parish minister perverted the gospel, instead of teaching it truly, yet the majority might seize the goods, or imprison the persons, of the minority, to support that blind guide! And the chief judge of each of our county courts have been required, from year to year, to charge the grand jury upon their oaths, to prosecute every parish in the county, that did not settle such a minister as the court called orthodox. Though, at the same time, if any church, together with the town or parish, was ever so unanimous in the choice of a gospel minister, yet there is an express law of this government that excludes him from being settled in their constitution, until he has an academical degree, or an approbation from the majority of the settled ministers in that county.

And this constitution has been so far from promoting our public welfare, that if the whole town of Chelsea, where Mr. Payson lives, was publicly sold for the most it would fetch, it would go but a little way towards paying the costs this government have been put to, only for the fitting of their legislature to form religious societies, and to hear and act upon quarrels and disputes of that nature, which they have no right to meddle with. And how can justice and righteousness ever have their free course among us, while men thus assume power to govern religion, instead of being governed by it?

I am as sensible of the importance of religion, and of the utility of it to human society, as Mr. Payson is. And I concur with him, that the fear and reverence of God; and the terrors of eternity, are the most powerful restraints upon the minds of men. But I am so far from thinking, with him that these restraints would be broken down, if equal religious liberty was established, that I am very certain we should heretofore have suffered much more than we have done, if the restraints of religion had not often constrained his party to act contrary to their ecclesiastical laws, or to suspend the execution of them. They often declare, that they allow us liberty of conscience, and also complain of injury, if we recite former and latter acts of their party to prove the contrary. Just so has Dr. Chandler done with regard to bishops; and he declares they had now no design of taxing America to them; yet he says, "Should a general tax be laid upon the country, and thereby a sum be raised sufficient for the purpose, I believe such a tax would not amount to more than four pence in one hundred pounds; and this would be no mighty hardship upon the country. He that could think much of giving the six thousandth part of his income to any use which the legislature of his country should assign, deserves not to be considered in the light of a good subject, or member of society." Put in answer hereto, Dr. Chauncey says, "If the country might be taxed four pence in one hundred pounds, it might for the same reason, and with as much justice, if it was thought support of bishops called for it, be taxed four shillings, or four pounds, and so on." All but tories will allow this to be good reasoning; and why is it not as good in a baptist as in a presbyterian? He goes back 150 years, and tells of the EPISCOPAL YOKE OF BONDAGE, which our forefathers came into this wilderness to avoid, and says, "Shall it be declared in the face of the world, that this would be *no hardship* to their posterity, and that they would be neither good subjects, nor good members of society, if they *thought much* of supporting that POWER which has been and may again be TERRIBLY OPPRESSIVE!" True, Doctor: There lies the difficulty. It is not the PENCE, but the POWER, that alarms us. And since the legislature of this State passed an act, no longer ago than last September, to continue a tax of FOUR PENCE a year, upon the baptists, in every parish where they live, as an acknowledgement of the POWER that they have long assumed over us in religious affairs, which we know has often been TERRIBLY OPPRESSIVE, how can we be blamed for refusing to pay that acknowledgement; especially when it is considered, that it is evident to us, that God never allowed any civil State upon earth, to impose religious taxes; but that he declared his vengeance against those in Israel, who presumed to use *force* in such affairs.—I Sam. ii. 16, 34.—Micah. iii. 5, 12.

Rulers, ministers and people, ought to improve all their influence, in their several stations, to promote and support true religion by gospel means and methods; but as the *teaching the fear of God by the precepts of man,* brought confusion and ruin upon the Jewish nation—Isaiah, xxix. 13, 21.—it surely is of infinite importance, that every lover of our dear country, be in earnest to have it saved from such iniquity, and from such ruin.

Middleborough, [Mass.] August 28, 1778

[11]
James Madison
A Memorial and Remonstrance on the Religious Rights of Man*

To the Honorable the General Assembly of the State of Virginia.

We, the subscribers, citizens of the said commonwealth, having taken into serious consideration a bill printed by order of the last session of the general assembly, entitled "A bill for establishing a provision for teachers of the Christian religion," and conceiving that the same, if finally armed with the sanctions of a law, will be a dangerous abuse of power, are bound, as faithful members of a free state, to remonstrate against the said bill—

Because we hold it for a "fundamental and undeniable truth," that religion, or the duty which we owe to our creator, and the manner of discharging it, can be directed only by reason and conviction, not by force or violence. The religion, then, of every man, must be left to the conviction and conscience of every man; and it is the right of every man to exercise it as these may dictate. This right is, in its nature, an unalienable right. It is unalienable, because the opinions of men, depending only on the evidence contemplated in their own minds, cannot follow the dictates of other men; it is unalienable, also, because what is here a right towards men, is a duty towards the creator. It is the duty of every man to

* From *Letters and Other Writings of James Madison* (Philadelphia, 1867), Vol. I, p. 162 ff.

render the creator such homage, and *such only,* as he believes
to be acceptable to him; this duty is precedent, both in order
of time and degree of obligation, to the claims of civil society. Before any man can be considered as a member of civil
society, he must be considered as a subject of the governor
of the universe; and if a member of civil society, who enters
into any subordinate association, must always do it with a
reservation of his duty to the general authority, much more
must every man who becomes a member of any particular
civil society do it *with the saving his allegiance to the universal sovereign.* We maintain, therefore, that in matters of
religion no man's right is abridged by the institution of civil
society; and that religion is wholly exempt from its cognizance.
True it is, that no other rule exists, by which any question
which may divide society can be ultimately determined, but
the will of the majority; but it is also true, that the majority
may trespass on the rights of the minority.

Because, if religion be exempt from the authority of the
society at large, still less can it be subject to that of the legislative body. The latter are but the creatures and vicegerents
of the former. Their jurisdiction is both derivative and limited.
It is limited with regard to the coordinate departments; more
necessarily is it limited with regard to the constituents. The
preservation of a free government requires not merely that
the metes and bounds which separate each department of
power be universally maintained; but more especially, that
neither of them be suffered to overleap the great barrier
which defends the rights of the people. The rulers who are
guilty of such an encroachment, exceed the commission from
which they derive their authority, and are tyrants. The people who submit to it are governed by laws made neither by
themselves, nor by an authority derived from them, and are
slaves.

Because it is proper to take alarm at the first experiment
on our liberties. We hold this prudent jealousy to be the first
duty of citizens, and one of the noblest characteristics of the
late revolution. The freemen of America did not wait till
usurped power had strengthened itself by exercise, and entangled the question in precedents. They saw all the conse-

quences by denying the principle. We revere this lesson too much soon to forget it. Who does not see that the same authority which can establish Christianity, in exclusion of all other religions, may establish, with the same ease, any particular sect of Christians, in exclusion of all other sects? That the same authority that can call for each citizen to contribute three pence only of his property for the support of only one establishment, may force him to conform to any one establishment, in all cases whatsoever?

Because the bill violates that equality which ought to be the basis of every law, and which is more indispensable in proportion as the validity or expediency of any law is more liable to be impeached. If "all men by nature are equally free and independent," all men are to be considered as entering into society on equal conditions, as relinquishing no more, and, therefore, retaining no less, one than another, of their rights. Above all, they are to be considered as retaining an "equal right to the free exercise of religion, according to the dictates of conscience." While we assert for ourselves a freedom to embrace, to profess, and to observe, the religion which we believe to be of divine origin, we cannot deny an equal freedom to those whose minds have not yet yielded to the evidence which has convinced us. If this freedom be abused, it is an offence against God, *not against man:* to God, therefore, *not to man,* must an account of it be rendered. As the bill violates equality by subjecting some to peculiar burdens, so it violates the same principle by granting to others peculiar exemptions. Are the Quakers and Menonists the only sects who think compulsive support of their religions unnecessary and unwarrantable? Can their piety alone be entrusted with the care of public worship? Ought their religions to be endowed, above all others, with extraordinary privileges, by which proselytes may be enticed from all others? We think too favorably of the justice and good sense of these denominations to believe that they either covet preeminence over their fellow citizens, or that they will be seduced by them from the common opposition to the measure.

Because the bill implies, either that the civil magistrate is a competent judge of truth, or that he may employ religion

as an engine of civil policy. The first is an arrogant preten-
sion, falsified by the contradictory opinions of rulers in all
ages, and throughout the world: the second is an unhallowed
perversion of the means of salvation.

Because the establishment proposed by the bill is not
requisite for the support of the Christian religion. To say
that it is, is a contradiction to the Christian religion itself;
for every page of it disavows a dependence on the powers
of this world: it is a contradiction to fact; for it is known that
this religion both existed and flourished, not only without the
support of human laws, but in spite of every opposition from
them; and not only during the period of miraculous aid, but
long after it had been left to its own evidence, and the ordinary care of Providence. Nay, it is a contradiction in terms;
for a religion not invented by human policy must have pre-
existed and been supported before it was established by human policy. It is, moreover, to weaken in those who profess
this religion a pious confidence in its innate excellence, and
the patronage of its author; and to foster in those who still
reject it, a suspicion that its friends are too conscious of its
fallacies to trust it to its own merits.

Because experience witnesseth that ecclesiastical establishments, instead of maintaining the purity and efficacy of religion, have had a contrary operation. During almost fifteen
centuries has the legal establishment of Christianity been on
trial. What have been its fruits? More or less, in all places,
pride and indolence in the clergy; ignorance and servility in
the laity; in both, superstition, bigotry, and persecution. Enquire of the teachers of Christianity for the ages in which it
appeared in its greatest lustre: those of every sect point to
the ages prior to its incorporation with civil policy. Propose
a restoration of this primitive state, in which its teachers depended on the voluntary rewards of their flocks; many of
them predict its downfall. On which side ought their testimony to have the greatest weight, when for, or when against,
their interest?

Because the establishment in question is not necessary for
the support of civil government. If it be urged as necessary
for the support of civil government only as it is a means of

supporting religion, and if it be not necessary for the latter purpose, it cannot be necessary for the former. If religion be not within the cognizance of civil government, how can its legal establishment be said to be necessary to civil government? What influences, in fact, have ecclesiastical establishments had on civil society? In some instances they have been seen to erect a spiritual tyranny on the ruins of civil authority; in many instances they have been seen upholding the thrones of political tyranny; in no instance have they been seen the guardians of the liberties of the people. Rulers who wished to subvert the public liberty may have found an established clergy convenient auxiliaries. A just government, instituted to secure and perpetuate it, needs them not. Such a government will be best supported by protecting every citizen in the enjoyment of his religion with the same equal hand that protects his person and property; by neither invading the equal rights of any sect, nor suffering any sect to invade those of another.

Because the proposed establishment is a departure from that generous policy which, offering an asylum to the persecuted and oppressed of every nation and religion, promised a lustre to our country, and an accession to the number of its citizens. What a melancholy mark is the bill, of sudden degeneracy. Instead of holding forth an asylum to the persecuted, it is itself a signal of persecution. It degrades from the equal rank of citizens all those whose opinions in religion do not bend to those of the legislative authority. Distant as it may be, in its present form, from the inquisition, it differs only in degree. The one is the *first* step, the other the *last,* in the *career of intolerance.* The magnanimous sufferer under this cruel scourge in foreign regions, must view the bill as a beacon on our coast, warning him to seek some other haven, where liberty and philanthropy, in their due extent, may offer a more certain repose from his troubles.

Because it will have a like tendency to banish our citizens. The allurements presented by other situations are every day thinning their numbers. To superadd a fresh motive to emigration, by revoking the liberty which they now enjoy, would be the same species of folly which has dishonored and de-populated flourishing kingdoms.

Because it will destroy the moderation and harmony which the forbearance of our laws to intermeddle with religion has produced among its several sects. Torrents of blood have been spilt in the world in vain attempts of the secular arm to ex-tinguish religious discord, by proscribing all differences in religious opinions. Time, at length, has revealed the true remedy. Every relaxation of narrow and rigorous policy, wherever it has been tried, has been found to assuage the disease. The American theatre has exhibited proofs, that equal and complete liberty, if it does not wholly eradicate it, suffi-ciently destroys its malignant influence on the health and prosperity of the state. If, with the salutary effects of this system under our own eyes, we begin to contract the bounds of religious freedom, we know no name that will too severely reproach our folly. At least, let warning be taken at the first fruits of the threatened innovation. The very appearance of the bill has transformed that "Christian forbearance, love, and charity," which of late mutually prevailed, into animosi-ties and jealousies, which may not soon be appeased. What mischiefs may not be dreaded, should this enemy to the public quiet be armed with the force of a law!

Because the policy of the bill is adverse to the diffusion of the light of Christianity. The first wish of those who enjoy this precious gift ought to be, that it may be imparted to the whole race of mankind. Compare the number of those who have as yet received it, with the number still remaining under the dominion of false religions, and how small is the former! Does the policy of the bill tend to lessen the dispro-portion? No: it at once discourages those who are strangers to the light of revelation from coming into the region of it: countenances, by example, the nations who continue in dark-ness, in shutting out those who might convey it to them. Instead of levelling, as far as possible, every obstacle to the victorious progress of truth, the bill, with an ignoble and un-christian timidity, would circumscribe it with a wall of de-fence against the encroachments of error.

Because attempts to enforce by legal sanctions acts obnoxious to so great a proportion of citizens, tend to enervate the laws in general, and to slacken the bands of society. If it be difficult to execute any law which is not generally deemed necessary or salutary, what must be the case where it is deemed invalid and dangerous? And what may be the effect of so striking an example of impotency in the government on its general authority?

Because a measure of such general magnitude and delicacy ought not to be imposed, without the clearest evidence that it is called for by a majority of citizens: and no satisfactory method is yet proposed, by which the voice of the majority in this case may be determined, or its influence secured. "The people of the respective counties are, indeed, requested to signify their opinion, respecting the adoption of the bill, to the next sessions of assembly;" but the representation must be made equal before the voice either of the representatives or the counties will be that of the people. Our hope is, that neither of the former will, after due consideration, espouse the dangerous principle of the bill. Should the event disappoint us, it will still leave us in full confidence that a fair appeal to the latter will reverse the sentence against our liberties.

Because, finally, "the equal right of every citizen to the free exercise of his religion, according to the dictates of conscience," is held by the same tenure with all our other rights. If we recur to its origin, it is equally the gift of nature; if we weigh its importance, it cannot be less dear to us; if we consult the "declaration of those rights which pertain to the good people of Virginia, as the basis and foundation of government," it is enumerated with equal solemnity, or, rather, studied emphasis.

Either, then, we must say that the will of the legislature is the only measure of their authority, and that, in the plenitude of this authority, they may sweep away all our fundamental rights; or, that they are bound to leave this particular right untouched and sacred: either we must say that they may control the freedom of the press, may abolish the trial by jury, may swallow up the executive and judiciary powers of the state; nay, that they may despoil us of our right of suf-

frage, and erect themselves into an independent and hereditary assembly: or, we must say, that they have no authority
to enact into law the bill under consideration. We, the subscribers, say, that the general assembly of this commonwealth
have no such authority; and that no effort may be omitted,
on our part, against so dangerous an usurpation, we oppose
to it in this remonstrance—earnestly praying, as we are in
duty bound, that the SUPREME LAWGIVER OF THE UNIVERSE,
by illuminating those to whom it is addressed, may, on the
one hand, turn their councils from every act which affronts
his holy prerogative, or violates the trust committed to them;
and, on the other, guide them into every measure that may
be worthy of his blessing, may redound to their own praise,
and may establish more firmly the liberties of the people, and
the prosperity and happiness of the commonwealth.

BIBLIOGRAPHICAL NOTE

The most thorough study of the literature of this period is
Alan Heimert, *Religion and the American Mind, from the
Great Awakening to the Revolution* (Cambridge, 1966).
Older works are A. L. Cross, *The Anglican Episcopate and
the American Colonies* (Cambridge, 1902) and Alice M.
Baldwin, *The New England Clergy and the American Revolution* (Durham, 1928). Leonard Trinterud, *The Forming of an
American Tradition* (Philadelphia, 1949) includes a discussion of the "threat" of an American episcopate in Chapter 13.
The first chapters of Sidney Mead, *The Lively Experiment*
(New York, 1963) are particularly suggestive. The most important examination of Baptist history in this period, with
attention given to Isaac Backus, is C. C. Goen, *Revivalism
and Separatism in New England, 1740–1800* (New Haven,
1962).

V. THE CALVINISTIC HERITAGE RE-EXAMINED

INTRODUCTION

The central issue between the Unitarians and "orthodox" Calvinists in the 1820s concerned the nature of man. Jonathan Edwards in his treatises, *The Great Christian Doctrine of Original Sin Defended* and *A Careful and Strict Inquiry into . . . Freedom of the Will,* rigorously defended the idea of original sin, though with a subtle modification of traditional Calvinism. He insisted, it is a "most Evident and acknowledged *Fact,* with respect to the state of all mankind, without exception of one individual among all the natural descendents of Adam, . . . that God actually deals with Adam and his posterity as one."[1] This theme of the unity of Adam and his descendents was viewed as an innovation by the Old Calvinists who held to the theory that the sin of Adam was imputed to his descendents. The Arminian party argued against any legal or constitutional relationship between Adam and his posterity; man is corrupted by sin, but he is not left in such a state that his good actions go unnoticed by the benevolent God. The intense controversy concerning freedom of the will has its root in the differing views of human nature.

William Ellery Channing (1780–1842) delivered the first major statement of Unitarianism in 1819, a sermon entitled *Unitarian Christianity.* Early in his life he had listened to the sermons of Samuel Hopkins (1721–1803), the defender of Edwardsean theology. Channing, while admiring the religious fervor of Hopkins, was not to become a disciple. After graduation from Harvard he became pastor of the Federal Street Church in Boston in 1803 and gradually began to formulate an

[1] Jonathan Edwards, "The Great Christian Doctrine of Original Sin . . . ," *The Works of Jonathan Edwards,* Vol. II. (New York, 1844), p. 484.

understanding of Christianity which differed sharply from the New Divinity themes of Edwards and Hopkins. The emphasis, argued Channing, must be on the parental and benevolent character of God, the divine and exemplary mission of Jesus but not the trinitarian formula, and the potential of man to fulfill the commands of Scripture.

Nathaniel William Taylor (1786–1858), graduate of Yale in 1807, became Professor of Theology at his Alma Mater in 1822. His theological task was to find a middle way between the Unitarian concerns and those of the heirs of the New Divinity tradition. Taylor's *Concio Ad Clerum* (1828) was a statement of the New Haven theology, where in more technical language than Channing, he argued against the view of man's nature as corrupted by being one with Adam and the doctrine of inherited depravity. He could not allow, however, the position of the Unitarians. Taylor had to deal with the Unitarian charge that Calvinism undercut human moral responsibility. Sidney Mead, quoting from Taylor, described his position: "if any two things are consistent, *certainty of action*, and *freedom of action*, are consistent. And Taylor went on to affirm: 'I believe in predestination and free agency at the same time because I believe this axiom'— certainty with power to the contrary."[2] This rather ambiguous phrase, "certainty with power to the contrary," became the slogan of the Taylorites. It was not a position which satisfied either the Unitarians or the "orthodox" Calvinists. The position of Taylor had great influence on the development of Calvinism in America, especially in shaping the theological foundations of nineteenth century revivalism.

[2] Sidney Mead, *Nathaniel William Taylor 1786–1858: A Connecticut Liberal* (Chicago, 1942), p. 190.

[12]

William Ellery Channing
Objections to Unitarian Christianity Considered*

It is due to truth, and a just deference to our fellow-Christians, to take notice of objections which are currently made to our particular views of religion; nor ought we to dismiss such objections as unworthy of attention on account of their supposed lightness; because what is light to us may weigh much with our neighbor, and truth may suffer from obstructions which a few explanations might remove. It is to be feared that those Christians who are called Unitarian have been wanting in this duty. Whilst they have met the labored arguments of their opponents fully and fairly, they have overlooked the loose, vague, indefinite objections which float through the community, and operate more on common minds than formal reasoning. On some of these objections remarks will now be offered; and it is hoped that our plainness of speech will not be construed into severity, nor our strictures on different systems be ascribed to a desire of retaliation. It cannot be expected that we shall repel with indifference what seem to us reproaches on some of the most important and consoling views of Christianity. Believing that the truths which through God's good providence we are called to maintain are necessary to the vindication of the divine character, and to the prevalence of a more enlightened and exalted piety, we are bound to assert them earnestly, and to speak freely of the opposite errors which now disfigure Christianity. What, then, are the principal objections to Unitarian Christianity?

* From *The Works of William E. Channing, D.D.* (Boston, 1901), pp. 401–405; 408. This essay was published in 1820.

1. It is objected to us, that we deny the divinity of Jesus Christ. Now what does this objection mean? What are we to understand by the divinity of Christ? In the sense in which many Christians, and perhaps a majority, interpret it, we do not deny it, but believe it as firmly as themselves. We believe firmly in the divinity of Christ's mission and office, that he spoke with divine authority, and was a bright image of the divine perfections. We believe that God dwelt in him, manifested himself through him, taught men by him, and communicated to him his spirit without measure. We believe that Jesus Christ was the most glorious display, expression, and representative of God to mankind, so that in seeing and knowing him, we see and know the invisible Father; so that when Christ came, God visited the world and dwelt with men more conspicuously than at any former period. In Christ's words we hear God speaking; in his miracles we behold God acting; in his character and life we see an unsullied image of God's purity and love. We believe, then, in the divinity of Christ, as this term is often and properly used. How, then, it may be asked, do we differ from other Christians? We differ in this important respect. Whilst we honor Christ as the Son, representative, and image of the Supreme God, we do not believe him to be the Supreme God himself. We maintain that Christ and God are *distinct beings,* two beings, not one and the same being. On this point a little repetition may be pardoned, for many good Christians, after the controversies of ages, misunderstand the precise difference between us and themselves. Trinitarianism teaches that Jesus Christ is the supreme and infinite God, and that he and his Father are not only one in affection, counsel, and will, but are strictly and literally one and the same being. Now to us this doctrine is most unscriptural and irrational. We say that the Son cannot be the same being with his own Father; that he, who was sent into the world to save it, cannot be the living God who sent him. The language of Jesus is explicit and unqualified. "I came not to do mine own will."—"I came not from myself." —"I came from God." Now we affirm, and this is our chief heresy, that Jesus was not and could not be the God from whom he came, but was another being; and it amazes us that

any can resist this simple truth. The doctrine that Jesus, who was born at Bethlehem; who ate and drank and slept; who suffered and was crucified; who came from God; who prayed to God; who did God's will; and who said, on leaving the world, "I ascend to my Father and your Father, to my God and your God;" the doctrine that this Jesus was the supreme God himself, and the same being with his Father, this seems to us a contradiction to reason and Scripture so flagrant, that the simple statement of it is a sufficient refutation. We are often charged with degrading Christ; but if this reproach belong to any Christians, it falls, we fear, on those who accuse him of teaching a doctrine so contradictory, and so subversive of the supremacy of our Heavenly Father. Certainly our humble and devout Master has given no ground for this accusation. He always expressed towards God the reverence of a son. He habitually distinguished himself from God. He referred to God all his powers. He said, without limitation or reserve, "The Father is greater than I."—"Of myself I can do nothing." If to represent Christ as a being distinct from God, and as inferior to him, be to degrade him, then let our opponents lay the guilt where it belongs, not on us, but on our Master, whose language we borrow, in whose very words we express our sentiments, whose words we dare not trifle with and force from their plain sense. Our limits will not allow us to say more; but we ask common Christians, who have taken their opinions from the Bible rather than from human systems, to look honestly into their own minds, and to answer frankly, whether they have not understood and believed Christ's divinity in the sense maintained by us, rather than in that for which the Trinitarians contend.

2. We proceed to another objection, and one which probably weighs more with multitudes than any other. It is this, that our doctrine respecting Christ takes from the sinner the only ground of hope. It is said by our opponents, "We and all men are sinners by our very nature, and infinitely guilty before God. The sword of divine justice hangs over us, and hell opens beneath us; and where shall we find a refuge but in an infinite Saviour? We want an infinite atonement; and in depriving us of this you rob us of our hope, you tear from the

Scriptures the only doctrine which meets our wants. We may burn our Bibles if your interpretation be true, for our case is desperate; we are lost for ever." In such warm and wild language, altogether unwarranted by Scripture, yet exceedingly fitted to work on common and terror-stricken minds, our doctrine is constantly assailed.

Now to this declamation, for such we esteem it, we oppose one plain request. Show us, we say, a single passage in the Bible, in which we are told that the sin of man is infinite, and needs an infinite atonement. We find not one. Not even a whisper of this doctrine comes to us from the sacred writers. Let us stop a moment and weigh this doctrine. It teaches us that man, although created by God a frail, erring, and imperfect being, and even created with an irresistible propensity to sin, is yet regarded by the Creator as an infinite offender, meriting infinite punishment for his earliest transgressions; and that he is doomed to endless torment, unless an infinite Saviour appear for his rescue! How can any one, we ask, charge on our benevolent and righteous Parent such a government of his creatures? We maintain that man is not created in a condition which makes an infinite atonement necessary; nor do we believe that any creature can fall into a condition from which God may not deliver him without this rigid expedient. Surely, if an infinite satisfaction to justice were indispensable to our salvation, if God took on him human nature for the very purpose of offering it, and if this fact constitute the peculiar glory, the life and essence, and the saving efficacy of the gospel, we must find it expressed clearly, definitely, in at least one passage in the Bible. But not one, we repeat it, can be found there. We maintain, further, that this doctrine of God becoming a victim and sacrifice for his own rebellious subjects, is as irrational as it is unscriptural. We have always supposed that atonement, if necessary, was to be made *to*, not by, the sovereign who has been offended; and we cannot conceive a more unlikely method of vindicating his authority, than that he himself should bear the punishment which is due to transgressors of his laws. We have another objection. If an infinite atonement be necessary, and if, consequently, none but God can make it, we see not but that God must become a sufferer, must take upon himself our pain and woe,—a thought from which a pious mind shrinks with horror. To escape this difficulty, we are told that Christ suffered as man, not as God; but if man only suffered, if only a human and finite mind suffered, if Christ, as God, was perfectly happy on the cross, and bore only a short and limited pain in his human nature, where, we ask, was the infinite atonement? Where is the boasted hope which this doctrine is said to give to the sinner?

The objection that there is no hope for the sinner unless Christ be the infinite God, amazes us. Surely, if we have a Father in heaven, of infinite goodness and power, we need no other infinite person to save us. The common doctrine disparages and dishonors the only true God, our Father, as if, without the help of a second and a third divinity, equal to himself, He could not restore his frail creature, man. We have not the courage of our brethren. With the Scriptures in our hands, with the solemn attestations which they contain to the divine Unity, and to Christ's dependence, we dare not give to the God and Father of Jesus an equal or rival in the glory of originating our redemption, or of accomplishing it by underived and infinite power. Are we asked, as we sometimes are, what is our hope if Christ be not the supreme God? We answer, it is the boundless and almighty goodness of his Father and our Father,—a goodness which cannot require an infinite atonement for the sins of a frail and limited creature. God's essential and unchangeable mercy, not Christ's infinity, is the Scriptural foundation of a sinner's hope. In the Scriptures, our Heavenly Father is always represented as the sole original, spring, and first cause of our salvation; and let no one presume to divide his glory with another. That Jesus came to save us, we owe entirely to the Father's benevolent appointment. That Jesus is perfectly adequate to the work of our salvation is to be believed, not because he is himself the supreme God, but because the supreme and unerring God selected, commissioned, and empowered him for this office. That his death is an important means of our salvation, we gratefully acknowledge; but ascribe its efficacy to the merciful disposition of God towards the human race. To build the hope of pardon on the independent and infinite sufficiency of Jesus Christ, is to build on an unscriptural and false foundation; for Jesus teaches us that of himself he can do nothing; that all power is given to him by his Father; and that he is a proper object of trust, because he came not of himself, or to do his own will, but because the Father sent him. We indeed lean on Christ, but it is because he is "a corner-stone, chosen by God and laid by God in Zion." God's forgiving love, declared to mankind by Jesus Christ and exercised through him, is the foundation of hope to the penitent on which we primarily rest, and a firmer the universe cannot furnish us.

3. We now proceed to another objection. We are charged with expecting to be saved by works, and not by grace. This charge may be easily despatched, and a more groundless one cannot easily be imagined. We indeed attach great importance to Christian works, or Christian obedience, believing that a practice or life conformed to the precepts and example of Jesus is the great end for which faith in him is required, and is the great condition on which everlasting life is bestowed. We are accustomed to speak highly of the virtues and improvements of a true Christian, rejecting with abhorrence the idea that they are no better than the outward Jewish righteousness, which the Prophet called "filthy rags;" and maintaining with the Apostle that they are, "in the sight of God, of great price." We believe that holiness or virtue is the very image of God in the human soul,—a ray of his brightness, the best gift which He communicates to his creatures, the highest benefit which Christ came to confer, the only important and lasting distinction between man and man. Still, we always and earnestly maintain that no human virtue, no human obedience, can give a legal claim, a right by merit, to the life and immortality brought to light by Christ. We see and mourn over the deficiencies, broken resolutions, and mixed motives of the best men. We always affirm that God's grace, benignity, free kindness, is needed by the most advanced Christians, and that to this alone we owe the promise in the gospel, of full remission and everlasting happiness to the penitent. None speak of mercy more

constantly than we. One of our distinctions is, that we magnify this lovely attribute of the Deity. So accustomed are we to insist on the infinity of God's grace and mercy, that our adversaries often charge us with forgetting his justice; and yet it is objected to us that, renouncing grace, we appeal to justice, and build our hope on the abundance of our merit!

4. We now proceed to another objection often urged against our views, or rather against those who preach them; and it is this, that we preach morality. To meet this objection, we beg to know what is intended by morality. Are we to understand by it, what it properly signified, our whole duty, however made known to us, whether by nature or revelation? Does it mean the whole extent of those obligations which belong to us as moral beings? Does it mean that "sober, righteous, godly life," which our moral Governor has prescribed to us by his Son, as the great preparation for heaven? If this be morality, we cheerfully plead guilty to the charge of preaching it, and of laboring chiefly and constantly to enforce it; and believing, as we do, that all the promises of the gospel are revealed for no other end than to make men moral, in this true and generous sense, we hope to continue to merit this reproach.

We fear, however, that this is not the meaning of the morality which is said to be the burden of our preaching. Some, at least, who thus reproach us, mean that we are accustomed to enjoin only a worldly and social morality, consisting in common honesty, common kindness, and freedom from gross vices; neglecting to inculcate inward purity, devotion, heavenly-mindedness, and love to Jesus Christ. We hope that the persons who thus accuse us speak from rumor, and have never heard our instructions for themselves; for the charge is false; and no one who ever sat under our ministry can urge it without branding himself a slanderer. The first and great commandment, which is to love God supremely, is recognized and enforced habitually in our preaching; and our obligations to Jesus Christ, the friend who died for us, are urged, we hope, not wholly without tenderness and effect.

It is but justice, however, to observe of many, that when they reproach us with moral preaching, they do not mean that we teach only outward decencies, but that we do not inculcate certain favorite doctrines, which are to them the very marrow and richness of the gospel. When such persons hear a sermon, be the subject what it may, which is not seasoned with recognitions of the Trinity, total depravity, and similar articles of faith, they call it moral. According to this strange and unwarrantable use of the term, we rejoice to say that we have for our pattern "him who spake as man never spake," and who, in his longest discourse, has dropped not a word about a Trinity, or inborn corruption, or special and electing grace; and, still more, we seriously doubt whether our preaching could with propriety be called moral, did we urge these doctrines, especially the two last; for, however warmly they may be defended by honest men, they seem to us to border on immorality; that is, to dishonor God, to weaken the sense of responsibility, to break the spirit, and to loosen the restraints on guilty passion.

. . . Unitarianism is Christianity stripped of those corrupt additions which shock reason and our moral feelings. It is a rational and amiable system, against which no man's understanding, or conscience, or charity, or piety revolts. Can the same be said of that system which teaches the doctrines of three equal persons in one God, of natural and total depravity, of infinite atonement, of special and electing grace, and of the everlasting misery of the non-elected part of mankind? We believe that unless Christianity be purified from these corruptions, it will not be able to bear the unsparing scrutiny to which the progress of society is exposing it. We believe that it must be reformed, or intelligent men will abandon it. As the friends of Christianity, and the foes of infidelity, we are therefore solicitous to diffuse what seem to us nobler and juster views of this divine system.

[13]

Nathaniel William Taylor
Advice to the Clergy*

The Bible is a plain book. It speaks, especially on the subject of sin, directly to human consciousness; and tells us beyond mistake, what sin is, and why we sin. In the text, the Apostle asserts the fact of the moral depravity of mankind, and assigns its cause. To be "the children of wrath" is to possess the character which deserves punishment; in other words, it is to be sinners, or to be entirely depraved in respect to moral character. The text then teaches; THAT THE ENTIRE MORAL DEPRAVITY OF MANKIND IS BY NATURE.

In illustrating this position, I shall attempt to show, First, in what the moral depravity of man consists; and Secondly, That this depravity is by nature.

I. By the moral depravity of mankind I intend generally, the entire sinfulness of their moral character,—that state of the mind or heart to which guilt and the desert of wrath pertain. I may say then negatively,

This depravity does not consist in any essential attribute or property of the soul—not in *any thing created* in man by his Maker. On this point, I need only ask,—does God create in men a sinful nature, and damn them for the very nature he creates? Believe this, who can.

Nor does the moral depravity of men consist in a sinful nature, which they have corrupted by being *one* with Adam,

---

* Nathaniel William Taylor, *Concio Ad Clerum. A Sermon Delivered in the Chapel of Yale College, September 10, 1828.* (New Haven, 1828), pp. 5–8; 12–18; 34–37. The text for the sermon was taken from Ephesians ii, 3, "And were by nature the children of wrath, even as others."

and by *acting in his act.* To believe that I am one and the same being with another who existed thousands of years before I was born, and that by virtue of this identity I truly acted in his act, and am therefore as truly guilty of his sin as himself,—to believe this, I must renounce the reason which my Maker has given me; I must believe it also, in face of the oath of God to its falsehood, entered upon the record.[1]

Nor does the moral depravity of men consist in any *constitutional propensities* of their nature. Whoever supposed himself or others to be guilty, for being hungry or thirsty after long abstinence from food or drink; or merely for desiring knowledge, or the esteem of his fellow-men, or any other good, abstractly from any choice to gratify such desires? Who does not know that a perfectly holy man must be subject to all these propensities? The man Christ Jesus was subject to every one of them, for he "was *in all points* tempted like as we are, yet without sin."

Nor does any degree of *excitement* in these propensities or desires, not resulting in choice, constitute moral depravity. Suppose them then, in the providence of God, excited in any degree, and yet the man to prefer doing the will of God to their gratification; all will admit that it is the noblest act of obedience conceivable in a moral being. All will agree, that the man, who always triumphs over excited propensity, who duly subordinates all his desires of inferior good to the will of God is a perfect man. It is the uniform sentiment of inspired truth, that this ruling of the spirit, this government of himself, imparts unrivalled glory to his character. We add the express declaration of the Apostle; "*Blessed* is the man that *endureth* temptation."

Nor does the moral depravity of men consist in any *disposition* or *tendency* to sin, which is *the cause of all sin.* It is important on this point to guard against error from the ambiguity of terms. There is an obvious distinction between a *disposition* or tendency to sin which is prior to *all* sin, and a *sinful* disposition. I am not saying then, that there is not, what with entire propriety may be called a disposition or

[1] Ezekiel xviii, 3, 4.

tendency to sin, which is the cause of *all* sin; nor that there is not, as a *consequence* of *this* disposition or tendency, what with equal propriety may be called a *sinful* disposition, which is the true cause of all *other* sin, itself excepted. But I say, that that which is the cause of *all* sin, is not itself sin. The cause of all sin, itself sin! Whence then came the first sin? Do you say, from a previous sin as its cause? Then you say, there is a sin before the first sin. Our first parents and fallen angels were once holy. Tell us now, whence came *their* first sin? Do you still repeat, from a previous sin? And what sort of philosophy, reason or common sense, is this—a sin before the first sin—sin before all sin?—Do you say there must be *difficulties* in theology?—I ask must there be *nonsense* in theology?

The question then still recurs, what is this moral depravity for which man deserves the wrath of God? I answer—*it is man's own act, consisting in a free choice of some object rather than God, as his chief good;—or a free preference of the world and of worldly good, to the will and glory of God. . . .*

And here we come to what I regard as the turning point of the whole controversy. So far as I know, the only argument in support of the opinion that sin pertains to something which is not preference, is based in a supposed decision of common sense. The decision claimed is, that all particular or specific sins, as fraud, falsehood, injustice, unbelief, envy, pride, revenge, result from a *wicked heart,*—from a *sinful disposition,* as the cause or source of such sinful acts.—To this fact, I yield unqualified assent, as "the dictate of the universal sense and reason of mankind," and by this universal judgment, I wish the present question to be decided. Let us then look at the fact in its full force and just application. There is a man then, whose course of life is wholly that of a worldling, his heart and hand shut against human woe, living without prayer, without gratitude, unmindful of God, and rejecting the Saviour of men, devising all, purposing all, doing all, for the sake of this world.—Why is it? You say, and *all* say, and say *right,* it is owing to his love of the world—to his worldly disposition—to a heart set on the world.—Now while all say this, and are right in saying it, we have one simple question to decide, viz. what do all *mean* by it? Every child can answer. Every child knows that the meaning is, that this man does freely and voluntarily fix his affections on worldly good, in preference to God; that the man has chosen the world as his chief good, his portion, his God. He knows that this is what is meant by a *worldly heart,* a *worldly disposition,* which leads to all *other* sins.—So when we ascribe the sins of the miser to his *avaricious disposition,* we mean his supreme love of money; or the crimes of the hero or conqueror to his *ambitious disposition,* we mean his supreme love of fame, a state of mind which involves *preference* for its object. And whatever previous tendency, or if you will previous disposition, there is to this state of mind; this state of mind itself and not any previous thing as the cause of it, is the *wicked heart*—the sinful disposition of men. They love the creature more than the Creator, when they can and ought to love the Creator most. This forbidden choice of worldly good, this preference of the low and sordid pleasures of earth to God and his glory—this love of the world which excludes the love of the Father,—*this—this* is man's depravity. This is that evil treasure of the heart, from which proceed evil things; this is the fountain, the source of all other abominations— man's free, voluntary preference of the world as his chief good, amid the revealed glories of a perfect God.

Having attempted to show in what the moral depravity of man consists, I now proceed to show

II. That this depravity is by nature. This I understand the Apostle to assert when he says, "and were by nature the children of wrath."

What then are we to understand, when it is said that mankind are depraved *by nature?*—I answer—*that such is their nature, that they will sin and only sin in all the appropriate circumstances of their being.*

To bring this part of the subject distinctly before the mind, it may be well to remark, that the question between the Calvinists and the Arminians on the point is this—whether the depravity or sinfulness of mankind is truly and properly ascribed to their *nature* or to their *circumstances* of *tempta-*

tion? And since, as it must be confessed, there can no more
be sin without circumstances of temptation, than there can
be sin without a nature to be tempted, why ascribe sin exclusively to nature?—I answer, it is truly and properly ascribed to *nature*, and *not* to circumstances because all mankind sin in all the appropriate circumstances of their being.
For all in the world ascribe an effect to the nature of a thing,
when no possible change in its appropriate circumstances will
change the effect; or when the effect is uniformly the same
in all its appropriate circumstances. To illustrate this by an
example: Suppose a tree, which in one soil bears only bad
fruit. Change its circumstances, transplant it to another soil,
and it bears very good fruit. Now we say, and all would say,
the fact that it bore bad fruit was owing to its situation,—to
its circumstances; for by changing its circumstances, you have
changed its fruit. Suppose now another tree, which bears bad
fruit place it where you will;—change its situation from one
soil to another, dig about it and dung it, cultivate it to perfection—do what you will, it still bears bad fruit only. Now
every one says, the fact is owing to *the nature* of the tree,
—the cause is in the tree, in its nature and *not* in its circumstances. So of mankind, change their circumstances as you
may; place them where you will within the limits of their
being; do what you will to prevent the consequence, you have
one uniform result, entire moral depravity. No change of condition, no increase of light nor of motives, no instructions nor
warnings, no any thing, within the appropriate circumstances
of their being, changes the result. Unless there be some interposition, which is not included in these circumstances, unless something be done which is above nature, the case is
hopeless. Place a human being any where within the appropriate limits and scenes of his immortal existence, and such
is his nature, that he will be a depraved sinner.

When therefore I say that mankind are entirely depraved
by nature, I do not mean that their nature is *itself* sinful, nor
that their nature is the *physical* or *efficient* cause of their
sinning; but I mean that their nature is the occasion, or reason of their sinning; that *such is their nature, that in all the*

appropriate circumstances of their being, they will sin and only sin.

Of this fact, I now proceed to offer some of the proofs.

1. I allege the text. It is here to be remarked, that the Apostle does not say, nor can he mean, that the nature of man is itself sinful. He is assigning the cause of all sin, and says it is *by nature.* If you say that he teaches that the *nature* itself is *sinful,* then as the cause must precede its effect you charge him with the absurdity of asserting that there is sin before sin.

The Apostle doubtless conforms his phraseology to common usage, and must mean just what every plain man, using the same language in any similar case would mean. His language too, must be understood with such restrictions as the nature of the subject and correct usage require. How then do we understand one another when using such language? We say the lion by nature eats flesh; the ox by nature eats grass; the tree by nature bears bad fruit; and so in a thousand cases. Now we mean by this, that the *nature* of the thing is such, that uniformly in all its circumstances, it will be the cause or occasion of that which we assert;—that the lion, for example, is of such a nature that he will eat flesh. So when the Apostle asserts, that mankind are by nature sinners, he must mean simply that such is their nature that uniformly in all the appropriate circumstances of their being, they will sin. He can no more mean that the nature itself is sinful, than we can mean in the example, that the nature of the lion is the same thing as the act of eating flesh, of which it is the cause. Still less can we suppose him to authorise the inference that the act of man in sinning, is not in some most important respects widely different from the act of a lion in eating flesh; so different that the one is sin, and the other not. This difference, the known nature of sin obliges us to suppose, it is intended not to deny, but to assume. The resemblance is simply in the *certainty* of the two things, and that which occasions this certainty; though in every other respect, especially in regard to the moral freedom and moral relations of man, the very nature of the acts spoken of, and the *mode* in which the certainty of them is occasioned, they are so diverse that the one is a moral act and has all the requisites of a moral act; the other cannot be a moral act.[2] The Apostle then, using language as all other men use it, traces the universal depravity of men to *their nature*, and thus most explicitly teaches, contrary to the Arminian view, that it is *not* owing to circumstances. If this be not his meaning he uses language as no one else uses it, and the world,

[2] With respect to the difficulty in which the doctrine of depravity *by nature* has been supposed to involve the free-agency of man, it may be remarked, that it can result only from a misapprehension of the terms. When we speak of the depravity or sinfulness of man *by nature*, no one, who correctly interprets the language, can understand us to mean that *nature* is the *physical* or *efficient cause* of sin, operating by absolute and irresistible compulsion. All that can be properly understood is, that *nature* is the *occasion* of sin, as a free act. The very nature of the predicate, *sin*, requires the restriction of the phrase to this import. Who ever supposes, when we speak of God as *by nature* holy, or of angels as *by nature* holy, that we intend that their nature is a *physical cause* of which holiness is a *physical effect?* or imagines that we intend to assert that which every one knows would annihilate the very nature of holiness? The known nature of the predicate and common sense of the speaker forbid such an interpretation. So in the present case, the Apostle cannot be understood to mean, nor can any one merely from using similar phraseology be properly or fairly understood to mean, that *nature* is a *physical cause* of which *sin* is a *physical effect*. The known nature of sin, the predicate, as a free act, is utterly at war with such a notion; we have a right to presume that no one can be so wanting in good sense as not to know this; or so uncandid as to suppose that we do not know it and assume it, or as to impute to us the opposite and palpably absurd view of sin. And as none ought ever to attribute flagrant absurdity to a writer or speaker whose language, according to correct usage, and just interpretation, expresses truth and good sense, (they pervert his language if they do,) they are obliged by the laws of interpretation, to understand *nature*, in the present case, to denote simply the *occasion* of sin. But if *nature* is not a *physical cause* of sin, but simply the *occasion* of sin, then since nothing but *physical* influence or efficiency can be supposed in the present case to be inconsistent with moral freedom, the consistency between sinning *by nature* and sinning freely, is apparent.

critics and all, may be safely challenged to tell what he does mean.

2. The Scriptures in many forms, teach the universal sinfulness of mankind in all the appropriate circumstances of their being.

First. They declare that "the imagination of man's heart is evil from his youth." And I need not cite passages from the word of God to show in how many forms it declares, that there is none that doeth good, no not one; that all have gone out of the way; that all depart from God and yield themselves to sin from the first moment of accountable action—sinning so early, that in the figurative language of the Scriptures they are said to "go astray as soon as they be born speaking lies." Thus God in his testimony, from the beginning to the end of it, asserts this appalling fact,—the absolute uniformity of human sinfulness, throughout the world and throughout all ages. Not a solitary exception occurs. Even those who become holy through grace are not noted as exceptions, and doubtless, because the object is to describe the character which without grace, is common to all. One character then, if God's record be true, prevails with absolute unvarying uniformity, from the fall in Eden till time shall be no longer. Let the circumstances of men be what they may, the eye of God sees and the voice of God declares that "there is no difference,—all are under sin." Now I ask, why is not the exception made—why, without intimating a single exempt case through favourable circumstances, or tracing sin in a single instance to adverse circumstances, why through all the tribes of men, is *all—all* sin—*all* depravity, in all the circumstances of their existence, according to God's testimony?—If then the absolute uniformity of an event proves that it is *by nature*, then does this uniformity of human sinfulness prove that man is depraved by nature. . . .

Now think of this, fellow sinner. God in adopting the present system with all the sin incidental to it, may have adopted the best possible. In giving to you the nature which he has, and in placing you in the circumstances in which he has, he may have done the best he could even for you.—Say then is your existence a curse, for which your Maker is to be reproached? Is it a curse at all, unless you make it so? Does not his preference of holiness to sin on your part, evince toward you, perfect benevolence? Listen to his calls and entreaties and say if this is not the voice of sincerity and truth. Listen to his oath, 'that he has no pleasure at all in your death,' and say if he would regret your return to duty and to life? Look around you and see what proofs of love, what intimations of grace and glory provided for you, gladden every moment of your being. Think what God has done to save you; how he has laid his wrath on one for your sake, how he has cleared away the darkness and tempest around his throne and with smiles of mercy invites you to himself, —how he bade angels sing in rapturous song "good will" to the guilty and the lost—how under his commission the swift messenger bears these tidings to you and to all,—how mercy with tears points you to that crown of life—how God himself with the earnestness of a suppliant father,—with the sincerity of a God entreats you to receive his great salvation. Say now, is he not good; is he not sincere?—What 'child of wrath,' will not trust in such a God to save him?

We see the importance of this view of man's depravity, compared with any other, in its bearing on the preaching of the Gospel. To what purpose, do we preach the Gospel to men, if we cannot reach the conscience with *its charge of guilt* and *obligations to duty*? And how I ask can this be done, unless sin and duty be shown to consist simply and wholly in acts and doings which are their own? Can this be done if we tell them and they believe us, that their sin is something which God creates before they existed? I care not what you call it, taste, disposition, volition, exercise, if it be that which *cannot* be unless God creates it, and cannot but be if he exerts his power to produce it, can we fasten the arrows of conviction in the conscience, and settle on the spirit the forebodings of a *merited* damnation? Can men be induced to make an effort to avoid sin which is thus produced in them, or to perform duties which must with the same passivity on their part, be produced in them? Does God charge on men, as that which deserves his endless indignation, what Himself does? Does God summon men to repentance with commands and entreaties, and at the same time tell them, that all efforts at compliance are as useless, as the muscular motions of a corpse to get life again. Does this book of God's inspiration, shock and appal the world, with the revelation of such things, respecting God and respecting man? Will the charge of *such sin* on man, touch the secret place of tears? Will the exhibition of such a God, allure the guilty to confide in his mercy? If so, preach it out—preach it consistently,—preach nothing to contradict it,—dwell on your message, that God creates men sinners and damns them for being so.—Tell them such is *their* nature and such the *modo* of his interposition, that there is no more hope from acting on the part of the sinner than from not acting; tell them they may as well sleep on, and sleep away these hours of mercy, as attempt any thing in the work of their salvation; that all is as hopeless with effort as without it. Spread over this world such a curtain of sackcloth, such a midnight of terror, and how as the appropriate effect, would each accountable immortal, either sit down in the sullenness of inaction, or take his solitary way to hell in the frenzy of despair!

But such is not the message of wrath and of mercy, by which a revolted world is to be awed and allured back to its Maker. The message we are to deliver to men is a message of wrath, because they are the perpetrators of the deed that deserves wrath.—It is a message of mercy to men who by acting, are to comply with the terms of it, and who can never hope to comply even through God's agency, without putting themselves to the doing of *the very thing* commanded of God.—And it is only by delivering such a message, that we, Brethren, can be "workers together with God." Let us then go forth with it; and clearing God, throw all the guilt of sin with its desert of wrath, upon the sinner's single self. Let us make him see and feel that he can go to hell only as a self-destroyer—that it is this fact, that will give those chains their strength to hold him, and those fires the anguish of their burning. Let us if we can, make this conviction take hold of his spirit, and ring in his conscience like the note of the second death. If he trembles at the sound in his ears, then let us point him to that mercy which a dying

Jesus feels for him, and tell him with the sympathies of men who have been in the same condemnation, that he need but to love and trust HIM, and heaven is his inheritance. Without derogating from the work of God's Spirit let us urge him to his duty—*to his duty—to his duty*, as a point-blank direction to business now on hand and now to be done. With the authorised assurance that 'peradventure God may give him repentance,' let us make known to him the high command of God "*strive* to enter in at the strait gate"—and make him hear every voice of truth and mercy in heaven and on earth, echoing the mandate.

Then shall the ministers of reconciliation be clad with truth as with a garment, and delivering their message not only in its substance but in its true manner and form, shall commend themselves to every man's conscience in the sight of God. Having his strength perfected in their weakness, they shall go forth 'as archangels strong,' and bidding the wide earth receive God's salvation, the bands of hell shall break, and a redeemed world return to the dominion of its God.

BIBLIOGRAPHICAL NOTE

Conrad Wright's *The Beginnings of Unitarianism in America* (Boston, 1955) and Sidney E. Mead, *Nathaniel William Taylor 1786–1858: A Connecticut Liberal* (Chicago, 1942) are especially important for this period, though Wright does not deal specifically with the controversy between the Unitarians and Taylorites. In Mead's volume, Chapter VII, "Old Calvinist to Taylorite," is an excellent brief statement of the changes occurring in New England theology at the end of the eighteenth and beginning of the nineteenth centuries.

For an introduction to William Ellery Channing consult Irving H. Bartlett, editor, *William Ellery Channing: Unitarian Christianity and Other Essays* (New York, 1957) and the Introduction of Conrad Wright, *Three Prophets of Religious Liberalism: Channing, Emerson, Parker* (Boston, 1961). David P. Edgell, *William Ellery Channing: An Intellectual*

Portrait (Boston, 1955) is probably the best general study of Channing's thought, though it should be complemented by Herbert W. Schneider, "The Intellectual Background of William Ellery Channing," *Church History*, vii (1938), pp. 3–23.

A sympathetic treatment of Taylor is Frank Hugh Foster, *A Genetic History of the New England Theology* (Chicago, 1907); a critical assessment is Joseph Haroutunian, *Piety Versus Moralism* (New York, 1932).

VI. REVIVALISM

The first half of the nineteenth century is frequently referred to as the period of westward expansion. In an increasingly mobile society the churches had to adopt new means to conduct their missionary and evangelistic tasks. Increased participation of the laity, a new image for the ministry, changing emphases in theology from the sovereignty of God to the responsibility and initiative of man, the use of interdenominational societies, and the adoption of revivalistic measures were some of the new characteristics of American Christianity.

The Camp Meeting was one "new measure." At these gatherings homesteaders would come to hear sermons delivered around the clock by clergy from various denominations. They were accompanied by emotional excesses and vivid recitals of conversion experiences. These Camp Meetings became more characteristic of the Baptist and Methodist churches and account, in part, for the rapid growth of these denominations. Frances Trollope (1780–1863), the English author, toured the United States at length in these years and wrote a brief account of her visit to a Camp Meeting, included here as Selection 14.

Charles Grandison Finney (1792–1875) was among the most well-known revivalists. Before his conversion in 1821 he taught school and prepared himself for a career in law. After studying theology with a Presbyterian pastor, George Gale, he was licensed by the St. Lawrence (New York) Presbytery and soon thereafter ordained. His uneasiness with prevailing interpretations of Calvinism, either of Princeton or New Divinity variety, led him gradually to adopt a theological position similar to that of Nathaniel William Taylor.[1] During the decade from 1825–35 Finney was in great de-

---

[1] See above, p. 138 ff.

mand as a preacher and his success as a revivalist was evident in the number of conversions he prompted. His use of the "Anxious Bench" was both imitated and criticized. He described it as "the appointment of some particular seat in the place of meeting (usually the front benches or pews) where the anxious may come and be addressed particularly and be made the subject of prayers and sometimes conversed with individually."[2] Finney was also instrumental in promoting revivals in urban centers, such as his extended visit to New York City in 1829–30. In 1835 he accepted an appointment as Professor at Oberlin and later became its President; there Finney served the cause of the abolitionists. His sermon, "Sinners Bound to Change their own Hearts," delivered in 1831, illustrates his departure from traditional Calvinistic expression.

One of Finney's critics was John Williamson Nevin (1803–1886), a graduate of Union College and Princeton Theological Seminary. Nevin taught at Princeton after graduation, followed by ten years at Western Theological Seminary in Allegheny, Pennsylvania, and then at the German Reformed seminary at Mercersburg, Pennsylvania. Nevin was sceptical of the fruits of revivalistic methods; his *The Anxious Bench* was a strong critique of these "new measures." His "high" doctrine of the church and stress on the importance and centrality of the sacraments in the life of the believer conflicted with the subjectivism which revivalism encouraged. Nevin was a leader in the group which sought to preserve denominational distinctiveness.

[2] Quoted in William G. McLoughlin, *Modern Revivalism: Charles Grandison Finney to Billy Graham* (New York, 1959), p. 95.

[14]

Frances M. Trollope
A Camp Meeting*

It was in the course of this summer that I found the opportunity I had long wished for, of attending a camp-meeting,
and I gladly accepted the invitation of an English lady and
gentleman to accompany them in their carriage to the spot
where it is held; this was in a wild district on the confines
of Indians.

The prospect of passing a night in the back-woods of
Indiana was by no means agreeable, but I screwed my courage to the proper pitch, and set forth determined to see with
my own eyes, and hear with my own ears, what a camp-
meeting really was. I had heard it said that being at a camp-
meeting was like standing at the gate of heaven, and seeing
it opening before you; I had heard it said, that being at a
camp-meeting was like finding yourself within the gates of
hell; in either case there must be something to gratify curiosity, and compensate one for the fatigue of a long rumbling
ride and a sleepless night.

We reached the ground about an hour before midnight, and
the approach to it was highly picturesque. The spot chosen
was the verge of an unbroken forest, where a space of about
twenty acres appeared to have been partially cleared for
the purpose. Tents of different sizes were pitched very near
together in a circle round the cleared space; behind them
were ranged an exterior circle of carriages of every description, and at the back of each were fastened the horses which
had drawn them thither. Through this triple circle of defence
we distinguished numerous fires burning brightly within it;

* Mrs. Trollope, *Domestic Manners of the Americans* (London,
1832), pp. 139–145.

and still more numerous lights flickering from the trees that were left in the enclosure. The moon was in meridian splendour above our heads.

We left the carriage to the care of a servant, who was to prepare a bed in it for Mrs. B. and me, and entered the inner circle. The first glance reminded me of Vauxhall, from the effect of the lights among the trees, and the moving crowd below them; but the second showed a scene totally unlike anything I had ever witnessed. Four high frames, constructed in the form of altars, were placed at the four corners of the inclosure; on these were supported layers of earth and sod, on which burned immense fires of blazing pine-wood. On one side a rude platform was erected to accommodate the preachers, fifteen of whom attended this meeting, and with very short intervals for necessary refreshment and private devotion, preached in rotation, day and night, from Tuesday to Saturday.

When we arrived, the preachers were silent; but we heard issuing from nearly every tent mingled sounds of praying, preaching, singing, and lamentation. The curtains in front of each tent were dropped, and the faint light that gleamed through the white drapery, backed as it was by the dark forest, had a beautiful and mysterious effect, that set the imagination at work; and had the sounds which vibrated around us been less discordant, harsh, and unnatural, I should have enjoyed it; but listening at the corner of a tent, which poured forth more than its proportion of clamour, in a few moments chased every feeling desired from imagination, and furnished realities that could neither be mistaken nor forgotten.

Great numbers of persons were walking about the ground, who appeared like ourselves to be present only as spectators; some of these very unceremoniously contrived to raise the drapery of this tent at one corner, so as to afford us a perfect view of the interior.

The floor was covered with straw, which round the sides was heaped in masses, that might serve as seats, but which at that moment were used to support the heads and the arms of the close-packed circle of men and women who kneeled on the floor.

Out of about thirty persons thus placed, perhaps half a dozen were men. One of these, a handsome-looking youth of eighteen or twenty, kneeled just below the opening through which I looked. His arm was encircling the neck of a young girl who knelt beside him, with her hair hanging dishevelled upon her shoulders, and her features working with the most violent agitation; soon after they both fell forward on the straw, as if unable to endure in any other attitude the burning eloquence of a tall grim figure in black, who, standing erect in the centre, was uttering with incredible vehemence an oration that seemed to hover between praying and preaching; his arms hung stiff and immoveable by his side, and he looked like an ill-constructed machine, set in action by a movement so violent as to threaten its own destruction, so jerkingly, painfully, yet rapidly, did his words tumble out; the kneeling circle ceasing not to call, in every variety of tone, on the name of Jesus; accompanied with sobs, groans, and a sort of low howling inexpressibly painful to listen to. But my attention was speedily withdrawn from the preacher, and the circle round him, by a figure which knelt alone at some distance; it was a living image of Scott's Macbriar, as young, as wild, and as terrible. His thin arms tossed above his head, had forced themselves so far out of the sleeves that they were bare to the elbow; his large eyes glared frightfully, and he continued to scream without an instant's intermission the word "Glory!" with a violence that seemed to swell every vein to bursting. It was too dreadful to look upon long, and we turned away shuddering.

We made the circuit of the tents, pausing where attention was particularly excited by sounds more vehement than ordinary. We contrived to look into many; all were strewed with straw, and the distorted figures that we saw kneeling, sitting, and lying among it, joined to the woful and convulsive cries, gave to each the air of a cell in Bedlam.

One tent was occupied exclusively by Negroes. They were all full-dressed, and looked exactly as if they were performing a scene on the stage. One woman wore a dress of pink gauze trimmed with silver lace; another was dressed in pale yellow silk; one or two had splendid turbans; and all wore a profusion of ornaments. The men were in snow white pantaloons, with gay coloured linen jackets. One of these, a youth of coal-black comeliness, was preaching with the most violent gesticulations, frequently springing high from the ground, and clapping his hands over his head. Could our missionary societies have heard the trash he uttered, by way of an address to the Deity, they might perhaps have doubted whether his conversion had much enlightened his mind.

At midnight, a horn sounded through the camp, which, we were told, was to call the people from private to public worship; and we presently saw them flocking from all sides to the front of the preachers' stand. Mrs. B. and I contrived to place ourselves with our backs supported against the lower part of this structure, and we were thus enabled to witness the scene which followed without personal danger. There were about two thousand persons assembled.

One of the preachers began in a low nasal tone, and, like all other Methodist preachers, assured us of the enormous depravity of man as he comes from the hands of his Maker, and of his perfect sanctification after he had wrestled sufficiently with the Lord to get hold of him, *et cætera*. The admiration of the crowd was evinced by almost constant cries of "Amen! Amen!" "Jesus! Jesus!" "Glory! Glory!" and the like. But this comparative tranquillity did not last long: the preacher told them that "this night was the time fixed upon for anxious sinners to wrestle with the Lord;" that he and his brethren "were at hand to help them," and that such as needed their help were to come forward into the "pen". . . . "The pen" was the space immediately below the preachers' stand; we were therefore placed on the edge of it, and were enabled to see and hear all that took place in the very centre of this extraordinary exhibition.

The crowd fell back at the mention of the *pen*, and for some minutes there was a vacant space before us. The preachers came down from their stand, and placed themselves in the midst of it, beginning to sing a hymn, calling upon the penitents to come forth. As they sung they kept turning themselves round to every part of the crowd, and, by degrees, the voices of the whole multitude joined in chorus.

This was the only moment at which I perceived any thing like the solemn and beautiful effect which I had heard ascribed to this woodland worship. It is certain that the combined voices of such a multitude, heard at dead of night, from the depths of their eternal forests, the many fair young faces turned upward, and looking paler and lovelier as they met the moonbeams, the dark figures of the officials in the middle of the circle, the lurid glare thrown by the altar fires on the woods beyond, did altogether produce a fine and solemn effect, that I shall not easily forget; but ere I had well enjoyed it, the scene changed, and sublimity gave place to horror and disgust.

The exhortation nearly resembled that which I had heard at "the revival," but the result was very different; for, instead of the few hysterical women who had distinguished themselves on that occasion, above a hundred persons, nearly all females, came forward, uttering howlings and groans so terrible that I shall never cease to shudder when I recall them. They appeared to drag each other forward, and on the word being given, "let us pray," they all fell on their knees; but this posture was soon changed for others that permitted greater scope for the convulsive movements of their limbs; and they were soon all lying on the ground in an indescribable confusion of heads and legs. They threw about their limbs with such incessant and violent motion, that I was every instant expecting some serious accident to occur.

But how am I to describe the sounds that proceeded from this strange mass of human beings? I know no words which can convey an idea of it. Hysterical sobbings, convulsive groans, shrieks and screams the most appalling, burst forth on all sides. I felt sick with horror. As if their hoarse and overstrained voices failed to make noise enough, they soon began to clap their hands violently. . . .

Many of these wretched creatures were beautiful young females. The preachers moved about among them, at once exciting and soothing their agonies. I heard the muttered "Sister! dear sister!" I saw the insidious lips approach the cheeks of the unhappy girls; I heard the murmured confessions of the poor victims, and I watched their tormentors, breathing into their ears consolations that tinged the pale cheek with red. Had I been a man, I am sure I should have been guilty of some rash act of interference; nor do I believe that such a scene could have been acted in the presence of Englishmen without instant punishment being inflicted; not to mention the salutary discipline of the tread-mill, which, beyond all question, would, in England, have been applied to check so turbulent and so vicious a scene.

After the first wild burst that followed their prostration, the moanings, in many instances, became loudly articulate; and I then experienced a strange vibration between tragic and comic feeling.

A very pretty girl, who was kneeling in the attitude of Canova's Magdalene immediately before us, among an immense quantity of jargon, broke out thus: "Wo! wo to the backsliders! hear it, hear it Jesus! when I was fifteen my mother died, and I backslided! take me home to my mother, Jesus! take me home to her, for I am weary! Oh! John Mitchel! John Mitchel! and after sobbing piteously behind her raised hands, she lifted her sweet face again which was as pale as death, and said, "Shall I sit on the sunny bank of salvation with my mother? my own dear mother? Oh Jesus, take me home, take me home!"

Who could refuse a tear to this earnest wish for death in one so young and so lovely? But I saw her, ere I left the ground, with her hand fast locked, and her head supported by a man who looked very much as Don Juan might, when sent back to earth as too bad for the regions below.

One woman near us continued to "call on the Lord," as it is termed, in the loudest possible tone, and without a moment's interval, for the two hours that we kept our dreadful station. She became frightfully hoarse, and her face so red as to make me expect she would burst a blood vessel. Among the rest of her rant, she said, "I will hold fast to Jesus, I never will let him go; if they take me to hell, I will still hold him fast, fast, fast!"

The stunning noise was sometimes varied by the preachers' beginning to sing; but the convulsive movements of the poor maniacs only became more violent. At length the atrocious wickedness of this horrible scene increased to a degree of grossness that drove us from our station; we returned to the carriage at about three o'clock in the morning, and passed the remainder of the night in listening to the very-increasing tumult at the pen. To speak was impossible. At daybreak the horn again sounded to send them to private devotion; and in about an hour afterward I saw the whole camp as joyously and eagerly employed in preparing and devouring their most substantial breakfasts as if the night had been passed in dancing; and I marked many a fair but pale face, that I recognized as a demoniac of the night, simpering beside a swain, to whom she carefully administered hot coffee and eggs. The preaching saint and the howling sinners seemed alike to relish this mode of recruiting their strength.

After enjoying abundance of strong tea, which proved a delightful restorative after a night so strangely spent, I wandered alone into the forest, and I never remember to have found perfect quiet more delightful.

We soon after left the ground; but before our departure we learned that a very *satisfactory* collection had been made by the preachers, for Bibles, Tracts, and *all other religious purposes.*

[15]

Charles G. Finney
Sinners Bound to Change Their Own Hearts*

Ezekiel xviii. 31, "Make you a new heart and a new spirit, for why will ye die?"

. . . The term *spirit,* in the Bible, is used in different senses; it sometimes means a spiritual being, or moral agent; in other places it is used in the sense in which we often employ it in

* From C. G. Finney, *Sermons on Important Subjects* (New York, 1836), pp. 4; 5; 7; 8; 10–13; 19–23; 39–42.

conversation. In speaking of the temper of a man, we say he has a good or bad spirit, a lovely or hateful spirit. It is evidently used in this sense in the text. The term *heart* is also employed in various senses: sometimes it appears to be used as synonimous with soul; sometimes it evidently means the will; sometimes the conscience, sometimes it seems to be used in such an extensive sense, as to cover all the moral movements of the mind; sometimes it expresses the natural or social affections. The particular sense in which it is to be understood in any place, may easily be determined by the connexion in which it stands. Our present business is, to ascertain its meaning as used in the text; for it is in this sense, that we are required to make us a new heart and a new spirit. I begin, therefore, by saying,

1. That it does not mean the fleshly heart, or that bodily organ which is the seat of animal life.

2. That it does not mean a new soul. We have one soul, and do not need another. Nor,

3. Are we required to create any new faculties, of body or mind. We now have all the powers of moral agency; we are just as God made us, and do not need any alteration in the substance of soul or body. Nor,

4. Does it mean that we are to bring to pass any *constitutional* change in ourselves. We are not required to add to the constitution of our minds or bodies any new principle or taste. Some persons speak of a change of heart as something miraculous—something in which the sinner is to be entirely passive, and for which he is to wait in the use of means, as he would wait for a surgical operation, or an electric shock. We need nothing added to the constitution of our body or mind; nor is it true in experience, that those who have a new heart, have any constitutional alteration of their powers whatever. They are the same identical persons, so far as both body and mind are concerned, that they were before. The alteration lies in the manner in which they are disposed to use, and do actually employ, their moral and physical powers. A constitutional change, either in body or mind, would destroy personal identity. A Christian, or one who has a new heart, would not be the same individual in regard to his powers of

moral agency, that he was before—would not be the same
agent, and under the same responsibilities. . . .

All holiness, in God, angels, or men, must be *voluntary*,
or it is not holiness. To call any thing that is a part of the mind
or body, holy—to speak of a holy substance, unless it be in a
figurative sense, is to talk nonsense. Holiness is virtue; it is
something that is praiseworthy; it cannot therefore be a part
of the created substance of body or mind, but must consist
in voluntary obedience to the principles of eternal righteousness. The necessary adaptation of the outward motive to the
mind, and of the mind to the motive, lies in the powers of
moral agency, which every human being possesses. He has
understanding to perceive and weigh; he has conscience to
decide upon the nature of moral opposites; he has the power
and liberty of choice. Now, to this moral agent, possessing
these faculties, the motives of the Gospel re-addressed; and
there is plainly a natural tendency in these weighty considerations to influence him to obey his Maker.

But I come now to show what we are to understand by
the command of the text. The Bible often speaks of the heart,
as a fountain, from which flow the moral affections and actions
or the soul, as in Matt. xv. 19, "Out of the heart proceed
evil thoughts, murders, adulteries, fornications, thefts, false
witness, blasphemies." The term *heart*, as applied to mind, is
figurative, and recognizes an analogy between the heart of
the body, and the heart of the soul. The fleshly organ of the
body called the *heart*, is the seat and fountain of animal life,
and by its constant action, diffuses life through the animal
system. *The spiritual heart, is the fountain of spiritual life, is
that deep-seated but voluntary preference of the mind, which
lies back of all its other voluntary affections and emotions,
and from which they take their character.* In this sense I
understand the term heart to be used in the text. It is evidently something over which we have control; something voluntary; something for which we are to blame, and which
we are bound to alter. Now, if the requirement is, that we are
to make some constitutional change in the substance of the
body or mind, it is evidently unjust, and enforced by a pen-
alty no less than infinite, as obedience is impossible, the re-

quirement is infinite tyranny. It is evident that the requirement here, is to change our *moral character;* our *moral* disposition; in other words, to change that abiding preference of our minds, which prefers sin to holiness; self-gratification to the glory of God. I understand a change of heart, as the term is here used, to be just what we mean by a change of mind in regard to the supreme object of pursuit; a change in the choice of an *end,* not merely in the choice of *means.* . . .

It is a change in the choice of a *Supreme Ruler.* The conduct of impenitent sinners demonstrates that they prefer Satan as the ruler of the world, they obey his laws, electioneer for him, and are zealous for his interest, even to martyrdom. They carry their attachment to him and his government so far as to sacrifice both body and soul to promote his interest and establish his dominion. A new heart is the choice of JEHOVAH as the supreme ruler; a deep-seated and abiding preference of his laws, and government, and character, and person, as the supreme Legislator and Governor of the universe.

Thus the world is divided into two great political parties; the difference between them is, that one party choose Satan as the god of this world, yield obedience to his laws, and are devoted to his interest. Selfishness is the law of Satan's empire, and all impenitent sinners yield it a willing obedience. The other party choose Jehovah for their governor, and consecrate themselves, with all their interests, to his service and glory. Nor does this change imply a constitutional alteration of the powers of body or mind, any more than a change of mind in regard to the form or administration of a human government.

There are certain things in regard to mind, with which we become familiar by experience. For instance, we know by experience that it is the nature of mind to be controlled in its individual exercises and affections, by a deep-seated *disposition* or *preference* of a particular course or object. It is not necessary here, to enter into the philosophy of this fact, but simply to recognize the fact itself. For instance, when Adam was first created, and awoke into being, before he had obeyed or disobeyed his Maker, he could have had no moral character at all; he had exercised no affections, no desires, nor put forth any actions. In this state he was a complete moral agent; and in this respect in the image of his Maker; but as yet could have had no moral character; for moral character cannot be a subject of creation, but attaches to voluntary action. Do not understand me to affirm, that any considerable time elapsed between the creation of Adam and his possessing a moral character. It is presumed, that as soon as he awoke into being, and had knowledge of the existence and character of his Maker, the evidences of which doubtless shone all around him, he chose *Him* as his supreme ruler, and voluntarily dedicated all his powers to his service. This preference of God, and his glory, and service, over his own self-interest and every thing else, constituted his *disposition,* or his moral character; in other words, it was a perfectly holy heart. Out of this heart, or preference, flowed as from a fountain the pure waters of obedience. All the subordinate movements, affections, choices, and purposes of the mind, and all the outward actions, flowed from this strong and governing preference for God and his service. Thus he went forth to dress God's garden, and keep it. Now, for a time, this preference of Adam was strong and abiding enough to insure perfect obedience in all things; for mind will act in consistency with an abiding preference, according to the strength and permanency of this preference. For instance, the strong preference that a man may have for home may forbid his entertaining any purpose of going abroad. The strength of his preference for his wife, may prevent his consenting to any improper intimacy with other women; and the probability, and I may say possibility, of betraying him into acts of infidelity to his wife, may depend upon the strength and abiding energy of his preference of her to all other women. So while the preference of Adam remained unshaken, its energy gave direction and character to all his feelings and to all his conduct; and that which must stamp perfection upon the obedience of heaven, is the great strength and continually abiding energy of their preference for God and his service. Indeed the continued holiness of God depends upon the same cause, and flows from the same fountain. His holiness does not consist in the substance of his nature, but in his preference of right. His holiness must be voluntary, and he is immutably holy, because he is infinitely so. In other words, his preference of right is infinitely strong, so strong and so abiding as never to admit of change; of any conduct inconsistent with it. Adam was perfectly holy, but not infinitely so. As his preference for God was not infinitely strong, it was possible that it might be changed, and we have the melancholy fact written in characters that cannot be misunderstood, on every side of us, that an occasion occurred on which he actually changed it. Satan, in the person of the serpent, presented a temptation of a very peculiar character. It was addressed to the constitutional appetites of both soul and body; to the appetite for food in the body, and for knowledge in the mind. These appetites were constitutional; they were not in themselves sinful, but their *unlawful indulgence* was sin. The proposal of the serpent was, that he should change his mind in regard to the supreme end of pursuit; and thus change his heart, or his whole moral character. "Yea, hath God said, ye shall not eat of every tree of the garden? and the woman said unto the serpent, we may eat of the fruit of the trees of the garden, but of the fruit of the tree which is in the midst of the garden, God hath said, ye shall not eat of it, neither shall ye touch it, lest ye die. And the serpent said unto the woman, ye shall not surely die: for God doth know that in the day ye eat thereof, then your eyes shall be opened, and ye shall be as Gods, knowing good and evil." Now the foundation of holiness in Adam, and that which constituted his holy heart, was the supreme choice that God should rule; the supreme preference of God and his glory to his own happiness or interest. It is easy to see, therefore, that the object aimed at by the serpent was to affect a change in the *supreme end* of pursuit. It was to prefer his own gratification to obedience to his Maker; to become as a god himself instead of obeying Jehovah; to pursue as a supreme end self-gratification instead of the glory of God. In yielding therefore to this proposal, in changing his mind upon this fundamental point, he changed his own heart, or that controlling preference which was at once the foundation, and

fountain, of all obedience. Now this was a real change of
heart; from a perfectly holy, to a perfectly sinful one. But
here was no constitutional change, no change in the substance of either body or mind. It was not a change in the
powers of moral agency themselves, but simply in the use
of them; in consecration their energies to a different end.
Now suppose God to have come out upon Adam with the
command of the text, "Make to you a new heart, for why will
you die." Could Adam have justly answered, Dost thou think
that I can change my own heart? Can I, who have a heart
totally depraved, can I change that heart? Might not the Almighty have answered him in words of fire, Rebel, you have
just changed your heart from holiness to sin, now change it
back from sin to holiness. . . .

How is this requirement, to "make to yourself a new
heart," consistent with the often repeated declarations of
the Bible, that a new heart is the gift and work of God. The
Bible ascribes conversion of a new heart, to four different
agencies. Oftentimes it is ascribed to the Spirit of God. And
if you consult the Scriptures, you will find it still more frequently ascribed to the truth; as, "Of his own will begat he us
by the word of truth"—"The truth shall make you free"—
"Sanctify them through thy truth"—"The law of God is perfect, converting the soul." It is sometimes ascribed to the
preacher, or to him who presents the truth; "He that winneth
souls is wise;" Paul says, "I have begotten you through the
Gospel"—"He that converteth a sinner from the error of his
ways, shall save a soul from death, and hide a multitude of
sins." Sometimes it is spoken of as the work of the sinner
himself; thus the apostle says, "Ye have purified yourselves
by obeying the truth;" "I thought on my ways," says the
Psalmist, "and turned unto the Lord." Again he says, "When
thou saidst, Seek ye my face; my heart replied, Thy face,
Lord, will I seek." Now the question is, Are all these declarations of Scripture consistent with each other? They are all
true; they all mean just as they say; nor is there any real disagreement between them. There is a sense in which conversion is the work of God. There is a sense in which it is the
effect of truth. There is a sense in which the preacher does

it. And it is also the appropriate work of the sinner himself.

The fact is, that the actual turning, or change, is the sinner's own act. The agent who induces him, is the Spirit of God. A secondary agent, is the preacher, or individual who presents the truth. The truth is the instrument, or motive, which the Spirit uses to induce the sinner to turn. Suppose yourself to be standing on the bank of the Falls of Niagara. As you stand upon the verge of the precipice, you behold a man lost in deep reverie, approaching its verge unconscious of his danger. He approaches nearer and nearer, until he actually lifts his foot to take the final step that shall plunge him in destruction. At this moment you lift your warning voice above the roar of the foaming waters, and cry out, *Stop.* The voice pierces his ear, and breaks the charm that binds him; he turns instantly upon his heel, all pale and aghast he retires, quivering, from the verge of death. He reels, and almost swoons with horror; turns and walks slowly to the public house; you follow him; the manifest agitation in his countenance calls numbers around him, and on *your* approach, he points to you, and says, That man saved my life. Here he ascribes the work to you; and certainly there is a sense in which you had saved him. But, on being further questioned, he says, *Stop!* how that word rings in my ears. Oh, that was to me the word of life. Here he ascribes it to the *word* that aroused him, and caused him to turn. But, on conversing still further, he said, had I not turned at that instant, I should have been a dead man. Here he speaks of it, and truly, as his own act; but directly you hear him say, O the mercy of God; if God had not interposed, I should have been lost. Now the only defect in this illustration is this: In the case supposed, the only interference on the part of God, was a *providential* one; and the only sense in which the saving of the man's life is ascribed to him, is in a providential sense. But in the conversion of a sinner there is something more than the providence of God employed; for here not only does the providence of God so order it, that the preacher cries, *Stop,* but the Spirit of God forces the truth home upon him with such tremendous power as to induce him to turn.

Not only does the preacher cry *Stop,* but, through the living voice of the preacher, the Spirit cries *Stop*. The preacher cries, "Turn ye, why will ye die." The Spirit pours the expostulation home with such power, that the sinner turns. Now, in speaking of this change, it is perfectly proper to say, that the Spirit turned him, just as you would say of a man, who had persuaded another to change his mind on the subject of politics, that he had converted him, and brought him over. It is also proper to say that the truth converted him; as in a case when the political sentiments of a man were changed by a certain argument, we should say, that argument brought him over. So also with perfect propriety may we ascribe the change to the living preacher, or to him who had presented the motives; just as we should say of a lawyer who had prevailed in his argument with a jury; he has got his case, he has converted the jury. It is also with the same propriety ascribed to the individual himself whose heart is changed; we should say that he had changed his mind, he has come over, he has repented. Now it is strictly true, and true in the most absolute and highest sense; the act is his own act, the turning is his own turning, while God by the truth had induced him to turn; still it is strictly true that he has turned and has done it himself. Thus you see the sense in which it is the work of God, and also the sense in which it is the sinner's own work. The Spirit of God, by the truth, influences the sinner to change, and in this sense is the efficient cause of the change. But the sinner actually changes, and is therefore himself, in the most proper sense, the author of the change. There are some who, on reading their Bibles, fasten their eyes upon those passages that ascribe the work to the Spirit of God, and seem to overlook those that ascribe it to man, and speak of it as the sinner's own act. When they have quoted Scripture to prove it is the work of God, they seem to think they have proved that it is that in which man is passive, and that it can in no sense be the work of man. Some months since a tract was written, the title of which was, "Regeneration is the effect of Divine Power." The writer goes on to prove that the work is wrought by the Spirit of God, and there he stops. Now it had been just as true, just as philosophical, and just as Scriptural, if he had said, that conversion was the work of man. It was easy to prove that it was the work of God, in the sense in which I have explained it. The writer, therefore tells the truth, so far as he goes; but he has told only half the truth. For while there is a sense in which it is the work of God, as he has shown, there is also a sense in which it is the work of man, as we have just seen. The very title to this tract is a stumbling block. It tells the truth, but it does not tell the whole truth. And a tract might be written upon this proposition that *"conversion or regeneration is the work of man;"* which would be just as true, just as Scriptural, and just as philosophical, as the one to which I have alluded. Thus the writer, in his zeal to recognize and honor God as concerned in this work, by leaving out the fact that a change of heart is the sinner's *own act*, has left the sinner strongly intrenched, with his weapons in his rebellious hands, stoutly resisting the claims of his Maker, and waiting passively for God to make him a new heart. Thus you see the consistency between the requirement of the text, and the declared fact that God is the author of the new heart. God commands you to do it, expects you to do it, and if it ever is done, you must do it. . . .

Few more mischievous sentiments have ever been broached, than that there is no philosophical connexion between means and end in the conversion of sinners; that there is no natural adaptedness in the motives of the Gospel to annihilate the sinner's selfishness, and lead him to submit to God. This idea is a part of the scheme of physical depravity. It considers regeneration as a change in the substance of the mind; as effected by the direct physical agency of the Spirit of God, irrespective of truth. If this were a correct view of regeneration, it would be manifest that there could be no connexion between the means and the end. For if the work be a physical creation, performed by the direct and physical power of the Holy Ghost, then certainly it is effected by *no means* whatever. But so far is this from truth, that no sinner ever was or ever will be converted, but by means wisely and philosophically adapted to this end.

The Spirit selects such considerations, at such times and under such circumstances, as are naturally calculated to dis-arm and confound the sinner; to strip him of his excuses, answer his cavils, humble his pride, and break his heart. The preacher should therefore acquaint himself with his refuges of lies, and as far as possible take into consideration his whole history, including his present views and state of mind; should wisely select a subject; so skilfully arrange, so simply and yet so powerfully present it, as to engage the sinner's whole attention, and then lay himself out to the utmost to bring him to yield upon the spot. He who deals with souls should study well the laws of mind, and carefully and prayerfully adapt his matter and his manner to the state and circumstances, views and feelings, in which he may find the sinner at the time. He should present that particular subject, in that connexion and in that manner, that shall have the greatest *natural tendency* to subdue the rebel at once. If men would act as wisely and as philosophically in attempting to make men Christians, as they do in attempting to sway mind upon other subjects; if they would suit their subject to the state of mind, conform "the action to the word and the word to the action," and press their subject with as much address, and warmth, and perseverance, as lawyers and statesmen do their addresses; the result would be the conversion of hundreds of thousands, and converts would be added to the Lord "like drops of the morning dew." Were the whole church and the whole ministry right upon this subject; had they right views, were they imbued with a right spirit and would they "go forth with tears, bearing precious seed, they would soon reap the harvest of the whole earth, and return bearing their sheaves with them."

The importance of rightly understanding that God converts souls by motives, is inconceivably great. Those who do not recognize this truth in *practice* at least, are more likely to hinder than to aid the Spirit in his work. Some have denied this truth in theory, but have happily admitted it in practice. They have prayed, and preached, and talked, as if they expected the Holy Spirit to convert sinners by the truth. In such cases, notwithstanding their theory, their practice was owned and blessed of God. But a want of attention to this truth in practice has been the source of much and ruinous error in the management of revivals and in dealing with anxious souls. Much of the preaching, conversation and exhortation have been irrelevant, perplexing and mystical. Sufficient pains have not been taken to avoid a diversion of public and individual attention. Sinners have been kept long under conviction, because their spiritual guides withheld those particular truths which at the time above all others they needed to know. They have been perplexed and confounded by abstract doctrines, metaphysical subleties, absurd exhibitions of the sovereignty of God, inability, physical regeneration and constitutional depravity, until the agonized mind, discouraged and mad from contradiction from the pulpit, and absurdity in conversation, dismissed the subject as altogether incomprehensible, and postponed the performance of duty as impossible. . . .

And now, sinner, while the subject is before you, will you yield? To keep yourself away from under the motives of the Gospel, by neglecting church, and neglecting your Bible, will prove fatal to your soul. And to be careless when you do attend, or to hear with attention and refuse to make up your mind and yield, will be equally fatal. And now, "I beseech you, by the mercies of God, that you at *this time* render your body and soul, a living sacrifice to God, which is your reasonable service." Let the truth take hold upon your conscience—throw down your rebellious weapons—give up your refuges of lies—fix your mind steadfastly upon the world of considerations that should instantly decide you to close in with the offer of reconciliation while it now lies before you. Another moment's delay, and it may be too late for ever. The Spirit of God may depart from you—the offer of life may be made no more, and this one more slighted offer of mercy may close up your account, and seal you over to all the horrors of eternal death. Hear, then, O sinner, I beseech you, and obey the word of the Lord—"Make you a new heart and a new spirit, for why will ye die?"

[16]
John W. Nevin
The Anxious Bench*

. . . It has been sometimes intimated, that it is not safe to
oppose and condemn the use of New Measures, because of
their connections and purpose. Their relation to the cause of
revivals, is supposed to invest them with a sort of sacred
character, which the friends of religion should at least respect, even if they may not be able in all cases, to approve.
The system has taken hold the "horns of the altar," and it
seems to some like sacrilege to fall upon it there, or to force
it away for the purposes of justice to any other place. It is a
serious thing, we are told, to find fault with any movement,
that claims to be animated by the Spirit of God. By so doing, we render it questionable whether we have ourselves
any proper sympathy with revivals, and furnish occasion to
the world also to blaspheme and oppose everything of the
kind. But this is tyrannical enough, to take for granted the
main point in dispute, and then employ it as a consideration
to repress inquiry or to silence objection. If New Measures
can be shown to proceed from the Holy Ghost, or to be
identified in any view with the cause of revivals, they may
well demand our reverence and respect. If they can be shown
even to be of *adiaphorous* character with regard to religion,
harmless at least if not positively helpful to the Spirit's work,
they may then put in a reasonable plea to be tolerated in
silence, if not absolutely approved. But neither the one nor
the other of these positions can be successfully maintained.
It is a mere trick unworthy of the gospel, for any one to

* John W. Nevin, *The Anxious Bench*. Second Edition, Revised
and Enlarged. (Chambersburg, Pa., 1844), pp. 21–22; 28–29;
112–121.

confound with the sacred idea of a revival, things that do not belong to it in truth at all, for the purpose of compelling a judgment in their favor. The very design of the inquiry now proposed, is to show that the Anxious Bench, and the system to which it belong, have no claim to be considered either salutary or safe, in the service of religion. It is believed, that instead of promoting the cause of true vital godliness, they are adapted to hinder its progress. The whole system is considered to be full of peril, for the most precious interests of the Church. And why then should there be any reserve, in treating the subject with such freedom as it may seem to require? We may well feel indeed that the subject is solemn. All that relates to the interests of revivals, and the welfare of souls, is solemn; and it becomes us to approach it in a serious way. But this is no reason, why we should close our eyes against the truth, or refuse to call things by their proper names. This would be to trifle with sacred things truly. . . . If Finneyism and Winebrennerism, the anxious bench, revival machinery, solemn tricks for effect, decision displays at the bidding of the preacher, genuflections and prostrations in the aisle or around the altar, noise and disorder, extravagance and rant, mechanical conversions, justification by feeling rather than faith, and encouragement ministered to all fanatical impressions; if these things, and things in the same line indefinitely, have no connection in fact with true serious religion and the cause of revivals, but tend only to bring them into discredit, let the fact be openly proclaimed. Only in this way, may it be hoped that the reproach put upon revivals and other evangelical interests by some, under cover of their pretended connection with this system of New Measures in the true sense, will be in due time fairly rolled away. . . .

The general system to which the Anxious Bench belongs, it may be remarked again, is unfavorable to deep, thorough and intelligent piety. This must be the case of course, if there be any truth in the observations already made with regard to its character. A system that leads to such a multitude of spurious conversions, and that makes room so largely for that low, gross, fanatical habit, which has just been described, cannot possibly be associated to any extent with the power of

godliness, in its deeper and more earnest forms. The religion
which it may produce, so far as it can be counted genuine,
will be for the most part of a dwarfish size and sickly complexion. The "experience" of the Anxious Bench is commonly
shallow. The friends of the new method often please themselves, it is true, with the idea that *their* awakenings include
a vast amount of power in this way; and they are not back-
ward to insinuate, that those who oppose their measures are
ignorant of what pertains to the "depths" of experimental
piety. Were such persons themselves experimentally acquainted with the pangs of the new birth, it is intimated,
they would not be so easily offended with the noise and disorder of poor souls *agonizing* at the altar; and if they had
ever themselves tasted the joys of pardoned sin, they might
be expected to have other ears than they now have, for the
shouts and hallelujahs of the redeemed, suddenly translated
in these circumstances from the power of Satan into the
glorious liberty of the family of God. But in fact no "experiences" are more superficial commonly, than those which belong to this whirlwind process. The foundations of the inward
life are not reached and moved by it at all. All that would
be wanted often to hush an "altar-full" of chaotic cries to
solemn stillness, would be that the hearts of the "agonizing"
mourners should be suddenly touched with some real sense
of the presence of God, and their own sins. "I have heard
of Thee," says Job, "with the hearing of the ear; but *now
mine eye seeth thee:* wherefore I abhor myself, and repent
in dust and ashes." Alas, it is not the *depth* of these anxious
bench and camp-meeting conversions, but their utter want
of depth, that exposes them to complaint. They involve little
or nothing of what the old divines call *heart work.* They bring
with them no self-knowledge. They fill the Church with lean
professors, who show subsequently but little concern to *grow*
in grace, little capacity indeed to understand at all the free,
deep, full life of the "new man" in Christ Jesus. Such converts, if they do not altogether "fall from grace," are apt to
continue at least babes in the gospel, as long as they live.
The natural fruit of the system is a sickly Christianity, that
is sure to be defective or one-sided, both in doctrine and

practice. It proceeds upon a wrong conception of religion from the start, and error and heresy, in the nature of the case, are wrought plentifully into the very texture of all that is reached by its operations. There is involved in it a spirit of delusion, which cannot fail to show its power disastrously, after a short time, in any community in which it is suffered to prevail.

Here is another most serious charge, demanding our special attention. I have denominated the system a *heresy*, not inconsiderately or for rhetorical effect simply, but with sober calculation and design. In religion, as in life universally, theory and practice are always inseparably intertwined, in the ground of the soul. Every error is felt practically; and wherever obliquity in conduct comes into view, it must be referred to some corresponding obliquity in principle. It is not by accident then that the system of New Measures is found producing so largely, the evil consequences which have been thus far described. Error and heresy, I repeat it, are involved in the system itself, and cannot fail sooner or later, where it is encouraged, to evolve themselves in the most mischievous results. Finneyism is only Taylorism reduced to practice, the speculative heresy of New-Haven actualized in common life. A low, shallow, pelagianizing theory of religion, runs through it from beginning to end. The fact of sin is acknowledged, but not in its true extent. The idea of a new spiritual creation is admitted, but not in its proper radical and comprehensive form. The ground of the sinner's salvation is made to lie at last in his own separate person. The deep import of the declaration, *That which is born of the flesh is flesh,* is not fully apprehended; and it is vainly imagined accordingly, that the flesh as such may be so stimulated and exalted notwithstanding, as to prove the mother of that spiritual nature, which we are solemnly assured can be born only of the Spirit. Hence all stress is laid upon the energy of the individual will, (the self-will of the flesh,) for the accomplishment of the great change in which regeneration is supposed to consist. The case is not remedied at all by the consideration, that due account is made at the same time *professedly* of the aids of God's Spirit, as indispensable in the work of conversion. The heresy lies involved in the system. This is so constructed as naturally, and in time inevitably, to engender false views of religion. Sometimes the mere purpose to serve God, in the same form with a resolution to sign a temperance pledge, is considered to be the ground of regeneration. At other times, it is made to stand in a certain state of feeling, supposed to be of supernatural origin, but apprehended notwithstanding mechanically, as the result of a spiritual process which begins and ends with the sinner himself. The experience of the supposed supernatural in this case, stands in the same relation to the actual power of the new birth, that magic bears to the true idea of a miracle. The higher force does not strictly and properly take possession of the lower, but is presumed rather to have been reduced to the possession and service of this last, to be used by it for its own convenience. Religion does not get the sinner, but it is the sinner who "gets religion." Justification is taken to be in fact by *feeling*, not by faith; and in this way falls back as fully into the sphere of self-righteousness, as though it were expected from works under any other form. In both the views which have been mentioned, as grounded either in a change of purpose or a change of feeling, religion is found to be in the end the product properly of the sinner himself. It is wholly subjective, and therefore visionary and false. The life of the soul must stand in something beyond itself. Religion involves the will; but not as self-will, affecting to be its own ground and centre. Religion involves feeling; but it is not comprehended in this as its principle. Religion is subjective also, fills and rules the individual in whom it appears; but it is not created in any sense by its subject or from its subject. The life of the branch is in the trunk. The theory we have been contemplating then, as included practically in the system of New Measures, is a great and terrible heresy; which it is to be feared is operating, in this connection, to deceive and destroy a vast multitude of souls.

The proper fruits of Pelagianism, follow the system invariably, in proportion exactly to the extent, in which it may be suffered in any case to prevail. A most ample field for instruction with regard to this point, for all who care to receive instruction, is presented in the history of the great religious movement, over which Mr. Finney presided some years ago, in certain parts of this country. Years of faithful pastoral service, on the part of a different order of ministers, working in a wholly different style, have hardly yet sufficed, in the Northern section of the State of New York, to restore to something like spiritual fruitfulness and beauty, the field, over which this system then passed, as a wasting fire, in the fulness of its strength. The perfectionism of Oberlin, with its low conceptions of the law of God, is but a natural development of the false life, with which it is animated. The wide West abounds, in every direction, with illustrations of its mischievous action, under all imaginable forms. In many places, a morbid thirst for excitement, may be said to exhaust the whole interest, that is felt in religion. The worst errors stand in close juxta-position, with the most bold pretensions to the highest order of christian experience. All might seem to begin in the Spirit, and yet all is perpetually ending in the flesh. It were an easy thing too, to gather exemplifications, supporting the same lesson, from the past history of the Church. For the system, properly speaking, is not new. The same theory of religion has led, in all ages, to substantially the same style of action, and this has been followed by substantially the same bad fruits.

The question of "New Measures" then, as it claims at this time particularly the attention of the German Churches, is one of much greater importance than some might be disposed to imagine. The truth is, this system, as we have said, has a life and spirit of its own. It may be associated to some extent, in certain hands, with the power of a more vigorous life derived from a different quarter, so as to seem comparatively sound and safe. But it ought not to be thought, on this account, that it may be incorporated practically with one order of thinking on the subject of religion, as easily as with another. It is not by accident only, that it is found connecting itself with the faults and defects that have now been mentioned. A false theory of religion is involved in it, which cannot fail to work itself out and make itself felt, in many hurtful results, wherever it gains footing in the Church. No religious

community can grow and prosper, in a solid way, where it is
allowed to have any considerable authority; because it will
always stand in the way of those deeper and more silent
forms of action, by which alone it is possible for this end to
be accomplished. It is a different system altogether that is
required, to build up the interests of Christianity in a firm
and sure way. A ministry apt to teach; sermons full of unction
and light; faithful, systematic instruction; zeal for the interests
of holiness; pastoral visitation; catechetical training; due attention to order and discipline; patient perseverance in the
details of the ministerial work; these are the agencies, by
which alone the kingdom of God may be expected to go
steadily forward, among any people. Where these are fully
employed, there will be revivals; but they will be only as it
were the natural fruit of the general culture going before,
without that spasmodic, meteoric character, which too often
distinguishes excitements under this name; while the life of
religion will show itself abidingly at work, in the reigning
temper of the Church, at all other times. Happy the congregation, that may be placed under such spiritual auspices!
Happy for our German Zion, if such might be the system
that should prevail, to the exclusion of every other, within
her borders! We may style it, for distinction sake, the system
of the *Catechism*.[1] It is another system wholly from that

[1] In the final chapter of *The Anxious Bench* John Nevin described in more detail the "system of the Catechism."

The theory of religion in which the system of the Catechism
stands, is vastly more deep and comprehensive, and of course
vastly more earnest also, than that which lies at the foundation
of the other system. This last we have seen to be characteristically
pelagian, with narrow views of the nature of sin, and confused ap-
prehensions of the difference between flesh and spirit; involving
in the end the gross and radical error, that conversion is to be
considered, in one shape or another, the product of the sinner's
own will, and not truly and strictly a new creation in Christ Jesus
by the power of God. . . . In opposition to this, the true theory
of religion carries us continually beyond the individual, to the
view of a far deeper and more general form of existence in which
his particular life is represented to stand. Thus sin is not simply
the offspring of a particular will, putting itself forth in the form

which we have been contemplating in this tract. We find the attempt made in some cases, it is true, to incorporate the power of the Catechism with the use of new measures. But the union is unnatural, and can never be inward and com-

---

of actual transgressions, but a wrong habit of humanity itself, a general and universal force, which includes and rules the entire existence of the individual man, from the very start. The disease is organic, rooted in the race, and not to be overcome in any case by a force less deep and general than itself. As well might we look for the acorn to forsake in growing the type of its proper species, and put forth the form of a mountain ash or stately elm. "That which is born of the flesh is flesh." So deep and broad is the ruin, from which man is to be delivered by the gospel. And here again, the same depth and breadth are presented to us also in the Christian salvation itself. Man is the subject of it, but not the author of it, in any sense. His nature is restorable, but it can never restore itself. The restoration to be real, must begin *beyond* the individual. In this case as in the other, the general must go before the particular, and support it as its proper ground. Thus humanity, fallen in Adam, is made to undergo a resurrection in Christ, and so restored, flows over organically, as in the other case, to all in whom its life appears. The sinner is saved then by an inward living union with Christ, as real as the bond by which he has been joined in the first instance to Adam. This union is reached and maintained, through the medium of the Church, by the power of the Holy Ghost. It constitutes a new life, the ground of which is not in the particular subject of it at all, but in Christ, the organic root of the Church. The particular subject lives, not properly speaking in the acts of his own will separately considered, but in the power of a vast generic life, that lies wholly beyond his will, and has now begun to manifest itself through him, as the law and type of his will itself, as well as of his whole being. As born of the Spirit, in contradistinction from the flesh, he is himself spiritual, and capable of true righteousness. Thus his salvation begins, and thus it is carried forward, till it becomes complete in the resurrection of the great day. From first to last, it is a power which he does not so much apprehend, as he is apprehended by it, and comprehended in it, and carried along with it, as something infinitely more deep and vast than himself. . . .

From first to last, the action now mentioned will go forward, under a due practical recognition of the truth, that both the ruin plete. The two systems involve at the bottom, two different theories of religion. The spirit of the Anxious Bench is at war with the spirit of the Catechism. Where it comes decidedly to prevail, catechetical instruction, and the religious training

---

of man and his recovery rest in a ground, which is beyond himself as an individual. If saved at all, he is to be saved by the force of a spiritual constitution, established by God for the purpose, the provisions of which go far beyond the resources of his own will, and are expected to reach him, not so much through the measure of his own particular life, as by the medium of a more general life, with which he is to be filled and animated from without. This spiritual constitution is brought to bear upon him in the Church, by means of institutions and agencies which God has appointed, and clothed with power, expressly for this end. Hence where the system of the Catechism prevails, great account is made of the Church, and all reliance placed upon the means of grace comprehended in its constitution, as all sufficient under God for the accomplishment of its own purposes. The means are felt to be something more than mere devices of human ingenuity, and are honoured and diligently used accordingly as the "wisdom of God and the power of God" unto salvation. Due regard is had to the idea of the Church as something more than a bare abstraction, the conception of an aggregate of parts mechanically brought together. It is apprehended rather as an organic life, springing perpetually from the same ground, and identical with itself at every point. In this view, the Church is truly the *mother* of all her children. They do not impart life to her, but she imparts life to them. Here again the general is felt to go before the particular, and to condition all its manifestations. The Church is in no sense the product of individual christianity, as though a number of persons should first receive the heavenly fire in separate streams, and then come into such a spiritual connection comprising the whole; but individual christianity is the product, always and entirely, of the Church, as existing previously, and only revealing its life in this way. Christ lives in the Church, and *through* the Church in its particular members; just as Adam lives in the human race generically considered, and through the race in every individual man. This view of the relation of the Church to the salvation of the individual, exerts an important influence, in the case before us, on the whole system of action, by which it is sought to reach this object. (pp. 123–126; 128–130.)

of the young generally, are not likely to be maintained with much effect; and it will not be strange, if they should be openly slighted even, and thrust out of the way as an incumbrance to the Gospel, rather than a help. What is wrought in the way of the Catechism is considered to be of man, what is wrought by the Bench is taken readily for the work of God. And the reason of this is near at hand. The Catechism is indeed weak in the hands of those who have this judgment. They have no inward power to make themselves felt, in this way. But they *seem* to have power in the use of the Bench; and it is no wonder they should magnify it accordingly. The systems are antagonistic. Particular men, standing under one standard, may be to some extent entangled in views and practices properly belonging to the other, but so far they must be inconsistent with themselves. Each system, as such, has its own life and soul, in virtue of which it cannot truly coalesce with the other. They cannot flourish and be in vigorous force together. The Bench is against the Catechism, and the Catechism against the Bench. I mean of course not the Catechism as a mere dead form, in the way in which the original order of the Church, has been too often abused; and it is silly, if not something worse, to insist upon *this* view of it, when the two systems are drawn into contrast, as though there could be no other alternative to the Bench than the Catechism without life. It is the living Catechism, the Catechism awakened and active, that is intended in this opposition. As such, it stands the representative and symbol of a system, embracing its own theory of religion, and including a wide circle of agencies, peculiar to itself, for carrying this theory into effect. These agencies, in the pulpit and out of it, will be understood, and honored, and actively applied, in proportion to the Christianity of the Church may be expected to show itself large, deep, full, vigorous and free. Between such a Christianity and that which is the product of the Bench, there can be no comparison; and it must be counted an immense misfortune, in the case of any religious denomination, when the views, feelings, and forms of action, that are represented by this, through the force of a perverse judgment, gain such ground, as to push the other system aside. It must be ever a wretched choice, when the *Bench* is preferred to the *Catechism*.

BIBLIOGRAPHICAL NOTE

There are several studies of nineteenth century revivalism. The most generally useful is William McLoughlin, *Modern Revivalism: Charles Grandison Finney to Billy Graham* (New York, 1959); a substantial part of his book deals with late nineteenth and twentieth century figures. McLoughlin's introduction to Charles Finney, *Lectures on Revivals of Religion* (Cambridge, 1960) is also instructive. In addition see: Whitney R. Cross, *The Burned Over District: The Social and Intellectual History of Enthusiastic Religion in Western New York, 1800–1850* (Ithaca, 1950; New York, 1965); Bernard A. Weisberger, *They Gathered at the River: The Story of the Great Revivalists and their Impact upon Religion in America* (Boston, 1958); and Charles A. Johnson, *The Frontier Camp Meeting* (Dallas, 1955). The source materials of four denominations compiled by William Warren Sweet, are unusually enlightening: *Religion on the American Frontier: The Baptists* (New York, 1931); *The Presbyterians* (New York, 1936); *The Congregationalists* (Chicago, 1939); and *The Methodists* (Chicago, 1946). A study of the entire period is Richard C. Wolf, "The Middle Period, 1800–1870: The Matrix of Modern Christianity," *Religion in Life*, xxii, Winter, 1952–1953, pp. 72–84.

For discussion of Nevin and the Mercersburg theology see James H. Nichols, *Romanticism in American Theology: Nevin and Schaff at Mercersburg* (Chicago, 1961) and George H. Richards, "The Mercersburg Theology: Its Purposes and Principles," *Church History*, xx, 1951, No. 3, pp. 42–55.

A suggestive article indicating some lasting effects of this period is William McLoughlin, "Pietism and the American Character," *American Quarterly*, xvii, Summer, 1965, pp. 163–186.

VII. SLAVERY

The conflict over slavery caused division in several Protestant churches near the middle of the nineteenth century. The selections included below are illustrations of southern views chosen from the Presbyterian and Baptist denominations.

In the South, especially the border states, anti-slavery groups were organized in the second and third decades of the nineteenth century. These societies declined in number and effectiveness as the work of the northern abolitionists became more polemical. The "Address" against Negro servitude by the Presbyterian Synod of Kentucky (1835) was one of the last strong statements by a southern denomination.

Southerners then turned their attention to a justification of slavery on Biblical grounds. One of the most vehement southern clerical defenders of the institution was James Henley Thornwell (1812–1862). A professor at the Presbyterian South Carolina College and later its president, Thornwell became Professor of Theology at the Presbyterian Theological Seminary at Columbia, South Carolina (1855–1862). He was instrumental in the formation of a policy statement by the Synod of South Carolina to endorse political secession at the Assembly of 1861 and became a leader in the organization of the Presbyterian Church in the Confederate States of America. The task of the southern apologists for slavery was to convince their opponents that if they argued that slavery was contrary to biblical teaching they could properly be classed as "infidels." A "biblical" defense of slavery was the key to much of their argument. The attempt was not, of course, successful in the minds of the northern abolitionists. Thornwell's "The Rights and Duties of Masters," was a defense of slavery on the ground that it was a fulfillment of God's providential plan.

"It [slavery] is not repugnant to the spirit of the Gospel, in its present relations to our race. It is one of the conditions in which God is conducting the moral probation of man—a condition not incompatible with the highest moral freedom, the true glory of the race, and, therefore, not unfit for the moral and spiritual discipline which Christianity has instituted. It is one of the schools in which immortal spirits are trained for their final destiny.[1]

We can note the change in perspective which occurred in the southern and border states by comparing the statement of the Presbyterian Synod of Kentucky (1835) with that of Thornwell (1850).

[17]
Synod of Kentucky
An Address Against Slavery*

We have exhibited fairly, but briefly, the nature and effects of slavery. For the truth of our facts, we refer to your own observations; for the correctness of our reasoning, we appeal to your judgments and consciences. What, then, must we conclude? Is slavery a system which Christians should sanction or even tolerate, if their efforts can avail to abolish it? The reply is often made, *'God's word sanctions slavery, it cannot therefore be sinful. It cannot be our duty to relinquish our power over our slaves, or the Bible would have enjoined it upon us to do so.'* We will not attempt to elaborate argument

[1] James Henley Thornwell, *The Rights and Duties of Masters, A Sermon Preached at the Dedication of A Church, erected in Charleston, S.C. for the Benefit and Instruction of the Coloured Population.* (Charleston, S.C., 1850), pp. 43-44.

* Quoted in Theodore D. Weld, *The Bible Against Slavery* (Pittsburgh, 1864). Appendix, pp. 149-154. The address is from the records of the Presbyterian Synod of Kentucky (1835).

against this plea for slavery—it needs no such answer. A few observations will suffice to show its utter fallacy.

We are told that the apostles gave to Christian masters and Christian servants directions for the regulation of their mutual conduct. True; and these directions will be valuable while the world lasts—for so long, we doubt not, will *the relation of master and servant exist*. But how do such directions license holding of *slaves? The terms which the apostles use in giving these precepts, are the same terms which they would have used had there been no slaves upon the earth.* Many of the masters of that day were indeed slaveholders, and many of the servants were slaves—but should that circumstance have prevented the inspired ambassadors from teaching the duties which devolved upon masters and servants, in every age, and under every form of service? If so, then the fact that rulers at that time were generally tyrants, and the people vassals, should have prevented them from laying down the duties of rulers and people. In the precepts of holy writ, neither *political tyranny* nor *domestic slavery* is countenanced. Nay, if masters complied with the apostolic injunction to them, and gave their servants, as they were directed to do, 'that which is just and equal,' there would be at once an end of all that is properly called slavery.

The divine right of kings to tyrannize over their subjects, and the unlawfulness of resistance to their authority on the part of the people, were formerly maintained by the very same kind of scriptural arguments which are now advanced in support of slavery. The arguments drawn from the Bible in favor of despotism, are, indeed, much more plausible than those in favor of slavery. We despised the former—how then should we regard the latter?

It has sometimes been said, that the 'New Testament does not condemn slaveholding in express terms.' And the practice has been advocated, because it has not been denounced. If this assertion were true, and if the Bible only *virtually* denounced it, it would be a sin. No man can righteously continue a practice which God disapproves of, no matter in what form the disapproval is expressed. But the assertion is not true. THE NEW TESTAMENT DOES CONDEMN

SLAVEHOLDING, AS PRACTISED AMONG US, IN THE
MOST EXPLICIT TERMS FURNISHED BY THE LAN-
GUAGE IN WHICH THE INSPIRED PEN MEN WROTE.
If a physician, after a minute examination, should tell a patient that his every limb and organ was diseased—if he should
enumerate the various parts of his bodily system, the arms,
the legs, the head, the stomach, the bowels, &c., and
should say of each one of these parts distinctly that it was
unsound; could the man depart and say, 'After all, I am not
diseased, for the physician has not said, in *express terms*,
that my *body* is unsound?' Has he not received a more clear
and express declaration of his entirely diseased condition,
than if he had been told, in merely general terms, that his
body was unsound? Thus has God condemned slavery. He
has specified the parts which compose it, and denounced
them, one by one, in the most ample and unequivocal form.
In the English language we have the term *servant*, which we
apply indiscriminately both to those held in voluntary subjection to another, and to those whose subjection is involuntary. We have also the term *slave*, which is applicable
exclusively to those held in involuntary subjection. The Greek
language had a word corresponding exactly in signification
with our word servant; but it had none that answered precisely to our term slave.[1] How then was an apostle, writing
in Greek, to condemn *our slavery*? Could it be done in the
way in which some seem to think it must be done, before they
will be convinced of its sinfulness? How can we expect to find
in Scripture the words 'slavery is sinful?' when the language
in which it is written contained no term which expressed the
meaning of our word slavery? Would the advocates of slavery

[1] The words *oiketos, andrapodon,* are those which most nearly
correspond, in the idea which they present, with our word slave.
But oiketos properly signifies a *domestic;* and andrapodon, *one
taken and enslaved in war.* The inspired writers could not have
denounced *our sort of slavery* by using either of these words. If
they had forbidden us to hold oiketai, they would have forbidden
us the use of all domestics—if they had forbidden us to hold
andrapoda, they might have been interpreted as forbidding our
use only of *such slaves as have been taken and enslaved in war.*

wish us to show that the apostles declare it to be unchristian to hold servants (douloi)? This would have been denouncing, as criminal, practices far different from slaveholding. But inspiration taught the holy pen men the only correct and efficacious method of conveying their condemnation of this unchristian system. They pronounce of each one of those several things which constitute slavery, that it is sinful—thus clearly and forever denouncing the system, wherever it might appear, and whatever name it might assume. If a writer should take up each part of our federal constitution separately and condemn it article by article, who would have the folly to assert that, after all, he had not expressly condemned the constitution? Who would say that this thorough and entire disapproval of every part of the instrument of confederation must pass for nothing, and is no proof of the writer's hostility to it, because he has never said exactly in so many words, 'I disapprove of the Constitution of the United States?' We see that he could condemn it most explicitly and thoroughly without even mentioning it by name.

Further, human language is so fluctuating that words often, in the lapse of time, change their meaning. The word tyrant expresses now a very different idea from that which it once conveyed. So the term Constitution of the United States, at some future period, from the alterations introduced into our government, may indicate something far different from that which it now indicates. It is true wisdom, then, when we wish to perpetuate our condemnation of a system or institution, to express our sentiments of the various *things* that constitute the system or institution, and not of the *mere name* by which it is now known. Thus our sentiments will be guarded from the misconceptions that may arise in the fluctuation of language. So that even if there were words in Greek, specifically set apart to designate the idea of slavery, inspiration would probably still have guided the apostles to their present form of expression in its condemnation. Had they used such language as this, 'slavery is sinful,' some modern apologists for the system might have alleged that our slavery was not such as existed among the Greeks—that slavery here was a different thing from that which the apostles denounced. But the course they pursued leaves no room for such a subterfuge. We have received the command, 'Love thy neighbor as thyself,' and we are conscious that we are violating the whole spirit as well as letter of this precept, when, for our own trifling pecuniary gain, we keep a whole race sunk in ignorance and pain. We are commanded to give our servants 'that which is just and equal,' and no sophistry can persuade us that we fulfil this towards those whom we deprive of the reward of their labor. We know that the idea of a bondman receiving a just and equal remuneration for his labor, never enters the minds of slaveholders. The precepts against fraud, oppression, pride, and cruelty, all cut directly through the heart of the slave system. Look back at the *constituents* and *the effects* of slavery, and ask yourself, 'Is not every one of these things directly at variance with the plainest commands of the gospel?' The maintenance of this system breaks not one law of the Lord, or two laws—it violates the whole code—it leaves scarcely one precept unbroken. And will any one, then, contend that slavery is not reprobated by God, and that he may participate in the system, and assist in its perpetuation, without deep criminality? Forbid it, conscience—forbid it, common sense! Gaming, horse-racing, gladiatorial shows in which men were hired to butcher each other, the selling of children by their parents, which was often practised in ancient days—all these things are condemned by the Scriptures, not by name, but (as slavery is condemned) by denouncing those crimes of which these acts are modifications and illustrations.

These views of the sinfulness of slavery place it beyond all doubt that it is the duty of every individual connected with the system to aid, vigorously and efficiently, in its abolition, and thus free himself from all participation in its criminality. How is this to be done? Certainly not by merely treating our slaves kindly, and thus mitigating the evils of their condition. You may say you have already, in the case of your own slaves, abolished the worst evils of the system, and that in every way you promote their comfort and welfare. Still duty absolutely requires at least one more step—a guarantee that their future happiness, and that of their children, shall not be at the mercy of another's caprice. And this can be effected only by a legal provision for their release from bondage. It is probable that the Romans were in a better condition under Titus than they would have been had they governed themselves. But the gentleness of his sway only aggravated the horrors of their situation, under his dark and bloody successors. Granting all that any man may urge in favor of his own kindness to his dependents, still he is, contrary to the laws of nature and of God, retaining them in a condition which is tolerable only under the most rare and favorable circumstances—which inevitably works woe and ruin, unless prevented by the singular virtue and generosity of an extraordinary master. Would we be willing that we and our children should be thus held? And remember that the fundamental principle of Christian morality is, that 'what things soever ye would that others should do unto you, do ye even so to them.' Are we complying with our Saviour's injunction, when we thus leave our fellow beings exposed to all the future miseries, which avarice, caprice, and cruelty may inflict? Yet we profess subjection to Christ's laws—'He that knoweth my will and *doeth* it,' says the divine Redeemer, 'he it is that loveth me.' The very best condition of a slave for life is like the condition of those unfortunate men that we sometimes read of, who have been unjustly condemned to die—but mercy or policy arresting the execution of the sentence, they have, for a time, been permitted to go at large, yet liable every moment to be remanded to prison and to death. This is the situation of a slave, at his best estate—and who will say that either mercy or justice permits us to retain him in such a situation?

It is often urged that our slaves are better off than our free negroes. If mankind had considered this plea for continuing to hold slaves a valid one, the whole world would have been still in slavery—for all nations have been at one time or other in some kind of slavery—and all despots urged this plea against their emancipation. Besides, no man ought to urge this as his reason for retaining his bondmen, unless he feels conscious that it is his real motive. And we willingly appeal to every man's conscience to say whether his own imagined interest is not his real motive for refusing to adopt any efficient measures for changing the condition of his servants. That our negroes, if emancipated, will be worse off, is, we feel, but the specious pretext for lulling our own pangs of conscience, and answering the argument of the philanthropist. None of us believe that God has so created a whole race, that it is better for them to remain in perpetual bondage. One mode of emancipation may be preferable to another—but any mode is preferable to the perpetuation, through generations to come, of a degrading bondage. History, with a hundred tongues, testifies that, as a general rule, to emancipate is to elevate. And it is vain for any man to argue against such a general law of nature by adducing the occasional departures, which have fallen under his own personal observation. We plant ourselves down on the broad and acknowledged principle, that God created all men capable of freedom—if, then, they have become unfit for this condition, it is by our fault they have become so; and our exertions, if we are willing to do our duty, can easily restore to them that fitness of which we have deprived them.

As the conclusion of all that has been advanced, we assert it to be the unquestionable duty of every Christian, to use vigorous and immediate measures for the destruction of the whole system, and for the removal of all its unhappy effects. Both these objects should be contemplated in his efforts.

[18]
James Henley Thornwell
The Rights and Duties of Masters*

The fundamental mistake of those who affirm slavery to be essentially sinful, is that the duties of all men are specifically the same. Though they do not state the proposition in so many words, and in its naked form would probably dissent from it, yet a little attention to their reasoning puts it beyond doubt, that this is the radical assumption upon which they proceed—all men are bound to do specifically the same things. As there are obviously duties of some men, in some relations, which cannot be practiced by a slave, they infer that the institution strips him of his rights, and curtails the fair proportions of his humanity. The argument, fully and legitimately carried out, would condemn every arrangement of society, which did not secure to all its members an absolute equality of position; it is the very spirit of socialism and communism.

The doctrine of the Bible, on the other hand, is that the specifick duties—the things actually required to be done, are as various as the circumstances in which men are placed. Moral perfection does not depend upon the number or variety of single acts, but upon the general habitudes of the soul. He is upright whose temper of mind is in conformity with the law, and whose prevailing disposition would always prompt him, in all the relations of life, to do what is right. There may be many right things which he may never be required to perform—but he is entitled to the praise of excellence if he cultivates a spirit which would lead him to perform them, if

* James Henley Thornwell, *The Rights and the Duties of Masters, A Sermon Preached at the Dedication of A Church, erected in Charleston, S.C. for the Benefit and Instruction of the Coloured Population.* (Charleston, S.C., 1850), pp. 35–37; 39–51.

circumstances should ever make them his duty. The heart
may be in full and perfect sympathy with the whole spirit of
the law, where the moral training has been confined to comparatively a narrow circle of actual duties. He may be full
of benevolence who has never had the means or opportunity
of costly alms to the poor—he may cherish the gentleness of
a lamb who has received no injuries to be forgiven—no
wrongs to be forgotten—and he may possess the patience of
a martyr, or the fortitude of a hero, whose virtue has never
been tried by severe suffering or danger. The circumstances
in which men are placed in this sublunary state are exceedingly diversified, but there is probably no external condition in which the actual discipline to which men are subjected may not terminate in the temper of universal holiness.
Some are tried in one way, some in another—some are
required to do one set of things, some another—but the spirit
of true obedience is universally the same—and the result of
an effectual probation is, in every case, a moral sympathy
with the moral perfections of God. The lesson is the same,
however different the text-books from which it has been
taught.

Now, unless slavery is incompatible with the habitudes of
holiness—unless it is inconsistent with the spirit of philanthropy
or the spirit of piety—unless it furnishes no opportunities for
obedience to the law, it is not inconsistent with the pursuit
or attainment of the highest excellence. It is no abridgement
of moral freedom; the slave may come from the probation
of *his* circumstances as fully stamped with the image of God,
as those who have enjoyed an easier lot—he may be as completely in unison with the spirit of universal rectitude, as if
he had been trained on flowery beds of ease. Let him discharge his *whole* duty in the actual circumstances of his
case, and he is entitled to the praise of a perfect and an
upright man. The question with God is—not *what* he has
done—but *how;*—man looketh at the outward circumstances,
but God looketh at the heart.

Hence those moralists are grievously in error, who have
represented slavery as inconsistent with the full complement
of human duty and as a consequent limitation upon the

spiritual freedom of man, because there are duties which God has not connected with this condition of society. To maintain that the same things are universally obligatory, without regard to circumstances or relations, that what is exacted of one must necessarily be exacted from another, however different or even incongruous their outward states, is to confound the obligations of rulers and subjects, of parents and children, of guardians and wards, and to plunge the community into irretrievable confusion. All that can be affirmed is, that the same temper of universal rectitude is equally incumbent upon all, while it must be admitted that the outward forms of its manifestations and expression must be determined by the relations which Providence has actually assigned to our state. The slave is to show his reverence for God—the freedom of his inward man—by a cheerful obedience to the lawful commands of his master;—the master, his regard for one who is his master in heaven, by rendering to the slave that which is just and equal. The character of both is determined, in the sight of God, by the spirit which pervades their single acts, however the acts may differ in themselves. . . .

All this the grace of God, through the instrumentality of the gospel, may accomplish in the person of one who is bound to labor under the direction and authority of another. The servant of men may be the freeman of the Lord. If his situation is compatible, as it confessedly is, with the achievement of the great end of his existence—if in the school of bondage he may be trained for the glorification and enjoyment of God, he is not divested of any of the rights which belong to him essentially *as man*. He may develope his moral and religious nature—the source and measure of all his rights—and must, consequently, retain every characteristick of essential humanity.

No proposition can be clearer than that the rights of man must be ultimately traced to his duties, and are nothing more than the obligations of his fellows to let him alone in the discharge of all the functions, and the enjoyment of all the blessings of his lot. Whatever puts an obstruction or hinderance to the complement of his duties, is an encroachment upon the complement of his rights as a *man*. Whatever is incompatible with the exercise of his moral nature is destructive of the fundamental law of his being. But as the moral discipline of man is consistent with the greatest variety of external condition, it is consistent with the greatest variety of contingent rights—of rights which spring from peculiar circumstances and peculiar relations—and in the absence of which a man may still be a man. These cannot be treated as a fixed and invariable quantity. Dependent as they are upon our duties—which, in turn, are dependent upon our circumstances, they fluctuate with the gradations and progress of society—being wider or narrower according to the spheres in which we move. It is only by postulating duties for the slave which God has not enjoined on him—that any show of decency can be given to the declamations against the robbery and fraud which have incapacitated him to perform them. The slave has rights—all the rights which belong essentially to humanity, and without which his nature could not be human, nor his conduct susceptible of praise or blame. In the enjoyment of these rights religion demands that he should be protected.

But then there are rights which belong to men in other situations, to which he is by no means entitled; the rights of the citizen, for example, and the free member of the commonwealth. They are not his, for the simple reason that they are not essential, but contingent; they do not spring from humanity simply considered, for then they would belong to women and children—but from humanity in such and such relations.

As to the influence of slavery upon the advancement of society, there can be no doubt, if the government of God be moral, that the true progress of communities and States, as well as the highest interests of individuals, depend upon the fidelity with which the duties are discharged, in every condition of life. It is the great law of providential education, that to every one that hath shall be given and he shall have abundance; but from him that hath not shall be taken away even that which he hath. In this way the reign of universal justice is promoted, and wherever that obtains, the developement of the individual, which is the great end of all social and political institutions, must infallibly take place. The prosperity of the State at the same time is secured, and secured, too, without the necessity of sudden changes or violent revolutions. It will be like the vigor of a healthful body, in which all the limbs and organs perform their appropriate functions, without collision or tumult, and its ascension to a high degree of moral elevation will be like the growth of such a body, silent and imperceptible, the natural result of the blessing of God upon the means He has appointed. Let masters and servants, each in their respective spheres, be impregnated with the principle of duty—let masters resolve to render unto their servants that which is just and equal, never transcending the legitimate bounds of their authority —and servants resolve to cherish sentiments of reverence for their masters according to the flesh—never falling short of the legitimate claims on their obedience, and the chief good of each, as individuals and as men, will be most surely promoted, while each will contribute an important share to the strength and stability of the commonwealth. The feet are as indispensable to the head as the head to the feet. The social fabrick is made up of divers ingredients, and the cement which binds them together in durability and unity is the cement of justice.

Beside the arguments drawn from considerations of justice and the essential rights of humanity, the incompatibility of slavery with the spirit and temper of the Gospel, is not unfrequently attempted to be made out, from the injuction of the Saviour to love our neighbor as ourselves, and to do unto others as we would have them to do unto us. The principle, however, upon which the precept of universal benevolence is interpreted in this case, makes it the sanction of the grossest wickedness. If we are to regulate our conduct to others by the arbitrary expectations which, in their circumstances, our passions and selfishness might prompt us to indulge, there ceases to be any other standard of morality than caprice. The humour of every man becomes law. The judge could not condemn the criminal, nor the executioner behead him—the rich man could not claim his possessions nor the poor learn patience from their sufferings. If I am bound to emancipate my slave because if the tables were turned and our situations reversed, I should covet this boon from him, I should be bound, upon the same principle, to promote my indigent neighbors around me, to an absolute equality with myself. That neither the Jews, in whose law the precept was first formally announced, nor the Apostles, to whom it was more fully expounded by the Saviour, ever applied it in the sense of the Abolitionists, is a strong presumption against their mode of interpretation. The truth is, it is nothing but the inculcation of *justice* from motives of love. Our Saviour directs us to do unto others what, in their situations, it would be right and reasonable in us to expect from them. We are to put ourselves in their situations, that we may duly weigh the circumstances of their case, and so be prepared to apply to it the principles of universal justice. We are to let no motives of indolence, ease or apathy prevent us from considering their condition. We are to take the same interest in them that we would take in ourselves—and are to extend to them the same protection of the Divine law which we would insist upon for ourselves. The rule then simply requires, in the case of slavery, that we should treat our slaves as we should feel that we had a right to be treated if we were slaves ourselves—it is only enforcing by benevolence the apostolick injunction—Masters give unto your servants, that which is just and equal. Do right, in other words, as you would claim right.

The instances which are usually urged to prove that slavery is inconsistent with the rights of man, unfortunately for the argument, are not peculiar to slavery. They are incidents to poverty, wherever it prevails in a distressing form; and a wise system of legislation could much more easily detach them from the system of slavery than from the deep indigence which is sure to crush the laborer where a crowded population obtains. They are, at best, only abuses in the one case which might be corrected, while in the other, they seem to be inseparable elements.

Enough has been said to show that slavery is not repugnant to the spirit of the Gospel, in its present relations to our race. It is one of the conditions in which God is conducting the moral probation of man—a condition not incompatible with the highest moral freedom, the true glory of the race, and, therefore, not unfit for the moral and spiritual discipline which Christianity has instituted. It is one of the schools in which immortal spirits are trained for their final destiny. If it is attended with severer hardships, these hardships are compensated by fewer duties, and the very violence of its temptations gives dignity and lustre to its virtues. The slave may be fitted, in his humble, and if you please, degraded lot, for shining as a star in the firmament of heaven. In his narrow sphere, he may be cherishing and cultivating a spirit which shall render him meet for the society of angels and the everlasting enjoyment of God. The Christian beholds in him, not a tool, not a chattel, not a brute or thing—but an immortal spirit, assigned to a particular position in this world of wretchedness and sin, in which he is required to work out the destiny which attaches to him, in common with his fellows, as a man. He is an actor on the broad theatre of life —and as true merit depends not so much upon the part which is assigned, as upon the propriety and dignity with which it is sustained—so fidelity in this relation, may hereafter be as conspicuously rewarded, as fidelity in more exalted stations. Angels and God look not upon the outward state of man; —the poverty, rags, and wretchedness of one—the robes, diadems and crowns of another, are nothing. True worth is the moral vesture of the soul. The spirit of obedience, the love of holiness, sympathy with God, these are the things which make men beautiful and glorious. This is true freedom—these are the things which shall endure and flourish with increasing lustre, when Thrones have crumbled in the dust and Republicks mouldered among the ruins of the past.

The important question among us is, that which relates to the discharge of our own duties as masters—what are the things which are just and equal that we are required to render to our slaves.

But before attending to this inquiry, it may be well to notice the popular argument against slavery, drawn from the fact, that as it must have begun in the perpetration of grievous wrong, no lapse of time can make it subsequently right. Prescription can never sanctify injustice. The answer turns upon the distinction between the wrong itself and the effects of the wrong. The criminal act, whatever it may have been, by which a man was reduced to the condition of bondage, can never cease to be otherwise than criminal, but the relations to which that act gave rise, may, themselves, be consistent with the will of God and the foundation of new and important duties. The relations of a man to his natural offspring, though wickedly formed, give rise to duties which would be ill-discharged by the destruction of the child. No doubt the principle upon which slavery has been most largely engrafted into society as an integral element of its complex constitution—the principle, that captivity in war gives a right to the life of a prisoner, for which his bondage is accepted in exchange, is not consistent with the truth of the case. But it was recognized as true for ages and generations—it was a step in the moral developement of nations, and has laid the foundation of institutions and usages, which cannot now be disturbed with impunity, and in regard to which, our conduct must be regulated by the fact of their existence, and not by speculation upon the morality of their origin. Our world exhibits, every where, the traces of sin —and if we tolerate nothing but what we may expect to find in a state of perfection and holiness, we must leave this scene of sublunary distraction. The education of States is a slow process. Their standards of rectitude slowly approximate the standard of God, and in their ages of infancy, ignorance and blindness, they establish many institutions upon false maxims, which cannot subsequently be extirpated without abandoning the whole of the real progress they have made, and reconstituting society afresh. These things, moreover, take place under the sleepless Providence of God, who is surely accomplishing His own great purposes, and who makes the wrath of man to praise Him, and restrains, at pleasure, the remainder of wrath.

In treating slavery as an existing institution, a fact involving most important moral relations, one of the prime duties of the State is to protect, by temporal legislation, the real rights of the slave. The moral sense of the country acknowledges them—the religion of the country to a large extent, ensures their observance, but until they are defined by law and enforced by penalties there is no adequate protection of them. They are in the category of imperfect and not of perfect rights. The effect of legal protection would be to counteract whatever tendencies slavery may be supposed to possess to produce servility and abjectness of mind. It would inspire a sense of personal responsibility—a certain degree of manliness and dignity of character, which would be, at once, a security to the master and an immense blessing to the slave. . . .

Our design in giving them the Gospel, is not to civilize them—not to change their social condition—not to exalt them into citizens or freemen—it is to save them. The Church contemplates them only as sinners, and she is straitened to declare unto them the unsearchable riches of Christ. She sees them as the poor of the land, under the lawful dominion of their masters; and she says to these masters, in the name and by the authority of God, give them what justice, benevolence, humanity would demand even for a stranger, an enemy, a persecutor—give them the Gospel, without which life will be a curse. Sweeten their toil—sanctify their lives—hallow their deaths. The solemnities of this night are a proof that the call has not been wholly disregarded among us. We have begun a good work, and God grant that it may never cease until every slave in the land is brought under the tuition of Jesus of Nazareth. None need be afraid of His lessons. It was said of Him on earth, that He should not cry, nor lift up, nor cause His voice to be heard in the streets. He was no stirrer up of strife, nor mover of sedition. His "religion on the other hand, is the pillar of society, the safeguard of nations, the parent of social order, which alone has power to curb the fury of the passions, and secure to every one his rights; to the laborious, the reward of their industry; to the rich, the enjoyment of their wealth; to nobles, the preservation of their honors; and to princes, the stability of their thrones." Insurrection, anarchy and bloodshed—revolt against masters, or treason against States, were never learned in the school of Him, whose

Apostles enjoined subjection to the magistrate, and obedience to all lawful authority, as characteristic duties of the faithful. Is any thing to be apprehended from the instructions of Him in whose text-book it is recorded: "let as many servants as are under the yoke, count their masters worthy of all honour?" Christian knowledge inculcates contentment with our lot; and in bringing before us the tremendous realities of eternity, renders us comparatively indifferent to the inconveniences and hardships of time. It subdues those passions and prejudices, from which all real danger to the social economy springs. "Some have objected," says a splendid writer,[1] "to the instruction of the lower classes, from an apprehension that it would lift them above their sphere, make them dissatisfied with their station in life, and by impairing the habits of subordination, endanger the tranquillity of the State; an objection devoid surely of all force and validity. It is not easy to conceive in what manner instructing men in their duties can prompt them to neglect those duties, or how that enlargement of reason which enables them to comprehend the true grounds of authority, and the obligation to obedience, should indispose them to obey. The admirable mechanism of society, together with that subordination of ranks which is essential to its subsistence, is surely not an elaborate imposture, which the exercise of reason will direct and expose. The objection we have stated, implies a reflection on the social order, equally impolitick, invidious and unjust. Nothing in reality renders legitimate governments so insecure as extreme ignorance in the people. It is this which yields them an easy prey to seduction—makes them the victims of prejudice and false alarms, and so ferocious withal, that their interference in a time of publick commotion is more to be dreaded than the eruption of a volcano."

Our highest security in these States, lies in the confidence and affection of our servants, and nothing will more effectually propitiate their regards than consistent efforts, upon our part, to promote their everlasting good. They will feel

[1] Robert Hall, "Advantages of Knowledge to the Lower Classes," *Works*, Vol. I. (New York, 1932), p. 202.

that those are not tyrants who are striving to bring them unto God; and they will be slow to cast off a system which has become associated in their minds with their dearest hopes and most precious consolations. Brutal ignorance is indeed to be dreaded—the only security against it, is physical force—it is the parent of ferocity, of rashness, and of desperate enterprizes. But Christian knowledge softens and subdues. Christ Jesus in binding his subjects to God, binds them more closely to each other in the ties of confidence, fidelity and love. We would say, then, to you and to all our brethren of the South, go on in your present undertaking; and though our common enemies may continue to revile, you will be consolidating the elements of your social fabrick, so firmly and compactly, that it shall defy the storms of fanaticism, while the spectacle you will exhibit of union, sympathy and confidence, among the different orders of the community, will be a standing refutation of all their accusations against us. Go on in this noble enterprise, until every slave in our borders shall know of Jesus and the resurrection, and the blessing of God will attend you—and turn back the tide of indignation which the public opinion of the world is endeavouring to roll upon you. Go on in this career, and afford another illustration of what all experience has demonstrated, that Christianity is the cheap defence of every institution which contributes to the progress of man.

BIBLIOGRAPHICAL NOTE

The literature on the abolition movement and emancipation of the Negro has increased greatly in recent years. Dwight L. Dumond, *A Bibliography of Anti-slavery in America* (Ann Arbor, Mich., 1961) is very helpful. Interpretive essays are: Gilbert Barnes, *The Anti-Slavery Impulse 1830–1844* (New York, 1933); Donald Mathews, *Slavery and Methodism: A Chapter in American Morality 1780–1845* (Princeton, 1965); Kenneth M. Stampp, *The Peculiar Institution: Slavery in the Ante-Bellem South* (New York, 1956). The list could be ex-

panded. For an insightful study of an abolitionist see Betty
Fladeland, *James Gillespie Birney: Slaveholder to Abolitionist* (New York, 1958).

For special treatments of southern views see William S.
Jenkins, *Pro-Slavery Thought in the Old South* (Chapel Hill,
N.C., 1935) which contains many quotations from sermons
and documents, and Alice Dana Adams, *The Neglected
Period of Anti-Slavery in America, 1800–1831* (New York,
1908), which discusses southern sentiment against slavery in
the earlier decades of the nineteenth century. Also: Kenneth
Stampp, "The Fate of the Southern Antislavery Movement,"
Journal of Negro History, xxxiii (1943), p. 18 ff. The writings
of James Henley Thornwell have been collected by John B.
Adger and John L. Girardeau, editors, *The Collected Writings
of James Henley Thornwell, D.D., L.L.D.,* Four Volumes,
(Richmond, Va., 1871–1873).

An important interpretive analysis of the later period is
Timothy L. Smith, *Revivalism and Social Reform* (Nashville,
1957), Chapters XII and XIII.

VIII. CONFLICT WITHIN LUTHERANISM

German immigration into the United States increased sharply in the period from 1820 to 1860: approximately 7000 arrived in the 1820s; 950,000 in the 1850s. Though most of the German Lutherans held firmly to the confessional standards of their church, they were confronted with a quite different religious environment in America. The separation of church and state had brought a voluntary principle to American church life: membership was by choice, not birth; new measures were needed to evangelize. For some American Lutherans the lines between denominations were becoming blurred.

Samuel Simon Schmucker (1799–1873), a graduate of Princeton Theological Seminary, was the leader of "American Lutheranism." He sought to minimize the normative character of the confessional "Symbols" of the church and to seek closer fellowship with other denominational groups. His *Fraternal Appeal to the American Churches, with a Plan for Catholic Union on Apostolic Principles,* published in 1838, proposed a platform for church union, including a confessional statement to which most denominations could subscribe. Though his proposal met with sympathetic hearing, it was not enacted. With the increase of German immigration Schmucker was gradually forced into a more polemical stance.

Why should there not be an *American* Lutheran church, as well as any other? There is a German, a Danish, a Swedish Lutheran church, each possessing its distinctive peculiarities, arising from their different civil governments, and the different views of those who founded them, to say nothing of the differences between one church in the several kingdoms and principalities of Germany. Then why should not American Lutherans be permitted to organize their church, in accordance with the principles of their own glorious civil institutions, in conformity to the dictates of their own consciences and their views of the inspired word of God? Are they less able to search the Scriptures with fidelity and success, than their brethren of other countries? Are we less competent to judge of what suits our peculiar circumstances, and the peculiar age of the world, and the signs of the eventful times in which we live than others?[1]

The culmination of Schmucker's efforts was the publication of the *Definite Synodical Platform* in 1855 which, circulated anonymously, sought a union of American Lutherans on a common confessional basis which included acceptance of the Old and New Testaments as the only Infallible Rule of Faith and Practice, the adoption of the Apostles' and Nicene-Constantinopolitan Creeds, and an "American Recension of the Augsburg Confession." This forthright statement brought immediate reaction from the "Old Lutherans" and hereafter Schmucker's influence was greatly diminished.

Charles Philip Krauth (1797–1867) was an early defender of "Old Lutheranism." He was a colleague of Schmucker on the faculty of Gettysburg Theological Seminary and editor of the *Evangelical Review,* founded in 1849 as a platform for the conservative point of view. His son, Charles Porterfield Krauth (1823–1883), a student of Schmucker, was Professor of Systematic Theology at the Lutheran Seminary at Mount Airy, Pennsylvania, which was established as a counter force to Gettysburg Seminary. The Krauths, father and son, did much to prevent the growth of American Lutheran sentiments.

The issue was one which confronted most immigrant church groups: the degree of accommodation which the church needed to make to the American scene.

[1] Quoted in Vergilius Ferm, *The Crisis in American Lutheran Theology* (New York, 1927), p. 172, from S. S. Schmucker, "The Doctrinal Basis and Ecclesiastical Position of the American Lutheran Church," in *The American Lutheran Church, Historically, Doctrinally and Practically Delineated, in Several Occasional Discourses* (Philadelphia, 1852), Fifth Edition, p. 234.

[19]
Samuel Simon Schmucker
Portraiture of Lutheranism*

Luther had wisely regarded the reformation as unfinished, and exhorted his followers to turn away from his works, and study the bible more attentively. Unfortunately for the cause of truth and peace, the admiration of many of his followers, degenerated into excessive veneration; and death, which translated him to the abode of peace in heaven, made his writings, the source of rancorous contention on earth, imparted a kind of canonical authority to them. Moreover, as the church, established by his instrumentality, was designated by his name, his works gradually were regarded as the standards of orthodoxy, and all attempts to continue the work of reformation so gloriously commenced by him, were denounced as treason to his cause! ! . .

Had not the church been dominated by the name of this distinguished servant of Christ; had not his works but the bible been regarded as the grand source of religious light, as the grand subject of continued study; and had the Augsburg Confession alone been received as an auxiliary test; the church would have enjoyed much more peace, and the whole field of doctrine, except the few points determined in that confession, would have been open to free continued study and scrutiny in the light of God's word. But instead of finding fault with those theological heroes, who vanquished the hosts of Rome, for not accomplishing everything; we should be grateful to God that they were enabled to effect so much.

* From Samuel Simon Schmucker, *The American Lutheran Church, Historically, Doctrinally, and Practically Delineated* (Philadelphia, 1852), pp. 59–70.

The *first* feature of improvement to which we will advert, is the *entire rejection of the authority of the Fathers in ecclesiastical controversy.* The grand mistake of the earlier reformers was their appeal to this authority. They were, indeed, enabled with these weapons, to overturn the corruptions introduced into the church after the rise of the papal hierarchy; but they also compelled themselves to retain such errors as were of earlier date. The writing of the fathers instead of being good authority for scripture doctrine, are a perfect labyrinth of theological errors, from which it is impossible to escape with safety, and in which we look in vain for that unanimous consent which Rome so loudly boasted. But it is easy to establish by authority of Antenicene fathers, the several errors retained by the earlier reformers, and since rejected by the mass of Protestants.

In short it is a principle which the experience of ages has clearly established, that in all controversies about the proper doctrines, or duties, or forms of christianity, *the bible, the whole bible, and nothing but the bible,* must be the armor of the Protestant. To concede to Romanists or others the necessity of an appeal to patristic authority, is a tacit denial of the word of God, as the sufficient and only rule of faith and practice, the only ground on which Protestantism can be permanently and triumphantly sustained.

Another feature of improvement in the Lutheran church consists in her *no longer requiring assent to the doctrine of the real presence of the Saviour in the eucharist.* On this subject her views have not unfrequently been misapprehended and misstated. It is indeed true, that she did entertain opinions on this topic different from the other churches. This difference was however by no means so great as is at present supposed by the less intelligent part of the community. Calvin and the early English reformers, employed language nearly, and in some cases, quite as strong as that found in the Lutheran symbols. The Augsburg Conference affirms, "that the body and blood of Christ are actually present (vere adsint), and the German copy adds, under the form or emblems of bread and wine and dispensed to the communicants." . . . At the present day, it is pretty generally agreed by Protestants, that to talk of the *spiritual* presence of a *material* body, of the *spiritual* eating and drinking of a *material* body and blood, is to employ language that conveys no distinct ideas. We, however, cheerfully concede that the other Protestant denominations relinquished these views of their reformers, more speedily and with less controversy than did the Lutheran church. It was indeed reported that Luther himself shortly before his death, in a confidential conversation with Melanchthon, acknowledged that he had gone too far in regard to the eucharist. But, much as we should be pleased to believe that our great and good reformer had made such an acknowledgment, the evidence appears unsatisfactory; or at most, he may have admitted, that he had exhibited too much warmth in the controversy, or overrated the importance of his peculiar views. At the present day, whilst some shades of difference exist in the Lutheran church, all are permitted to enjoy their opinions in peace, and the most generally received view, if we mistake not, is: "That there is no presence of the glorified *human* nature of the Saviour, either substantial or influential; nor anything mysterious or supernatural in the eucharist; yet, that whilst the bread and wine are merely symbolic representations of the Saviour's absent body, by which we are reminded of his sufferings, there is also a special spiritual blessing bestowed by the divine Saviour on all worthy communicants, by which their faith and Christian graces are confirmed."

The *third* item of improvement is the relinquishment of a much abused custom connected with the preparation for communion. The reformers and their successors had substantially repudiated as unscriptural and corrupting what constituted the essential features of Romish *private confession,* namely: the pretence that the priest is in the place of God; that every individual sin, even the secret thoughts and feelings of the heart must individually be detailed to the priest, as essential to pardon; and that the priest possesses the absolute power to forgive these sins. Yet the reformers deemed it useful, that before communion, each communicant should have a private interview with the pastor, and give him an account of the state of his soul, and his progress in the divine life; in order that the minister might give him instruction and advice, and if the case warranted it, encourage the applicant with the promise of pardon from God. This custom, in order to give as little offense as possible, they denominated, though very inappropriately, confession. They had rejected the thing, and therefore it would have been more consistent not to retain the name. Yet, against this custom, it would be difficult to allege any valid objection, except its misapprehension and consequent abuse by the ignorant. Thus explained, confession was approved by Calvin, Peter Martyr, Werenfels, Heidegger, Hornbeck, Jurien, and other distinguished Reformed divines. But even this custom has been almost entirely abandoned, and the preparation for communion consists of a public preparatory discourse, public and united confession of sins, and rehearsal of the promises of divine mercy, similar to the preparatory exercises of other churches. The only difference is, that in the Lutheran and Episcopal churches, which use liturgies, these exercises of confession of sins and exhibition of divine promises of pardon, are conducted according to a settled form, whilst in others they are extemporaneous. Yet in the numerous Lutheran liturgies we have seen, including those of Sweden and Norway, the minister never professes to forgive sins himself, nor even to announce the divine promises of pardon unconditionally to all, but limits them to truly penitent believers; whilst the impenitent and unbelieving are expressly told that God will not pardon their sins, but inflict deserved punishment on them. This formal annunciation of the divine promise of forgiveness, thus conditionally made, is edifying to intelligent minds, especially as the Saviour himself, in the words of the institution, mentions "remission of sins" as the design of that death which we are to commemorate in the eucharist. Yet as it is easily perverted into certain pardon by the less informed, who may erroneously conceive themselves penitent, and as the scriptures contain no special promise of pardon at communion, more than in the performance of any other duty; the utmost caution should be observed against misapprehension, and the annunciation itself is very properly often thrown into the form of a prayer, as is also done in the Episcopal liturgy.

The *fourth* item of *improvement* is the entire rejection of every remnant of papal superstition in the administration of baptism. The Romanists maintain, that unbaptized persons are possessed by evil spirits, and that the priest possesses the power by adjuration to expel them. This ceremony, termed exorcism, is performed by the priest with a multitude of formalities. Luther, and the other early reformers, rejected both these principles; yet retained some kind of adjuration as a symbolic acknowledgment of the natural depravity of all men. To this they were probably led by their lingering regard for the early fathers. For, something of this kind was practiced even in the third century, when the corrupting influence of the New Platonists was first felt in the church; and it was defended by such men as Cyprian and Augustine. Yet many of our churches were from the beginning unwilling to retain the semblance of this ceremony, even as a declaration of natural depravity, and accordingly it was totally rejected from the liturgy and directory for worship, published at Augsburg seven years after the celebrated diet of that place, namely in 1537; as also in that of Strasburg, published in 1543, of Nuremberg, published in the same year, and in many others. In different kingdoms it was long since wholly rejected, whilst in others, phraseology more or less resembling it was long retained.

The *fifth* item of improvement in the Lutheran church is the more *systematic adjustment of her doctrines*. Luther was so incessantly employed in the great work of reforming the church from the corruptions and superstitions of Rome, that he had little leisure for abstract reflections on the reciprocal relations of the scripture doctrines, and on the entire and minute consistency of his views with each other. It is certain that in the earlier part of his life, he believed the Augustinian view of predestination. His work, on the Bondage of the Will, published in 1525, must put this question to rest. But he at the same time entertained other views inconsistent with this. Melanchthon, who had embraced Luther's unadjusted views of doctrine, led the way in the process of harmonizing their conflicting elements, by the rejection of absolute predestination. Luther himself adopted these modifications, and long before he died, preached and taught what have ever since been the doctrines of the Lutheran standards. The particulars of this interesting process are detailed in Dr. Plank's invaluable History of the Rise, Changes and Formation of the Protestant System of Doctrines. During the reign of infidelity in Europe, when an unbaptized philosophy had desecrated the sanctuary of God, and so far effaced all lineaments and extinguished all attachment to genuine protestant Christianity, that even a Buonaparte could contemplate as a matter of state policy the re-establishment of the Romish religion over all protestant Germany; the doctrines of great reformers were forsaken by many. But thanks be to God, the cause of truth is again prospering, orthodoxy is again preponderant in Germany; and in the Lutheran church in this country the great doctrines of the reformation are taught as universally, as in any other denomination of Christians in our land.

The *sixth* feature of improvement is the adoption of a more regular and rigid system of church government and discipline in this country. The union between church and state has prevented the adoption of an independent and thoroughly scriptural discipline in the Lutheran, as well as in all the other established churches of Europe. Kings and princes are not willing to be disciplined by humble ministers and lay elders. Accordingly, the systems of discipline in different provinces and kingdoms are different, and generally very lax. In this country our General Synod has adopted and recommended a system, which, it is believed, contains all the prescriptions of the Saviour and his apostles, and all that appeared most valuable in the systems of the different other churches. The government and discipline of each individual church, is essentially like that of our Presbyterian brethren. Our Synods, also, in structure and powers, most resemble their Presbyteries, having fewer formalities in their proceedings, and frequently couching their decisions in the form of recommendations. Our General Synod is wholly an advisory body, resembling the consociations of the Congregational churches of New England. In addition to these regular ecclesiastical bodies, constituting our system of government, we having special Conferences, for the purpose of holding stated protracted meetings. These are subdivisions of Synods, containing ordinarily from five to ten ministers each, who are annually to hold several protracted meetings within the bounds of their district. The chief object of these meetings is, to awaken and convert sinners, and to edify believers by close, practical preaching. This feature mainly resembles the quarterly meetings of our Methodist brethren, and presents to pious and zealous ministers, who are thirsting for the salvation of souls, the most direct opportunity they can desire, to glorify God, and advance his spiritual kingdom. Yet all these meetings are to be conducted as the scriptures enjoin, "decently and in order." This system of government is not yet adopted by all our Synods; yet Its general features, with perhaps a greater admixture of Congregationalism, substantially pervade those Synods also, which have not yet united with the General Synod.

The *last* item of improvement to which we shall refer, Is the practice of the Lutheran church in this country, not to bind her ministers to the minutiae of any human creed. The bible and the belief that the fundamental doctrines of the bible are taught in a manner substantially correct in the Augsburg Confession, is all that is required. On the one hand, we regard it as certain, that if we would be faithful to the injunction of our text, "not to receive any who come to us bringing other doctrine," and examination of applicants for admission among us is indispensable. Such an examination is virtually a requisition of their creed, that we may compare it with our own. Now, whether the articles to which we require their assent be few or many, be written or oral, they are a creed, and obviously its reduction to paper, presents some material facilities in the examination. A written creed, therefore, seems necessary to the purity of the church. On the other hand, history informs us, that for several hundred years after the days of the apostles, no other creed was used in the whole church than that called the Apostle's Creed, because admitted by all to contain the principal doctrines taught by the apostles. This creed embodied only the cardinal doctrines of the gospel, which all the so called orthodox denominations of the present day do actually believe; and yet the assent to these few doctrines did for centuries after the apostolic age, secure admission to any and every part of the Catholic, that is, the universal church on earth. By what authority then did the several Protestant denominations after the Reformation adopt creeds ten, and some of them, a hundred times as long as that used in the earlier ages, and require assent to these interminable instruments as a condition of admission to their churches? The bible certainly confers no such authority. But does the experience of three centuries prove their influence to be salutary? Have they not rather been the occasion of endless strife in all the churches adopting them? Have they not proved wedges of dissension to split asunder the body of Christ? It is matter of historical certainty, that the orthodox denominations of the present day coincide as much in doctrinal views, as did the Christians in the golden age of Christianity. If they could walk together in love, and their minor differences created no difficulty then; why should not Christians in the present day unite in the same manner, instead of rending the body of Christ asunder, creating separate and conflicting interests among brethren in Christ, alienation and prosecutions for minor differences, which would not have been noticed in the apostolic and primitive, and purest age of the church. The duty of all parts of the Christian church seems therefore to be, to return to the use of shorter doctrinal creeds as tests of ecclesiastical, ministerial, and sacramental communion. This noble course the Lutheran church has already virtually taken, by requiring assent only to the fundamental doctrines of the Augsburg Confession, together with an approval of our principles of government and worship. This course cannot fail to promote brotherly love, and fraternal appreciation between different denominations, by giving prominence to their actual unity in doctrine, and restoring a proper unity of spirit among the disciples of Christ. Happy, thrice happy too is the Lutheran church, that she, who was first to cast off the yoke of Roman superstition and oppression, should lead the way in breaking the bonds of Protestant sectarianism; be first in practically teaching the world: that the apostolic injunction to "receive a brother that is weak in the faith, but not for the purpose of doubtful disputation," does not mean to prosecute and expel him. And happy are all in every denomination who raise their voice in behalf of the lacerated body of Christ, and teach Christians to remember the solemn injunction of the Saviour to love one another; and not only to profess but to practise the principle of our blessed Lord, "one is our Master Christ, and ye are all brethren."

Such, my brethren, are the features of the Lutheran church, of that church, to whose service this chaste and beautiful ediface has been dedicated. She may be emphatically styled the church of the Reformation. She holds the grand doctrines of Christianity, with fewer appended peculiarities than most other denominations. With the Calvinist she holds the graciousness of salvation; with the Congregationalist she believes that Christ tasted death for every men; with the Methodist she approves of regularly recurring protracted meetings; with the Episcopalian she occasionally employs a liturgy and forms of prayer; with the German Reformed she agrees in the instruction and confirmation of Catechumens; and with all she unites in ascribing all the glory of our privileges on earth and hopes in heaven, to that Lamb of God, that taketh away the sins of the world. Long may those blessed doctrines be taught within these sacred walls! Long may they be taught throughout our favored land, purifying and elevating our political and social institutions, providing for our citizens, security of person and property, and especially the privilege of worshiping God under our own vine and fig tree, making it the land of refuge to the virtuous oppressed of all nations.

[20]

Charles Philip Krauth

The Lutheran Church in the United States*

The time has, perhaps, arrived, in which it becomes the duty of the Lutheran Church in the United States to examine its position, and to determine its future course . . .

The Lutheran Church in this country traces its origin to the Lutheran Church in Germany. . . . Coeval with the Reformation, and established upon the doctrinal system of Luther, as expressed in the Augsburg Confession, its Apology, the Smalcald Articles and the Catechism of Luther, as developed and explained in the Formula Concordiae, its history has been illustrious. . . . Its first ministers, educated in the schools of sound Lutheran theology, designed to transfer the same to this country. . . . That the orthodoxy of the olden time was gradually lost sight of, that the Confessions were practically superseded, that formal subscription was entirely abandoned, are facts which admit of no controversy. It is true, since the commencement of the era, as it has been called, of the General Synod, the Augsburg Confession has again been brought into notice, and a limited subscription to it enforced; but it cannot be regarded as anything more than an approximate return to the ancient landmarks. . . .

The Lutheran church in this country is in a state of reaction. She has passed, in some parts, through an extreme subjectivity, an extreme leaning to the emotional in religion; she permitted herself, to some extent, to be carried away by the surges of animal feeling, and lost much of her ancient propriety. She is now retracing her steps, acknowledging her error, seeking release from crude views and objectionable

* Charles Philip Krauth, "The Lutheran Church in the United States," *Evangelical Review,* Vol. ii, July, 1850, p. 1 ff.

measures. She is hunting amongst the records of the past for the faith of former days, and endeavoring to learn what she was in her earliest form. The desire for the symbols of our Church, the attention that is paid to them, the admiration that has been expressed of them, the candor with which they are viewed, the expressed willingness on the part of many, only to dissent when it cannot be avoided, all indicate a new state of things—and are adapted to produce the conviction that the Church is disposed to renew her connection with the past, and in her future progress to walk under the guidance of the light which it has furnished. There is no fear of any doctrine which our symbols contain, no unwillingness to give it a fair examination, and a predisposition, rather than the contrary, to receive and assent. If these statements are correct, it certainly shows a remarkable state of things in our Lutheran Zion, it must awaken the enquiry, whither do these things tend, and what will be the issue? How we should demean ourselves under existing circumstances, what part we should perform in this great movement, are important enquiries, and bring us to that division of our subject in which we propose to treat of the duties which are obligatory upon us as a Church, in the condition in which we find ourselves, in the providence of God.

It is our duty, we think, holding fast what we have, abandoning no ground that we fairly occupy, to aim at union in view and harmony of action. The points in which we agree are so numerous—our predilections as theologians are so much alike, our principles are so uniform, that it does not appear improbable that we may be brought to as perfect a coincidence as can be expected of humanity; and in the way of harmony of action, we can perceive no impediment. Those views, to which we have referred as peculiar to one class of Lutherans, the views about the Lord's Supper and the person of the Redeemer, so strenuously asserted by the Lutheran Fathers, men of great ability, profound students of the Word of God, and holy men too—asserted in view of as powerful objections, and as powerfully wielded as can well be conceived, revived so extensively abroad, and amongst the best men and the ablest divines of our Church—ought not to be considered as absolutely incredible by us, but rather we should give them a candid examination, try the arguments by which they are supported, test the modifications with which they are reasserted, and then, and only then, determine where truth lies. We are satisfied that we have had an imperfect understanding of these opinions, have examined too carelessly, or not at all, the grounds of them, have caught too readily at the perverted views of their opponents, and have too hastily identified them with doctrines from which they differ very widely. It is due to our Church, it is due to our symbols, it is due to our brethren, that we should pursue this course. It is due, too, to the memory of our Fathers, if we do dissent from them, that we should nevertheless be able to vindicate them from those objections which are based upon a one-sided and very inadequate understanding of what they taught.

To bring about the state of things which we desire, it is obviously the duty of those on the opposite side to remember, that their doctrines were not universally received, that even amongst those who fought under the same banner there was occasionally a dissenting voice, that the great Melanchthon himself gradually departed from the doctrine of the presence, as held by his most celebrated coadjutor, and that death alone prevented his expression of that view of Christ's presence, which has been ascribed to Calvin—not a real spiritual presence, but, as it has been called by the Mercersburg school of theology, in our country, which has promulgated it as the ancient faith of the German Reformed Church—"a spiritual real presence." The controversies in the Church on the subject of Christ's presence in the Eucharist, the fact that even in the Romish Church, during the middle ages, able men appeared against the settled opinion, should teach us moderation, induce us to bear with those who may differ from us, lead us to believe that uniformity of faith is not unattended with difficulty, to feel persuaded that though there may be a difference in explanation, all realize the same results, because all true Christians display the same character, and to be persuaded that, if we have so much the superiority in argument over our opponents, they will not hold out long against us.

We are satisfied that, if primitive Lutheranism is to make progress in this country, it will at first be amongst Lutherans; if converts to the doctrine of the real presence are to be made, they will not soon be derived from any other quarter. In them we will have an unprejudiced auditory, men who will hear our proofs, who will calmly weigh them, and will give their acquiescence, if they believe it right. In the meantime, let us cultivate peace and harmony, let us endeavor to act together, let us be united and seek to do each other good. Let us aim to diffuse a spirit of harmony, concord, and peace amongst our people, and the God of peace will bless us.

It is our duty to avoid controversy of a bitter, alienating character. We do not object to controversy, but to such as tends to alienate and embitter feeling. Contend should we for the faith, but in a meek and gentle spirit. Treating our opponents with fairness, seeking to do full justice to their views, we should abstain from all reproachful epithets, and endeavor by honest arguments to vindicate our position. We are to contend for truth, not for victory; for the glory of God, not our own. We are to aim to persuade men, not to compel them. It is said that the truth is mighty, and will prevail; we believe both: it is mighty and it will prevail. With an ardent love of it, with a sincere desire to propagate it, we should make it our constant employment to bring it before those to whom we have access. If we are to be members of the same Christian household, if we would dwell comfortably together, it will be necessary to avoid all heated strife, and all condemnatory language.

We entertain no doubt that the utmost good will is cherished by that part of the Church which has least of the Lutheran element, toward that which has most. They have no desire that they should be alienated, that they should stand aloof, that they should not be regarded and treated in the fullest sense as brethren. They would have them partake in the operations in which all can participate, and be associated in every organization designed for concentrated action. They claim reciprocity in the feelings and actions of the others. They ask that both may grow together till the harvest. They believe that it will be best for all. They are persuaded that it will tend to the glory of the ascended Redeemer, to the welfare of His Church, to the best interests of the German population of our country, and therefore do they urge that One should be regarded as our Master, even Christ, and that we should look upon ourselves as brethren.

Another duty, we think, is to use the great symbol of the Church, the Augsburg Confession, allowing such latitude in the subscription as is compatible with harmony. We believe that there has been too much looseness in our Church in regard to the necessity and utility of creeds in general. The change from the original ground occupied by the Church, the disuse of the symbols, the latitudinarianism about them were calculated to be productive of much evil. That this has not occurred may be said to be happy for the Church. We believe that the evils to be dreaded from the neglect of the symbols have not followed in a very great degree, yet they have in some. That orthodoxy which we retain, strongly tinctured as it is with Lutheranism, has various phases, never running, perhaps, into Calvinism on the one hand, or Pelagianism on the other, but sometimes passing almost into the region of the one, and at others hardly steering clear of the other.

Now, we suppose that this requires a remedy, and we can suggest no other, in the present state of our Church, than the use of the Augsburg Confession as a creed, and requiring the subscription of it, within certain limits, by every minister of Jesus Christ who serves at our altars. It may be said that it has been used, that it has received the sanction of the General Synod of our Church, and that it is subscribed by the ministers of those synods which are connected with the General Synod. This is true; but we object to the liberty allowed in that subscription. Thus far it has been without serious injury, but it is liable to very great abuse. The terms of the subscription are such as to admit of the rejection of any doctrine or doctrines which the subscriber may not receive. It is subscribed or assented to, as containing the doctrines of the Word of God substantially; they are set forth in substance; the understanding is that there are some doctrines in it not contained in the Word of God, but there is no specification concerning them. Everyone could omit from his assent whatever he did not believe. The subscription did not preclude this. It is at once evident that a creed thus presented is no creed; that it is anything or nothing; that its subscription is a solemn farce. It is true that the views of subscribers were ascertained in advance of their subscription, and the dangers were avoided which otherwise might have ensued; but then they were ascertained under no circumstances of special solemnity, under none that bind the conscience as does an oath of subscription to a creed, and consequently nothing was gained; or, if there was a previous conviction as to the soundness of the candidate, the subscription was superseded as entirely supererogatory. To set aside this great, this venerated symbol, would meet with no favor in the Church; an *ex animo* subscription is not possible to all. What, then, is to be done? We insist upon a creed; we consider it a *sine qua non*; the Church cannot operate harmoniously, efficiently without it; the only course that we can devise is to give normative authority. It may be subscribed *ex animo* by all who can do so; it may be subscribed by others with the privilege of dissenting from certain doctrines, which shall be stated or specified. The doctrines from which there may be dissent cannot be any that are essential to the orthodox system—cannot be any which, if received and rejected in the same Church, would tend to confusion. Different views may be allowed in regard to our relation to the first man, and the manner in which we became involved in his sin, but not in regard to the sinfulness of man, original sin, and the necessity of regeneration. Different views may be entertained as respects the *Communicatio idiomatum* in the nature of Christ, but not in regard to those natures. Carefully must we exclude every form of Arianism, high and low, Socinianism and rationalism, and anti-trinitarianism of all kinds.

These are the conclusions to which we have come upon this subject; we confess its difficulty, and can only say to any or to all, If you have anything better, candidly impart it; if not, use this with us. It was a different course which led to the division of the Presbyterian Church in this country; it was in a position very much like our own, and we suppose that such a plan as we propose would have prevented a separation neither necessary nor profitable, but which may, in the end, be conducive to the glory of God.

It is our duty to exert a conservative influence. The true position of the Lutheran Church is conservative. It should hold fast the form of sound words which it has received, and display its doctrinal and ritual moderation. Occupying a middle position between prelatical Episcopacy and *jure divino congregationalism;* extreme neither in the one direction nor the other; conceding to utility all that it can ask without detriment to order; avoiding in doctrine the errors of Calvinism, and those of low Arminianism and Pelagianism; repudiating a mere animal religion whilst it shows no countenance to a morality cold and religionless—these, its true position, its very essence and form, adapt it to exert an influence favorable to doctrinal soundness and religious purity. We do not claim for it too much when we ascribe to it a capacity to uphold a true, living system of Christianity, when we regard it as adapted to exert an influence opposed to extremes in the one direction or the other. It might appear invidious to ascribe such a power to the Lutheran Church exclusively. This we do not do; but, at the same time, we think that in no other is there capacity to do so much, and upon so extensive a scale. No other church occupies, we think, so nearly the central point between Roman Catholic and Protestant extremes. No other so central a point between the High-Churchism of Protestantism and the extremes of Protestantism, and therefore we suppose that no other can more fairly regard itself as summoned to act a conservative part—conservative not only by upholding a moderate orthodoxy in doctrine, ecclesiastical government and ceremonies, but by preventing extremes, either on the one hand subversive of human liberty, or on the other of the grace of God. It neither makes man independent of means or of God. It connects not his salvation with direct influences without means, nor does it grow out of means without the influences of God.

BIBLIOGRAPHICAL NOTE

The most comprehensive discussion of the "Americanism" controversy in the Lutheran Church is Vergilius Ferm, *The Crisis in American Lutheran Theology* (New York, 1927). The author has included many quotations from documents of the period. The biography of Adolph Spaeth, *Charles Porterfield Krauth,* Two Volumes (New York, 1898), is a thorough study of this key figure in American Lutheran history, with significant attention also given to his father, Charles Philip Krauth. Unfortunately both of these titles are presently out of print.

An excellent bibliographical aid is Herbert H. Schmidt, "The Literature of Lutherans in America," *Religion in Life,* Vol. 27, no. 4, Autumn, 1958, pp. 583–603. The most adequate history of American Lutheranism is Abdel Ross Wentz, *The Lutheran Church in American History,* 2nd edition (Philadelphia, 1933).

IX. LIBERALISM

INTRODUCTION

In the latter decades of the nineteenth century the Protestant churches were confronted by a variety of new intellectual interests. Charles Darwin's *The Descent of Man* (1871) and his theory of biological evolution was viewed by many as a direct challenge to the authority of Scripture; others welcomed his work. New critical approaches to biblical studies called into question traditional uses of the Bible. The missionary movement of the nineteenth century had brought American churches into closer contact with non-western religions and in this period the study of comparative religion became popular and, indirectly, a challenge to the uniqueness of Christianity. Theologians turned their attention to sociological and psychological analyses of religious phenomena. Many of the leading philosophical figures of this period also had intense interest in religious questions and brought a rigorous and fresh perspective to the study of theological themes. These new interests cut across denominational lines; they were not the special concern of any one church. It is interesting to note that many of the early "liberals" were pastors of churches, not theological professors.

Though no one can be called the "father" of liberalism it may be said that Horace Bushnell (1802–1876), pastor of the North Congregational Church in Hartford, Connecticut, through his numerous sermons and theological essays became the theological tutor for many in the liberal era. One central figure was Theodore T. Munger (1830–1910), pastor of the United Church (Congregational) in New Haven, Connecticut. His essay, "The New Theology," sought to show that the liberal wanted to conserve the values in the Christian tradition while making accommodation to the newer intellectual concerns.

The Social Gospel was an expression of the "new theology."

The problems of an increasingly industrial and urbanized society had not been met by the churches and resulted in a separation between the laboring classes and the industrialists. Samuel Gompers of the AFL commented: "My associates have come to look upon the church and the ministry as the apologists and defenders of the wrong committed against the interests of the people."[1] On the other side George F. Baer of the Reading Railroad wrote that the poor would be "protected and cared for not by the labor agitators, but by the Christian man to whom God in his infinite wisdom has given the control of the property interests of the country."[2]

Among the many names associated with the "Social Gospel" Washington Gladden (1836–1918) and Walter Rauschenbusch (1861–1918) stand out. Gladden was pastor of churches in Massachusetts before becoming minister to the First Congregational Church in Columbus, Ohio. He was a prolific writer. The Selection from Gladden included below was an address he delivered at the National Council of the Congregational Churches at Cleveland, Ohio, in October of 1907; Gladden had just retired from a three year term as Moderator of the Church.

Walter Rauschenbusch is noted as the foremost theological interpreter of the Social Gospel. A Baptist minister and graduate of Rochester Seminary, he became pastor of a small Second German Church in New York City. During his pastorate from 1886–1897 he was intimately involved in the problems of the church in an area of abject poverty and began to formulate a different interpretation of the Christian faith. A central theme of his thought was the Kingdom of God.

The Kingdom of God is not confined within the limits of the Church and its activities. It embraces the whole of human life. It is the Christian transfiguration of the social order. The Church is one social institution alongside of the family, the

[1] Quoted in C. Howard Hopkins, *The Rise of the Social Gospel in American Protestantism, 1865–1915* (New Haven, 1940), p. 85.
[2] Quoted in Robert M. Miller, *American Protestantism and Social Issues 1919–1939* (Chapel Hill, 1958), p. 12.

industrial organization of society, and the State. The Kingdom of God is in all these, and realizes itself through them
all.[3]

Rauschenbusch occupies a central place in American Protestant history.

Russell Conwell (1843–1925) was a figure of fascination
to many Americans. He graduated from Yale and practiced
law for a number of years until 1872 when, after a conversion
experience, he took charge of a Baptist Church in Lexington,
Massachusetts. Shortly after his ordination in 1879 he was
called to the Grace Baptist Church in Philadelphia. There
he became a lecturer and preacher in great demand. His
address, "Acres of Diamonds," was delivered more than 5000
times and his advocacy of the "Gospel of Wealth" put him
into sharp conflict with the "Social Gospel" movement.

By the 1920s the issue between the "liberals" and "conservatives" had moved beyond the irenic spirit of T. T. Munger.
Shailer Mathews' (1863–1941) *The Faith of Modernism*,
though not a literary gem, was a statement of one in the
forefront of the modernist movement. Mathews wrote: "liberal theology uses the methods of modern science to find,
state and use the permanent and central values of inherited
orthodoxy in meeting the needs of the modern world."[4] The
accommodation of theology to the scientific method was characteristic of prominent theologians, for example, the Professor of Theology at Yale Divinity School, Douglas Clyde
Macintosh, published *Theology as an Empirical Science* in
1919. Shailer Mathews was Professor of Historical Theology
and Dean of the Divinity School, University of Chicago.
In an autobiographical statement he remarked:

As a result of historical critical study the Bible had already
lost its authority as an infallible revelation to be used as a
theological oracle, but now the basis of religious loyalty itself
was subject to examination. If one accepted evangelical or-

[3] Walter Rauschenbusch, *A Theology for the Social Gospel* (New
York, 1917), pp. 144–145.
[4] Shailer Mathews, *The Faith of Modernism* (New York, 1923),
p. 23.

thodoxy it could only be because of the authority of a group or a literature rather than because of any demonstration of its truth. But if the decisions of the group themselves were functional, a method by which the social mind of a given period adapted religion for its own good, what was there left of Christianity for our own day? The only answer that I could see would be that ecclesiastical authority must be replaced by some intelligible method by which one would be able to distinguish between the form and the content of an inherited religious group belief, and then determine as to the truth of its content by such criteria as were applicable.[5]

Mathews' liberal sentiments were not well received by conservative theologians.

There were unsophisticated attacks on the work of the Biblical critics by popular figures of the time. William Jennings Bryan remarked: "Why should the Bible, which the centuries have been unable to shake, be discarded for scientific works that have to be revised and corrected every few years."[6] One of the articulate and learned defenders of "orthodoxy" was J. Gresham Machen. Machen, a graduate of Princeton Theological Seminary in 1905, taught at his Alma Mater until 1929 and then later at Westminster Theological Seminary which was organized by the newly founded Orthodox Presbyterian Church. His most well-known work, *Christianity and Liberalism*, attempted to show that these were radically different and "sprang from different roots."

[5] Shailer Mathews, "Theology as Group Belief," in Vergilius Ferm, *Contemporary American Theology: Theological Autobiographies*, Second Series (New York, 1933), p. 173.

[6] Quoted in Norman Furniss, *The Fundamentalist Controversy, 1918–1931* (New Haven, 1954), p. 17.

[21]
Theodore T. Munger
The New Theology*

The purpose of this Essay is to state, so far as is now possible, some of the main features of that phase of present thought popularly known as "The New Theology:" to indicate the lines on which it is moving, to express something of its spirit, and to give it so much of definite form that it shall no longer suffer from the charge of vagueness.

I will first refer to certain negative features, indicating what it is *not;* and then more fully to its positive character.

1. It does not propose to do without a theology.

It seeks no such transformation of method or form that it can no longer claim the name of a science. It does not resolve belief into sentiment, nor etherealize it into mysticism, nor lower it into mere altruism; yet it does not deny an element of sentiment, it acknowledges an element of mysticism, and it insists on a firm basis in ethics. It is the determined foe of agnosticism, yet it recognizes a limitation of human knowledge. While it insists that theology is a science, and that therefore its parts should be coordinate and mutually supporting, and an induction from all the facts known to it, it realizes that it deals with eternal realities that cannot be wholly compassed, and also with the mysteries and contradictions of a world involved in mystery and beset by contradictory forces. If it finds itself driven into impenetrable mystery, as it inevitably must, it prefers to take counsel of the higher sentiments and better hopes of our nature, rather than project into it the frame-work of a formal logic, and insist on its conclusion. It does not abjure logic, but it refuses to be held

* From Theodore T. Munger, *The Freedom of Faith* (Boston, 1883), pp. 3; 7–14; 16–17; 19–20; 22–28; 31–37; 43–44.

by what is often deemed logic. While it believes in a harmony of doctrines, it regards with suspicion what have been known as systems of theology, on the ground that it rejects the methods by which they are constructed. It will not shape a doctrine in order that it may fit another which has been shaped in the same fashion,—a merely mechanical interplay, and seeking a mechanical harmony. Instead, it regards theology as an induction from the revelations of God—in the Bible, in history, in the nation, in the family, in the material creation, and in the whole length and breadth of human life. It will have, therefore, all the definiteness and harmony it can find in these revelations, but it will have no more, since it regards these revelations as under a process still enacting, and not as under a finality.

2. The New Theology does not part with the historic faith of the church, but rather seeks to put itself in its line while recognizing a process of development. It does not propose to commit "retrospective suicide" at every fresh stage of advance. It holds to progress by slow and cosmic growth rather than by cataclysmal leaps. It allies itself even with the older rather than the later theologies, and finds in the early Greek theology conceptions more harmonious with itself than those in the theology shaped by Augustine.

3. It does not reject the specific doctrines of the church of the past. It holds to the Trinity, though indifferent to the use of the word, but not to a formal and psychologically impossible Trinity; to the divine sovereignty, but it does not make it the corner-stone of its system, preferring for that place the divine righteousness, *i.e.*, a moral rather than a dynamic basis; to the Incarnation, not as a mere physical event, for that has entered into many religions, but as the entrance into the world through a person of a moulding and redeeming force in humanity,—the central and broadest fact of theology; to the Atonement as a divine act and process of ethical and practical import—not as a mystery of the distant heavens and isolated from the struggle of the world, but a comprehensible force in the actual redemption of the world from its evil; to the Resurrection as covering the whole essential nature of man; to Judgment as involved in the de-

velopment of a moral nature; to the eternal awards of conduct considered as laws and principles of character, but not necessarily set in time-relations; to human sinfulness under a conception of moral freedom; to Justification by faith in the sense of a faith that, by its law, induces an actual righteousness—a simple, rational process realized in human experience; to Regeneration and Sanctification by the Spirit as most imperative operations based on the utmost need, and on the actual presence and power of the Spirit in the life of humanity. It does not explain away from these doctrines their substance, nor minimize them, nor aim to do else than present them as revealed in the Scriptures and as developed in history and in the life of the church and of the world.

4. It is not iconoclastic in its temper; it is not pervaded by a spirit of denial, but is constructive—taking away nothing without supplying its place; it does not, indeed, find so much occasion to take away and replace as to uncover and bring to light. Believing that revelation is not so much *from* God as *of* God, its logical attitude is that of seeing and interpreting.

5. It is not disposed to find a field and organization outside of existing churches, conscious that it is building on that Eternal Foundation which alone has given strength to the church in every age. It claims only that liberty whereunto all are called in the church of Christ. It asserts that the real ground of membership in the church is fidelity to the faith, and that this ground is not forfeited because it refuses to assent to human and formal conditions that the church has taken on, and which are not of the substance of the faith.

I pass now to the positive features of the New Theology.

1. It claims for itself a somewhat larger and broader use of the reason than has been accorded to theology.

And by reason we do not mean mere speculation nor a formal logic, but that full exercise of our nature which embraces the intuitions, the conscience, the susceptibilities, and the judgment, *i.e.*, man's whole inner being. Especially it makes much of the intuitions—the universal and spontaneous verdicts of the soul; and in this it deems that it allies itself with the Mind through which the Christian revelation is made.

If Christianity has any human basis it is its entire reason-ableness. It must not only sit easily on the mind, but it must ally itself with it in all its normal action. If it chafes it, if it is a burden, if it antagonizes, it detracts from itself; the human mind cannot be detracted from. Man is a knower; the reason never ceases to be less than itself without losing all right to use itself as reason. Consequently a full adjustment between reason and Christianity is steadily to be sought. If there is conflict, uneasiness, burdensomeness, the cause is to be looked for in interpretation rather than in the human reason. For, in the last analysis, revelation—so far as its ac-ceptance is concerned rests on reason, and not reason on revelation. The logical order is, first reason, and then revela-tion—the eye before sight. . . . In brief, we accept the Chris-tian faith because of the reasonableness of its entire substance, and not because we have somehow become persuaded that a revelation has been made. It is impossible to conceive of it as gaining foothold in the mind and heart in any other way, nor can faith in it be otherwise secured. And the reve-lation will be forever appealing to the reason; playing into it as flame mingles with flame, and drawing from it that which is kindred with itself. The inmost principle of revela-tion is that the mind of God reveals itself to the mind of man; and the basis of this principle is that one mind is made in the image of the other, and therefore capable of similar processes of thought and feeling. Revelation is not a dis-closure of things to be done, or of bare facts pertaining to eternity, but is rather an unveiling of the thought and feeling of God to men, in response to which they become sons of the Most High. This is the hold that it has on humanity, and this is the method of its acting. Hence, in simple phrase, it must be on friendly terms with the human reason and heart. It is on such terms; it is only through misinterpretation that it antagonizes the sober conclusions of universal reason and evokes the protest of the universal human heart.

2. The New Theology seeks to interpret the Scriptures in what may be called a more natural way, and in opposition to a hard, formal, unsympathetic, and unimaginative way.

Its strongest denial and its widest divergence from the Old

Theology lie here. It holds profoundly to inspiration, but it also holds that the Scriptures were written by living men, whose life entered into their writings; it finds the color and temper of the writer's mind in his work; it finds also the temper and habit of the age; it penetrates the forms of Oriental speech; it seeks to read out of the mind and conception and custom of the writer instead of reading present conceptions into his words. In brief, it reads the Scriptures as literature, yet with no derogation from their inspiration. It refuses to regard the writers as automatic organs of the Spirit,—"moved," indeed, but not carried outside of themselves nor separated from their own ways and conceptions. It is thus that it regards the Bible as a *living* book; it is warm and vital with the life of a divine humanity, and thus it speaks to humanity. But as it was written by men in other ages and of other habits of speech, it needs to be interpreted; it is necessary to get back into the mind of the writer in order to get at the inspiration of his utterance; for before there is an inspired writing there is an inspired man, through whom only its meaning can be reached. This is a very different process from picking out texts here and there, and putting them together to form a doctrine; yet it is by such a process that systems of theology have been formed, and cast on society for acceptance. The New Theology does not proceed in such a way. The Old Theology reads the Scriptures with a lexicon, and weighs words as men weigh iron; it sees no medium between the form of words and their first or preconceived meaning. It looks into the Bible as one looks through space, beyond the atmosphere, upon the sun,—seeing one point of glowing light, but darkness on every side; one text of burning sense, but no atmosphere of context, or age, or custom, or temper of mind, or end in view. The New Theology does not tolerate the inconsistency of the Old, as it slowly gives up the theory of verbal inspiration, but retains views based on verbal inspiration. It will not remove foundations and prop up the superstructure with assertions.

Another principle is that the Bible, like the order of history, is a continually unfolding revelation of God; it is a book of eternal laws and facts that are evolving their truth and reality in the process of history. Its full meaning is not yet disclosed; it is an ever-opening book. It is always leading man in the right direction, but it does not show him at once, in clear light, the whole domain of truth. It is therefore a book to be constantly and freshly interpreted; it may mean to-morrow more than it means to-day.

3. The New Theology seeks to replace an excessive individuality by a truer view of the solidarity of the race.

It does not deny a real individuality, it does not predicate an absolute solidarity, but simply removes the emphasis from one to the other. It holds that every man must live a life of his own, build himself up into a full personality, and give an account of himself to God: but it also recognizes the blurred truth that man's life lies in its relations; that it is a derived and shared life, that it is carried on and perfected under laws of heredity and of the family and the nation; that while he is "himself alone" he is also a son, a parent, a citizen, and an inseparable part of the human race; that in origin and character and destiny he cannot be regarded as standing in a sharp and utter individuality. It differs from the Old Theology in a more thorough and consistent application of this distinction. That holds to an absolute solidarity in evil, relieved by a doctrine of election of individuals; this holds to a solidarity running throughout the whole life of humanity in the world,—not an absolute solidarity, but one modified by human freedom. It is not disposed wholly to part company with the Old in respect to the "fall in Adam" (when the Scriptures, on this point, are properly interpreted), and hereditary evil, and the like; it sees in these conceptions substantial truths, when freed from their excessiveness and their formal and categorical shapes, but it carries this solidarity into the whole life of man. If it is a fallen world, it is a saved world; the Christ is no less to it than Adam; the divine humanity is no smaller than the Adamic humanity; the Spirit is as powerful and as universal as sin; the links that bind the race to evil are correlated by links equally strong binding it to righteousness. It goes, in a certain manner, with the Old Theology in its views of common evil, but it diverges from it in its conceptions of the redemptive and delivering forces by ascribing to them corresponding sweep. To repeat: it does not admit that Christ is less to the race than Adam, that the Gospel is smaller than evil; it does not consign mankind as a mass to a pit of common depravity, and leave it to emerge as individuals under some notion of election, or by solitary choice, each one escaping as he can and according to his "chance," but the greater part not escaping at all. It does not so read revelation and history and life, finding in them all a corporate element, "a moving altogether when it moves at all,"—an interweaving of life with life that renders it impossible wholly to extricate the individual. It allies itself with the thought of the present age and the best thought of all ages, that mankind is moved by common forces, and follows common tendencies falling and rising together, partakers together in all good and ill desert, verifying the phrase, "the life of humanity." It believes that the Spirit broods over the "evil world" as it brooded upon the chaos of old; that humanity is charged with redemptive forces, wrought into the soul and into the divine institutions of the family and the nation, and whatever other relation binds man to man; and it believes that these forces are not in vain.

4. This theology recognizes a new relation to natural science; but only in the respect that it ignores the long apparent antagonism between the kingdoms of faith and of natural law,—an antagonism that cannot, from the nature of things, have a basis in reality. But while it looks on the external world as a revelation of God and values the truth it may reveal; while even it recognizes in it analogies to the spiritual world and a typical similarity of method, it does not merge itself in natural science. It is not yet ready, and it shows no signs that it ever will be ready, to gather up its beliefs, and go over into the camp of natural science, and sit down under the manipulations of a doctrine of evolution, with its one category of matter and one invariable force. It is not ready to commit itself to a finite system, a merely phenomenal section of the universe and of time, with no *whence*, or *whither*, or *why*,—a system that simply supplies man with a certain kind of knowledge, but solves no problem that weighs on his heart, answers no question that he much cares to ask,

and throws not one glimmer of additional light on his origin, his nature, or his destiny. It accepts gratefully the knowledge it discloses of the material universe, its laws, and its processes; it admits that science has anticipated theology in formulating the method of creation known as evolution, that it has corrected modern theology by suggesting a closer and more vital relation between God and creation, and so has helped it throw off a mechanical theory and regain its forgotten theory of the divine immanence in creation. But farther than this it does not propose to go, for the simple reason that it is the end of its journey in that direction. The New Theology, like the old, refuses to merge itself in a system that is both material and finite, and therefore incapable of a moral and spiritual conception. It denies that the universe can be put into one category, that matter is inclusive of the spiritual, or what is deemed spiritual; it denies that the material world is the only field of knowledge, and that its force is the only force acting in the world. It asserts the reality of the spiritual as above the material, of force that is other than that lodged in matter, of truth realized in another way than by induction from material facts, however fine their gradation, of an eternal existence and a human self-consciousness correlated in mutual knowledge and freedom and power. It makes these assertions on scientific grounds and as inductions from phenomena, and therefore claims for itself the possession of knowledge that is such in reality.

5. The New Theology offers a contrast to the Old in claiming for itself a wider study of man.

It is the characteristic fault of the Old Theology that it touches human life as a sphere touches a plane,—at one point only; as in the doctrine of divine sovereignty, the whole being of God resting on man in that one truth. The New Theology would present them as plane resting on plane,—the whole of God in contact with the whole of man. It thus allies itself not only with the Scriptures, and with philosophy and science and human consciousness, but it awakens a sense of *reality*, the securing of which lies at the basis of the Incarnation,— the divine life made a human life, the Son of man eating and drinking, a *living* way, that is, a way lived out in very fact in all the processes of human life, and so leading to eternal life.

This full and direct look at humanity induces what may be called the ethical habit of thought. The New Theology seeks to recover spiritual processes from a magical to a moral conception. It insists that these processes and facts are governed and shaped by the eternal laws of morality. It would have a moral God, a divine government truly moral, a moral atonement, and not one involving essential injustice, nor clouded with mysteries that put it outside of human use; an atonement resting on God's heart, and calling into play the known laws and sentiments of human nature, and not one constructed out of a mechanical legality; an atonement that saves men by a traceable process, and not one that is contrived to explain problems that may safely be left with God; an atonement that secures oneness with the Christ, and not one framed to buttress some scheme of divine government constructed out of human elements. It regards faith as a moral act, a direct acceptance and laying hold of God in trusting obedience, a simple and rational process; and it opposes the view which regards it as simply a belief that an atonement has been made, a holy life being merely its proper adjunct. It would make faith an actual entering into and fellowship with the life of the Christ, and the individual's justification by faith the actual realization and consequent of this oneness. It does not differ essentially from the Old Theology in its treatment of regeneration, but it broadens the ground of it, finding its necessity not only in sin, but in the undeveloped nature of man, or in the flesh. It is disposed also to regard it as a process, involving known laws and analogies, and to divest it of that air of magical mystery in which it has been held; a plain and simple matter, by which one gets out of the lower world into the higher by the Spirit of God.

6. The New Theology recognizes the necessity of a restatement of belief in Eschatology, or the doctrine of Last Things.

It is not alone in this respect; it is the position of nearly every school and organ of theological thought. The New Version compels it, the thought of the age demands it. But while there are enough who urge the necessity, whenever a champion appears in the lists he receives but a cold welcome from those who summoned him. The New Theology recognizes the necessity, but its work is not summed up in meeting this need. In the popular conception it is identified with mere criticism of existing views of everlasting punishment. No mistake could be greater; still, seeing the necessity in common with others, it does not withhold itself from the subject, and if its essays, though largely negative and tentative, are met by contradiction and ecclesiastical censure, it does not stay its hand nor heed the clamor. "Truth hath a quiet breast."

First, and broadly, the New Theology does not propound any new doctrine relative to future eternal salvation or eternal punishment. It is popularly supposed to concern itself chiefly with the future condition of men, but it rather draws away from such a field. It is less assertive here than in any other region of theological thought. It is, however, critical of the Old Theology, deeming it to be wise above what is written and out of line with the logic of the Faith; but it does not follow it into the future existence, with denials that imply a statement of the contrary, nor with positive assertions of its own. And the reason is that it transfers, to a large extent, the scene of the action of the truths pertaining to the subject from the future world conceived as a world of time and space to a world above time and not set in dimensions of space. In briefer phrase, it does not regard the *future* world as identical with the *eternal* world. Hence, its constructions on the subject turn largely on the word "eternal," which it does not regard wholly as a time-word, but as a word of moral and spiritual significance; it has little to do with time, but rather has to do with things that are above time; there is no more and no other relation between time and eternity in the future world than there is in the present world. This conception of the word does not necessarily imply that eternal punishment will not be everlasting; only, if that belief is entertained, it does not rest on this word, but is to be based on other grounds. And the battle waged over it is due simply to the mistaken anxiety of one side lest it shall be robbed of a text. But this rendering of the word does not antagonize the doctrine it has been held to teach; it simply separates it from the doctrine.

Such are some of the features of this fresh movement in the realm of theology, for it can scarcely be called more than a movement, an advance to meet the unfolding revelation of God. It is not an organization, it is little aggressive, it does not herald itself with any Lo here or Lo there, it does not crowd itself upon the thought of the age, it is not keyed to such methods. It has no word of contempt for those who linger in ways it has ceased to walk in; it has no sympathy with those who have forsaken the one way. It does not destroy foundations, nor sap faith, nor weaken motives; it does not reduce the proportions of evil nor dim the glory of righteousness; it does not chill the enthusiasm of faith, nor hold it back from its mightiest effort of sacrifice. It seeks no conquest represented in outward form, but is content to add its thought to the growing thought of the world, and, if it speaks, content to speak to those who have ears to hear. It makes no haste, it seeks no revolution, but simply holds itself open and receptive under the breathing of the Spirit that has come, and is ever coming, into the world; passive, yet quick to respond to the heavenly visions that do not cease to break upon the darkened eyes of humanity.

THE SOCIAL GOSPEL

[22]
Russell H. Conwell
Acres of Diamonds*

As I come here to-night and look around this audience I am seeing again what through these fifty years I have continually seen—men that are making precisely that same mistake. I often wish I could see the younger people, and would that the Academy had been filled to-night with our high-school scholars and our grammar-school scholars, that I could have them to talk to. While I would have preferred such an audience as that, because they are most susceptible, as they have not grown up into their prejudices as we have, they have not gotten into any custom that they cannot break, they have not met with any failures as we have; and while I could perhaps do such an audience as that more good than I can do grownup people, yet I will do the best I can with the material I have. I say to you that you have "acres of diamonds" in Philadelphia right where you now live. "Oh," but you will say, "you cannot know much about your city if you think there are any 'acres of diamonds' here."

I was greatly interested in that account in the newspaper of the young man who found that diamond in North Carolina. It was one of the purest diamonds that has ever been discovered, and it has several predecessors near the same locality. I went to a distinguished professor in mineralogy and

* Russell H. Conwell, *Acres of Diamonds* (New York, 1915), pp. 15–25; 29. This lecture was delivered many times and there is no standard text.

asked him where he thought those diamonds came from. The professor secured the map of the geologic formations of our continent, and traced it. He said it went either through the underlying carboniferous strata adapted for such production, westward through Ohio and the Mississippi, or in more probability came eastward through Virginia and up the shore of the Atlantic Ocean. It is a fact that the diamonds were there, for they have been discovered and sold; and that they were carried down there during the drift period, from some northern locality. Now who can say but some person going down with his drill in Philadelphia will find some trace of a diamond-mine yet down here? Oh, friends! you cannot say that you are not over one of the greatest diamond-mines in the world, for such a diamond as that only comes from the most profitable mines that are found on earth.

But it serves simply to illustrate my thought, which I emphasize by saying if you do not have the actual diamond-mines literally you have all that they would be good for to you. Because now that the Queen of England has given the greatest compliment ever conferred upon American woman for her attire because she did not appear with any jewels at all at the late reception in England, it has almost done away with the use of diamonds anyhow. All you would care for would be the few you would wear if you wish to be modest, and the rest you would sell for money.

Now then, I say again that the opportunity to get rich, to attain unto great wealth, is here in Philadelphia now, within the reach of almost every man and woman who hears me speak to-night, and I mean just what I say. I have not come to this platform even under these circumstances to recite something to you. I have come to tell you what in God's sight I believe to be the truth, and if the years of life have been of any value to me in the attainment of common sense, I know I am right; that the men and women sitting here, who found it difficult perhaps to buy a ticket to this lecture or gathering to-night, have within their reach "acres of diamonds," opportunities to get largely wealthy. There never was a place on earth more adapted than the city of Philadelphia to-day, and never in the history of the world did a poor man without capital have such an opportunity to get rich quickly and honestly as he has now in our city. I say it is the truth, and I want you to accept it as such; for if you think I have come to simply recite something, then I would better not be here. I have no time to waste in any such talk, but to say the things I believe, and unless some of you get richer for what I am saying to-night my time is wasted.

I say that you ought to get rich, and it is your duty to get rich. How many of my pious brethren say to me, "Do you, a Christian minister, spend your time going up and down the country advising young people to get rich, to get money?" "Yes, of course I do." They say, "Isn't that awful! Why don't you preach the gospel instead of preaching about man's making money?" "Because to make money honestly is to preach the gospel." That is the reason. The men who get rich may be the most honest men you find in the community.

"Oh," but says some young man here to-night, "I have been told all my life that if a person has money he is very dishonest and dishonorable and mean and contemptible." My friend, that is the reason why you have none, because you have the wrong idea of people. The foundation of your faith is altogether false. Let me say here clearly, and say it briefly, though subject to discussion which I have not time for here, ninety-eight out of one hundred of the rich men of America are honest. That is why they are rich. That is why they are trusted with money. That is why they carry on great enterprises and find plenty of people to work with them. It is because they are honest men.

Says another young man, "I hear sometimes of men that get millions of dollars dishonestly." Yes, of course you do, and so do I. But they are so rare a thing in fact that the newspapers talk about them all the time as a matter of news until you get the idea that all the other rich men got rich dishonestly.

My friend, you take and drive me—if you furnish the auto—out into the suburbs of Philadelphia, and introduce me to the people who own their homes around this great city, those beautiful homes with gardens and flowers, those magnificent homes so lovely in their art, and I will introduce you to the very best people in character as well as in enterprise in our city, and you know I will. A man is not really a true man until he owns his own home, and they that own their homes are made more honorable and honest and pure, and true and economical and careful, by owning the home.

For a man to have money, even in large sums, is not an inconsistent thing. We preach against covetousness, and you know we do, in the pulpit, and oftentimes preach against it so long and use the terms about "filthy lucre" so extremely that Christians get the idea that when we stand in the pulpit we believe it is wicked for any man to have money—until the collection-basket goes around, and then we almost swear at the people because they don't give more money. Oh, the inconsistency of such doctrines as that!

Money is power, and you ought to be reasonably ambitious to have it. You ought because you can do more good with it than you could without it. Money printed your Bible, money builds your churches, money sends your missionaries, and money pays your preachers, and you would not have many of them, either, if you did not pay them. I am always willing that my church should raise my salary, because the church that pays the largest salary always raises it the easiest. You never knew an exception to it in your life. The man who gets the largest salary can do the most good with the power that is furnished to him. Of course he can if his spirit be right to use it for what it is given to him.

I say, then, you ought to have money. If you can honestly attain unto riches in Philadelphia, it is your Christian and godly duty to do so. It is an awful mistake of these pious people to think you must be awfully poor in order to be pious.

Some men say, "Don't you sympathize with the poor people?" Of course I do, or else I would not have been lecturing these years. I won't give in I admit, but what I sympathize with the poor, but the number of poor who are to be sympathized with is very small. To sympathize with a man whom God has punished for his sins, thus to help him when God would still continue a just punishment, is to do wrong, no doubt about it, and we do that more than we help those who are deserving. While we should sympathize with God's poor —that is, those who cannot help themselves—let us remember there is not a poor person in the United States who was not made poor by his own shortcomings, or by the shortcomings of some one else. It is all wrong to be poor anyhow. Let us give in to that argument and pass that to one side.

A gentleman gets up back there, and says, "Don't you think there are some things in this world that are better than money?" Of course I do, but I am talking about money now. Of course there are some things higher than money. Oh yes, I know by the grave that has left me standing alone that there are some things in this world that are higher and sweeter and purer than money. Well do I know there are some things higher and grander than gold. Love is the grandest thing on God's earth, but fortunate the lover who has plenty of money. Money is power, money is force, money will do good as well as harm. In the hands of good men and women it could accomplish, and it has accomplished, good.

I hate to leave that behind me. I heard a man get up in a prayer-meeting in our city and thank the Lord he was "one of God's poor." Well, I wonder what his wife thinks about that? She earns all the money that comes into that house, and he smokes a part of that on the veranda. I don't want to see any more of the Lord's poor of that kind, and I don't believe the Lord does. And yet there are some people who think in order to be pious you must be awfully poor and awfully dirty. That does not follow at all. While we sympathize with the poor, let us not teach a doctrine like that.

Yet the age is prejudiced against advising a Christian man (or, as a Jew would say, a godly man) from attaining unto wealth. The prejudice is so universal and the years are far enough back, I think, for me to safely mention that years ago up at Temple University there was a young man in our theological school who thought he was the only pious student in that department. He came into my office one evening and sat down by my desk, and said to me: "Mr. President, I think it is my duty sir, to come in and labor with you." "What has happened now?" Said he, "I heard you say at the Acad-

emy, at the Peirce School commencement, that you thought
it was an honorable ambition for a young man to desire to
have wealth, and that you thought it made him temperate,
made him anxious to have a good name, and made him in-
dustrious. You spoke about man's ambition to have money
helping to make him a good man. Sir, I have come to tell
you the Holy Bible says that 'money is the root of all evil.' "

I told him I had never seen it in the Bible, and advised
him to go out into the chapel and get the Bible, and show
me the place. So out he went for the Bible, and soon he
stalked into my office with the Bible open, with all the bigoted
pride of the narrow sectarian, or of one who founds his Christianity on some misinterpretation of Scripture. He flung the
Bible down on my desk, and fairly squealed into my ear:
"There it is, Mr. President; you can read it for yourself." I
said to him: "Well, young man, you will learn when you get a
little older that you cannot trust another denomination to read
the Bible for you. You belong to another denomination. You
are taught in the theological school, however, that emphasis
is exegesis. Now, will you take that Bible and read it yourself,
and give the proper emphasis to it?"

He took the Bible, and proudly read, " 'The love of
money is the root of all evil.' "

Then he had it right, and when one does quote aright
from that same old Book he quotes the absolute truth. I have
lived through fifty years of the mightiest battle that old Book
has ever fought, and I have lived to see its banners flying free;
for never in the history of this world did the great minds
of earth so universally agree that the Bible is true—all true—
as they do at this very hour.

So I say that when he quoted right, of course he quoted
the absolute truth. "The love of money is the root of all
evil." He who tries to attain unto it too quickly, or dishonestly, will fall into many snares, no doubt about that. The
love of money. What is that? It is making an idol of money,
and idolatry pure and simple everywhere is condemned by
the Holy Scriptures and by man's common sense. The man
that worships the dollar instead of thinking of the purposes
for which it ought to be used, the man who idolizes simply

money, the miser that hordes his money in the cellar, or hides it in his stocking, or refuses to invest it where it will do the world good, that man who hugs the dollar until the eagle squeals has in him the root of all evil.

I think I will leave that behind me now and answer the question of nearly all of you who are asking, "Is there opportunity to get rich in Philadelphia?" Well, now, how simple a thing it is to see where it is, and the instant you see where it is it is yours. Some old gentleman gets up back there and says, "Mr. Conwell, have you lived in Philadelphia for thirty-one years and don't know that the time has gone by when you can make anything in this city?" "No, I don't think it is." "Yes, it is; I have tried it." "What business are you in?" "I kept a store here for twenty years, and never made over a thousand dollars in the whole twenty years."

"Well, then, you can measure the good you have been to this city by what this city has paid you, because a man can judge very well what he is worth by what he receives; that is, in what he is to the world at this time. If you have not made over a thousand dollars in twenty years in Philadelphia, it would have been better for Philadelphia if they had kicked you out of the city nineteen years and nine months ago. A man has no right to keep a store in Philadelphia twenty years and not make at least five hundred thousand dollars, even though it be a corner grocery up-town." You say, "You cannot make five thousand dollars in a store now." Oh, my friends, if you will just take only four blocks around you, and find out what the people want and what you ought to supply and set them down with your pencil, and figure up the profits you would make if you did supply them, you would very soon see it. There is wealth right within the sound of your voice.

. . . . To be great at all one must be great here, now, in Philadelphia. He who can give to this city better streets and better sidewalks, better schools and more colleges, more happiness and more civilization, more of God, he will be great anywhere. Let every man or woman here, if you never hear me again, remember this, that if you wish to be great at all, you must begin where you are and what you are, in Philadelphia, now. He that can give to his city any blessing, he who can be a good citizen while he lives here, he that can make better homes, he that can be a blessing whether he works in the shop or sits behind the counter or keeps house, whatever be his life, he who would be great anywhere must first be great in his own Philadelphia.

[23]

Walter Rauschenbusch
The Social Aims of Jesus*

Jesus began his preaching with the call: "The time is fulfilled; the kingdom of God is now close at hand; repent and believe in the glad news." The kingdom of God continued to be the centre of all his teaching as recorded by the synoptic gospels. His parables, his moral instructions, and his prophetic predictions all bear on that.

We have no definition of what he meant by the phrase. His audience needed no definition. It was then a familiar conception and phrase. The new thing was simply that this kingdom was at last on the point of coming.

We are not all in that situation to-day. Any one who has tried to grasp the idea will have realized how vague and elusive it seems. It stands to-day for quite a catalogue of ideas. To the ordinary reader of the Bible, "inheriting the kingdom of heaven" simply means being saved and going to heaven. For others it means the millennium. For some the organized Church; for others "the invisible Church." For the mystic it means the hidden life with God. The truth is that the idea in the sense in which Jesus and his audiences understood it almost completely passed out of Christian thought as soon as Christianity passed from the Jewish people and

* Walter Rauschenbusch, *Christianity and the Social Crisis* (New York: 1907), pp. 54–68; 70–71.

found its spiritual home within the great Graeco-Roman world. The historical basis for the idea was wanting there. The phrase was taken along, just as an emigrant will carry a water-jar with him; but the water from the well of Bethlehem evaporated and it was now used to dip water from the wells of Ephesus or from the Nile and Tiber. The Greek world cherished no such national religious hope as the prophets had ingrained in Jewish thought; on the other hand it was intensely interested in the future life for the individual, and in the ascetic triumph over flesh and matter. Thus the idea which had been the centre of Christ's thought was not at all the centre of the Church's thought, and even the comprehension of his meaning was lost and overlaid. Only some remnants of it persisted in the millennial hope and in the organic conception of the Church.

The historical study of our own day has made the first thorough attempt to understand this fundamental thought of Jesus in the sense in which he used it, but the results of this investigation are not at all completed. There are a hundred critical difficulties in the way of a sure and consistent interpretation that would be acceptable to all investigators. The limits of space and the purpose of this book will not permit me to do justice to the conflicting views. I shall have to set down my own results with only an occasional reference to the difficulties that beset them.

We saw in the previous chapter that the hope of the Jewish people underwent changes in the course of its history. It took a wider and more universal outlook as the political horizon of the people widened. It became more individual in its blessings. It grew more transcendent, more purely future, more apocalyptic and detached from present events, as the people were deprived of their political autonomy and health. Moreover it was variously understood by the different classes and persons that held it. Because this hope was so comprehensive and all-embracing, every man could select and emphasize that aspect which appealed to him. Some thought chiefly of the expulsion of the Roman power with its despotic officials, its tax-extorters, and its hated symbols. Others dwelt on the complete obedience to the Law which would prevail when all the apostates were cast out and all true Israelites gathered to their own. And some quiet religious souls hoped for a great outflow of grace from God and a revival of true piety; as the hymn of Zacharias expresses it: "that we, being delivered out of the hand of our enemies, should serve him without fear, in holiness and righteousness before him all our days." But even in this spiritual ideal the deliverance from the national enemies was a condition of a holy life for the nation. Whatever aspect any man emphasized, it was still a national and collective idea. It involved the restoration of Israel as a nation to outward independence, security, and power, such as it had under the Davidic kings. It involved that social justice, prosperity, and happiness for which the Law and the prophets called, and for which the common people always long. It involved that religious purity and holiness of which the nation had always fallen short. And all this was to come in an ideal degree, such as God alone by direct intervention could bestow.

When Jesus used the phrase "the kingdom of God," it inevitably evoked that whole sphere of thought in the minds of his hearers. If he did not mean by it the substance of what they meant by it, it was a mistake to use the term. If he did not mean the consummation of the theocratic hope, but merely an internal blessedness for individuals with the hope of getting to heaven, why did he use the words around which all the collective hopes clustered? In that case it was not only a misleading but a dangerous phrase. It unfettered the political hopes of the crowd; it drew down on him the suspicion of the government; it actually led to his death.

Unless we have clear proof to the contrary, we must assume that in the main the words meant the same thing to him and to his audiences. But it is very possible that he seriously modified and corrected the popular conception. That is in fact the process with every great, creative religious mind: the connection with the past is maintained and the old terms are used, but they are set in new connections and filled with new qualities. In the teaching of Jesus we find that he consciously opposed some features of the popular hope and sought to make it truer.

For one thing he would have nothing to do with bloodshed and violence. When the crowds that were on their way to the Passover gathered around him in the solitude on the Eastern shore of the lake and wanted to make him king and march on the capital, he eluded them by sending his inflammable disciples away in the boat, and himself going up among the rocks to pray till the darkness dispersed the crowd. Alliance with the Messianic force-revolution was one of the temptations which he confronted at the outset and repudiated; he would not set up God's kingdom by using the devil's means of hatred and blood. With the glorious idealism of faith and love Jesus threw away the sword and advanced on the intrenchments of wrong with hand outstretched and heart exposed.

He repudiated not only human violence, he even put aside the force which the common hope expected from heaven. He refused to summon the twelve legions of angels either to save his life or to set up the kingdom by slaying the wicked. John the Baptist had expected the activity of the Messiah to begin with the judgment. The fruitless tree would be hewn down; the chaff would be winnowed out and burned; and there was barely time to escape this. Jesus felt no call to that sort of Messiahship. He reversed the programme; the judgment would come at the end and not at the beginning. First the blade, then the ear, and then the full corn in the ear, and at the very last the harvest. Only at the end would the tares be collected; only when the net got to shore would the good fish be separated from the useless creatures of the sea. Thus the divine *finale* of the judgment was relegated to the distance; the only task calling for present action was to sow the seed.

The popular hope was all for a divine catastrophe. The kingdom of God was to come by a beneficient earthquake. Some day it would come like the blaze of a meteor, "with outward observation," and they could say: "Lo, there it is!" We have seen that the prophetic hope had become catastrophic and apocalyptic when the capacity for political self-help was paralyzed. When the nation was pinned down helplessly by the crushing weight of the oppressors, it had to

believe in a divine catastrophe that bore no causal relation to
human action. The higher spiritual insight of Jesus reverted
to the earlier and nobler prophetic view that the future was
to grow out of the present by divine help. While they were
waiting for the Messianic cataclysm that would bring the
kingdom of God ready-made from heaven, he saw it growing
up among them. He took his illustrations of its coming from
organic life. It was like the seed scattered by the peasant,
growing slowly and silently, night and day, by its own ger-
minating force and the food furnished by the earth. The
people had the impatience of the uneducated mind which
does not see processes, but clamors for results, big, thun-
derous, miraculous results. Jesus had the scientific insight
which comes to most men only by training, but to the elect
few by divine gift. He grasped the substance of that law of
organic development in nature and history which our own
day at last has begun to elaborate systematically. His parables of the sower, the tares, the net, the mustard-seed, and
the leaven are all polemical in character. He was seeking to
displace the crude and misleading catastrophic conceptions
by a saner theory about the coming of the kingdom. This
conception of growth demanded not only a finer insight, but
a higher faith. It takes more faith to see God in the little
beginnings than in the completed results; more faith to say
that God is now working than to say that he will some day
work.

Because Jesus believed in the organic growth of the new
society, he patiently fostered its growth, cell by cell. Every
human life brought under control of the new spirit which he
himself embodied and revealed was an advance of the kingdom of God. Every time the new thought of the Father and
of the right life among men gained firmer hold of a human
mind and brought it to the point of action, it meant
progress. It is just as when human tissues have been broken
down by disease or external force, and new tissue is silently
forming under the old and weaving a new web of life. Jesus
incarnated a new type of human life and he was conscious
of that. By living with men and thinking and feeling in their
presence, he reproduced his own life in others and they

gained faith to risk this new way of living. This process of assimilation went on by the natural capacities inherent in the social organism, just as fresh blood will flow along the established arteries and capillaries. When a nucleus of like-minded men was gathered about him, the assimilating power was greatly reenforced. Jesus joyously felt that the most insignificant man in his company who shared in this new social spirit was superior to the grandest exemplification of the old era, John the Baptist. Thus Jesus worked on individuals and through individuals, but his real end was not individualistic, but social, and in his method he employed strong social forces. He knew that a new view of life would have to be implanted before the new life could be lived and that the new society would have to nucleate around personal centres of renewal. But his end was not the new soul, but the new society; not man, but Man.

The popular hope was a Jewish national hope. Under the hands of Jesus it became human and therefore universal. John the Baptist had contradicted the idea that a Jew was entitled to participation in the good time coming by virtue of his national descent. Every time Jesus met a Gentile, we can see the Jewish prejudices melt away and he gladly discovered the human brotherhood and spiritual capacity in the alien. "Verily I say unto you, I have not found so great faith, no, not in Israel," and he immediately makes room at the Messianic table-round for those who shall come from the east and the west to sit down with the patriarchs, while the sons of the kingdom, the Jews who were properly entitled to it, would be cast out. He reminded the indignant audience at Nazareth that the great Elijah had found his refuge with a heathen Phœnician and Elisha had healed only a Syrian leper. When one leper out of ten thanked him, he took pains to point out that this one was a Samaritan foreigner, and when he wanted to hold up a model of human neighborliness, he went out of his way to make him a Samaritan, an alien, and a heretic. Thus the old division of humanity into Jews and Gentiles began to fade out in his mind, and a new dividing line ran between the good and the evil, between those who opened their heart to the new life and those who closed it. He approached the bold cosmopolitanism of Paul, that "in Christ Jesus there is neither Jew nor Greek." But as soon as religion was thus based, not on national prerogatives, but on human needs and capacities, the kingdom of God became universal in scope, an affair of all humanity. This was a modification of immense importance.

Another subtle and significant change in the conception of the kingdom came through the combination of all these changes. If the kingdom was not dependent on human force nor on divine catastrophes, but could quietly grow by organic processes; if it was not dependent on national reconstruction, but could work along from man to man, from group to group, creating a new life as it went along; then the kingdom in one sense was already here. Its consummation, of course, was in the future, but its fundamental realities were already present.

This is the point on which scholars are most at odds. Was the kingdom in Christ's conception something eschatological, all in the future, to be inaugurated only by a heavenly catastrophe? Or was it a present reality? There is material for both views in his sayings. It is important here to remember that the sayings of Jesus were handed down by oral repetition among Christians for thirty or forty years before they were recorded in our gospels. But any one can test for himself the fact that with the best intentions of veracity, a message or story changes a little when it passes from one mind to another, or even when it is repeated often by the same man. Something of his tastes and presuppositions flows into it. Unless we assume an absolute divine prevention of any such change, we must allow that it is wholly probable that the Church which told and retold the sayings of Jesus insensibly moulded them by its own ideas and hopes. And if that is true, then no part of the sayings of Christ would be so sure to be affected as his sayings about his return and the final consummation of the kingdom. That was the hottest part of the faith of the primitive Church and anything coming in contact with it would run fluid. But any modifications on this question would all be likely to be in the direction of the catastrophic hope. That was the form of the Jewish hope before Christ touched it; he certainly did not succeed in weaning his disciples from it; it was the form most congenial to cruder minds; it chimed best with the fervid impatience of the earliest days; its prevalence is attested by the wide circulation of the Jewish apocalyptic literature among Christians. It is thus exceedingly probable that the Church spilled a little of the lurid colors of its own apocalypticism over the loftier conceptions of its Master, and when we read his sayings to-day, we must allow for that and be on the watch against it.

Like the old prophets, Jesus believed that God was the real creator of the kingdom; it was not to be set up by man-made evolution. It is one of the axioms of religious faith to believe that. He certainly believed in a divine consummation at the close. But the more he believed in the supreme value of its spiritual and moral blessings, and in the power of spiritual forces to mould human life, the more would the final act of consummation recede in importance and the present facts and processes grow more concrete and important to his mind. It was an act of religious faith for John the Baptist to assert that the long-desired kingdom was almost here. It was a vastly higher act of faith for Jesus to say that it was actually here. Others were scanning the horizon with the telescope to see it come; he said, "It is already here, right in the midst of you." Any one who reversed the direction of his life and became as a child could enter into it. Any one who saw that love to God and man was more than the whole sacrificial ritual was not far from the kingdom. The healing power going out to the demonized was proof that a stronger one had come upon the lord of this world and was stripping him of his property, and that the kingdom was already come upon them. Thus the future tense was changing to the present tense under the power of faith and insight into spiritual realities. In the gospel and epistle of John we have a confirmation of this translation of the future tense into the present. The expected antichrist is already here; the judgment is now quietly going on; the most important part of the resurrection is taking place now. The discourse about the future coming of the Lord in the Synoptists is replaced in John by the discourse about the immediate coming of the Comforter.

This, then, is our interpretation of the situation. Jesus, like all the prophets and like all his spiritually minded countrymen, lived in the hope of a great transformation of the national, social, and religious life about him. He shared the substance of that hope with his people, but by his profounder insight and his loftier faith he elevated and transformed the common hope. He rejected all violent means and thereby transferred the inevitable conflict from the field of battle to the antagonism of mind against mind, and of heart against lack of heart. He postponed the divine catastrophe of judgment to the dim distance and put the emphasis on the growth of the new life that was now going on. He thought less of changes made *en masse*, and more of the immediate transformation of single centres of influence and of social nuclei. The Jewish hope became a human hope with universal scope. The old intent gaze into the future was turned to faith in present realities and beginnings, and found its task here and now.

All the teaching of Jesus and all his thinking centred about the hope of the kingdom of God. His moral teachings get their real meaning only when viewed from that centre. He was not a Greek philosopher or Hindu pundit teaching the individual the way of emancipation from the world and its passions, but a Hebrew prophet preparing men for the righteous social order. The goodness which he sought to create in men was always the goodness that would enable them to live rightly with their fellow-men and to constitute a true social life.

All human goodness must be social goodness. Man is fundamentally gregarious and his morality consists in being a good member of his community. A man is moral when he is social; he is immoral when he is anti-social. The highest type of goodness is that which puts freely at the service of the community all that a man is and can. The highest type of badness is that which uses up the wealth and happiness and virtue of the community to please self. All this ought to go without saying, but in fact religious ethics in the past has largely spent its force in detaching men from their community, from marriage and property, from interest in political and social tasks.

The fundamental virtue in the ethics of Jesus was love, because love is the society-making quality. Human life originates in love. It is love that holds together the basal human organization, the family. The physical expression of all love and friendship is the desire to get together and be together. Love creates fellowship. In the measure in which love increases in any social organism, it will hold together without coercion. If physical coercion is constantly necessary, it is proof that the social organization has not evoked the power of human affection and fraternity.

Pride disrupts society. Love equalizes. Humility freely takes its place as a simple member of the community. When Jesus found the disciples disputing about their rank in the kingdom, he rebuked their divisive spirit of pride by setting a little child among them as their model; for an unspoiled child is the most social creature, swift to make friends, happy in play with others, lonely without human love. When Jesus overheard the disciples quarrelling about the chief places at the last meal, he gave them a striking object lesson in the subordination of self to the service of the community, by washing their dusty sandalled feet.

All these acts and sayings receive their real meaning when we think of them in connection with the kingdom of God, the ideal human society to be established. Instead of a society resting on coercion, exploitation, and inequality, Jesus desired to found a society resting on love, service, and equality. These new principles were so much the essence of his character and of his view of life, that he lived them out spontaneously and taught them in everything that he touched in his conversations or public addresses. God is a father; men are neighbors and brothers; let them act accordingly. Let them love, and then life will be true and good. Let them seek the kingdom, and all things would follow. Under no circumstance let them suffer fellowship to be permanently disrupted. If an individual or a class was outside of fraternal relations, he set himself to heal the breach. The kingdom of God is the

true human society; the ethics of Jesus taught the true social
conduct which would create the true society. This would be
Christ's test for any custom, law, or institution: does it draw
men together or divide them?

[24]

Washington Gladden

The Church and the Social Crisis*

. . . It is idle, it is fatuous, to hide from ourselves the fact
that we are facing, here in the United States of America, a
social crisis. The forces which are at work here—the forces
whose operation I have been pointing out—mean destruction.
The tendencies which have been gathering strength since the
Civil War—the tendencies to the accumulation of power in
the hands of a few; the tendencies to use this power preda-
ceously; the tendencies to boundless luxury and extravagance;
the tendencies to the separation and the antagonism of social
classes—must be arrested and that speedily, or we shall soon
be in chaos. A social order which makes possible the rise of
a Harriman or a Rockefeller is a social order which cannot
long endure. These swollen fortunes that many are gloating
over are symptoms of disease; they are tumors, wens, goiters;
the bigger they are the deadlier. They are not the reward of
social service; they are the fruit of plunder. We have made
them possible only by permitting the gate of opportunity to
be made narrower and the burden of toil more unrequiting
for millions of the poor. They exist only because by our acts
we approve or by our indifference we consent to monumental
injustice. A society which tolerates such conditions cannot live.

It is because we have begun to have some dim conception of this truth that we are moving, now, toward the

* From Washington Gladden, *The Church and the Social Crisis*
(Boston, 1907), pp. 19–36; 41–42.

correction, by law, of these grave injustices. We must exterminate them; that is the fight in which there must be no faltering. If we would not be destroyed, we must destroy the destroyers. This is the truth which our brave President, by word and deed, is always enforcing upon us, and he is entirely and everlastingly right about it. He means that the law shall do all that law can do to prevent and punish the rapacity of the strong. He means that our democracy shall not harbor subtle and cryptic tyrannies, forms of robbery with webs like gossamer, that drop on us out of the dark, and entangle us when we are asleep; impalpable spoliations that drain away our earnings in driblets and leave us not only poor but ignorant of what has impoverished us. These are the arts by which swollen fortunes are heaped up in these days, and our President is bound to put an end to them. He means that the gate of opportunity shall not be shut; that the ways of freedom shall be kept clear for the climbing feet of the high and the lowly. If he has any worse purpose than this he has well concealed it, and though there are many who hate him and malign him, those to whom justice is dearer than policy and courage than finesse honor him and trust him and thank God for him.

Everything that law can do to restrain and extirpate these unsocial forces must be done—this is President Roosevelt's policy, and I trust we are all with him in it. The least we can do to save this country from destruction is to enforce with all rigor the law which punishes every kind of robbery and extortion, and especially those artistic schemes of plunder by which our plutocracy has been created. But after President Roosevelt and those who now stand with him and who may come after him have done all that law can do to extirpate these social injustices, I greatly fear that their roots will be found imbedded in the soil and their sprouts springing up right and left and growing amain. Law can do something, but there is a great deal that it cannot do, because, as Paul says, it is weak through the flesh. It deals only with the external act, it cannot touch the inward motive. What our social order most needs is not more and better laws, nor a more rigorous enforcement of law; it needs to be permeated by a better morality; to have its whole conception of the meaning and purpose of life revolutionized. The trouble with this social order of ours is not a matter of forms and methods; its ruling ideas are wrong ideas. Ever since we got rid of absolutism and feudalism and paternalism we have been trying to build our civilization on the basis of moral individualism. Self-interest has been recognized as the regulative principle of the social organism. All our laws, all our civic and industrial organizations, have been based on this principle. That self-love is the mainspring of human action, and that all rules of conduct must be adjusted to this as the supreme controlling motive, has been the assumption of all our political and practical philosophy. We have not denied the existence of good-will and kindness, but we have contended that these were minor and subordinate forces; that no reliance could be placed on them as regulative principles of human action; that society was rightly organized by giving practically unrestricted play to the working of self-interest. In the family, of course, and to some extent in the church, we have recognized the supremacy of altruistic motives, and we have set them free in our philanthropies; but these are lesser interests; in all the central, masterful, absorbing affairs of life, in industry, traffic, politics, the spheres in which by far the largest part of our activities find exercise, we have insisted on enthroning the principle of self-interest.

That this principle had not worked very well through the old days of absolutism and aristocratic feudalism we could see; but we laid that failure to the monarchs and the aristocrats. When one man behaved selfishly, there was trouble, that was evident; but there was a fond hope that when all men had free rein to be as selfish as they chose, all would be well. Our notion was that when all political yokes were broken and democracy came to its own, the principle of "every man for himself" would give us universal welfare. We have had, now, a few generations of democracy, long enough to test the operation of this principle. The phenomena upon which we have been looking give us the result. Here, on this broad continent, with every vestige of political privilege swept away, under a pure democracy, such social conditions as those which we have been considering have been developed. Inequalities of the most glaring sort, oppressions that are continental in their reach, a race of plunderers more powerful and more cunning than ever before appeared in history, with great lawyers to aid them in their predatory schemes; a reign of debilitating luxury that would put to the blush the Romans of the decadence, and, as the fruit of the tree, misery and poverty at the other end of the social scale, and deadly class hatreds steadily deepening, and threatening revolution—this is the logical, natural, inevitable outcome of the moral individualism on which we have been trying to build society. Instead of its being true that democracy will transfigure egoism, we have found that no form of society can march hellward faster than a democracy under the banner of unbridled individualism.

That, past all doubt, is the way we have been going. That, and nothing else, has precipitated the social crisis which we are confronting. You will hear a great many other explanations of it, but they are all superficial; the bottom trouble with it all is that we have been trying to found a social order on selfishness. The word to be spoken to this industrial and social order of ours is the word that John the Baptist spoke, and that Jesus caught from his lips and repeated: "Repent! Change your minds! Your idea of what life means is fundamentally wrong. You are building your whole civilization on a false basis. You imagine that human beings can live together usefully and happily when every man lives for himself. You cannot live together in that way. You will simply devour one another. The weak will always be the prey of the strong. You will have strife, confusion, misery as your perpetual portion.

"You were made to share in one another's good, to be helpers, one of another; not to strive and fight but to coöperate. It is not that you are to neglect your own interests in promoting your neighbors'; simply to identify yourselves in interest with your neighbors; to love your neighbors, not better than yourselves, but *as* yourselves. This law of goodwill, which is simply the law of justice, nothing more, will bring peace and welfare to all."

Such was the challenge of Jesus Christ to the social order which he found existing, which was, in its fundamental principles, the same social order that exists to-day, the same social order out of which have grown our rotten cities and our insurance piracies, and our rebate robberies and our meat trusts and our labor wars. He condemned it as radically wrong; he called for its reconstruction upon a ruling idea which would *change the direction of human conduct*. And this, as any one may see who will read the Synoptic Gospels, was the main thing that he came into the world to do. To establish in this world the kingdom of heaven was his mission; he assumed that men would be ready for heaven if they lived the heavenly life upon earth.

If the world could only have learned from him that great truth, what ages of strife and misery would have been spared us! But, alas for human stupidity, the truth which he meant that we should learn first, the headstone of the corner of his teaching, has been ignored or rejected through all the generations. We have learned many things of this great Teacher. We have learned much about the ordering of our homes; his love and peace abide in many of them. We have learned to honor womanhood, and to hold sacred and precious the life of little children; we have learned to show compassion to the sick and the blind and the deaf and those of clouded mind; we have learned to be merciful to the criminal and kind to the needy; we have learned to trust, for ourselves, in the love of our Father in heaven; to believe that he is ready to forgive our sins, to comfort us in trouble, and to take care of us when this life is ended; all this and far more is precious gain; no word can tell how much it is worth to our sinning and sorrowing humanity.

But he has always wanted to give us so much more! If we could but have taken his yoke upon us and have learned of him how to order the relations of our social lives, how to live together in factory and shop and counting-room, how much happier and better off we should have been! Some of us would not have been so rich, many of us would not have been so poor.

To this part of the teaching of Jesus we have, however,

persistently turned a deaf ear. For other parts of our lives we confess that he has good gifts; but in all this part of our lives—and it includes by far the larger portion of our thoughts and energies—we do not yield to his authority. Here, we have insisted, another law than his must rule—the law of strife, the law that gives dominion to the strongest. So it has come to pass that through all these centuries the chief part of the work that Jesus came to do has been left undone, practically unattempted. The consequences we have seen, in that culmination of the world's selfishness which to-night we have been reviewing.

But how has it happened that the chief thing which Jesus came to do has been left undone? Was there no agency here to which this work had been entrusted? Had he no representatives in the world on whom he could depend for the application to human society of the saving truth which he came to teach? It would seem that the Christian Church must have been intended to be such an agency. We often speak of it as the Body of Christ; we mean that it is a social organism which his mind controls and in which his spirit dwells. Doubtless that was what he meant his Church to be.

That his life has been, in some imperfect way, manifested to the world through the Church, most of us believe. How very imperfect the revelation has been, all of us know. The Church is the light of the world, but often it has been but a dark lantern, quenching the ray that it ought to have reflected. Doubtless our Master knew that it would be so; human nature in its crude condition is hardly transparent to the heavenly beam; ages of cleansing and purification must pass before the light will shine through.

Therefore the Church, which is, after all, only a human agency, has very dimly understood its Lord, and very imperfectly represented him. Often and often it has utterly misplaced the emphasis of his teachings; it has put first things last and lowest things highest; it has spent its energies on trifles and shirked the great tasks for which it was commissioned.

Thus it is that the truth which Jesus always made central in his teachings has never yet been made central in the teach-

ing and the life of his Church. For many centuries it waited
for him to return in power and capture by miracle the kingdoms of the world; then it suffered this expectation to die
out and shifted its hope to the regions beyond our sight,
putting all the stress of its appeal upon the escape of the
faithful from this world to another.

It is this overdone unworldliness of which the Church of
the present day is the inheritor. For while we must make
no sweeping statements, and must thankfully and hopefully
recognize the existence of a strong minority of disciples to
whom, as to their Master, the establishment of his kingdom
in the world is the chief concern, it still remains true that
to the vast majority of modern Christians the main business
of religion is to keep people out of contact with the life of
this world, and to get them safely away from it when they
die. And while there are now not a few of the leaders of
the Church who are interested in the real work that Jesus
came to do, there is still a host of them like the occupant of
one of the most conspicuous pulpits of Christendom, who,
when asked if his church had any institutional features, answered, "God forbid! My own deep conviction is that the
institutional church is the devil's own invention," and who
then went on to testify: "I detest these semi-social and semi-
political subjects. I have never touched them in the pulpit.
Of course, as a private individual I have my own private
opinions, and I vote. But when God makes a minister he is
to declare the unsearchable riches of God in Christ Jesus,
and he is limited to that." That is the tone; you hear it continually; the business of the Church is saving souls for heaven;
it has nothing to do with making a better world of this. How
little such a man knows of what "the unsearchable riches of
God in Christ Jesus" really are!

It is because the Church, to so large an extent, has long
been under the control of such a sentiment as this; because
it has turned its gaze away from the world that Christ came
to save and has fixed it so intently upon the heaven for which
it hopes or the hell which it dreads, that the work which he
came to do in the regeneration of human society has not
been done. We can forgive the medieval saints for forgetting

their social obligations; most of them had but few; but how a Christian man in a democracy, with the chrism upon his head of God's ordination to rule this world rightly, can separate his religion from his social obligations is hard to understand. And we cannot forgive the Christian Church—the Christian Church must not forgive herself—for failing, in these great years of freedom and opportunity, to leaven human society with the truth as it is in Jesus.

What has the Christian Church been doing while these powers of piracy and plunder have been gathering their forces and spreading their nets and heaping up their spoils? Where was the Christian Church when the grafters were ravaging the cities and the rebate robbers and the frenzied financiers and the insurance sharks were getting in their work? For the most part she has been standing by and looking on, winking her eyes and twiddling her thumbs, and wondering whether she had any call to interfere.

The prophets of old had no such embarrassment in defining their function. Here and there a prophetic voice has been heard, in our own time, but against these monumental injustices with which the nation is now in a life and death grapple, the Church has lifted up no clear and effectual protest. Indeed, she has gathered into her communion many of the most conspicuous of the perpetrators of these injustices —they are nearly all church-members—and has made herself a pensioner upon their bounty, and has been content with preaching to them the "simple gospel" that such men always love to hear!

It is a sad business, brethren, a sad and shameful business; and I am afraid that most of us have had some part in it. But I wonder if it is not true that in this hour of the nation's testing, the Church is beginning to awake to some sense of her past infidelity and her present opportunity. I wonder if she knows that *now*, NOW, is for her the accepted time and the day of salvation. Is she not aware that the treasure with which she has been entrusted is for the redemption of the society in which she is living? Does she not comprehend the fact that the morbid and threatening social conditions which have been appearing during the last three years are due simply to the absence from industrial and civil society of those elements which it is her business to supply? If she had made men hate robbery as they ought to hate it there would have been no rebate robbers. If she had enforced upon the world, as she ought to have done, and could have done, the social ideas of Jesus, there would have been no frenzied financiers. If the Christian Church, with her present membership and social influence, would but accept, heartily, for herself, the simple truth that Jesus taught about life, and would begin honestly and bravely to put it into practise, society would soon be filled with ideas and sentiments in which such unsocial evils as those which we are now confronting could not long endure.

And this is the work to which in this great day the Church of Jesus Christ is summoned. It is a day of judgment. Those who have ears to hear can hear a great voice saying: "Now is the judgment of this world: now shall the prince of this world be cast out." What we are witnessing is nothing other than the culmination and collapse of the existing social order which rests on moral individualism. And the Church of Jesus Christ is called to replace this principle of selfishness and strife with the principle of good-will and service. It is called to give to society a new organic law, the law of love. It is called to organize industrial and civil society on Christian principles. This is its business in the world, a business too long neglected, but not now impossible, if the Church can discern this time and gird herself for the work.

This social change cannot be an instantaneous metamorphosis; the processes of growth are never so; but it can begin at once, and the vitalizing, transforming energy will soon make itself felt in every part of the social organism. It will be a great thing if the Church can grasp the idea of the thing to be done, and can believe that it is possible. It is not necessary to work out the methods, all at once; let them be developed as needs arise. It is only necessary that the Church shall know that she is here in the world to seek first the kingdom of God and his righteousness; to seek it, not by turning her eyes to the skies but by fixing them upon the world; to seek it and find it here, in shop and store and factory and mine, in bank and counting-room, in kitchen and drawing-room, in sanctum and studio, in public office and private station, wherever human beings join hands or touch elbows in the tasks and pleasures and comradeships of our daily life. To fill all these human relations with the spirit of good-will and kindness, of unselfish ministry; to make men and women feel that the great joy of life is not the joy of strife but the joy of service; to populate this world with a race of people whose central purpose it shall be, not to get as much as they can but to give as much as they can—this is what Jesus came into this world to do, and what his Church will be doing as soon as she comprehends her mission.

When she takes up this task with full purpose she will get some light on questions that now puzzle her. She will be able to see that while these social injustices which now disturb our peace have been culminating, her own growth has been seriously retarded. The Christian Church has not been making, during the last decades, the kind of progress that she ought to make. Her membership increases very slowly; her benevolences languish; there are signs of decrepitude that none of us is willing to confess. The strenuous efforts that have been made to replenish her forces by evangelism have not been effectual. Upon the outside masses the appeal has little power. It does not now appear that an evangelism whose objective is the individual sinner is likely to accomplish much until some things are done for which the world has long been waiting. The fact is plainly apparent that the Church has lost her grip on the world, and she is not going to regain it until she finds out what is her real business in the world. Her enfeeblement is due to her failure to dress herself to that with faith and courage and she will soon find her resources returning. It seems to me that the responsibility now resting on the Church in America is something tremendous. If this nation is destroyed the guilt will lie at the door of the Church.

. . . If, as we talk together here, we can come to a clearer understanding of the truth as it is in Jesus; if we can learn to believe in him; to feel that his way of living is the right way; to seek first the kingdom of God and his righteousness, as Jesus has shown it to us in the Sermon on the Mount; to feel that the simple life, the quiet life, the loving life, into which Jesus invites us is the best and happiest life; if we can consider all our missionary work and our philanthropic work and our educational work as methods by which we are seeking to guide men into the way of Jesus; if we can go home from this place, at the end of our sojourn here, with the new purpose in our hearts of raising up a generation of men and women who believe in Jesus Christ as Lord and Ruler of this world, and who are ready to accept his law of love and govern their lives by it, then it will be well for us and for the world that we have come together.

MODERNISM AND CONSERVATISM

[25]

J. Gresham Machen
History and Faith*

The student of the New Testament should be primarily an historian. The centre and core of all the Bible is history. Everything else that the Bible contains is fitted into an historical framework and leads up to an historical climax. The Bible is primarily a record of events.

That assertion will not pass unchallenged. The modern Church is impatient of history. History, we are told, is a dead thing. Let us forget the Amalekites, and fight the enemies that are at our doors. The true essence of the Bible is to be found in eternal ideas; history is merely the form in which those ideas are expressed. It makes no difference whether

* The Princeton Theological Review, Vol. xiii, July, 1915, pp. 337–351.

the history is real or fictitious; in either case, the ideas are the same. It makes no difference whether Abraham was an historical personage or a myth; in either case his life is an inspiring example of faith. It makes no difference whether Moses was really a mediator between God and Israel; in any case the record of Sinai embodies the idea of a covenant between God and His people. It makes no difference whether Jesus really lived and died and rose again as He is declared to have done in the Gospels; in any case the Gospel picture, be it ideal or be it history, is an encouragement to filial piety. In this way, religion has been made independent, as is thought, of the uncertainties of historical research. The separation of Christianity from history has been a great concern of modern theology. It has been an inspiring attempt. But it has been a failure.

Give up history, and you can retain some things. You can retain a belief in God. But philosophical theism has never been a powerful force in the world. You can retain a lofty ethical ideal. But be perfectly clear about one point you can never retain a gospel. For gospel means "good news", tidings, information about something that has happened. In other words, it means history. A gospel independent of history is simply a contradiction in terms.

We are shut up in this world as in a beleaguered camp. Dismayed by the stern facts of life, we are urged by the modern preacher to have courage. Let us treat God as our Father; let us continue bravely in the battle of life. But alas, the facts are too plain—those facts which are always with us. The fact of suffering! How do you know that God is all love and kindness? Nature is full of horrors. Human suffering may be unpleasant, but it is real, and God must have something to do with it. The fact of death! No matter how satisfying the joys of earth, it cannot be denied at least that they will soon depart, and of what use are joys that last but for a day? A span of life—and then, for all of us, blank, unfathomed mystery! The fact of guilt! What if the condemnation of conscience should be but the foretaste of judgment? What if contact with the infinite should be contact with a dreadful infinity of holiness? What if the inscrutable cause of all things should turn out to be a righteous God? The fact of sin! The thraldom of habit! This strange subjection to a mysterious power of evil that is leading resistlessly into some unknown abyss! To these facts the modern preacher responds—with exhortation. Make the best of the situation, he says, look on the bright side of life. Very eloquent, my friend! But alas, you cannot change the facts. The modern preacher offers reflection. The Bible offers more. The Bible offers news—not reflection on the old, but tidings of something new; not something that can be deduced or something that can be discovered, but something that has happened; not philosophy, but history; not exhortation, but a gospel.

The Bible contains a record of something that has happened, something that puts a new face upon life. What that something is, is told us in Matthew, Mark, Luke and John. It is the life and death and resurrection of Jesus Christ. The authority of the Bible should be tested here at the central point. Is the Bible right about Jesus?

The Bible account of Jesus contains mysteries, but the essence of it can be put almost in a word. Jesus of Nazareth was not a product of the world, but a Saviour come from outside the world. His birth was a mystery. His life was a life of perfect purity, of awful righteousness, and of gracious, sovereign power. His death was no mere holy martyrdom, but a sacrifice for the sins of the world. His resurrection was not an aspiration in the hearts of His disciples, but a mighty act of God. He is alive, and present at this hour to help us if we will turn to Him. He is more than one of the sons of men; He is in mysterious union with the eternal God.

That is the Bible account of Jesus. It is opposed to-day by another account. That account appears in many forms, but the essence of it is simple. Jesus of Nazareth, it maintains, was the fairest flower of humanity. He lived a life of remarkable purity and unselfishness. So deep was His filial piety, so profound His consciousness of a mission, that He came to regard himself, not merely as a prophet, but as the Messiah. By opposing the hypocrisy of the Jews, or by imprudent obtrusion of His lofty claims, He suffered martyrdom. He died on the cross. After His death, His followers were discouraged. But His cause was not lost; the memory of Him was too strong; the disciples simply could not believe that He had perished. Predisposed psychologically in this way, they had visionary experiences; they thought they saw Him. These visions were hallucinations. But they were the means by which the personality of Jesus retained its power; they were the foundation of the Christian Church.

There, in a word, is the issue. Jesus a product of the world, or a heavenly being come from without? A teacher and example, or a Saviour? The issue is sharp—the Bible against the modern preacher. Here is the real test of Bible authority. If the Bible is right here, at the decisive point, probably it is right elsewhere. If it is wrong here, then its authority is gone. The question must be faced. What shall we think about Jesus of Nazareth?

From the middle of the first century, certain interesting documents have been preserved; they are the epistles of Paul. The genuineness of them—the chief of them at any rate—is not seriously doubted, and they can be dated with approximate accuracy. They form, therefore, a fixed starting-point in controversy. These epistles were written by a remarkable man. Paul cannot be brushed lightly aside. He was certainly, to say the least, one of the most influential men that ever lived. His influence was a mighty building; probably it was not erected on the sand.

In his letters, Paul has revealed the very depths of a tremendous religious experience. That experience was founded, not upon a profound philosophy or daring speculation, but upon a Palestinian Jew who had lived but a few years before. That Jew was Jesus of Nazareth. Paul had a strange view of Jesus; he separated Him sharply from man and placed Him clearly on the side of God. "Not by man, but by Jesus Christ", he says at the beginning of Galatians, and he implies the same thing on every page of his letters. Jesus Christ, according to Paul, was man, but He was also more.

That is a very strange fact. Only through familiarity have we ceased to wonder at it. Look at the thing a moment as though for the first time. A Jew lives in Palestine, and is executed like a common criminal. Almost immediately after

His death He is raised to divine dignity by one of His contemporaries—not by a negligible enthusiast either, but by one
of the most commanding figures in the history of the world.
So the thing presents itself to the modern historian. There is
a problem here. However the problem may be solved, it can
be ignored by no one. The man Jesus deified by Paul—that
is a very remarkable fact. The late H. J. Holtzmann, who
may be regarded as the typical exponent of modern naturalistic criticism of the New Testament, admitted that for the
rapid apotheosis of Jesus as it appears in the epistles of Paul
he was able to cite no parallel in the religious history of the
race.[1]

The raising of Jesus to superhuman dignity was extraordi-
narily rapid even if it was due to Paul. But it was most emphatically not due to Paul; it can be traced clearly to the
original disciples of Jesus. And that too on the basis of the
Pauline Epistles alone. The epistles show that with regard to
the person of Christ Paul was in agreement with those who
had been apostles before him. Even the Judaizers had no
dispute with Paul's conception of Jesus as a heavenly being.
About other things there was debate; about this point there
is not a trace of a conflict. With regard to the supernatural
Christ Paul appears everywhere in perfect harmony with all
Palestinian Christians. That is a fact of enormous significance.
The heavenly Christ of Paul was also the Christ of those
who had walked and talked with Jesus of Nazareth. Think
of it! Those men had seen Jesus subject to all the petty limitations of human life. Yet suddenly, almost immediately after
His shameful death, they became convinced that He had
risen from the tomb and that He was a heavenly being. There
is an historical problem here—for modern naturalism, we venture to think, an unsolved problem. A man Jesus regarded as
a heavenly being, not by later generations who could be deceived by the nimbus of distance and mystery, but actually
by His intimate friends! A strange hallucination indeed! And

[1] In *Protestantische Monotshefte*, iv (1900), p. 465 ff., and in
Christliche Welt, xxiv (1910), column 153.

founded upon that hallucination the whole of the modern world!

So much for Paul. A good deal can be learned from him alone—enough to give us pause. But that is not all that we know about Jesus; it is only a beginning. The Gospels enrich our knowledge; they provide an extended picture.

In their picture of Jesus the Gospels agree with Paul; like Paul, they make of Jesus a supernatural person. Not one of the Gospels, but all of them! The day is past when the divine Christ of John could be confronted with a human Christ of Mark. Historical students of all shades of opinion have now come to see that Mark as well as John (though it is believed in a lesser degree) presents an exalted Christology, Mark as well as John represents Jesus clearly as a supernatural person.

A supernatural person, according to modern historians, never existed. That is the fundamental principle of modern naturalism. The world, it is said, must be explained as an absolutely unbroken development, obeying fixed laws. The supernatural Christ of the Gospels never existed. How then explain the Gospel picture? You might explain it as fiction— the Gospel account of Jesus throughout a myth. That explanation is seriously being proposed to-day. But it is absurd; it will never convince any body of genuine historians. The matter is at any rate not so simple as that. The Gospels present a supernatural person, but they also present a real person—a very real, a very concrete, a very inimitable person. That is not denied by modern liberalism. Indeed it cannot possibly be denied. If the Jesus who spoke the parables, the Jesus who opposed the Pharisees, the Jesus who ate with publicans and sinners, is not a real person, living under real conditions, at a definite point of time, then there is no way of distinguishing history from sham.

On the one hand, then, the Jesus of the Gospels is a supernatural person; on the other hand, He is a real person. But according to modern naturalism, a supernatural person never existed. He is a supernatural person; He is a real person; and yet a supernatural person is never real! A problem here! What is the solution? Why, obviously, says the modern historian—

obviously, there are two elements in the Gospels. In the first place, there is genuine historical tradition. That has preserved the real Jesus. In the second place, there is myth. That has added the supernatural attributes. The duty of the historian is to separate the two—to discover the genuine human traits of the Galilean prophet beneath the gaudy colors which have almost hopelessly defaced His portrait, to disentangle the human Jesus from the tawdry ornamentation which has been hung about Him by naive and unintelligent admirers.

Separate the natural and the supernatural in the Gospel account of Jesus—that has been the task of modern liberalism. How shall the work be done? We must admit at least that the myth-making process began very early; it has affected even the very earliest literary sources that we know. But let us not be discouraged. Whenever the mythical elaboration began, it may now be reversed. Let us simply go through the Gospels and separate the wheat from the tares. Let us separate the natural from the supernatural, the human from the divine, the believable from the unbelievable. When we have thus picked out the workable elements, let us combine them into some sort of picture of the historical Jesus. Such is the method. The result is what is called "the liberal Jesus". It has been a splendid effort. I know scarcely any more brilliant chapter in the history of the human spirit than this "quest of the historical Jesus". The modern world has put its very life and soul into this task. It has been a splendid effort. But it has also been—a failure.

In the first place, there is the initial difficulty of separating the natural from the supernatural in the Gospel narrative. The two are inextricably intertwined. Some of the incidents, you say, are evidently historical; they are so full of local color; they could never have been invented. Yes, but unfortunately the miraculous incidents possess exactly the same qualities. You help yourself, then, by admissions. Jesus, you say, was a faith-healer of remarkable power; many of the cures related in the Gospels are real, though they are not really miraculous. But that does not carry you far. Faith-healing is often a totally inadequate explanation of the cures.

And those supposed faith-cures are not a bit more vividly, more concretely, more inimitably related than the most uncompromising of the miracles. The attempt to separate divine and human in the Gospels leads naturally to a radical scepticism. The wheat is rooted up with the tares. If the supernatural is untrue, then the whole must go, for the supernatural is inseparable from the rest. This tendency is not merely logical; it is not merely what might naturally be; it is actual. Liberal scholars are rejecting more and more of the Gospels; others are denying that there is any certainly historical element at all. Such scepticism is absurd. Of it you need have no fear; it will always be corrected by common sense. The Gospel narrative is too inimitably concrete, too absolutely incapable of invention. If elimination of the supernatural leads logically to elimination of the whole, that is simply a refutation of the whole critical process. The supernatural Jesus is the only Jesus that we know.

In the second place, suppose this first task has been accomplished. It is really impossible, but suppose it has been done. You have reconstructed the historical Jesus—a teacher of righteousness, an inspired prophet, a pure worshipper of God. You clothe Him with all the art of modern research; you throw upon Him the warm, deceptive, calcium-light of modern sentimentality. But all to no purpose! The liberal Jesus remains an impossible figure of the stage. There is a contradiction at the very centre of His being. That contradiction arises from His Messianic consciousness. This simple prophet of yours, this humble child of God, thought that He was a heavenly being who was to come on the clouds of heaven and be the instrument in judging the earth. There is a tremendous contradiction here. A few extremists rid themselves easily of the difficulty; they simply deny that Jesus ever thought He was the Messiah. An heroic measure, which is generally rejected! The Messianic consciousness is rooted far too deep in the sources ever to be removed by a critical process. That Jesus thought He was the Messiah is nearly as certain as that He lived at all. There is a tremendous problem there. It would be no problem if Jesus were an ordinary fanatic or unbalanced visionary; He might then have deceived Himself as well as others. But as a matter of fact He was no ordinary fanatic, no megalomaniac. On the contrary, His calmness and unselfishness and strength have produced an indelible impression. It was such an one who thought that He was the Son of Man to come on the clouds of heaven. A contradiction! Do not think I am exaggerating. The difficulty is felt by all. After all has been done, after the miraculous has carefully been eliminated, there is still, as a recent liberal writer has said, something puzzling, something almost uncanny, about Jesus.[2] He refuses to be forced into the mould of a harmless teacher. A few men draw the logical conclusion. Jesus, they say, was insane. That is consistent. But it is absurd.

Suppose, however, that all these objections have been overcome. Suppose the critical sifting of the Gospel tradition has been accomplished, suppose the resulting picture of Jesus is comprehensible—even then the work is only half done. How did this human Jesus come to be regarded as a superhuman Jesus by His intimate friends, and how, upon the foundation of this strange belief was there reared the edifice of the Christian Church?

In the early part of the first century, in one of the petty principalities subject to Rome, there lived an interesting man. Until the age of thirty years He led an obscure life in a Galilean family, then began a course of religious and ethical teaching accompanied by a remarkable ministry of healing. At first His preaching was crowned with a measure of success, but soon the crowds deserted Him, and after three or four years, He fell victim in Jerusalem to the jealousy of His countrymen and the cowardice of the Roman governor. His few faithful disciples were utterly disheartened; His shameful death was the end of all their high ambitions. After a few days, however, an astonishing thing happened. It is the most astonishing thing in all history. Those same disheartened men suddenly displayed a surprising activity. They began preaching, with remarkable success, in Jerusalem, the very scene of their disgrace. In a few years, the religion that they preached burst the bands of Judaism, and planted itself in

[2] Heitmüller, *Jesus,* 1913, p. 71.

the great centres of the Graeco-Roman world. At first despised, then persecuted, it overcame all obstacles; in less than
three hundred years it became the dominant religion of the
Empire; and it has exerted an incalculable influence upon
the modern world.

Jesus, Himself, the Founder, had not succeeded in winning
any considerable number of permanent adherents; during
His lifetime, the genuine disciples were comparatively few.
It is after His death that the origin of Christianity as an influential movement is to be placed. Now it seems exceedingly
unnatural that Jesus' disciples could thus accomplish what
He had failed to accomplish. They were evidently far inferior
to Him in spiritual discernment and in courage; they had not
displayed the slightest trace of originality; they had been
abjectly dependent upon the Master; they had not even succeeded in understanding Him. Furthermore, what little understanding, what little courage they may have had was
dissipated by His death. "Smite the shepherd, and the sheep
shall be scattered." How could such men succeed where their
Master had failed? How could they institute the mightiest
religious movement in the history of the world?

Of course, you can amuse yourself by suggesting impossible hypotheses. You might suggest, for instance, that after
the death of Jesus His disciples sat quietly down and reflected on His teaching. "Do unto others as you would have
others do unto you." "Love your enemies." These are pretty
good principles; they are of permanent value. Are they not
as good now, the disciples might have said, as they were
when Jesus was alive? "Our Father which art in heaven." Is
not that a good way of addressing God? May not God be our
Father even though Jesus is now dead? The disciples might
conceivably have come to such conclusions. But certainly
nothing could be more unlikely. These men had not even
understood the teachings of Jesus when He was alive, not
even under the immediate impact of that tremendous personality. How much less would they understand after He
had died, and died in a way that indicated hopeless failure!
What hope could such men have, at such a time, of influenc-
ing the world? Furthermore, the hypothesis has not one jot

of evidence in its favor. Christianity never was the continuation of the work of a dead teacher.

It is evident, therefore, that in the short interval between the death of Jesus and the first Christian preaching, something had happened. Something must have happened to explain the transformation of those weak, discouraged men into the spiritual conquerors of the world. Whatever that happening was, it is the greatest event in history. An event is measured by its consequences—and that event has transformed the world.

According to modern naturalism, that event, which caused the founding of the Christian Church, was a vision, an hallucination; according to the New Testament, it was the resurrection of Jesus from the dead. The former hypothesis has been held in a variety of forms; it has been buttressed by all the learning and all the ingenuity of modern scholarship. But all to no purpose! The visionary hypothesis may be demanded by a naturalistic philosophy; to the historian it must ever remain unsatisfactory. History is relentlessly plain. The foundation of the Church is either inexplicable, or else it is to be explained by the resurrection of Jesus Christ from the dead. But if the resurrection be accepted, then the lofty claims of Jesus are substantiated; Jesus was then no mere man, but God and man, God come in the flesh.

We have examined the liberal reconstruction of Jesus. It breaks down, we have seen, at least at three points.

It fails, in the first place, in trying to separate divine and human in the Gospel picture. Such separation is impossible; divine and human are too closely interwoven; reject the divine, and you must reject the human too. To-day the conclusion is being drawn. We must reject it all! Jesus never lived! Are you disturbed by such radicalism? I for my part not a bit. It is to me rather the most hopeful sign of the times. The liberal Jesus never existed—that is all it proves. It proves nothing against the divine Saviour. Jesus was divine, or else we have no certain proof that He ever lived. I am glad to accept the alternative.

In the second place, the liberal Jesus, after he has been reconstructed, despite His limitations is a monstrosity. The

Messianic consciousness introduces a contradiction into the very centre of His being; the liberal Jesus is not the sort of man who ever could have thought that He was the Messiah. A humble teacher who thought He was the Judge of all the earth! Such an one would have been insane. To-day men are drawing the conclusion; Jesus is being investigated seriously by the alienists. But do not be alarmed at their diagnosis. The Jesus they are investigating is not the Jesus of the Bible. They are investigating a man who thought He was Messiah and was not Messiah; against one who thought He was Messiah and was Messiah they have obviously nothing to say. Their diagnosis may be accepted; perhaps the liberal Jesus, if He ever existed, was insane. But that is not the Jesus whom we love.

In the third place, the liberal Jesus is insufficient to account for the origin of the Christian Church. The mighty edifice of Christendom was not erected upon a pin-point. Radical thinkers are drawing the conclusion. Christianity, they say, was not founded upon Jesus of Nazareth. It arose in some other way. It was a syncretistic religion; Jesus was the name of a heathen god. Or it was a social movement that arose in Rome about the middle of the first century. These constructions need no refutation; they are absurd. Hence comes their value. Because they are absurd, they reduce liberalism to an absurdity. A mild-mannered rabbi will not account for the origin of the Church. Liberalism has left a blank at the beginning of Christian history. History abhors a vacuum. These absurd theories are the necessary consequence; they have simply tried to fill the void.

The modern substitute for the Jesus of the Bible has been tried and found wanting. The liberal Jesus—what a world of lofty thinking, what a wealth of noble sentiment was put into His construction! But now there are some indications that He is about to fall. He is beginning to give place to a radical scepticism. Such scepticism is absurd; Jesus lived, if any history is true. Jesus lived, but what Jesus? Not the Jesus of modern naturalism! But the Jesus of the Bible! In the wonders of the Gospel story, in the character of Jesus, in His mysterious self-consciousness, in the very origin of the Christian Church, we discover a problem, which defies the best efforts of the naturalistic historian, which pushes us relentlessly off the safe ground of the phenomenal world toward the intellectual abyss of supernaturalism, which forces us, despite the resistance of the modern mind, to recognize a very act of God, which substitutes for the silent God of philosophy the God and Father of our Lord Jesus Christ, who, having spoken at sundry times and in divers manners unto the fathers by the prophets, hath in these last days spoken unto us by His Son.

The resurrection of Jesus is a fact of history; it is good news; it is an event that has put a new face upon life. But how can the acceptance of an historical fact satisfy the longing of our souls? Must we stake our salvation upon the intricacies of historical research? Is the trained historian the modern priest without whose gracious intervention no one can see God? Surely some more immediate certitude is required.

The Objection would be valid if history stood alone. But history does not stand alone; it is confirmed by experience.

An historical conviction of the resurrection of Jesus is not the end of faith, but only the beginning; if faith stops there, it will probably never stand the fires of criticism. We are told that Jesus rose from the dead; the message is supported by a singular weight of evidence. But it is not just a message remote from us; it concerns not merely the past. If Jesus rose from the dead, as He is declared to have done in the Gospels, then He is still alive, and if He is still alive, then He may still be found. He is present with us to-day to help us if we will but turn to Him. The historical evidence for the resurrection amounted only to probability; probability is the best that history can do. But the probability was at least sufficient for a trial. We accepted the Easter message enough to make a trial of it. And making trial of it we found that it is true. Christian experience cannot do without history, but it adds to history that directness, that immediateness, that intimacy of conviction which delivers us from fear. "Now we believe, not because of thy saying: for we have heard him ourselves, and know that this is indeed the Christ, the Saviour of the world."

The Bible, then, is right at the central point; it is right in its account of Jesus; it has validated its principal claim. Here, however, a curious phenomenon comes into view. Some men are strangely ungrateful. Now that we have Jesus, they say, we can be indifferent to the Bible. We have the present Christ; we care nothing about the dead documents of the past. You have Christ? But how, pray, did you get Him? There is but one answer; you got Him through the Bible. Without the Bible you would never have known so much as whether there be any Christ. Yet now that you have Christ you give the Bible up; you are ready to abandon it to its enemies, you are not interested in the findings of criticism. Apparently, then, you have used the Bible as a ladder to scale the dizzy height of Christian experience, but now that you are safe on top you kick the ladder down. Very natural! But what of the poor souls who are still battling with the flood beneath? They need the ladder too. But the figure is misleading. The Bible is not a ladder; it is a foundation. It is buttressed, indeed by experience; if you have the present Christ, then you know that the Bible account is true. But if the Bible *were* false, your faith would go. You cannot, therefore, be indifferent to Bible criticism. Let us not deceive ourselves. The Bible is at the foundation of the Church. Undermine that foundation and the Church will fall. It will fall, and great will be the fall of it.

Two conceptions of Christianity are struggling for the ascendency to-day; the question that we have been discussing is part of a still larger problem. The Bible against the modern preacher! Is Christianity a means to an end, or an end in itself, an improvement of the world, or the creation of a new world? Is sin a necessary stage in the development of humanity, or a yawning chasm in the very structure of the universe? Is the world's good sufficient to overcome the world's evil, or is this world lost in sin? Is communion with God a help toward the betterment of humanity, or itself the one great ultimate goal of human life? Is God identified with the world, or separated from it by the infinite abyss of sin? Modern culture is here in conflict with the Bible. The Church is in perplexity. She is trying to compromise. She is saying, Peace, peace, when there is no peace. And rapidly she is losing her power. The time has come when she must choose. God grant she may choose aright! God grant she may decide for the Bible! The Bible is despised—to the Jews a stumbling-block, to the Greeks foolishness—but the Bible is right. God is not a name for the totality of things, but an awful, mysterious, holy Person, not a "present God", in the modern sense, not a God who is with us by necessity, and has nothing to offer us but what we have already, but a God who from the heaven of His awful holiness has of His own free grace had pity on our bondage, and sent His Son to deliver us from the present evil world and receive us into the glorious freedom of communion with Himself.

[26]

Shailer Mathews

Modernism and the Bible*

Deep within the Modernist movement is a method of appreciating and using the Bible. This is inevitable. Even the most superficial observer knows that the Bible is the basis upon which much of our religion has been built. But how shall men accustomed to scientific methods of thought use it for religious ends? Need they use it at all? They would be foolish not to. In using it, shall they give up their scientific attitude? That is impossible. Shall they treat the Bible merely as one of the ethnic literatures? That would be of incalculable injury to the religious life.

The true method is followed by the Modernist: to study the Bible with full respect for its sanctity but with equal respect for the student's intellectual integrity. We must begin with the facts concerning it, interpret its actual value and

* From Shailer Mathews, *The Faith of Modernism* (New York, 1924), pp. 37–53.

use it for what it is actually worth. Only thus can it properly minister to our spiritual needs.

I

The Modernist, when he appeals to biblical teachings, wants, first of all, to find the facts concerning the Bible.

For nearly a century the Bible has been studied scientifically. Such study has not started from the assumption of supernatural revelation, but has sought information regarding the origin, time of writing, and the integrity of the biblical material. No one doubts the legitimacy of such attempts. They do not spring from theological bias; they do not deny doctrine; they simply seek to obtain information. They are those used by all students of literature and history and are no more anti-religious than a textbook in chemistry is anti-chemical. But no sooner do men thus study the Bible than facts appear which make belief in its verbal inerrancy untenable. As facts they naturally must be accounted for. In consequence there has grown up a general view of the Bible which is basis of the Modernist position. It was never voted upon or formally adopted by any group of scholars. Like views commonly held in biology or any other science, it is the result of investigators working, without collusion, sometimes in rivalry, but without dogmatic assumptions, seeking to find and organize facts by scientific methods. Now that their work in the critical field is largely done, we find general agreement as to how the Bible originated, how it was composed, where it was written, why it was written. Differences as to details exist but the world of undogmatic biblical scholarship is certainly as much at one as to these matters as are the various theologies. How complete is the result of this study can be seen from the fact that there is no serious attempt to refute its conclusions by its own methods. There is plenty of anti-critical literature, plenty of denunciation of higher critics as enemies of the faith, plenty of attempts to enforce conformity in views of doctrines declared to be the teaching of the Bible; but there is little appeal to method and facts. It could not be otherwise. One cannot use the methods of

critical scholarship without adopting them. Once adopted
they can be trusted to give trustworthy results.

At the present time, although men may differ in their
theology, in the extent to which they follow their methods,
and in the frankness with which they give utterance to their
views, there is no recognized biblical investigator who does
not use the methods of criticism when studying the Bible to
obtain knowledge of its origin, time of writing and composition, or who does not accept the general theory of the
structure of the Pentateuch and synoptic gospels. Even so
conservative a theologian as A. H. Strong declares "we may
concede the substantial correctness" of the Pentateuchal
analysis, and limits inspiration to religious ends.

II

By their historical and critical study men have found that
the Bible is composed of literature gradually gathered in the
course of centuries. But, in fact, if one wished to be academi-
cally accurate one should speak of Bibles rather than a Bible.
The Hebrew Old Testament is composed of three collections.
To these collections were added in the Septuagint or Greek
Old Testament, another, The Apocrypha, containing eleven
more writings. Thus the Jews had two sacred collections,
the Hebrew and the Septuagint. There does not seem to have
been any hesitancy in using the Greek translation of the
Hebrew Old Testament, but the eleven extra books of the
Greek Old Testament were not regarded as possessing the
same authority as the others.

The writers of the New Testament used both of these Old
Testaments. Many of the quotations of the New Testament
are from the Septuagint.

When the Christian movement started it had no New Testament and its first literature seems to have consisted in letters written by Paul to some church on issues suggested by
the new faith in Jesus. There were also various collections
of sayings and anecdotes concerning Jesus circulating among
the churches, some of which came from the apostles. Gradually these collections coalesced and took permanent literary
form in different parts of the Roman Empire. Christian lit-

erature, however, by the second century was considerable, and there arose the question as to which of the writings that were circulating among the churches were trustworthy and authoritative. It took centuries for final answers to be given the question, and even then the answers were not identical. By the middle of the second century the churches seem to have agreed that the collections of biographical material which we now know as the four Gospels were from the apostles, and that there were thirteen Pauline Epistles, an apostolic Book of Acts, an Epistle of Peter and another of John. Beyond this there was a wide difference of opinion and no final agreement. None of the great churches except those of the West accepted the book of Revelation. Some churches wished to include in their New Testament other writings such as First Clement, Barnabas, the Gospel of the Hebrews and the Shepherd of Hermas. Thus it came to pass that there were different canons for the New Testament approved by various churches, none of which was that adopted by the Roman Catholic church and now held by Protestants. A final decision as to these books was reached in the Roman church at the Third Council of Carthage in 397, but the same church at the Council of Trent added to the collection those so called Apocrypha which were in the Greek Old Testament. Thus we have at the present time the Bibles of the Roman Catholic church, of the Protestant churches, of the Armenian church, of the Coptic church, and of the Syrian church. *There is no single Bible accepted universally by Christians.*

The test of admission of a book to the canon was simple. Out from a large number of writings which circulated among Christians of the second century as the works of Peter, James, Barnabas and other contemporaries of Jesus, the churches gradually selected those which they regarded as authentic. The test was, therefore, in essence, critical.

The dogmatic mind rests content with giving authority to this grouping. But such passivity is impossible for one who would test the trustworthiness of this decision of Christians who lived hundreds of years after the books were written, and almost as many years after the original manuscripts had disappeared. He, as well as the Christians of the fourth century, would seek to discover the real contribution of the Bible to his faith, and therefore he seeks to discover the authorship and the time of writing of the biblical literature.

Nor is such investigation fruitless. Practically the same general results have been reached by independent scholars. True, details of their findings vary, but there is practical unanimity in the belief that the Pentateuch and many other Old Testament writings are combinations of much older material; that the biblical material has been subjected to successive editings; that many of the Old Testament writings are centuries younger than the events they record; and that several of the New Testament books did not spring from apostolic sources in the sense that they were written by the apostles themselves.

These results of the study of facts are a starting point for any real understanding of the Scriptures, and should be a common-place among all ministers and church members. The object of such study is not "to cut the Book to pieces" but to arrange it chronologically. At the end of thirty years of widespread critical and historical study of the Scriptures it would seem as if ministers, at least, would know these conclusions. The fact that the rank and file of ministers are not only unacquainted with a scientific study of the Bible, but are ignorant of some of the more elementary facts concerning the Scriptures is a commentary on the working of the dogmatic mind.

III

The Modernist believes in studying the Bible according to accredited historical and literary methods. These methods, though not theological but scientific, are used in the interest of the religious life.

One does not need to be learned in order to see that biblical literature often expresses religious truth in ways that are not literal. We instinctively feel that expressions attributing to God face, hands, hair, back and kidneys are figurative. Few persons assert the legitimacy of interpreting such expressions literally. But what limits are to be set this concession? If the Bible is to be taken as verbally inerrant, then we must hold that God has hands large enough to cover the cleft in the rock in which a prophet hides. Not to take it literally is to abandon the principle of inerrancy formulated as a doctrine. That opens up the whole question as to the proper method of interpretation of all the biblical situations. It is this method which the Modernist endeavors to shape and use. His aim is to do intelligently and methodically throughout the entire Bible what the average Bible student does instinctively or allegorically in certain passages. When his work is done he has an intelligent view of the development of the biblical literature. By its use he can see the growing faith in God, and what is far more important, the growing revelation of God's character through the prophets and Jesus Christ. No one, of course, will claim that any method is beyond the range of human frailty. Historians and critics are men of like passions with the theologians. The ultimate question is whether we have the right to use responsible literary methods in interpreting the Bible as a record of the growing knowledge of God sufficient, when properly understood, to be regulative in our own lives. To such a question the Modernist unhesitatingly replies that he has such a method and that it gives facts upon which a helpful use of the Bible can be based.

The value of such a conclusion has been questioned on the ground that if the Bible is not historically and literally accurate at one point it cannot be trusted at others. Such an opinion evidences the dogmatic type of mind, but it cannot be respected by those who seek to know the facts. The Bible has always been seen to contain material of different value for the spiritual life. From the days of the allegorists of Alexandria to our own day, Christians have adopted other than literal interpretations of the Bible although most of these ingenious methods have been abandoned as artificial and untrustworthy. The Modernist having adopted a method approved in all similar studies, *finds in the Bible the product and the record of a religion;* and this religion he not only traces through the biblical period, but can project into his own day and the day of his children. For his method enables him to distinguish trustworthy from questionable beliefs of an ancient civilization recorded in a literature.

IV

The Modernist studies the Bible to discover the characteristics of his religion and to share in the faith of its founders.

The understanding of the literary nature of the Bible as well as of the literary methods of the contemporaries of Biblical writers determine the Modernist's treatment of the Bible material. He knows that its literary forms and methods are those of the time of writing. When, therefore, he finds that among the literary habits of the time is the use of symbols, of rewritten history, of folk-tales, he is prepared to examine the biblical material impartially and without apprehension. Whatever may have been the estimate of such literary forms on the part of those to whom they were immediately addressed, there is no doubt that they express a genuinely religious attitude. A study of the pre-Christian and Jewish literary methods results in the discovery of what this attitude and this ultimate purpose were. If it should appear that certain stories of the Bible were legend rather than sober history, this would simply mean that the past expressed its religious attitude and conviction by the use of legend. Similarly in the case of pictures of the future which characterized the preaching of the early church. Certainly they are no more literal when found in the New Testament than when found in the non-biblical pre-Christian writings of Judaism with which recent studies have made us so familiar.

And so throughout the entire Bible. Having discovered the time of authorship and the type of literature of a biblical book it is easy to determine the way in which it is to be used. To say that this is a denial of the Bible is, of course, easy. It is urged that if one portion of the Bible is folk-tale and so cannot be given full historical weight, we cannot be sure that all of the Bible is not of the same sort. The answer is simple: The dogmatic mind cannot be sure. It does not recognize or correctly use the facts of the Bible.

But there are methods by which we can tell whether the Bible is history or not. Such methods require intellectual attention and training as truly as any other scientific procedure. The inability of the uninstructed to understand Christianity has always been asserted by dogmatic authority. What the Modernist is doing is, therefore, nothing new. The Christian church in its study of the Scriptures has never delivered itself into the hands of the unintelligent leader. The work of men like Clement of Alexandria, Chrysostum, Ambrose, Augustine, Bernard, Francis, Thomas Aquinas, the Schoolmen, Luther, Melanchthon, Calvin and Wesley, that is to say, of the very men who have shaped Western Christianity, makes it plain that their treatment of the Scriptures is no farther from that of the believer in literal inerrancy than from that of the Modernist's. They all insisted that revelation must conform to realities of the universe and in their interpretation they took pains to show that such agreement existed with the universe as they knew it. If ordinary grammatical interpretation left them in any uncertainty, they promptly found an allegorical meaning in the Scriptures which satisfied the demands of what they regarded as truth. The Modernist rather than the champion of verbal inerrancy is a true successor of such fathers of orthodoxy. His regard for the Bible is just as sincere, his use of the Bible for building up the spiritual life is no farther removed from an assumption of inerrancy, his attempt to understand the experiences of God in the Bible are no less intellectual than theirs. And he knows how to separate between the permanent and the temporary in its pages.

The real issue in the case of the Bible is deeper than the question as to whether it is inerrantly inspired. What we are really concerned to gain is a conception of the Christian salvation.

The Bible when properly arranged on the basis of satisfactory evidence is a trustworthy record of human experience of God. In point of literary character and method it is just what might have been expected from our knowledge of the literary habits of the periods in which its component parts were written. Thus annals, history, laws, poetry, folk-tales, preaching, although incomparably superior in content, are of the same literary class as the contemporary literature in so far as it has been recovered. By a comparison of such facts the Modernist is able to use the Bible as furnishing trustworthy material for the discovery of what its writers thought or recorded others as thinking.

The mere fact, however, that a belief has been recorded in the Bible accurately does not guarantee its permanency or accuracy. That must wait upon other than literary tests. A legitimate distinction can therefore be drawn between the words of the Bible and the teaching of the Bible. The latter is to be found in the experience recorded in the Scriptures properly estimated in its historical surrounding.

It is well to reassert this difference as the heart of the Modernist's position regarding the Bible. It is not negative but positive. He does not deny the truth of the Scriptures. On the contrary, he is devoted to the Scriptures and the endeavor to place them in their true position in modern life. Many of the most spiritually helpful studies in the field of biblical study are from the Modernists. The difference between the Modernist and the dogmatic theologian does not lie in degrees of loyalty to or respect for the Bible, but in *the method of using it and the presuppositions with which it is studied.* Confessional theology uses the Scripture as itself supernaturally given. The Modernist uses Scripture as the trustworthy record and product of a developing religion. Here again he is at one with many so-called conservative theologians who explicitly say that the writings of inspired men are the record of a progressive revelation and not the revelation itself. *Through the Bible, as through all historical documents, the historian gets to the actual current of human experience, attitudes, convictions.* By such study he is enabled not only to describe what this experience was, but also to discern the tendency of the historical process shown in the succession of institutions, hopes, and beliefs of the religion of which the Bible is the record.

This distinction between a literature which is final in itself and a literature which is a door through which one enters the earlier stages of the Christian religion, is of great help to one who seeks God in human experience. It opens the way for using the fullest intellectual equipment in understanding not only the Bible but the total religious movement of which the student himself is a part. There grows upon one a new conviction of the worth of that religion the origin and the earlier stages of which the Bible records. Through the critical and historical study of the Bible the Christian scholar finds himself the heir of those men of faith whose lives he has come to understand. Christianity becomes not the acceptance of a literature but a reproduction of attitudes and faith, a fellowship with those ancient men of imperfect morals whose hearts found God, whose lives were strengthened by the divine spirit, whose words point out the way of life, and who determined the inner character of the Christian religion. From such sources the major doctrines of Christians are derived. Other elements are secondary accretions from contemporary religions, easily and repeatedly separated from the religion of Jesus Christ.

It is difficult to make this plain to those who know nothing of the scientific use of documents. True, as Protestants, they distinguish between the major and secondary elements of the theology they inherited from the Roman Catholic church, but to them any statement in the Scriptures is material to be used for the construction of any theological edifice. To the Modernist any statement of Scriptures is to be located in its proper historical environment and seen as the expression of the religious attitude of men in that environment. The Bible sprang from our religion, not our religion from the Bible.

The unity of the Christian revelation is found in the unity of a growing religion. In discovering this experience of God and accepting it as his own religious ancestry the Modernist affirms the trustworthiness of the Scripture. He is forced by the discovery and estimate of facts to be loyal to the spirit of the biblical religion. It is this concrete religion which, like all progenitors, has set the sharp limits within which Christianity has developed. The Bible is, therefore, of incalculable value to a modern Christian. He draws inspiration from its pages. But since the religion of biblical characters is distinct from the Bible as its product and record, in reproducing as best we can the faith of prophets and apostles, the spirit of

Jesus and the loyalty of the early disciples to Jesus, we are not burdened with the impossible task of proving that the Bible is an infallible text-book in all fields of human knowledge. It is a trustworthy record of a developing experience of God which nourishes our own faith. It is all the more trustworthy because it makes plain that God was experienced and His will taught through a variety of social institutions, scientific beliefs, ethical ideals and the literary methods, each dependent upon contemporary culture.

There is no static religion or standardized formula in the Bible. In that fact is one of the most significant of the Modernist points of view, *viz.*, that the true attitude toward God and the true experience of his presence are possible and discernible in the midst of imperfect and even mistaken scientific and other views. The author of Genesis may declare that the sun and stars were created after the creation of the earth and plant life, a conception which our knowledge of astronomy shows is incorrect. But this error does not prevent our sharing in the author's faith that in the shaping of the universe, God was present. So, too, it is only something to be expected when we find in the religious experiences of men who lived before the siege of Troy conceptions of God which to our Christian morality seem unworthy. Such conceptions are, however, no bar to the discovery that with all the human infirmities attributed to Him, the Jahweh of the Book of Judges possessed qualities which had only to be expanded as men's experience expanded, to give the righteous monotheism of the prophets. Belief in the providence of God can be expressed in poetry, folk-tale and legend just as truly as in literal statement.

In consequence, the Modernist enjoys the spiritual ministry of the Bible quite undisturbed by objections which the believer in the inerrancy of the Scriptures has either to answer or to denounce. Poetical statements as to the sun standing still, the story of Jonah, miracles like those of Elijah and Elisha and some of those of the New Testament, can be used at their full religious value. Whether they are sober history or not they are current ways of expressing belief in God's care for men. They are material for understanding the de-

veloping consciousness of God and a growing religion. They
were contemporary ways of expressing religious faith. In them
the Bible is recording trust in a good God whose law is righteous and whose love and power are coextensive. From such a
trust we gain help as we seek to have a kindred faith in our
day. We face our different tasks and problems in accordance
with their trust in God. Our knowledge has grown, but we
are still "sons of the faithful Abraham."

Thus, although the historical and critical study of the
Scriptures does not begin with a doctrine of inspiration,
Modernists believe in inspiration rather than inerrancy. But
in the inspiration of men, not of words. Men were inspired
because they inspire. In this Modernists are one with writers
of the Bible themselves, for inspiration within the Bible is
always regarded as the experience of the Spirit of God on the
part of some individual.

With confidence, therefore, and with the enthusiasm of
those who intelligently open up a treasure of religious inspiration and moral guidance, we approach the Bible. We
read it not only for its spiritual appeal; we honor it, so to
speak, as the germ-plasm of a developing religion. We seek
to discover in it information regarding the origin, development and nature of the Christian faith in order that attitudes
and convictions which grew with its characters' growing
understanding of God and found fullest and effective expression in Jesus Christ and inspired the religious group he
founded, may be more influential in our own lives and in
our modern world. We search the Scriptures that we may
have life and find them testifying to him whose words are
spirit and life.

BIBLIOGRAPHICAL NOTE

The works of Daniel Day Williams, *The Andover Liberals*
(New York, 1941) and Frank Hugh Foster, *The Modern
Movement in American Theology* (New York, 1939) are use-
ful for the early period. Barbara Cross, *Horace Bushnell:*

Minister to a Changing America (Chicago, 1958) is the most adequate study of this precursor of liberal theology. See also the excellent articles of Arthur Schlesinger, "A Critical Period in American Religion," *Proceedings of the Massachusetts Historical Society,* lxiv, June, 1932 and Bert J. Loewenberg, "Darwinism Comes to America, 1858–1900," *Mississippi Valley Historical Review,* xxvii, 1941, pp. 339–368.

For the Social Gospel Robert T. Handy, *The Social Gospel in America* (New York, 1966) includes selections from Washington Gladden, Walter Rauschenbusch, and Richard T. Ely; his Introduction is especially helpful. Two earlier essays may be consulted: C. Howard Hopkins, *The Rise of the Social Gospel in American Protestantism, 1865–1915* (New Haven, 1940) and Henry F. May, *Protestant Churches and Industrial America* (New York, 1949). Winthrop Hudson's *The Great Tradition of the American Churches* (New York, 1953) is an excellent study of the changing religious scene in the latter part of the nineteenth and early twentieth centuries: see especially, Chapter VIII, "Princes of the Pulpit." For discussion of Russell Conwell see: Clyde Nelson, "Russell H. Conwell and the 'Gospel of Wealth'," *Foundations,* v, January, 1962, pp. 39–51.

Vergilius Ferm's *Contemporary American Theology* Volume I (New York, 1932) and Volume II (New York, 1933) contain theological autobiographies which shed considerable light on the period. Norman Furniss, *The Fundamentalist Controversy 1918–1931* (New Haven, 1954) is the most adequate study available, though Ernest R. Sandeen, "Towards a Historical Interpretation of the Origins of Fundamentalism," *Church History,* xxxvi, March, 1967, takes a new look at the nineteenth century roots of the movement. See also Robert T. Handy, "Fundamentalism and Modernism in Perspective," *Religion in Life,* xxiv, Summer, 1955, pp. 381–394. Of the several studies of the changes in theological concerns I have found Edwin Aubrey's *Present Theological Tendencies* (New York, 1936) the most judicious.

X. THEOLOGICAL CHANGE

INTRODUCTION

In the 1930s a remarkable change occurred in American theology. The confidence in the possibility of social reordering and the optimism of the liberals were shattered, largely by the effects of the Depression and the beginnings of the European struggles.

American theologians sought to recapture and reaffirm more traditional Christian beliefs. The uniqueness and scandal of the Gospel were asserted. Awareness of the sinfulness of man, stress on the redemptive role of Jesus Christ, reconsideration of the doctrine and nature of the church, its liturgy and sacramental life, were some of the new motifs.

The German theologian, Karl Barth, prompted many to rethink their liberal affirmations. In one of his first books translated into English he wrote:

"It is not the right human thoughts about God which form the content of the Bible, but the right divine thoughts about men. The Bible tells us not how we should talk with God but what he says to us; not how we find the way to him, but how he has sought and found the way to us; not the right relation in which we must place ourselves to him, but the covenant which he has made with all who are Abraham's spiritual children and which he has sealed once and for all in Jesus Christ. It is this which is within the Bible. The word of God is within the Bible.[1]

The biblical revelation was the starting point for the theologian's task.

Edwin Lewis (1881–1959), Professor of Systematic Theology at Drew Seminary (Methodist) published the essay, "The Fatal Apostasy of the Modern Church" in 1933. It is a

[1] Karl Barth, *The Word of God and the Word of Man*, translated by Douglas Horton (New York, 1956), p. 43.

stringent attack on the presuppositions of the liberals and uncompromising in its affirmation of a Christocentric theology.

Reinhold Niebuhr (1892–   ), after attending Yale Divinity School, assumed a pastorate in Detroit where he was confronted by the problems of the laboring classes in a rapidly growing industrial complex.[2] It was not long before he saw that the emphases of the Social Gospel were not realistic; his *Moral Man and Immoral Society* (1932) applied the changing theological interests to the problems of the social order. Niebuhr has remained a central figure in contemporary American Protestantism. His essay of 1939, "Ten Years that Shook My World," described the forces that altered his theological and social perspectives.

Harry Emerson Fosdick (1878–   ) was a preacher of eminent power and persuasion. During his interim pastorate at the First Presbyterian Church in New York he delivered his famous sermon, "Shall the Fundamentalists Win?" (1922), which set off a lengthy controversy with fundamentalists in the Presbyterian Church. At the General Assembly of the Presbyterian Church in 1924 Fosdick was asked to become a member of the church which involved subscribing to the confessional standards of the denomination; he declined the invitation. He continued his career at the Park Avenue Baptist Church (Riverside Church) until 1946. His sermon, "Beyond Modernism," shows the influence that the newer theological concerns had on his own understanding of the Christian faith.

[2] For his observations on this period of his life see Reinhold Niebuhr, *Leaves from the Notebook of a Tamed Cynic* (New York, 1957).

[27]
Edwin Lewis
The Fatal Apostasy of the Modern Church*

Modern theological liberalism undoubtedly rendered the
church an important service. It helped to break the strangle-
hold of empty shibboleths. It re-established, after the fashion
of the thirteenth century, the rights of the intellect in the
evaluation of the things of the spirit. It garnered for the use
of the church the right harvest of scholarship in many fields
—biblical, historical, sociological, psychological. It served notice to a world too often skeptical that a man could believe
in Jesus and at the same time be fully aware of all the amazing kaleidoscopic changes occurring in contemporary life. For
such a service we cannot but be grateful. Nevertheless, all
is not well with us. Liberalism has not brought us to the
Promised Land. We may have gained a battle, but the cam-
paign is still on, and there is more than a suspicion that the
gain made at one point involved a serious loss elsewhere.
We yielded positions whose strategic significance is becoming more and more manifest. We so stressed the Bible as
coming to us in "the words of men" that the sense in which
it is also "the word of God" has become increasingly vague.
We so freely allowed the influence of contemporary forces in
the development of doctrine as to have endangered the continuity of that living core of truth and reality for which contemporary forces were but the *milieu*. We exposed all the
delicate nuances of spiritual experience to the cold dispassionate gaze of psychology, until it has become a question
whether psychology of religion is not in danger of destroying

* Edwin Lewis, "The Fatal Apostasy of the Modern Church,"
Religion in Life, Vol. ii, No. 4, Autumn, 1933, 483–492. Copyright
1933 by Abingdon Press. Used by permission.

the very thing it lives by. And in particular we were so determined to recover for the church "the human Jesus" that we lost sight of the fact that the church is the creation of "the divine Christ," or at least of faith in Christ as divine. Have we sown the wind, and is the whirlwind now upon us?

THE GOSPELS AND THE CHURCH

The *Hibbert Journal* symposium of a generation ago, "Jesus, or Christ?" was a sign of the times. It showed very clearly the results of the "Jesus-study" of the latter part of the nineteenth century. It prophesied an increasing emphasis on "the religion of Jesus," a prophecy which has been abundantly fulfilled. In many quarters of the modern church it is now taken for granted that "the Jesus of the Gospels" is the primary datum for Christianity. This would not be disturbing if Jesus were given his complete significance, but before he can become a datum he must be passed through the alembic of critical investigation. By that time, he has become a hardly recognizable Figure, as Schweitzer himself—notwithstanding his own arbitrary construction—so vigorously contends. But such as he is, he is given to us. We are asked to suppose that one who may have been anything from the energetic "go-getter" of Bruce Barton to "the Man of Genius" in the Middleton Murry sense, is the adequate explanation—plus certain "tendencies" in the time—of the genesis of Christianity and of its historical growth. Let us therefore "return to Jesus." Let us eliminate from Christianity everything not agreeable to the "Portrait" we have had reconstructed for us. Let us be done with the majestic Figure of the Epistles. Let us admit that the Prologue of the Fourth Gospel, and the Kenosis passage in Philippians, and the daring flights of Colossians, and the introduction to Hebrews, represent simply so much mythologizing—understandable enough in the circumstances, but corresponding to nothing in the world of actual reality. Having thus arrived at "the essence of Christianity"—Harnack's familiar grouping, "the Fatherhood of God, the value of the soul, the righteousness of the heart, and the commandment of love"—let us "re-think" the whole Christian enterprise in the appropriate terms. Let us be realistic. Let us frankly change our direction. Let us abandon definitely and forever, the whole concept of the supernatural; and as men who will tolerate no illusions, comforting and inspiring though they may be, let us set ourselves anew to the church's unfinished task. What is—what?

But perhaps the case is not so simple as it seems. Say what we will, the stubborn fact remains that the Gospels are themselves the product of a community which already had "seated Christ at the right hand of God," and that, failing that audacious act of their mind and heart, we had had no Gospels at all. If the dangerous expression may be permitted, it was "Christ" who saved "Jesus" to us. That is to say, although Jesus was saved to posterity by "the Christian community," that community organized itself not around the fact that a man named Jesus had lived and taught and wrought and died, but around the belief that in that same Jesus had "dwelt all the fullness of the Godhead bodily." But for that belief, Jesus would have disappeared from human ken, for not one single unimpeachable reference to Jesus of any independent value do we possess from the first century outside of the Christian literature. We may object to the faith of that early community. We cannot but admit, however, that it is to this community that we owe the Synoptic Gospels. They produced for us and saved to us the very documents by which we propose to discredit their dynamic faith! They produced them, used them, loved them, circulated them, at the same time that they were integrating their Lord with the very being of the Godhead, saying of him that he *is* the Spirit, that he *is* the Ever-living One, that by him the invisible God is apprehended, and nowhere is there the least evidence that they felt any incongruity in doing this. By the Gospels they accounted for their historical origin and justified their claims, but the community preceded the Gospels. There was a Church of the Living Christ before there was any attempt made to collate the traditions respecting Jesus. Apply to the Gospel Portrait all the historicism and psychologism you will: you cannot thereby get rid of that confident faith in a Redeemer-God which is the sole reason why we have the Portrait at all. Take the Synoptic Gospels, discriminate their sources, lay bare their inconsistencies and contradictions, explain away their mighty works, find the Rabbinic parallels of their teachings, "reduce" Jesus to what level you will—and you have not destroyed Christianity thereby, because Christianity was born not of these documents but of contact with the Personality whom the documents attempt to describe. And be it added that although in the order of *time* the contact with him was "in the flesh" first and "in the spirit" second, nevertheless the *fundamental* contact was the second because it was through that that the first came to its full understanding and appreciation.

The Fourth Gospel therefore receives its justification. No attack on its historicity can rob it of its significance as a permanent obstacle in the way of those who, having duly sifted out of the Synoptic Gospels all subjectivism and supernaturalism, would take what is left as sufficient both to explain and to perpetuate Christianity. It would almost seem as though the Ephesian seer who wrote "the spiritual Gospel" anticipated the possibility of this proposal, and set himself the task of providing for its defeat. In any case he rewrote the Gospel history in the light of what had for long been the central conviction of the church, namely, that in a human life that had been "full of grace and truth" something of God's own self, called by him the eternal "Word," had "become flesh"; that the ending of that life in a shameful death was not the ending of the Word; that this Word, visualized to men in that perfect human life, was now active in the church as "Spirit"; and that he who now thinks of God and deals with God may think of him and deal with him as One in whose very bosom lay "the only-begotten Son." It is, of course, open to anyone who insists on it to say that in thus re-writing the Gospel history "John" took such liberties with the "facts" as renders his work historically worthless. But one who says that will necessarily assume the completeness and the adequacy of the Synoptic Gospels. *What is the basis of that assumption?* Also, he will deny any absolute interpretive significance to the experience of the church in its most fruitful period, namely, the beginning. *And what is the basis of that denial?*

THE ORIGINAL CHRISTIAN MESSAGE

The Christian "facts" are not to be limited to what fell between Bethlehem and Calvary. What was then said and done was but part of a larger whole—of a movement taking place within the very being of God. Men believed that this was implied in the indubitable historical and experiential facts. They therefore wrought out the idea of "pre-existence" as applied to their Lord, identified him as the permanently active occasion of that life of fellowship in which the church as they knew it was constituted, and from this were led on step by step to formulate finally the doctrine of the Trinity. It is easy enough to complain that this was to transform "the simple Gospel" into a *Weltanschauung,* yet we have no evidence that the so-called simple Gospel was ever preached, even at the beginning, apart from at least some of the elements of this philosophy. Not that unlettered apostles suddenly found themselves possessed of a full-blown philosophy that answered all questions in the world and out of it. But they were making affirmations of such an astounding character as that inevitably before long took to themselves coherence, and the original Christocentric religion became a Christocentric philosophy.

As to this, the New Testament is the evidence, and the New Testament reflects the life and faith of the primitive church. Here we read of a God who had an eternal purpose respecting mankind, a purpose that had to do specifically with delivering men from the power of sin and bringing them to holiness. We read that such a deliverance could not be an arbitrary act upon the part of God, since in all that he does he must be true to the demand of his own holy nature. We read that God himself was so constituted that he could enter in the most intimate and personal way into the stream of human life both to experience all its limitations and struggles and to establish within the stream the principle of its purification, and that the point of this entry was the man Jesus, who would never have existed at all but for the eternal purpose of God. We read that the ensuing intimacy of relationship between the Eternal God and this human life was

such that the experience of the man thereupon became the
experience of God—which makes it actually true to say that
the Infinite knows finitude, that the All-Holy knows moral
trial, that the Creator knows creatureliness, that the Death-
less knows death. We read that therefore something has
"happened to" God which makes his relation to men different
from what it would have been had this *not* "happened." And
we read that henceforth in speaking of God men may speak
of him as One who was in Christ reconciling the world unto
himself: therefore the Christian God is God suffused with all
the qualities men saw in Jesus, and a God so suffused and
transformed is also that divine Christ who is the very source
and center of the life of the redeemed.

What then is the object of Christian faith? Not a man who
once lived and died, but a Contemporary Reality, a God
whose awful holiness is "covered" by one who is both our
representative and his, so that it is "our flesh that we see in
the Godhead," that "flesh" which was historically Jesus of
Nazareth but is eternally the divine Christ whose disclosure
and apprehension Jesus lived and died to make possible. I
do not deny for a single moment that this overwhelming conception lent itself to all sorts of crudities of expression, impossible analogies, and gross materialisms. But he is blind
indeed who cannot see what the New Testament is trying
to say. Though language were not adequate to the thought,
we can see what the thought aimed to be. It was that thought
that created and sustained the church, and the church lan-
guishes to-day because it has substituted that thought with
one of lesser power as it is of lesser truth.

THE REPUDIATION OF CHRISTIANITY

Many reasons are alleged for the modern turning away
from Christianity as thus understood. Not one of these reasons can touch its intrinsic credibility. A philosophical view
that precludes it is quite possible. A philosophical view that
allows for it is equally possible. Why is the first view so
generally accepted? Because Christianity, with the view of
things it necessarily calls for, makes such a terrific onslaught
upon human pride. We would fain be self-sufficient, and this

means that we are not. We would fain be the masters of our fate and the captains of our souls, and this says that our fate is in another's hands and that our souls are not our own but have been bought with a price. We do not like Christianity, not because it is intrinsically incredible but because it is so vastly humiliating. We do not *want* it to be true that "the Son of Man came to give himself a ransom for many," and so we find "critical" reasons for doubting that the words were ever spoken—as though by proving that Jesus did not say them we should prove that they were not true! We do not *want* it to be true that "the Word became flesh and dwelt among us": therefore we get rid of one of the most profound, heart-searching, and revolutionary truths ever uttered—the truth which must always be the touch-stone of any proposed Christology—by the simple device of labeling it "Platonism." We do not *want* it to be true that "through one act of righteousness the free gift came unto all men to justification of life": this being so, we ask by what right Paul "distorted" the simple Gospel of brotherhood and service and good will by introducing into it misleading analogies from temple and law-court.

No; we do not like Christianity. We do not like its cosmic audacity. We do not like its moral pessimism. We do not like the way it smashes the beautiful orderliness of our metaphysical systems. We do not like its uncompromising insistence on the possibility of our being damned souls, whose only hope is in the sovereign grace of God—a God who voluntarily endured self-immolation as the cost of his own graciousness. We be *men*—men whose prerogative it is to stand before God, face him without a tremor, and *demand;* not slaves whose duty it is to kneel before him with covered face, humbly and reverently and gratefully to *accept*. Away with this doctrine of grace! Away with this whole mythology of Incarnation! Away with this outworn notion of Atonement! Make way for emancipated man!

THE PLIGHT OF THE CHURCH

But in this pride lies our shame, our weakness, and our defeat. What has it done for us? What has it done for the

church—at least, for evangelical Protestantism? How far
have we gotten with our various substitutes? Look over our
churches: they are full of people, who, brought up on these
substitutes, are strangers to those deeper experiences without
which there had been no New Testament and no Church of
Christ. Thousands of clergymen will go into their pulpits next
Sunday morning, but not as prophets. There will be no burning fire shut up in their bones, by reason of which they cannot forbear to speak. Those who come to listen will not be
brought face to face with eternal verities. Hungry sheep will
look up, but will not be fed. Men harassed with a thousand
problems and seeking not inexpert advice on how to solve
them but the sense of another world in whose light they can
see this one and find strength to cope with it and remold it
nearer to the heart's desire, will go away as impotent as they
came for anything the preacher has to say. Grievous is the
hurt of the daughter of God's people, and slight is the
proffered healing. They go to Gilead, and there is no balm.
They go to the fountain of waters, and they find there a
broken cistern. They cry for bread, and behold a stone.

And to a large extent, this plight of the church is traceable
to a weakening of its dogmatic basis. Whether the phrase
"humanitarian Christology," is defensible or not is a question.
Unless Christ is conceived as one who "stands on the divine
side of causality in effecting redemption," it is difficult to see
why we need a doctrine of him at all. If Jesus is not specifically related to God's eternal purpose to enter sacrificially the
stream of our humanity, to the end that he might thereby
change its direction and set it flowing toward himself, then
we no more need a doctrine of Jesus than we need a doctrine
of Jeremiah or a doctrine of Paul. There is no permanent
resting-place between *some form* of the Logos Christology
and a "humanitarian Christology" (allowing the phrase)
which in effect surrenders the whole idea of direct divine
sacrificial saving activity. And what we mean theologically
by a Logos Christology we mean practically by a Christ-
centered religion rather than a "religion of Jesus." If the
emulation of "the religion of Jesus" were presented as the
possible end of a Christ-centered faith, that would be dif-

ferent. What we are actually doing, however, is supposing that unregenerate men can be "like Jesus"! Even a casual acquaintance with great sections of modern Protestantism makes it evident that it has departed very widely from the Christocentric emphasis. We must recover that emphasis, or perish. The divine Christ saved the human Jesus from disappearing, and if the human Jesus is to continue to mean for men all that he should, it must still be through the divine Christ. Christ must continue to save Jesus!

It is not that men cannot live "the good life" without faith in the divine Christ. It is not that there cannot be a profound appreciation of the character of Jesus without it. But Christianity does not consist simply in the good life and in moral appreciation and endeavor. It *is* this, of course. One of the incredible suppositions of our day is that the only persons who are interested in the wellbeing of their fellows are the so-called "humanists." No one who really knows what Christianity has done for the world could possibly make that supposition. It is sadly true that on countless occasions Christians have failed to recognize the logic of their own belief. They have professed to be "sons of God," and they have not seen that because of that they must also be "brothers" of their kind. It is that failure which justifies many of the savage strictures of the "humanistic" critic of Christianity. But the other side is there, as anyone may see who will take the trouble to read Charles Loring Brace's *Gesta Christi.* Did the mediæval monks do nothing but sing psalms and pray—or squander and carouse? They who answer "Yes" simply do not know all the story. Was "the evangelical movement" entirely without social results? Were there no devoted Churchmen in Great Britain in the last century known as "Christian Socialists," lay and cleric—Kingsley, Maurice, Hare, Hughes, Ludlow, Neale? Have not Weber and Troeltsch written of "the Protestant ethic," and not altogether to its discredit? Has our time seen three men more thoroughly committed to "historical" Christianity than William Temple, W. R. Inge, and the late Charles Gore, and would anyone even suggest that they were not men of the clearest social vision? The sacramentarianism of the Anglo-Catholics may cause us some anxiety at certain points, but before you denounce them too severely, read of the sacrificial service that many of them are rendering the poor of their land. Certainly we need "humane religion," but what could possibly be more "humane" than a Christocentric religion that accepted its own implicates? If anyone has surrendered a "high" doctrine of Christ in the interests of "the social Gospel," then he has fully realized neither the meaning of the doctrine he has surrendered nor the staggering demands that his message makes both on himself and on others.

Yes; Christocentric religion means human devotion carried to its ultimate issue—say a Damien with a crucifix on his breast the while he dresses the rotting stumps of a leper, a Damien who, as R. L. Stevenson says in his noble defense of the man, "shut to with his own hand the doors of his own sepulcher." But it means an "experience" as well—an experience falling within that "unleaguerable fortress" of the innermost soul "whose keys are at the cincture hung of God," and which is something one can better know for oneself than describe to another. And this experience, whence comes it? It comes of *belief.* If we are going to psychologize religion, well and good; but by what imaginable psychological process can there be "spiritual experience" completely independent of all intellectual assent? It were absurd to say that Christianity is *only* credal; to say that it is in no sense credal would be equally false. And to say that "it does not matter what one believes" so long as one "lives the good life" and "has a religious experience" reveals rather an amazing *naïveté* than any profound insight into the life-movement.

But what *does* the modern church believe? The church is becoming creedless as rapidly as the innovators can have their way. The "Confession of Faith"—what is happening to it? Or what about the "new" confessions that one sees and hears—suitable enough, one imagines, for, say, a fraternal order. And as for the Apostles' Creed—"our people will not say it any more": which means, apparently, that "our people," having some difficulties over the Virgin Birth and the resurrection of the body, have elected the easy way of believing in nothing at all—certainly not in "the Holy Catholic Church."

So we are going to allow them to be satisfied with "The Social Creed of the Churches," quite forgetful of the fact that unless the church has a "religious" creed besides a "social" creed the church as such will cease to exist long before it has had time to make its "social" creed effective in the life of the world. "But the social creed *is* religious." Yes; but has its religion proved dynamic enough, impelling enough, to maintain itself at the high point—the Himalayanly high point —necessary to make its creed effective? The church has set itself to do more at the very time that it is lessening its power to do anything.

"WHAT MUST WE DO TO BE SAVED?"

The church, especially the American evangelical churches, must re enthrone Christ, the divine Christ, in the life and thought of the people, or cease to exist. Not that the church merely as an institution is the necessary desideratum. But the church in the high New Testament sense of "the body of Christ"—this *must* be saved for the sake of the world. Here is the world's one redeeming force because here is the world's one redeeming message—if the message be *complete*. It is that completeness whose lack is the secret of our impotence. Can we recover it? Nay rather, do we here highly resolve that we *will* recover it? Let us be done with compromise, and let us affirm—affirm magnificently, affirm audaciously. Let us affirm God—his unchanging love for men, his unchanging hatred of sin, his sacrificial presence in all the life and work of Jesus. Let us affirm Christ—Christ as the meaning of God, Christ as what God *is* in virtue of that mysterious "kenosis" by which he made himself one with a human life, and at the same time that he was doing the utmost he could do for men endured the worst—a Cross—that men could do against him. Let us affirm the Spirit—the divine concern to bring to bear upon the hearts and consciences of men the impact of what God in Christ has done and is forever doing on their behalf, to the end that they may be moved to repentance, to that faith which ensures forgiveness, to that love which brings moral empowerment, and to that surrender of the will which makes God's purposes their purposes. Let us affirm the church

—the community of the redeemed, those who in all their life seek the regnancy of the spirit of Jesus, carrying on and extending the mystery of the Incarnation against that day when God, the Christ-God, shall be all and in all. Let us affirm the Kingdom—the Christianizing of life everywhere, children with straight backs and happy faces, women released from drudgery and set free for creative living, industry conducted for the good of all, war and kindred evils done away, racial antipathies lost in a universal brotherhood, the rich heritage of culture made available to the last man. O there is no limit to the affirmations, and, better still, no limit to the dynamic needful to make them effective, once we grasp the profound structural coherence of Christianity, the wide sweep of its thought, the absoluteness of its demands, the revolutionary results of its consistent application. "That in all things he, who is the image of the invisible God, might have the preeminence."

"O Church of Rome, would that thy creed were sound!" So cried Newman, distracted, uncertain, seeking a light amid the encircling gloom. But his lament was too narrow in its reference. O Church of Christ *everywhere*, on the avenue, down the side-street, in the town-square, at the country cross-roads, would that thou believedst as thou should! For of believing comes feeling, and of feeling comes being, and of being comes doing.

Not willingly does one write what has here been written. It may be so easily misunderstood, by friend and by foe alike. If there be any extenuation, it is in the prophet's simile: "The lion hath roared: who will not fear? The Lord Jehovah hath spoken: who can but prophesy?"

[28]

Harry Emerson Fosdick
Beyond Modernism*

If we are successfully to maintain the thesis that the church must go beyond modernism, we must start by seeing that the church had to go as far as modernism. Fifty years ago, a boy, seven years of age, was crying himself to sleep in terror lest, dying, he should go to hell, and his solicitous mother, out of all patience with the fearful teachings which brought such apparitions of the mind, was trying in vain to comfort him. That boy is preaching to you today and you may be sure that to him the achievements of Christian modernism in the last half century seem not only important but indispensable.

Fifty years ago the intellectual portion of western civilization had turned one of the most significant mental corners in history and was looking out on a new view of the world. The church, however, was utterly unfitted for the appreciation of that view. Protestant Christianity had been officially formulated in pre-scientific days. The Augsburg confession was a notable statement but the men who drew it up, including Luther himself, did not even believe that the earth went around the sun. The Westminster confession, for the rigorous acceptance of which the Presbyterian rearguard still contends, was a memorable document but it was written forty years before Newton published his work on the law of gravitation. Moreover, not only were the mental patterns of Protestant Christianity officially formulated in pre-scientific days but, as is always true of religion, those patterns seemed sacred to their believers and the changes forced by the new science seemed impious and sacrilegious.

Youths, like myself, therefore, a half century ago, faced an appalling lag between our generation's intellect on one side and its religion on the other, with religion asking us to believe incredible things. Behind his playfulness the author of "Through the Looking Glass" had this serious matter in mind when he represented the White Queen as saying to Alice, "I'm just one hundred and one, five months and a day." Said Alice, "I can't believe *that!*" Said the Queen pityingly, "Can't you? Try again: draw a long breath, and shut your eyes." So the church seemed to be speaking to us.

Modernism, therefore, came as a desperately needed way of thinking. It insisted that the deep and vital experiences of the Christian soul, with itself, with its fellows, with its God, could be carried over into this new world and understood in the light of the new knowledge. We refused to live bifurcated lives, our intellect in the late nineteenth and our religion in the early sixteenth century. God, we said, is a living God who has never uttered his final word on any subject; why, therefore, should pre-scientific frameworks of thought be so sacred that forever through them man must seek the Eternal and the Eternal seek man? So we said, and, thanks to modernism, it became true of many an anxious and troubled soul in our time that

> He saw the boundless scheme dilate,
> In star and blossom, sky and clod;
> And as the universe grew great,
> He dreamed for it a greater God.

The church thus had to go as far as modernism but now the church must go beyond it. For even this brief rehearsal of its history reveals modernism's essential nature; it is primarily an adaptation, an adjustment, an accommodation of Christian faith to contemporary scientific thinking. It started by taking the intellectual culture of a particular period as its criterion and then adjusted Christian teaching to that standard. Herein lies modernism's shallowness and transiency: it arose out of a temporary intellectual crisis; it took a special type of scientific thinking as standard; it became an adaptation to, a harmonization with, the intellectual culture of, a particular generation. That, however, is no adequate religion to represent the Eternal and claim the allegiance of the soul. Let it be a modernist who says that to you! Unless the church can go deeper and reach higher than that it will fail indeed.

I

In the first place, modernism had been excessively preoccupied with intellectualism. Its chosen problem has been somehow to adjust Christian faith to the modern intellect so that a man could be a Christian without throwing away his mind. Modernism's message to the church has been after this fashion: When long ago, the new music came, far from clinging to old sackbuts and psalteries, you welcomed Palestrina, Bach, Beethoven and their successors to the glory of God; when the new art came you did not refuse it but welcomed Cimabue, Giotto, Raphael and Michelangelo to the enrichment of your faith; when the new architecture came, far from clinging to primitive catacombs or old romanesque, you greeted the gothic with its expanded spaces and aspiring altitudes; so now, when the new science comes take that in too, and, however painful the adaptations, adjust your faith to it and assimilate its truths into your Christian thinking.

Surely, that has been a necessary appeal but it centers attention on one problem only—intellectual adjustment to modern science. It approaches the vast field of man's experience and need headfirst, whereas the deepest experiences of man's soul, whether in religion or out of it, cannot be approached headfirst. Friendship, the love that makes a home, the enjoyment of music, delight in nature, devotion to moral causes, the practice of the presence of God—name as you will the list of the soul's deepest experiences and needs, and while, if we are wise, we use our heads on them, we do not approach them mainly headfirst but heart first, conscience first, imagination first. A man is vastly greater than his logic and the sweep and ambit of his spiritual experience and need are incalculably wider than his rational processes. So modernism, as such, covers only a segment of the spiritual field and does not nearly compass the range of religion's meaning.

Indeed, the critical need of overpassing modernism is evident in the fact that our personal spiritual problems do not lie there any more. When I was a student in the seminary, the classrooms where the atmosphere grew tense with excitement concerned the higher criticism of the Bible and the harmonization of science and religion. That, however, is no longer the case. The classrooms in the seminary where the atmosphere grows tense today concern Christian ethics and the towering question whether Christ has a moral challenge that can shake this contemporary culture to its foundations and save us from our deadly personal and social sins. So the world has moved far to a place where mere Christian harmonizers, absorbed with the intellectual attempt to adapt faith to science and accommodate Christ to prevalent culture, seem trivial and obsolete. Our modern world, as a whole, cries out not so much for souls intellectually adjusted to it as souls morally maladjusted to it, not most of all for accommodators and adjusters but for intellectual ethical challengers.

When Paul wrote his first letter to the Corinthians he said that he had become a Jew to the Jews that he might win the Jews, and a Greek to the Greeks that he might win the Greeks. "I am become," he said, "all things to all men, that I may by all means save some." That is a modernistic passage of adjustment and accommodation. But that is not all Paul said. Had it been all, Paul would have sunk from sight in an indistinguishable blend with the Greco-Roman culture of his day and we should never have heard of him. When he wrote the second time to the Corinthians he said something else:

> Come ye out from among them, and be ye separate,
>   saith the Lord,
> And touch no unclean thing.

Church of Christ, take that to yourself now! Stop this endeavor to harmonize yourself with modern cultures as though *that* were a standard and criterion. Rather, come out from among them. Only an independent standing-ground from which to challenge modern culture can save either it or you.

II

In the second place, not only has modernism been thus predominantly intellectualistic and therefore partial, but, strange to say, at the same time it has been dangerously sentimental. The reason for this is easy to explain. One of the predominant elements in the intellectual culture of the late nineteenth and early twentieth centuries, to which modernism adjusted itself, was illusory belief in inevitable progress. So many hopeful and promising things were afoot that two whole generations were fairly bewitched into thinking that every day in every way man was growing better and better. Scientific discovery, exploration and invention, the rising tide of economic welfare, the spread of democracy, the increase of humanitarianism, the doctrine of evolution itself, twisted to mean that automatically today has to be better than yesterday and tomorrow better than today—how many elements seduced us in those romantic days into thinking that all was right with the world!

In the intellectual culture to which modernistic Christianity adapted itself, such lush optimism was a powerful factor, and the consequences are everywhere present in the natural predispositions of our thought today. In the little village of Selbourne, England, the visitor is shown a row of lovely trees planted by a minister so that from his parsonage windows he need not look upon the village slaughter-house. Those trees are suggestive and symbolic of the sentimental illusions we plant to hide from our eyes the ugly facts of life. Especially we modernistic Christians, dealing as we were with thoughts of a kindly God by evolution lifting everything and everybody up, were deeply tempted to live in a fool's paradise behind our lovely trees!

For example, modernistic Christianity largely eliminated from its faith the God of moral judgment. To be sure, in the old theology, the God of moral judgment had been terribly presented so that little children did cry themselves to sleep at night for fear of him and of his hell. Modernism, not content with eliminating the excrescences of a harsh theology, became softer yet and created the general impression that there is nothing here to fear at all. One of the most characteristic movements of the nineteenth century heralded this summary of faith:

> The Fatherhood of God.
> The Brotherhood of Man.
> The Leadership of Jesus.
> Salvation by Character.
> The Progress of Mankind—
> Onward and upward forever.

Well, if that is the whole creed, this is a lovely world with nothing here to dread at all.

But there are things here to dread. Ask the physicians. They will tell us that in a law-abiding world are stern conditions whose fulfilment involves bodily destiny. Ask the novelists and dramatists, and at their best they are not lying to us as they reveal the inexorable fatality with which character and conduct work out their implied consequence. Ask the economists. They will tell us there are things to dread which lead to an inevitable economic hell. Ask even the historians and they will talk at times like old preachers about the God of moral judgment as James Anthony Froude did when he said: "One lesson, and only one, history may be said to repeat with distinctness: that the world is built somehow on moral foundations; that, in the long run, it is well with the good; in the long run, it is ill with the wicked."

Indeed, cannot we use our own eyes to see that there are things here to fear? For this is no longer the late nineteenth and early twentieth centuries. This is the epoch after the first world war has shaken the earth to its foundations and the God of judgment has spoken. My soul, what a world, which the gentle modernism of my younger ministry, with its kindly sentiments and lush optimism, does not fit at all! We must go beyond that. Because I know that I am speaking here to many minds powerfully affected by modernism, I say to you as to myself: Come out of these intellectual cubicles and sentimental retreats which we built by adapting Chris-

tian faith to an optimistic era. Underline this: *Sin is real.*
Personal and social sin is as terribly real as our forefathers
said it was, no matter how we change their way of saying
it. And it leads men and nations to damnation as they said
it did, no matter how we change their way of picturing it.
For these are times, real times, of the kind out of which man's
great exploits have commonly been won, in which, if a
man is to have a real faith he must gain it from the very
teeth of dismay; if he is to have real hope, it must shine,
like a Rembrandt portrait, from the dark background of fearful apprehension; if he is to have real character, he must
achieve it against the terrific down-drag of an antagonistic
world; and if he is to have a real church, it must be not
harmonized with the world but standing out from the world
and challenging it.

III

In the third place, modernism has even watered down
and thinned out the central message and distinctive truth of
religion, the reality of God. One does not mean by that, of
course, that modernists have been atheists. One does mean,
however, that the intellectual culture of the late nineteenth
and early twentieth centuries, to which modernism adjusted
itself, was predominantly man-centered. Man was blowing on
his hands and doing such things at such a rate as never had
been done or dreamed on earth before. Man was pioneer-
ing new truth and building a new social order. You young
people who were not here then can hardly imagine with
what cheerful and confident trust we confided to man the
saving of the world. So the temptation was to relegate God
to an advisory capacity, a kind of chairman of the board of
sponsors of our highly successful human enterprise. A poet
like Swinburne could even put the prevailing mood into candid words:

Thou art smitten, thou God, thou art smitten; thy death is
   upon thee, O Lord.
And the love-song of earth as thou diest resounds through
   the wind of her wings—
Glory to Man in the highest! for Man is the master of things.

Look out on the world today and try, if you can, to repeat those words of Swinburne and still keep your face straight! At any rate, if ever I needed something deeper to go on than Swinburne's sentimental humanism about man as the master of things, it is now—a philosophy, namely, a profound philosophy about what is ultimately and eternally real in this universe. We modernists were so disgusted with the absurdities of the old supernaturalistic theology as a whole and threw it away. But theology means thinking about the central problem of existence—that is ultimately and eternally real in this universe. And in the lurid light of days like these it becomes clearer, as an increasing number of atheists are honestly saying, that if the eternally real is merely material, if the cosmos is a physical fortuity and the earth an accident, if there is no profounder reason for mankind's being here than just that at one stage in the planet's cooling the heat happened to be right, and if we ourselves are "the disease of the agglutinated dust," then to stand on this temporary and accidental earth in the face of this vast cosmos and try lyrically to sing, "Glory to man in the highest, for man is the master of things," is an absurd piece of sentimental tomfoolery. And because I have been and am a modernist it is proper that I should confess that often the modernistic movement, adjusting itself to a man-centered culture, has encouraged this mood, watered down the thought of the Divine, and, may we be forgiven for this, left souls standing, like the ancient Athenians, before an altar to an Unknown God!

On that point the church must go beyond modernism. We have been all things to all men long enough. We have adapted and adjusted and accommodated and conceded long enough. We have at times gotten so low down that we talked as though the highest compliment that could be paid to Almighty God was that a few scientists believed in him. Yet all the time, by right, we had an independent standing-ground and a message of our own in which alone is there hope for humankind. The eternally real is the spiritual. The highest in us comes from the deepest in the universe. Goodness and truth and beauty are not accidents but revelations of creative reality. God is! On that point come out from among them and be ye separate! As the poet imagined Paul saying:

> Whoso has felt the Spirit of the Highest
> Cannot confound nor doubt Him nor deny:
> Yea with one voice, O world, tho' thou deniest,
> Stand Thou on that side, for on this am I.

IV

Finally, modernism has too commonly lost its ethical standing-ground and its power of moral attack. It is a dangerous thing for a great religion to begin adjusting itself to the culture of a special generation. Harmonizing slips easily into compromising. To adjust Christian faith to the new astronomy, the new geology, the new biology, is absolutely indispensable. But suppose that this modernizing process, well started, goes on and Christianity adapts itself to contemporary nationalism, contemporary imperialism, contemporary capitalism, contemporary racialism—harmonizing itself, that is, with the prevailing social *status quo* and the common moral judgments of our time—what then has become of religion, so sunk and submerged in undifferentiated identity with this world?

This lamentable end of a modernizing process, starting with indispensable adaptations and slipping into concessions and compromise, is a familiar phenomenon in religious history. For the word "modernism" may not be exclusively identified with the adjustment of Christian faith and practice to the culture of a single era. Modernization is a recurrent habit in every living religion. Early Protestantism, itself, emerging along with the new nationalism and the new capitalism was in its day modernism, involving itself and us in entanglements and compliances with political and economic ideas in whose presence we still are tempted to be servile. Every era with powerful originative factors evokes from religion indispensable adaptations, followed by further concessive acquiescences, which in time must be superseded and out grown. Early Christianity went out from an old Jewish setting into a new Greek culture and never would have survived if it had not carried up into its faith the profound insights of

Greek philosophy. So in the classic creeds, like that of Nicea, we have a blending of the old faith with the new philosophy, and in that process John and Paul themselves had already played a part. But, alas, early Christianity in its adjustment of its faith to Greek culture did not stop with adaptations to the insights of philosophy. At last it adapted itself to Constantine, to the imperial court, to war, to the lucrative enjoyment of imperial favors, to the use of bloody persecutions to coerce belief. One after another, it threw away the holiest things that had been entrusted to it by its Lord, until, often hardly distinguishable from the culture it lived in, it nearly modernized itself into moral futility. Lift up that history, as it were a mirror, in which to see the peril of our American churches.

It is not in Germany alone that the church stands in danger of being enslaved by society. There the enslavement is outward, deliberate, explicit, organized. Here it is secret, quiet, pervasive, insidious. A powerful culture—social, economic, nationalistic, militaristic—impinging from every side upon the church, cries with persuasive voices, backed by all the sanctions and motives most urgent to the self-interest of man, adjust yourself, adapt yourself, accommodate yourself!

When Great Britain was as mad about the Boer war as Italy is mad today about the Ethiopian war and all the forces of propaganda had whipped up the frenzy of the people to a fever heat, John Morley one night in Manchester faced an indignant, antagonistic crowd, and pleaded with his countrymen against the war. This in part is what he said:

You may carry fire and sword into the midst of peace and industry: it will be wrong. A war of the strongest government in the world against this little republic will bring you no glory: it will be wrong. You may make thousands of women widows and thousands of children fatherless: it will be wrong. You may add a new province to your empire: *it will still be wrong.*

John Morley did not call himself a Christian. He called himself an agnostic. But he was nearer standing where Christ intended his church to stand than the church has often been.

We modernists had better talk to ourselves like this. So

had the fundamentalists—but that is not our affair. We have already largely won the battle we started out to win; we have adjusted the Christian faith to the best intelligence of our day and have won the strong minds and the best abilities of the churches to our side. Fundamentalism is still with us but mostly in the backwaters. The future of the churches, if we will have it so, is in the hands of modernism. Therefore, let all modernists lift a new battle cry: We must go beyond modernism! And in that new enterprise the watchword will not be, Accommodate yourself to the prevailing culture! but, Stand out from it and challenge it! For this inescapable fact, which again and again in Christian history has called modernism to its senses, we face: we cannot harmonize Christ himself with modern culture. What Christ does to modern culture is to challenge it.

[29]

Reinhold Niebuhr
Ten Years That Shook My World*

The editor has suggested that this series of articles shall survey the currents of theological thought and life during the past decade in autobiographical terms, in the sense that they shall express the author's own reactions to theological winds of doctrine and give some account of how he arrived at his own convictions.

I

I can do this most simply by confessing that about midway in my ministry which extends roughly from the peace of Versailles to the peace of Munich, measured in terms of Western history, I underwent a fairly complete conversion of

* Copyright 1939 by Christian Century Foundation. Reprinted by permission from the April 26, 1939 issue of *The Christian Century*.

thought which involved rejection of almost all the liberal theological ideals and ideas with which I ventured forth in 1915. I wrote a book, my first, in 1927 which when now consulted is proved to contain almost all the theological windmills against which today I tilt my sword. These windmills must have tumbled shortly thereafter for every succeeding volume expresses a more and more explicit revolt against what is usually known as liberal culture.

While my critics accuse me of inconstancy my own biased judgment is that there is no inconstancy in the development of my thought since that day, though there is a gradual theological elaboration of what was at first merely socio-ethical criticism. Since the war was the revelation of the internal anarchy of Western civilization, the existence of which bourgeois culture was inclined to deny, and since the peace of Versailles was the revelation of vindictive passions which liberalism imagined were banished from the world, and since the peace of Munich proves that one cannot simply correct the injustices of conquest by the injustice which results from capitulation to tyranny, I conclude that the whole of contemporary history proves that liberal culture has not seen the problem of mankind in sufficient depth to understand its own history. Its too simple moralism has confused issues at almost every turn.

The contemporary problem is brought into theological focus if it is recognized that liberal Christianity is essentially an appropriation of the genuine achievements, and an accommodation to the characteristic prejudices, of this bourgeois culture which first came to flower in the Renaissance, which gained some triumphs and suffered some checks in the Reformation, which reached its zenith in the early part of this century, which revealed its internal anarchy in the World War and its inability to defend itself against lower forms of civilization in the present hour. In terms of politics and economics the bourgeois world is the world of the business man, of expanding commerce and industry, of economic imperialism, transmuted in a period of decay into economic nationalism.

II

In terms of culture, the bourgeois civilization produced what is generally known as liberalism. This liberalism, I must hasten to add, is something more than either the spirit of tolerance on the one hand or liberal economic theory on the other hand. The liberalism of classical economics, upon which capitalism is built (though it must disavow its own presuppositions in its period of decay) is only one characteristic fruit of the liberal culture. The faith of classical economic theory, that economic activity left to itself, without political interference, would gradually achieve a perfect harmony and justice, was merely one, though a very fateful, error derived from the general liberal assumption that man is essentially a very harmless animal, if only he can be held within the harmonies of nature and of reason from which the fanaticism of religion had beguiled him.

The spirit of tolerance in the liberal culture is of course a real gain. It belongs by right to any profound Christianity which understands the ambiguity of all human actions, the imperfection of all human ideals and the peril of self-righteous fanaticism in all human conflict. It must be admitted, however, that traditional Christianity, both Catholic and Protestant, had so frequently allowed the loyalty and worship, which belongs to God alone, to be appropriated for relative, social, political, economic and theological positions, that it had given rationalists good reason to believe that fanatic cruelty was the chief by-product, or possibly even the chief product, of religion.

It may be observed, however, that those who move away from a liberal culture have both the obligation and the possibility of proving that they have a securer foundation for the spirit of tolerance than traditional liberalism afforded. In secular liberalism the spirit of tolerance is either rooted in a deep skepticism and pessimism which must finally culminate in the intolerable sneer of Pilate, "What is truth?" or it is based on an untenable optimism which believes, with Professor Dewey, that men of good will must, if they meditate upon the issues of life long and profoundly enough, arrive

at a "common faith." Professor Dewey's notion that divisions
in the human family are chiefly derived from anachronistic
religious dogmas ought, incidentally, to be fairly well refuted
now by the force of the tragic events of contemporary
history.

In any profound Christianity the spirit of tolerance must be
derived from the knowledge that, however necessary it may
be to judge one another and even to fight one another on the
moral and political level, we are all sinners who stand under
God's ultimate judgment. It is this consciousness of a divine
judgment which must persuade us to recognize the validity
of Christ's admonition, "Judge not that ye be not judged," or
of St. Paul's exhortation: "Therefore thou art inexcusable, O
man, whosoever thou art that judgest; for wherein thou
judgest another, thou condemnest thyself; for thou that judgest doest the same thing."

III

If liberalism as a creed is more than the liberal spirit of
toleration on the one hand and more than laissez faire economics on the other, what is it? I should say primarily faith
in man; faith in his capacity to subdue nature, and faith that
the subjection of nature achieves life's final good; faith in
man's essential goodness, to be realized either when man
ceases to be spiritual and returns to nature (romanticism),
or when he ceases to be natural and becomes rational; and
finally, faith in human history which is conceived as a movement upward by a force immanent within it. Whether this
faith rests upon Darwin or upon Hegel, that is, whether
nature is believed to guarantee progress or whether progress
is conceived of as man's "gradual spiritualization" and his
emancipation from natural impulses, prejudices and parochial
attachments, the optimistic conclusion is the same.

It is instructive to note that liberal culture was always
divided against itself on the question whether it should regard
human nature and human history primarily from the standpoint of man's relation to nature or from the standpoint of his
rational transcendence over nature. In this conflict between
the naturalists and idealists, the idealists had something of the

Christian doctrine of the dignity of man as made in the image of God, and the naturalists had something of the Christian doctrine of man as a creature who must not pretend to be more than he is. But between them they lost the uneasy conscience of the Christian and expressed themselves in terms of an easy conscience. Whatever was wrong with man, the cause was some defect in his social organization or some imperfection in his education which further social history and cultural development would correct.

I may say that though I express my opposition to liberal civilization politically in terms of Marxian politics, I regard Marxian culture as participating essentially in all the liberal illusions. It also believes in the goodness of man, once capitalism has been destroyed. It also believes in an inevitable progress on the other side of the revolution. It has a catastrophic view of history, but only provisionally so. The destruction of capitalism is, for it, the final destruction of evil. This error must not be taken lightly, even by those of us who believe that the Marxian analysis of the relation of economics to politics is essentially correct.

The Marxian misunderstanding of man has contributed to the development of a tyranny in Russia which almost, though not quite, rivals fascist tyranny. Objectively it cannot be as bad, because it is impossible to destroy all the universal hopes in communism, which distinguish it from the franker tribal mania of fascism. Subjectively, this decay in Russia may be worse, because it extinguishes a new hope in which all the old lights are going out. I feel genuinely sorry for my friends who seem to be under a spiritual necessity to deny obvious facts about Russian tyranny.

IV

In a sense, the really tragic end of a liberal culture is to be found in the peace of Munich. What was best in that culture was outraged by the peace of Versailles and what was shallowest in it came to the conclusion that the horrors of a peace of conquest could be expiated by a peace of capitulation. Thus it lost its last chance to save what is genuine and universal in its life against the threat of a new

barbarism. It fondly imagines that the decay of the modern
world may still be healed by belatedly yielding "justice" to
Germany, when it is obvious that Germany, and the fascist
world in general, is no longer interested in justice, but bent
upon the display of its power and the exercise of a dominion
which asks no questions about justice in either the Christian
or the liberal sense.

Liberal moralism is, in short, unable to cope either with
man's immediate political or with his ultimate religious problems. It does not know how to check evil and historical injustice in politics, because it would like to operate against
injustice in terms of perfect moral purity. The ultimate religious problem of evil in man does not arise for it, because it
is always waiting for the perfect education or perfect social
order which will make man moral. It does not understand
man in the full dimension of his spirit, and does not see that
precisely because he is a child of God and made in God's
image, he cannot be contained in, or easily checked by, either
the harmony of nature or the prudence of reason.

It would, of course, be grossly unfair not to recognize that
liberal Christianity made a genuine contribution to true Christianity by appropriating some of the achievements of this
culture. Through some of these appropriations liberal Christianity purified Christian theology of some of its grievous
historical errors. One of these was the insistence of Christian
orthodoxy that a religious explanation of natural events was
also a scientific explanation and obviated the necessity of tracing the natural sequence of events and their secondary causation.

But religion is constitutionally indifferent to the problem of
secondary causation. This indifference becomes a sin when
theology is made into a bad science and the sense of ultimate
meaning and creation is allowed to obscure the problem of
natural causation. In accommodating itself to the "scientific
spirit," liberal Christianity therefore rightly clarified an ancient confusion, though it must be admitted that it was
frequently betrayed thereby into a world view in which its
essential theism was transmuted into a vague pantheism.

A second great gain of liberal Christianity, derived from

the achievements of modern culture, was the application of
the scientific historical method to its own records. Ethi-
cally, this emancipated Christianity from the necessity of regarding any moral attitude, fortuitously enshrined in its own
canon, as final and authoritative. It permitted the Christian
law of love to stand out in Christian ethics as the only final
norm. Theologically, this scientific spirit saved Christianity
from the corruption of the profound principle, *credo ut in-
telligam*, into a tyranny of theological authority over human
reason. These gains of liberal Christianity must not be imperiled. It would be truer to say that they must not be
sacrificed, though they will be imperiled. Frantic and hysterical retreats to orthodoxy are bound to imperil them. This
advance must be protected against those who think it a gain
to return to theological obscurantism from the shallows of a
too simple rationalism.

But liberal Christianity quite obviously accepted the
prejudices as well as the achievements of modern culture. It
was pathetically eager to justify itself before the "modern
mind" and failed to realize that this modern mind was involved in a very ancient human sin. It imagined itself the
final mind. It thought of itself as God, the final arbiter of
truth and destiny.

v

In seeking to persuade the modern mind that Christianity
is respectable and intelligent, the liberals sacrificed most of
the essential Christian positions. Christ was transmuted into
the good man Jesus, who could charm all men to become as
good as he was. The classic Christology of the God-man was
repudiated, though innumerable reservations sought to hide
the repudiation. It was not recognized that this absurd
doctrine of the God-man Christ contains the whole essence of
the Christian faith—its belief that God transcends history and
yet makes himself known in history; that history measured
by Christ is tragic and ends tragically for it crucifies Christ;
that only God is able to resolve the conflict between what
man is and what he ought to be, a conflict in which all men
stand; that God cannot do this by simply wiping out history

and transmuting it into eternity, but by redeeming history, but that the redemption of history involved more than persuading man to follow the law of God. It involved God's taking upon himself the inevitable violation of that law.

Liberal Christianity, in short, tended to follow modern culture in estimating both the stature and the virtue of man. It did not recognize that man is a spirit who can find a home neither in nature nor in reason, but only in God. The power of human self-transcendence (the true image of God) is such that man can and does break every restraint set by nature or reason. His very capacities are occasions for sin in him. It is because he is made in the image of God that man can be tempted to make himself God, to seek to overcome his natural insecurity by pretensions of power which involve him in more insecurity; to seek to hide the finiteness of his intelligence by pretensions of absolute truth, which involve him in cruel fanaticisms; to seek to transcend his insignificance by claims of importance which are both ridiculous and dangerous.

All these things man does, not because his pure mind is impeded by the inertia of his animal nature, but because he is the only animal who is involved in history and yet stands outside of it, the only creature who has a glimpse of the eternal beyond the finite and is incited to pretend an eternal significance for all his finite interests, values and ideals.

For this reason, the simple reinterpretation of the Kingdom of God into the law of progress, in the thought of liberal Christianity, is an equally serious betrayal of essential insights of the Christian faith to the prejudices of modern culture. Obviously there is progress of all kinds in human history, including progress in aerial bombing and the effective use of the radio for the dissemination of political lies. There is progress from immaturity to maturity in every field of endeavor. But there is not a single bit of evidence to prove that good triumphs over evil in this constant development of history. History points to a goal beyond itself, and not merely to an eternity which negates history.

This is what all biblical religion tries to say in words and symbols which outrage reason, as they must. For reason cannot contain this idea, though, if it is astute enough, it can uncover the absurdity of alternative propositions. Liberal Christianity sought to efface these irrationalities of biblical apocalypticism by discovering that Jesus had, indeed, some difficulty in freeing his thought about the Kingdom of God from outworn forms of Jewish thought, but that he is to be commended for almost achieving this desirable emancipation in the end and thus approximating what an enlightened modern man believes about history.

Yet from the standpoint of mere history the final story about this Jesus is that he was crucified. That he was raised from the dead and will come again in glory—*that* faith belongs to another dimension which is beyond history, and yet without which history would be either meaningless or filled with tragic meaning only.

VI

Christianity, in short, faces the tremendous task of extricating itself from the prejudices and illusions of a culture which is rapidly sinking with the disruption of the civilization which gave it birth. This is not yet fully realized in America, because the prospects and hopes of our civilization are sufficiently brighter than in Europe to give liberal illusions a tougher vitality and a slower death here. This task of emancipation is a tremendous one, partly because liberalism as a culture is still superior to many of the cultures which threaten to displace it politically. It is certainly superior to the primitive and Nietzschian romanticism which expresses itself in fascist politics. It may even prove superior to socialism, if socialism sacrifices the achievements of democracy as it has done in Russia.

One of the real tragedies of our era is that the very democracy which is the great achievement of liberalism cannot be maintained if liberalism is not transcended as a culture. The problem of achieving economic justice is obviously more difficult than liberalism had imagined. The prerequisite of economic justice is a tolerable equilibrium of economic power, which in a technical age means the socialization of property. The excessive moralism of liberalism makes it impossible to see either the necessity of this end or the rigorous means which will be required to achieve it. Liberalism seems unable to move toward the economic democracy which is required to maintain its political democracy. Nor does it seem able to protect what is still left of its political democracy against the threat of a new barbarism; which is what makes the peace of Munich so significant.

If I believe that the Christian understanding of man could help solve some of these crucial issues and could conserve the best achievements of liberalism better than traditional liberalism can conserve them, I do not for that reason wish merely to hitch Christian faith to this or to that political task. Christianity faces ultimate issues of life which transcend all political vicissitudes and achievements. But the answer which Christian faith gives to man's ultimate perplexities and the hope which it makes possible in the very abyss of his despair, also throw light upon the immediate historical issues which he faces. Christianity is not a flight into eternity from the tasks and decisions of history. It is rather the power and the wisdom of God which makes decisions in history possible and which points to proximate goals in history which are usually obscured either by optimistic illusions or by the despair which followed upon the dissipation of these illusions. Christianity must therefore wage constant war, on the one hand against political religions which imagine some proximate goal and some conditioned good as man's final good, and on the other hand against an otherworldliness which by contrast gives these political religions a seeming validity.

VII

For this reason, any new orthodoxy which seeks to persuade men that because all men must finally be made manifest before the judgment seat of Christ, they are not to regard the momentary judgments, the proximate goals and the relative values of history seriously, must be regarded as a heresy as dangerous as any simple optimism. In every experience of life, Christ appears in many guises to the believer. He is the judge in comparison with whom I am found to fall short and to be an unprofitable servant. He is the redeemer who gives my life a new center of loyalty and a new source of power. He is, however, also the law, the logos, the essential structure of life, which I must seek to obey, even though I fall short in my obedience. He is what I am essentially, and therefore what I ought to be.

Liberal Christianity emphasized that fact rather too simply. The new orthodoxy rightly insists that he is also what I can never be. He is therefore the source of my despair. Only in that despair and in repentance can he become the source of of a new hope. This second emphasis is true enough. Only it will tempt us "to continue to sin that grace may abound" if we do not preserve what is genuinely Christian in liberal Christian moralism: the insistence that Christ is our law, our ideal, our norm, and the revelation of our essential being.

All this is not very autobiographical, after all. The only autobiographical note which I can add, in conclusion, is that such theological convictions which I hold today began to dawn upon me during the end of a pastorate in a great industrial city. They dawned upon me because the simple little moral homilies which were preached in that as in other cities, by myself and others, seemed completely irrelevant to the brutal facts of life in a great industrial center. Whether irrelevant or not, they were certainly futile. They did not change human actions or attitudes in any problem of collective behavior by a hair's breadth, though they may well have helped to preserve private amenities and to assuage individual frustrations.

These convictions which dawned in my pastorate have been further elaborated in a teaching position in a theological seminary. Greater leisure has given me opportunity to discover the main currents and emphases of the classical ages of Christian thought, and to find insights there which have been long neglected and which are yet absolutely essential to modern man, or indeed to man of any age.

However, since I am not so much scholar as preacher, I must confess that the gradual unfolding of my theological ideas has come not so much through study as through the pressure of world events. Whatever measure of Christian faith I hold today is due to the gradual exclusion of alternative beliefs through world history. As did Peter, I would

preface my confession, "Thou hast words of eternal life,"
with the question, "Lord, to whom shall we go?" Even while
imagining myself to be preaching the gospel, I had really ex-
perimented with many modern alternatives to Christian faith,
until one by one they proved unavailing.

BIBLIOGRAPHICAL NOTE

There is considerable literature on this period. The reader
may wish to consult Daniel Day Williams, *What Present Day
Theologians are Thinking*, revised edition (New York, 1959),
and the introductory essay by Hans Frei in Paul Ramsay,
editor, *Faith and Ethics: The Theology of H. Richard
Niebuhr* (New York, 1957). A thorough study of the changing views of sin is Mary Frances Thelen, *Man As Sinner in
Contemporary American Realistic Theology* (New York,
1946). George Ernest Wright, *God Who Acts* (London,
1952) shows the concern of the biblical theologian. Robert T.
Handy, "The American Religious Depression 1925–35,"
Church History, xxix, 1960, pp. 2–16, places the change in
the wider context of American religious life.

Much has been written about Reinhold Niebuhr. Of special importance are the contributions of several critics of
Niebuhr's work in Charles Kegley and Robert Bretall, editors,
The Theology of Reinhold Niebuhr (New York, 1956). Harry
Emerson Fosdick's *The Living of These Days* (New York,
1956) is an enjoyable and illuminating biographical statement.

XI. THE ECUMENICAL MOVEMENT

INTRODUCTION

Though the nineteenth century brought the formation of many indigenous American denominations and the division of other church groups there were also efforts to encourage church unity. The Plan of Union (1801) aided joint Congregational-Presbyterian missionary work in the "Western Reserve"; the Evangelical Alliance, founded in 1849 with an American branch in 1867, encouraged interdenominational co-operation; the conflicts within the missionary movement also prompted organizational structures which attempted to overcome competing activities. The Federal Council of Churches (1908) consisted of thirty-three Protestant denominations attempting to deal with the witness of the church in industrial society.

A major date in the history of the ecumenical movement is 1948, the formation of the World Council of Churches at Amsterdam. It included one hundred and forty seven churches from forty four countries. The WCC brought American Protestantism into intimate conversation with churches from other nations. In Assemblies since 1948 the ties and mutual understanding among denominations have been enhanced. Within the United States, the National Council of Churches (1950) made possible joint statements on national and international issues. No attempt was made to unite denominations into one church or to require doctrinal uniformity. The selection included below from the Second Assembly of the World Council of Churches, held in Evanston, Illinois, in 1954, illustrates the theological concerns of the contemporary ecumenical movement.

Many within American Protestantism have not supported these efforts. Those of highly conservative theological positions formed the American Council of Christian Churches in 1941. The most prominent figure among the conservatives is

Carl McIntire (1906–   ), a graduate of Park College and
Westminster Seminary. After a bitter battle within the judi-
catories of the Presbyterian Church in the 1930s he was removed from its rolls and formed the Bible Presbyterian
Church. The recurring theme in McIntire's attack on the
World Council of Churches and National Council of Churches
is that "modernist" and "socialistic" views dominate the organizations. His position received modest international attention with the formation of the International Council of Christian Churches in August, 1948, a week before the First
Assembly of the World Council of Churches; both groups
met in Amsterdam. The vehemence and character of his attack is seen in the selection from Carl McIntire's *Servants of
Apostasy*.

[30]

The Evanston Assembly
World Council of Churches
Faith and Order: Our Oneness
in Christ and Our Disunity as Churches*

"Christ in you, the hope of glory" (Col. 1: 27)

INTRODUCTION

1. We speak as those who have met together in the
World Council of Churches and have known for a fact that
we have been given a "oneness in Christ," in spite of our
"disunity as churches."

* From *The Evanston Report: The Second Assembly of the
World Council of Churches 1954.* Edited by W. A. Visster
'T Hooft, copyrighted © 1955 Harper & Brothers, Publishers, Inc.,
pp. 82–91. Reprinted with the permission of Harper & Brothers,
Publishers, Inc., New York.

This oneness is no mere unity of sentiment. We become aware of it because it is given to us by God as the Holy Spirit reveals to us what Christ has done for us. In this report we have tried to make clearer what we believe about this given unity, in the prayer that if we, and the churches from which we come, strive earnestly to lay hold upon the meaning of that which is already given, the Spirit of God will open our eyes to still deeper understanding, and our hearts to still fuller enjoyment of the unity which is ours in Christ.

To that end:

First, we speak together with one mind and in accordance with the witness of the New Testament, of the oneness of the Church, as grounded in the whole work of Christ, as growth into the fulness of Christ and as partially realized even in our present divided state.

Secondly, we speak of our disunity as churches as partaking of that disobedience over which Christ has won His victory, granting us even in our disunity some foretaste of our ultimate unity in Him.

Thirdly, we speak of some of the consequences for us, in the obedience of faith, as we meet together in His saving Name to beg Him to fulfil His unifying work in us.

I. Our Oneness in Christ

A. CHRIST'S UNIFYING WORK

2. The New Testament conceives of the unity of the Church, not as sociological, but as having its essential reality in Christ Himself and in His indissoluble unity with His people (Acts 9: 4 ff.; 1 Cor. 12: 12; Jn. 15: 1 f.). Hence we must still ask Paul's question about division in the Church: "Is Christ divided?" (1 Cor. 1: 13), and assert with the Apostle the indestructible unity that belongs to the Church in Christ. Christ is the *one* Lord who represents and gathers to Himself the *many* of redeemed humanity, and it is therefore He alone who makes the many to be one in the Church (1 Cor. 12: 12; Eph. 1: 10, 22; cf. Jn. 14: 20; 17: 4 ff.; 1 Cor. 6: 16 f.).

3. The New Testament speaks in many ways of the relationship of Christ and His people to describe their unity in Him. The Church is many members in one body (1 Cor. 12: 12); the several members are subject to the one Lord as Head of the body (Eph. 1: 22; 4: 15; 5: 23; Col. 1: 18; 2: 19); the Church is His bride, to be united to Him, the bridegroom (Mk. 2: 19; Rev. 19: 7; cf. Mt. 22: 2 ff.; 25: 10 f.; Lk. 12: 36; Eph. 1: 22 ff.) the faithful are His people (1 Pet. 2: 9 f.; Col. 3: 12; Rom. 11: 2, 11 f., 32); He is the new temple in whom true worship is offered (Jn. 2: 19 ff.; cf. 4: 21 ff.) or the one building of which the believers constitute living stones (1 Pet. 2: 5; Eph. 2: 20; cf. 1 Cor. 3: 9); He is the vine, of which we are the branches (Jn. 15: 1 ff.), or the shepherd whose flock we are (Jn. 10: 1 ff.).

4. The New Testament thinks of the one life of the Church as deriving from the whole Person and work of Jesus Christ as Saviour and Lord. The Church's unity is grounded in His taking of our nature upon Him; in His own words and works by which the power and life of His kingdom were manifested; in His calling of men into the fellowship of His kingdom, and in the appointing of the Twelve to share in His messianic ministry and work; in His passion and death, where sin was finally conquered and the power of divisiveness defeated; in His resurrection, where He manifested the new man unto whom we all grow (Eph. 4: 11 ff.), in whom all human divisions are done away (Gal. 3: 28); in His ascension and heavenly reign, by which all history is brought under His authority; in His outpouring of the Holy Spirit on the whole Church at Pentecost, which gives to each subsequent baptismal rite its deepest significance; and in His promise to come again as the triumphant and glorious king. Through the indwelling Spirit, the Comforter, who leads the Church into all truth, the unity of the Church even now is a foretaste of the fulness that is to be because it already is; therefore, the Church can work tirelessly and wait patiently and expectantly for the day when God shall sum up all things in Christ.

B. THE ONENESS OF THE CHURCH IN ITS EARTHLY PILGRIMAGE

5. From the beginning the Church has been given an indissoluble unity in Christ, by reason of His self-identification with His people. But the Church has never realized the fulness of that unity. From the beginning discord has marred the manifested unity of Christ's people (Lk. 22: 24 ff.; Mk. 10: 35 ff.). Thus we may speak of the oneness of the Church in its earthly pilgrimage as a growth from its unity, as given, to its unity, as fully manifested (Eph. 4: 3, 13). In this way we may think of the Church as we are able to think of the individual believer, who may be said at one and the same time to be both a justified man and a sinner (*simul justus et peccator*). In each Christian there is both the "new man" who has been created and yet must be put on daily (2 Cor. 5: 17) and also the "old man" who has been crucified with Christ and yet must be daily mortified (Col. 3: 1–5). So the Church is already one in Christ, by virtue of His identification of Himself with it (Jn. 14: 20; 15: 1–5) and must become one in Christ, so as to manifest its true unity (Eph. 4: 11–16) in the mortification of its divisions.

6. Christ of His love and grace has given His Church such gifts as it needs for its growth from unity to unity. The gifts are severally and together none other than Christ Himself, but each has its place and its function in the life of the Church as it strives to give obedience to its Lord. Christ has given His Spirit, which is the bond of peace and love, and the guide to all truth. He has given apostles, prophets, evangelists, pastors and teachers, that the unity of the body may be continually built up. He has given the Scriptures, the preaching of the Word, Baptism and Eucharist by which the Church proclaims the forgiveness of sins and by which, in the power of the Holy Spirit, faith is quickened and nourished. He has given the Church the gift and power of prayer, by which the Church can plead both for its own unity and for the reconciliation of men to God and to one another. He has given it faith and hope and love, that in its own life a new divine unity shall be manifest in deeds, and that its service to

the world shall be both a manifestation of unity and a summons to it.

7. The New Testament, therefore, testifies to us that the Church shares in the life both of this world and of that which is to come. Indeed the Church's life is encompassed by a "great cloud of witnesses" (Heb. 12: 2)—and the Church must never forget that its citizenship is really there, in the heavenly places (Eph. 2: 6). Its responsibilities must be discharged in this present world, but it must never become conformed to the world.

8. Thus the fellowship (*koinonia*) that the members of the Church have is not simply human fellowship; it is fellowship with the Father and with His Son Jesus Christ through the Holy Spirit and fellowship with the saints, in the Church triumphant. In all the Church's life there is being manifested not simply the activity of mortal men, but the life of the whole Church, militant on earth, triumphant in heaven, as it has its unity in the one Lord of the Church, who is its life.

9. But all this cannot be asserted without understanding that the unity given to the Church in Christ, and gifts given to the Church to help and enable it to manifest its given unity, are not for the sake of the Church as an historical society, but for the sake of the world. The Church has its being and its unity in the "Son of Man, who came not to be ministered unto, but to minister and to give his life a ransom for many." The being and unity of the Church belong to Christ and therefore to His mission, to His enduring the Cross for the joy that was set before Him. Christ wrought "one new man" for us all by His death, and it is by entering into His passion for the redemption of a sinful and divided world that the Church finds its unity in its crucified and risen Lord.

C. THE ONENESS OF THE CHURCH PARTIALLY REALIZED

10. Jesus Christ has given to His Church the gift of Himself and thereby the means of corporate life. These gifts were given not solely to the Church of New Testament days, nor are they reserved for the Church in some ideal state which ought to exist but unhappily does not. We acknowledge these gifts as being in a real sense present possessions.

11. It would be ungrateful to a merciful God if we did not speak now of those gifts which assure us that the undivided Christ is present amongst us, pouring His life into us all, in spite of our divisions.

12. We all wait upon one Father, through the one Holy Spirit, praying that we may be ready to hear and obey when He takes of the things of Christ and shows them to us. We all read the Holy Scriptures and proclaim the gospel from them in the faith that the Word speaking through them draws us to Himself and into the apostolic faith. We all receive His gift of Baptism whereby, in faith, we are engrafted in Him even while we have not yet allowed it fully to unite us with each other. We all hear His command to "do this" and His word "This is my body . . . this is my blood" in the Sacrament of the Eucharist, even whilst our celebration of the Lord's Supper is not yet at one Table. We all receive a ministry of the Word and Sacraments, even whilst our ministries are not yet recognized by all and not understood in the same sense. We all are called to be imitators of Christ and to follow Him in moral obedience as we confess Him before men even though we are still unprofitable servants.

13. As we have come to know each other better in the World Council of Churches, we have come to appreciate the immense range of common practice and intention which we share. The *fact* of our common (though diverse) use of these gifts is a powerful evidence of our unity in Christ and a powerful aid to reminding us that unity lies in His work and not in our own achievements. We have also discovered that the old confessional divisions are being criss-crossed by new lines of agreement and disagreement.

14. We give thanks to our Father for these evidences that our unity in Christ is a present reality, both in the World Council of Churches and in relation to other Christians whose fellowship we do not as yet fully enjoy. But the very fact that, in every case, our benefit from these mercies is marred by our separation from each other, compels us now to examine seriously how it is that our disunity as churches contradicts our unity in Christ.

II. *Our Disunity as Churches*

15. Only in the light of the oneness of the Church in Christ can we understand the difference between diversity and division in the Church, and their relation to sin. There is diversity which is not sinful but good because it reflects both the diversities of gifts of the Spirit in the one body and diversities of creation by the one Creator. But when diversity disrupts the manifest unity of the body, then it changes its quality and becomes sinful division. It is sinful because it obscures from men the sufficiency of Christ's atonement, inasmuch as the gospel of reconciliation is denied in the very lives of those who proclaim it.

16. Divisions in the Church have been caused and are perpetuated, to a large degree, by sincere concern for the gospel. Some believed that others were departing from the God-given structure and faith of the Church by unwarrantable claims and unfounded doctrines. So came the schism between East and West. Some believed that God had called them to such reformation of the faith and order of the Church as would restore it to its primitive purity. They found their work could not be completed within the framework of Roman Catholicism; thus came the separate churches of the Reformation. Some believed that the faith must indeed be reformed but within the framework of ancient and historic episcopacy. So the Anglican and Old Catholic communions became separated both from Rome and from many of the Reformed churches. Some believed that the established churches of their day would not give free course to the Word of salvation. So the older free churches and the Methodist connexion felt themselves forced to adopt independent church orders. Similar acts of conscientious obedience to the will of God have likewise resulted, even if unintended, in breaches of Christian fellowship in doctrine, sacraments and order. God in His mercy has used such decisions to save souls, to build up communities who worship Him, and to preserve or recover aspects of His truth. All this we can and must say. But He has also given to us today a fresh awareness of the sin which

characterizes the divided state which we have inherited. We shall never, in this life, escape from our sinfulness, but we can repent of sin when it is revealed to us. Even when we have done that which we thought it right to do, we must remember that we are culpably implicated in sin not wholly of our own making and cannot dissociate ourselves from the sin of division. Confession of oneness with Christ carries with it confession of solidarity with our brethren in sin.

17. We ask each other whether we do not sin when we deny the sole lordship of Christ over the Church by claiming the vineyard for our own, by possessing our "church" for ourselves, by regarding our theology, order, history, nationality, etc., as our own "valued treasures," thus involving ourselves more and more in the separation of sin. The point at which we are unable to renounce the things which divide us, because we believe that obedience to God Himself compels us to stand fast—this is the point at which we come together to ask for mercy and light. So what we believe to be our "faithfulness" must bring us together at the foot of the Cross. The Cross tells us that where the dividing power of sin was most manifest, there God has gained the victory. By the same Cross He is able to make all things to work together for good—even our divisions. By planting the Cross of Christ in the midst of our divisions we believe He will overrule all their sin and make them serve His purpose of unity.

18. Concretely, this means that when churches, in their actual historical situations, reach a point of readiness and a time of decision, then their witnessing may require obedience unto death. They may then have to be prepared to offer up some of their accustomed, inherited forms of life in uniting with other churches without complete certainty as to all that will emerge from the step of faith. Otherwise, acts of apparent re-union might be merely acts of calculated self-aggrandizement and a betrayal of the true calling of the Church. But when churches have been ready in this sense "to die with Christ," they have found that He who raised Jesus from the dead is faithful and powerful still.

19. It is certain that the perfect unity of the Church will not be totally achieved until God sums up all things in Christ.

But the New Testament affirms that this unity is already being realized within the present historical order. By the power of His resurrection, Christ has granted this grace to His Church even now, and the signs of His work are discernible to him who has eyes to see. In the upheavals of the present hour, Jesus Christ is gathering His people in a true community of faith and obedience without respect for existing divisions.

We must not assume that the divisions which now separate Christians from one another correspond to those which Christ brings about in times of tribulation. Still less can we think that they will coincide with the separation finally to be made by the Son of Man. In this eschatological perspective all our human divisions are provisional.

III. *The Action of Faith*

20. Christ has made us one by breaking down walls of partition. We are nevertheless disunited as churches. How are we to act in the obedience of faith and hope in our one Lord?

21. At least we all ought to be united in thinking of our divisions with repentance: not the repentance we may expect of others, but that which *we* undertake ourselves—cost what it may—even when others are unwilling to follow. True repentance is the acknowledgment before God that we have sinned so as to be caught in the net of inexplicable evil and rendered unable to heal our divisions by ourselves. But we cannot in sincerity and truth repent of our various understandings of God's will for His Church, unless the Spirit Himself reveals that our understandings have been in error. Penitence cannot be hypocrisy. Neither can it truly be expressed without desire for forgiveness and amendment of life.

22. All of us as members of churches believe that we have been entrusted by God with certain elements of the one Church of Christ which we cannot forfeit. But at least we in the World Council of Churches are committed to a fellowship in which we are ready to bring our convictions under scrutiny in the presence of our fellow Christians and in the presence of the living Christ. In common we seek to know the judg-

ment of the Word of God upon these convictions as to any error which may be involved in them.

23. Together we suggest the following ways in which, being both united and divided, we all must seek to be obedient:

(i) In thanking God joyfully for the actual oneness He has given us in the World Council of Churches, we must try to understand the theological implications of this ecumenical fact and to implement it in the concrete relations of neighbour churches. With the Lund Conference on Faith and Order, we ask the churches "whether they should not act together in all matters except those in which deep differences of conviction compel them to act separately." We do not minimize the deep differences separating some churches. Nor do we ignore the numerous attempts to unite churches and the achievements of such reunion. In the World Council of Churches we still "intend to stay together." But beyond that, as the Holy Spirit may guide us, we intend to unite. "The World Council of Churches is not . . . a Super-Church."[1] Hence we do not ask the World Council of Churches to initiate plans for union, but to keep providing occasions for honest encounter between divided Christians.

24. (ii) We must all listen together in the midst of our disunity to our one Lord speaking to us through Holy Scripture. This is a hard thing to do. We still struggle to comprehend the meaning and authority of Holy Scripture. Yet whenever we are prepared to undertake together the study of the Word of God and are resolved to be obedient to what we are told, we are on the way toward realizing the oneness of the Church in Christ in the actual state of our dividedness on earth. In this connection we need also to study together the significance of Christian tradition and our various traditions, as reflected in liturgy, preaching and teaching.

25. (iii) We must consider frankly the influence of social and cultural differences upon the matters of faith and order which cause divisions, and also perceive how the events and

[1] See "The Church, the Churches, and the World Council of Churches," W.C.C. Central Committee, Toronto, 1950.

developments of current history make disunity a most urgent
question.

26. (iv) We must speak the truth in love with one another
and practise that love towards those with whom we disagree
(Eph. 4: 15, 25). Sometimes this involves us in judgments
which fellow Christians cannot recognize as being made in
love. At other times, we are so conscious of both the sin and
the cultural conditioning with which all our judgments are
infected that we are tempted to be more tolerant than truth
allows.

27. (v) We must learn afresh the implications of the one
Baptism for our sharing in the one Eucharist. For some, but
not for all, it follows that the churches can only be conformed
to the dying and rising again in Christ, which both Sacraments set forth, if they renounce their eucharistic separateness. We must explore the deeper meaning of these two
sacramental gifts of the Lord to His Church as they are
rooted in His own redeeming work.[2]

28. (vi) We must seek to acknowledge beyond the
bounds of our own church each ministry that preaches the
gospel of reconciliation as a means whereby Christ performs
His saving deeds. Especially need we to discover the meaning
of the ministry of the laity for Christian unity.

29. (vii) We must bear witness together to the gospel of
Him who has already overcome our sins and divisions and
who graciously uses sinners as His servants. Our divided witness is a necessarily defective witness, and indeed a scandal
in the face of the non-Christian world. We have scarcely begun to work out the essential connection between "mission"
and "unity." Our Lord's own prayer (Jn. 17: 21 f.) must become our own, not only on our lips but in our lives.

30. (viii) The measure of our concern for unity is the
degree to which we pray for it. We cannot expect God to
give us unity unless we prepare ourselves to receive His gift
by costly and purifying prayer. To pray *together* is to be
drawn together. We urge, wherever possible, the observance
of the Week of Prayer for Christian Unity, January 18–25

[2] Cf. Lund Report, Chapter V.

(or some other period suited to local conditions) as a public testimony to prayer as the road to unity.

31. We cannot discern all that will be disclosed to us when we look to Him who is the Head of the body and affirm our oneness in Him. We know that we shall be changed, but wherein we shall be changed we cannot know until, in the act of faith and self-denial, we are given to discern, through crucifixion and resurrection, the lineaments of the one true Body of Christ which our sinful dividedness obscures from ourselves and from the world. Rejoicing in the grace which has been bestowed upon us in His various gifts even in our sin and separateness, we here set our hope on our one Lord Jesus Christ, who comes to take control over our divided and broken estate and to heal it by His grace and power. At Amsterdam we said that we intend to stay together. He has kept us together. He has shown Himself again as our Hope. Emboldened by this Hope, we dedicate ourselves to God anew, that He may enable us to grow together.

[31]

Carl McIntire
The Dividing Line*

The Jews answered him, saying, For a good work we stone thee not; but for blasphemy; and because that thou, being a man, makest thyself God.—John 10:33.

Two movements of a world-wide nature have arisen within this twentieth century to challenge and command the Christian churches. The first is the Ecumenical Movement, represented in the World Council of Churches and the International Missionary Council. The second is the Twentieth

* From Carl McIntire, *Servants of Apostasy* (Collingswood, N. J., 1955), pp. 1–4; 7–15. Used by permission of Dr. Carl McIntire.

Century Reformation movement, represented in the International Council of Christian Churches and its related organizations. Ecumenical means "the inhabited world," or world wide. The ecumenical church means "The World Church." The World Council was formally constituted in Amsterdam, August 22 to September 4, 1948. Just previous to this, August 11 to 19, in the historic English Reformed Church in Amsterdam, where the Pilgrims worshiped before coming to America, the International Council of Christian Churches was formally established.

The World Council is a council of churches which includes the Greek Orthodox churches and is publicly referred to as a council of Protestant and Greek Orthodox churches; the International Council of Christian Churches is made up exclusively of Protestant bodies. The I.C.C.C. held its Second Plenary Congress in Geneva, Switzerland, August 16 to 23, 1950, and its Third Plenary Congress in Philadelphia, August 3 to 12, 1954. This preceded by a few days the Second Assembly of the W.C.C. which met in Evanston, just north of Chicago, August 15 to 31, 1954. At the Evanston Assembly, the World Council received two additional bodies, making a total of 163 denominations. At the Philadelphia Assembly, the International Council of Christian Churches received into its membership 12 new bodies, and now numbers 54 self-governing, evangelical denominations.

The World Council is large. It includes most of the major church bodies, and presumes to speak for the non-Roman churches. It claims to speak for 170,000,000 people scattered over the face of the earth. The International Council of Christian Churches is small, several of its denominations in the United States having withdrawn from denominations which are in places of leadership in the World Council of Churches itself. The two groups are rivals in many respects. When the question is asked, "What is the difference?" one is immediately confronted with basic questions concerning the Christian faith, the nature of the church, and the preservation of human freedom. The Twentieth Century Reformation movement is what its name suggests—an effort to restore the Protestant churches to their original historic positions in the light of the Scriptures.

The Evanston Assembly took as its theme, "Christ, the Hope of the World," but used no text of Scripture. The Philadelphia Congress took as its theme, "The Historic Christian Faith," and for its theme text, Revelation 1: 9, "For the word of God, and for the testimony of Jesus Christ." The World Council of Churches met on the campus of Northwestern University, in McGaw Memorial auditorium, for its plenary sessions. The International Council of Christian Churches met on the campus of Faith Theological Seminary, Elkins Park, the former home of P. A. B. Widener, the world-famous Widener Estate, and held its plenary sessions in a large cathedral tent.

Both of these groups speak of Christian co-operation and unity, but the basis of the co-operation and the concept of unity are entirely different.

In this world in which we live there is such a person as a Christian—a Christian. What is a Christian? A Christian is an individual who has accepted Jesus Christ as his personal Saviour, believed that Christ died for his sins, and seeks, in all things, to obey the commands of Christ. A Christian is one who has been born again. He is a new creature in Christ, and his salvation has come by faith—by faith alone. He believes God's Word, and in faith he accepts it for what it represents itself to be: the verbally inspired Scriptures of the Old and New Testaments.

All who are Christians, regardless of their color, their race, or where they may live, are brethren—worshiping and serving one Lord and Master. As such, they belong to one another. They have an interest and a concern one for another. They are going to spend eternity together. They are members of His body, the Church invisible.

There is such a thing as the historic Christian faith. The Christian religion consists of certain definite and specific tenets, or doctrines. The various churches of different denominational complexion—which have come out of the history of the Church—have all stood, in their beginnings, for the great doctrines which are distinctive of the Christian faith. And each, within its own particular emphasis, has stood for its own denominational testimony. But as such, these churches have recognized one another as Christian churches.

There are Christian churches. There are Presbyterian, Reformed, Lutheran, Independent, Congregational, Baptist, Methodist, Brethren, Evangelical, and a wide range of others. These churches seek to preach the Gospel, to honor the name of Jesus Christ, to worship God, and to administer the sacraments. Is there anything wrong, therefore, with Christian co-operation among Christian churches? Absolutely nothing. It is a normal, natural development, especially with the elimination of distance by the development in our century of speedy means of communication and transportation. With the shrinking of the world, the churches of the world have been brought to each other's doorsteps; and it has become possible for churches and groups of many different nationalities that name the name of Christ to meet each other in the flesh, to rejoice together in the faith once delivered to the saints, and to sing together—as a little foretaste of the heavenly habitation—the song of Moses and the Lamb.

Why, then, must there be two councils of churches on the world level: the World Council of Churches and the International Council of Christian Churches? Is it not a tragedy that two councils should be formed when all should work together in unity, harmony, and peace, for the glory of God? Yes, indeed. There should be only one, and there would have been only one except for a definite historic development. There arose, as a result of what is called higher criticism, the philosophy generally called "modernism." It is not Christianity. It is also called, in certain circles, "liberalism."

An assault was made, within the church itself, upon the most fundamental doctrines of the Christian religion. The Bible was attacked, its truth and authority questioned and denied. The person of our Lord was disputed. His deity, His place in the Trinity, His virgin birth, His ministry and work were all perverted. His sinless life was besmirched. His blood, shed for the redemption of the race, became a scandal. Subtly, deliberately, this unbelief—for such it is—found its way into the life stream of church after church. In many churches, the struggle led to total victory on the part of the liberals and those who accepted an inclusivist church. Some believers were ready to practice coexistence with the unbelievers within the church and accepted a modernist leadership. The little leaven leavened the lump. It was the leadership on the part of the liberals, or modernists, that gave birth in its dream to the Ecumenical Movement, with the basis of co-operation so broad that what has no right to be called Christianity has been honored as Christianity. Using a legitimate concept of Christian co-operation, the program for bringing the churches together nullified the Reformation, by including in its fellowship the Greek Orthodox churches, and by extending an invitation of fellowship to the Roman Catholic pontiff himself. . . .

The necessity for a true council of churches can be seen in considering the doctrinal foundation of the two movements.

The International Council has worked out, as its platform, a summary statement of the great evangelical doctrines. None can deny that these truths have been held in common by the historic Church through the centuries.

The I.C.C.C.'s declaration in full follows:

DOCTRINAL STATEMENT

Among other equally Biblical truths, we believe and maintain the following:

a. The plenary Divine inspiration of the Scriptures in the original languages, their consequent inerrancy and infallibility; and, as the Word of God, the supreme and final authority in faith and life;

b. The Triune God: Father, Son, and Holy Spirit;

c. The essential, absolute, eternal Deity; and the real and proper, but sinless, humanity of our Lord Jesus Christ;

d. His birth of the virgin Mary;

e. His substitutionary, expiatory death, in that He gave His life "a ransom for many";

f. His resurrection from among the dead, in the same body in which He was crucified; and the second coming of this same Jesus in power and great glory;

g. The total depravity of man through the fall;

h. Salvation, the effect of regeneration by the Spirit and the Word, not by works but by grace through faith;

i. The everlasting bliss of the saved, and the everlasting suffering of the lost;

j. The real spiritual unity in Christ of all redeemed by His precious blood;

k. The necessity of maintaining, according to the Word of God, the purity of the Church in doctrine and life;

And, still believing the Apostles' Creed to be a statement of Scriptural truth, we therefore incorporate it in these articles of faith.

On the other hand, the World Council of Churches has as its only doctrinal foundation the following:

"The World Council of Churches is a fellowship of churches which accept our Lord Jesus Christ as God and Saviour."

This in itself is insufficient and inadequate as a basis for a strong, co-operative movement of Christian churches. If the basis were to be understood in the truly evangelical sense, a fuller statement of evangelical truth such as the I.C.C.C.'s would be most natural, desirable, and for God's glory.

But the World Council of Churhces, in its inception, in an official declaration, made it clear to all churches of the world that it did not define its foundation. The declaration said:

a. "That the foundation is not a touchstone, whereby the faith of churches or persons can be judged;

b. "That the World Council does not concern itself with the manner in which the churches will interpret the foundation;

c. "That it is left to the responsibility of every Church to decide whether it will co-operate on this basis."[1]

Thus we must say in all charity that the doctrinal foundation is utterly meaningless as a platform for uniting any body or any churches. Though the Council has words to front its movement, the movement is built on another basis, actually no basis at all so far as Christ's name is concerned, for

[1] *The World Council of Churches* (p. 182); published by the World Council of Churches, Geneva, Switzerland.

it means just what anybody wants to make it mean. The lone doctrinal sentence of the W.C.C. is nullified and, in effect, does not exist.

It is fundamentally dishonest to make such a confession and then withdraw it in qualifying explanations. The World Council would be honest with itself and the churches of the world if it declared that it had no doctrinal statement at all but was simply an association or organization of churches. At least honesty could be claimed for such a position. But the Council is caught in the dilemma of trying to be something that in the very nature of its composition it cannot be. To be or not to be is the question! It is also equally dishonest, from the other horn of the dilemma, for the Council to publish, as it constantly does, that it accepts Jesus Christ as "God and Saviour." On the face of it, as it now stands, its creedal claim is merely a propaganda weapon to impress the rank and file in the pews of the churches and to deceive evangelical groups. . . .

There is, therefore, in the World Council's declaration nothing more than a union of meaningless words; and this is supposed to be the basis for a world-wide movement of Christian co-operation, which will lead the nations and direct the affairs of mankind for the glory of God. We must say that we believe it is indeed an offense to God and His Christ so to trifle with His name. His name is used to deny Him, for there is no agreed substance for its meaning or use.

Because of this falsification of the name of Christ—and that is all it can properly be called—it is absolutely essential that God's people everywhere who love each other, who delight in the Church, who honor the name of Christ, and who rejoice in Christian co-operation be fully alerted to what the Ecumenical Movement is doing; and, on the other hand, what the International Council of Christian Churches is, what the Twentieth Century Reformation movement proposes to accomplish, how it has already suffered for the name of Christ, and how God is working through it.

There is, however, another reason why the doctrinal statement of the World Council of Churches is so brief. It is, in fact, not an evangelical statement at all and was never in-

tended to be such. The so-called basis was so phrased and
designed that the Council could include the Greek Catholic
Church and also the Roman Catholic Church. To have added
any other statements that might in any way be interpreted as
defining or stating what the Council meant by the word "Saviour," would have been a hindrance to the Greek Orthodox
or the Roman Catholics. For instance, in the I.C.C.C.'s doctrinal statement, it is said, concerning Christ, that the
churches believe in "His substitutionary, expiatory death, in
that He gave His life 'a ransom for many'"; and "Salvation,
the effect of regeneration by the Spirit and the Word, not by
works but by grace through faith." Any such statements
would immediately have blocked the Greek Orthodox and
Roman Catholic churches, which do not believe that salvation is alone by grace through faith—but offer works, too.
Furthermore, the truth stated in the International Council's
doctrinal platform has been degraded by some of these
churches in the W.C.C. to the realm of a theory. The World
Council's statement then was carefully designed to open the
way for an inclusivist co-operation among all kinds of Protestant bodies, including those that have gone into liberalism,
together with the Greek Catholic and the Roman Catholic
churches—which hold to their traditions and worship and
pray to the saints, thus being simply *not* evangelical. Actually, those who planned and dreamed of the Ecumenical
Movement saw that if there ever were to be a bringing together of these churches into one world-wide body, there
would have to be at the beginning such a platform enumerated and such a general, nondescript interpretation given to
it that they could then undertake their arduous struggle to
bring the churches together into one body, where the
World Council of Churches some day would give place to
the World Church.

The impact of this evaluation of the Council's brief creedal
statement has been felt in various ways.

On one hand there are some who believe that the Council
should eliminate its creedal statement entirely, and as such
it would be a forum where churches would discuss and debate the various problems confronting them. It is question-

able, however, first, whether a "council of churches" could exist without giving in its "cooperation" a witness of some kind or other and, second, whether a "council of churches" should exist without seeking to give a clear witness as the I.C.C.C. has done. Those who would like to think of the World Council as being just a forum, at the present moment, are confronted with the fact that it is not, and in its dishonest and deceptive handling of the name of Christ it is an organization with which no true, evangelical church should affiliate or in which it should assist in any way, if it would be loyal to the Church's only Head and King.

On the other hand, Bishop Eivind Josef Berggrav of Norway has sought to strengthen the creedal statement.

Some months before Evanston, he announced a proposed amendment that would introduce an appeal to the Scriptures. The full text of his proposal reads:

"The World Council of Churches is a fellowship of churches which, in accordance with Holy Scripture, confess our Lord Jesus Christ as God and Saviour."

At Evanston this proposal was ruled out on the technicality that it had not been sent to the constituent churches at least six months before the Assembly met, as required by Article VIII of the constitution. The Central Committee is to study the question and report to the Third Assembly in 1960.

But, the Berggrav amendment does not meet the situation. It still leaves the open question to cover many shades of opinion—modernist, liberal, neo-orthodox, Barthian, evangelical—as to what the Scriptures teach? What is in accordance with Holy Scripture? Any statement concerning "Jesus Christ as God and Saviour" should be so precise and so delineated that those who do not agree with what the Scriptures clearly teach would be offended and kept out! There should be no room for them in a council of churches bearing the name of Christ. Because of this open gap still left by the Berggrav amendment, which continues to shield and protect the liberals, and all others, we do not see why there should be any serious objection, from the W.C.C. position, to its adoption. In our opinion it is designed further to appease the evangelicals who are troubled by just the questions we are discussing here, but who are themselves willing to accept such continued deception. When all that the church holds dear concerning Jesus Christ is at stake, what is said "in accordance with Holy Scripture" must be specifically and unmistakably set forth for His glory, in order that there may be no trifling, compromising, or debauching of His name. God has "given him a name which is above every name"! At this point there should be no hesitancy or disagreement on the part of any who are truly begotten of the Father.

It is just this—so beautifully done—that the I.C.C.C. included in its doctrinal statement when it said: "We believe and maintain . . . the essential, absolute, eternal Deity, and real and proper, but sinless, humanity of our Lord Jesus Christ," and as to His work as Saviour, "His substitutionary, expiatory death, in that He gave His life 'a ransom for many.'" There is no doubt whatever that this is what the Scriptures teach when they are received as the infallible Word of God.

It is this basic, fundamental, original flaw in the World Council's setup, their disagreement over Christ Himself, His person and His work, that must be seen by all who love the Lord.

If there is disagreement over Christ, then there is no fellowship in Christ, and this reality, for it certainly was evident at Evanston, forces upon us a consideration of another aspect of this creedal statement. The World Council of Churches claims to be "a fellowship of churches," and this fellowship is supposed to be, according to their creedal statement, among those who accept "Jesus Christ as God and Saviour."

The meaning of fellowship for God's people and the churches must be understood from Scripture. The Apostle John makes the conditions of fellowship exclusive and immutable. "If we say that we have fellowship with him, and walk in darkness, we lie, and do not the truth: but if we walk in the light, as he is in the light, we have fellowship one with another, and the blood of Jesus Christ his Son cleanseth us from all sin" (1 John 1: 6, 7). To walk, therefore, as the World Council is attempting to do, in confusion and disagreement over Christ, and to claim that such is a fellowship, is, in the light of John's statement, a lie.

The beloved disciple relates, in his first Epistle, this fellowship to Him who "was from the beginning . . . the Word of life." This Christ is "that eternal life, which was with the Father, and was manifested unto us"; and "that which we have seen and heard declare we unto you, that ye also may have fellowship with us: and truly our fellowship is with the Father, and with his Son Jesus Christ. And these things write we unto you, that your joy may be full" (1 John 1: 1–4).

Had Evanston participated in this kind of fellowship there would have been joy. Fellowship is impossible between those who have varying opinions and viewpoints concerning Jesus Christ, His person and work. Paul explains, "God is faithful, by whom ye were called unto the fellowship of his Son Jesus Christ our Lord" (1 Cor. 1: 9). But a church is unfaithful when it unites with that which calls itself a fellowship, when true fellowship is impossible. How can a true church, which delights in the fellowship of Jesus Christ as presented in the Scriptures, be a party to a council of churches which attempts to unite light and darkness. It is God's Word which says, "Have no fellowship with the unfruitful works of darkness, but rather reprove them" (Eph. 5: 11). Those who would take the position that the World Council of Churches is only a public forum, or platform of discussion, in order to justify their membership and fellowship with those who deny the essentials of the faith must consider the restrictions which the Scriptures place upon the word "fellowship."

It was this disagreement over Christ, and this alone, that is at the bottom of all the difficulties of the World Council of Churches, and which was seen in Evanston in the most startling fashion. The Ecumenical Movement was embarrassed before the Christian public and the world as it talked of unity. Moreover, the Council was so confused it could not define its own theme—"Christ, the Hope of the World."

BIBLIOGRAPHICAL NOTE

The history of the ecumenical movement may be found in Ruth Rouse and Stephen C. Neill, editors, *A History of the Ecumenical Movement, 1517–1948* (Philadelphia, 1954). A sociological discussion of church unity movements is Robert Lee, *The Social Sources of Church Unity: An Interpretation of Unitive Movements in American Protestantism* (New York, 1960); it is instructive to read this in connection with H. Richard Niebuhr's interpretation of an earlier period in *Social Sources of Denominationalism* (New York, 1929). The future of the ecumenical movement is discussed by several of its leading figures in Keith Bridston and Walter Wagoner, editors, *Unity in Mid-Career* (New York, 1963). For a severe critique of the American Council of Churches see Ralph L. Roy, *Apostles of Discord* (Boston, 1953), pp. 181–202.

XII. THE CONTEMPORARY SCENE

INTRODUCTION

The 1960s have been years of ferment in American Protestantism, a decade of criticism and reflection when many assumptions have been rigorously and openly challenged. Mutual understanding between Roman Catholics and Protestants has increased; new forms of the ministry are appearing; the "death of God" theology has attracted wide public interest; and lengthy and involved discussions concerning church union among major Protestant denominations are now under way.

In the late 1950s and early 1960s much was written in criticism of the "culture religion" of American Protestants. These critics decried the "surge of piety," marked by the increase of church membership to 63 percent of the population in the late 1950s as compared with 10 to 15 percent at the beginning of the nineteenth century. Will Herberg's study of American religion, *Protestant-Catholic-Jew*, attracted wide attention and was a serious indictment of the "religion of democracy."[1] Sidney Mead has written a critique of the theses of Herberg and others in an article entitled: "The Post-Protestant Concept and America's Two Religions." A central argument of Mead's article is "that the bedrock assumptions on which the legal structure of the United States rests never were Protestant in any particularistic sense, and, therefore, there always has been an unresolved tension between the theology of the republic and that professed in the denominations."[2]

Individual theologians have also created much excitement.

[1] The article of Will Herberg, Selection 32, is a summary of the thesis of his book.

[2] See Selection 33. Sidney Mead, "The Post-Protestant Concept and America's Two Religions," *Religion in Life*, Spring, 1964, pp. 191 ff.

The 1960s are a time of probing and questioning, where theological systems are no longer dominant, but new and tentative explorations are undertaken. H. Richard Niebuhr (1894–1962), for many years Professor of Theology and Christian Ethics at Yale Divinity School, was the teacher of many, both in the classroom and through his many essays. His own theological pilgrimage is similar to others of his generation: from liberalism through neo-orthodoxy to a search for new ways to articulate the Christian faith. Niebuhr's essay, "Reformation: Continuing Imperative," indicates where his creative energies were directed.

Another important contemporary theological figure is Daniel Day Williams, Professor of Theology at Union Theological Seminary. His recent essay, included as Selection 35, offers an analysis of the many fronts of contemporary theological reflection and his own views of where the most fruitful avenues of investigation are.

[32]

Will Herberg

Religion and Culture
in Present-Day America*

I

Whatever may be true about the religious situation, it certainly cannot be doubted that religion is enjoying a boom of unprecedented proportions in America today. Well over 95 per cent of the American people identify themselves religiously, as Protestants, Catholics, or Jews—an incredibly high figure by all available standards of comparison. The proportion of Americans who are church members—that is, actually

* From Thomas T. McAvoy, editor, *Roman Catholicism and the American Way of Life* (Notre Dame, Indiana: University of Notre Dame Press, 1960). Used by permission of the publisher.

on the rolls of the churches—has nearly doubled in the past half century; in the last twenty years indeed, church membership has been increasing twice as fast as population. Church and synagogue attendance is rising rapidly, Sunday school enrollment is rising even more rapidly, and religious giving has reached a formidable figure, even allowing for the inflationary devaluation of the dollar. Interest in religion and religious thinking is widespread on all cultural levels. Whatever the criterion of religiousness we take—and by religiousness I mean the "externals" of religion, using this term in a neutral sense, without prejudice—we cannot escape the conclusion that we are today witnessing an upsurge of religion without precedent in recent times.

But it is a curious kind of religion. The very same people who are so unanimous in identifying themselves religiously, who are joining churches at an accelerating rate, and who take it for granted that religion is a "very important" thing, do not hesitate to acknowledge that religion is quite peripheral to their everyday lives; more than half of them quite frankly admit that their religious beliefs have no influence whatever on their ideas in economics and politics, and a good proportion of the remainder are obviously uncertain. The very same people who distribute the Bible in vast quantities, largely by voluntary effort, are unable in their majority to give the name of one single book of the New Testament, and the showing is not very different when you take the Bible as a whole. The very same people who, four out of five, say they regard Jesus as divine, when asked to name the most important event in all universal history, place the Christ-event —the birth or crucifixion of Christ—fourteenth on the list, tied with the Wright brothers' invention of the airplane; the Number 1 event, almost without exception, is given as Columbus' discovery of America.[1]

This is the problem: America is in the grip of a great religious boom, that is obvious; yet equally obvious, though

[1] Data illustrating both sides of the contemporary religious situation will be found in Will Herberg, *Protestant-Catholic-Jew: An Essay in American Religious Sociology* (Doubleday, 1955), esp. chaps. I, IV, and V.

not so easy to establish by facts and figures, is the continuing "trend toward secularism in ideas," to use Professor Handlin's phrase[2]—it is really a trend toward secularism not only in ideas, but in attitudes and values as well. This is the problem: the religiousness of a secularist society, the "strengthening of the religious structure in spite of increasing secularization."[3] Thinking through this paradox will take us a long way toward understanding the present religious situation in this country.

II

The best approach to the problem, I think, is to try to understand something of the role that religious belonging plays in the social structure and functioning of contemporary America. I well recognize that religion has its transcendent dimension, which escapes all external scrutiny and analysis; but I am deliberately limiting my inquiry at this point to those aspects that are subject to such scrutiny and analysis, and I think that these aspects are significant in the total picture. What, then, is it that strikes one about the new function of religion in the life of the American people today? It is, I think, that religion, in its tripartite form of Protestant-Catholic-Jew, is rapidly becoming the primary context of self-identification and social location in present-day America. Let us see what this really means.

By and large, since the latter part of the nineteenth century at any rate, Americans have tended to identify and locate themselves in terms of race, ethnicity, and religion. "When asked the simple question, 'What are you?'," Gordon W. Allport has noted, referring to certain recent researches, "only ten per cent of four-year-olds answer in terms of racial, ethnic, or religious membership, but 75 per cent of nine-year-olds do so"[4]—and the percentage is even higher for

[2] Oscar Handlin, *The American People in the Twentieth Century* (Harvard, 1954), p. 222.

[3] Marshall Sklare, *Conservative Judaism: An American Religious Movement* (Free Press, 1955), p. 39.

[4] Gordon W. Allport, *The Resolution of Intergroup Tensions*, p. 7.

adults. "Race" in America today means color, white vs. non-white, and racial stigmatization has introduced an element of caste-like stratification into American life. For white Americans, ethnicity (immigrant origin) and religion have been, and remain, the major sources of pluralistic diversity, and therefore the major forms of self-identification and social location. But the relation between the two has changed drastically in the course of the past generation, and it is this change that provides a clue to the new role of religion in American life.

As long as large-scale immigration continued, and America was predominantly a land of immigrants, in the days when "the immigrants were American history," as Handlin puts it,[5] the dominant form of diversity, and therefore the dominant form of self-identification, was immigrant ethnicity. The always interesting question about a new family moving into the neighborhood—"What are they?"—was regularly answered in terms of ethnic-immigrant origin. Religion was felt to be an aspect of ethnicity, a part of the ethnic heritage, recent or remote. The enthusiasts of the "melting pot" were eager to eliminate these diverse heritages as quickly as possible; the "cultural pluralists" were determined to perpetuate them; but both alike moved within a pluralism based substantially on ethnicity, ethnic culture, and ethnic religion.

Within the past generation, the picture has been radically transformed. The stoppage of mass immigration during the first World War, followed by the anti-immigration legislation of the 1920's, undermined the foundations of immigrant ethnicity and the immigrant ethnic group with amazing rapidity; what it did was to facilitate the emergence of third and post-third generations, with their characteristic responses and attitudes, as a decisive influence on American life, no longer threatened with submergence by the next new wave of immigration. Within the threefold American scheme of race, ethnicity, and religion, a shift took place, a shift is taking place, from ethnicity to religion as the dominant form of

[5] Oscar Handlin, *The Uprooted: The Epic Story of the Great Migrations That Made the American People* (Little Brown, 1951), p. 3.

self-identification—as the dominant way of answering the question, "What am I? how do I differ from 'one man's family'? where do I fit in in the totality of American society?" Ethnic identifications and traditions have not disappeared; on the contrary, with the third generation, they are enjoying a lively popularity as symbols of "heritage." But now the relation between ethnicity and religion has been reversed: religion is no longer an aspect of ethnicity; it is ethnicity, or rather what remains of it, that is taken up, redefined, and expressed through religious identifications and institutions. Religion, or at least the tripartite differentiation of Protestant, Catholic, and Jew has (aside from race) become the prevailing form of defining one's identity as an American in contemporary American society.

Keeping this in mind, we can begin to understand one of the most striking facts in the religious history of this country during the past half century—the transformation of America from a *Protestant* country into a *three-religion* country.

Writing just thirty years ago, André Siegfried described Protestantism as America's "national religion,"[6] and he was largely right, despite the ban on religious establishment in the Constitution. Normally, to be born an American meant to be a Protestant; this was the religious identification that in the American mind quite naturally went along with being an American. Non-Protestants felt the force of this conviction almost as strongly as did the Protestants; Catholics and Jews, despite their vastly increasing numbers, experienced their non-Protestant religion as a problem, even as an obstacle, to their becoming full-fledged Americans: it was a mark of their foreignness. (This was true despite the much esteemed colonial heritage of both Jews and Catholics, since it was not the "old American" elements in these two groups that influenced American attitudes, but the newer immigrant masses.) In the familiar Troeltschean sense, Protestantism—not any one of the multiplying denominations, but Protestantism as a whole—constituted America's "established church."

---

[6] André Siegfried, *America Comes of Age* (Harcourt Brace, 1927), p. 33.

This is no longer the case. Today, to be born an American is no longer taken to mean that one is necessarily a Protestant; Protestantism is no longer the obvious and "natural" religious identification of the American. Today, the evidence strongly indicates, America has become a three-religion country: the normal religious implication of being an American today is that one is either a Protestant, a Catholic, or a Jew. These three are felt to be, by and large, three different forms of being religious in the American way; they are the three "religions of democracy," the "three great faiths" of America. Today, unlike fifty years ago, not only Protestants, but increasingly Catholics and Jews as well, feel themselves, and are recognized to be, Americans not apart from, or in spite of, their religion, but because of it. If America today possesses a "church" in the Troeltschean sense—that is, a form of religious belonging which is felt to be involved in one's belonging to the national community—it is the tripartite religious system of Protestant-Catholic-Jew.

This transformation of America from a Protestant into a three-religion country has come about not because of any marked increase in Catholics or Jews—the Protestant-Catholic ratio has remained pretty well the same for the past thirty years, and the proportion of Jews in the general population has probably been declining. It has come about, as I have suggested, through the emergence of a stabilized American third generation, which is able to set its mark on American life because it is no longer threatened with dissolution by recurrent waves of mass immigration.

The immigrant generation, and this is true of all immigrant nationalities, established itself in America as an ethnic group with an ethnic culture, of which the ethnic language and the ethnic religion were generally the most significant elements. For the first, the immigrant generation, religion was part of ethnicity; for the Italian immigrant, in other words, his Catholicness was part of his Italianness; for the Jewish immigrant, his Judaism, his Jewish religion, was part of his *Yiddishkait*, his ethnic culture. You remember the movie "Marty." You remember how Marty brings home the girl Clara to introduce her to his mother. His mother is a good church-going Catholic, but what is the question she asks about Clara? Not "Is she Catholic?," but "Is she Italian?" Why? Because to the mother, the first-generation immigrant, if she's Italian, then she's Catholic, and if she's Catholic without being Italian, it doesn't do any good anyway! This is the outlook on ethnicity and religion characteristic of the immigrant generation.

The second generation is in a very different position. The second generation is marginal—"too American for the home and too foreign for the school," in Marcus Hansen's celebrated phrase. It is doubly alienated, belonging to two communities but at home in neither, torn away from the old moorings and not yet anchored in the new reality. The second generation responds to its marginality in a number of ways, but by and large it may be said that what the second generation wants most of all is to get rid of its foreignness and become American. This obviously influences its attitude to religion. Just because in the immigrant home, in which the second generation grows up, religion is understood to be a part of ethnicity, to be a part of the immigrant foreignness, the second generation takes a negative view of religion, sometimes breaking with it entirely, usually retaining an uneasy connection, mixed with hostility and embarrassment. The second generation—and that holds true for every immigrant group in America—is characteristically the least religious of American generations.

But now comes the third generation. The third generation—and with it we must include the post-third generations that have arisen on American soil—is again in a very different position. It is at last American, securely American, secure as any American is in his Americanness. But it is faced with a new problem, the problem of defining its identity. Ethnic identifications will no longer serve, as in one way or another they served the first and second generations. What then?—how is the third generation to answer the question, "What am I? how do I differ from 'one man's family'? where do I fit in the totality of American society?" In an effort to define its social identity—without which no tolerable life is possible—the American third generation goes in search of a "heritage."

In a sensational reversal of earlier attitudes, the third generation seeks a "return." Some two decades ago, Marcus Lee Hansen, studying not Italians or Jews on the east coast, but Scandinavian Lutherans in the Midwest in the twenties and thirties, expressed this reversal in a classic formula: "What the son wishes to forget, the grandson wishes to remember."[7] The "son," constituting the second generation, wishes to "forget" because he wants so passionately to get rid of his foreignness; the "grandson," belonging to the third generation, wishes to "remember" because he needs a "heritage." But what of the grandfather can the grandson "remember"?— what of his grandfather's legacy can he take over and use for the purpose of giving himself a "heritage" and defining his identity? Not his grandfather's nationality, language, or culture; the American pattern of assimilative acculturation obviously makes that impossible. But the grandfather's religion is a very different thing: America not only permits, it even encourages, the perpetuation of one's religious diversity and distinctiveness without danger to one's Americanness. Of course, it is not the grandfather's religion as the grandfather would have recognized it; it is the grandfather's religion brought up to date and Americanized. But it serves; and so religion becomes the characteristic symbol of "heritage" for the third generation, and its return to its heritage becomes a return to religion. With Catholics and Jews, the process, however complex, is relatively unambiguous. With Protestants, however, there is a double movement: on the one side, a return to ethnically associated religion, as among Lutherans; on the other side, because of the confusion, blurring, and growing meaninglessness of denominational lines, a "return" to Protestantism rather than to any particular group within it as a form of religious identification. William H. Whyte's account, in *The Organization Man*, of the emergence of the United Protestant Church in Park Forest, Ill., a story which could be duplicated in so many other suburban communities, well illustrates this pattern of development; but

[7] M. L. Hansen, *The Problem of the Third Generation Immigrant* (Augustana Historical Society, 1938), p. 9.

even where denominational affiliations are still maintained, the basic identification is still Protestant, especially among the younger people. And so a three-religion America has emerged, an America in which being a Protestant, being a Catholic, and being a Jew are the three recognized alternative ways of being an American.

A word of caution is necessary. It should not be imagined that just because America has become, or is becoming, a three-religion country, all ethnic or religious group tensions are at an end. Anti-Semitism runs deeper than any merely sociological analysis can penetrate, and even on the sociological level, the new tripartite system would, for the time being at least, seem to make almost as much for the exacerbation as for the alleviation of intergroup tensions. Anti-Jewish manifestations are, for the moment, at a low ebb, but Protestant-Catholic antagonisms appear to be growing sharper. This accentuation of Protestant-Catholic tensions seems to me to be very largely a reflection of the painful transition period through which we are passing; there is every reason to hope that with the stabilization of the new situation, these hostilities too will abate. Yet we should not overlook the fact that the new system of tripartite coexistence is bound to raise its own problems and breed its own tensions with which we will have to cope in the time to come.

III

What has the transformation of America from an ethnic into a religious pluralism, and concomitantly from a Protestant into a three-religion country, meant so far as the status and character of religion in this country are concerned?

Very obviously, it has made for a boom in religious belonging. To have a "name" in American society today—to have an identity, to be able to answer the question "What am I? where do I belong?"—means increasingly to identify oneself in religious terms, as Protestant, Catholic, or Jew. These are three alternative ways of being an American. This is eminently true of the burgeoning suburban sector of American society, least true in the rural areas, and measurably true in the older urban centers. It is certainly the over-all pattern of American life. Obviously, such self-identification in religious terms engenders a new sense of belonging to one's religious community; obviously, too, it impels to institutional affiliation, characteristically expressed in terms of concern for the children: "We have to join a church (or a temple) for the sake of the children." There is profound sociological wisdom in this remark, though its theological implications may be dubious. "The church," Oscar Handlin points out, "supplies a place where the children come to learn what they are"[8]—what kind of Americans they are. The mechanisms of other-directed conformity to which David Riesman has called attention serve to give religious belonging the compelling power it is acquiring in the pattern of suburban "sociability," but the new role of religion in this process is the result of the more basic factors I have tried to indicate in my remarks on the third generation and the transformation of America into a three-religion country.

Just as Americans are coming more and more to think of being a Protestant, being a Catholic, and being a Jew as three alternative ways of being an American, so they are coming to regard Protestantism, Catholicism, and Judaism, the "three great faiths," as three alternative (though not necessarily equal) expressions of a great overarching commitment which they all share by virtue of being Americans. This commitment is, of course, democracy or the American Way of Life. It is the common allegiance which (to use Professor Williams' phrase) provides Americans with the "common set of ideas, rituals, and symbols" through which an "overarching sense of unity" is achieved amidst diversity and conflict.[9] It is, in a sense far more real than John Dewey ever dreamed of, the "common religion" of Americans.

Let me illustrate this point with two texts borrowed from President Eisenhower, who may, I think, be taken as a repre-

[8] Oscar Handlin, *The American People in the Twentieth Century,* p. 222.

[9] Robin M. Williams, Jr., *American Society: A Sociological Interpretation* (Knopf, 1951), p. 312.

sentative American really serious about religion. "Our government," Mr. Eisenhower declared shortly after his election in 1952, "makes no sense unless it is founded in a deeply felt religious faith, *and I don't care what it is.*"[10] It is the last phrase which I have emphasized—"and I don't care what it is"—to which I want to call your attention. Of course, President Eisenhower did not mean that literally; he would have been much disturbed had any sizable proportion of Americans become Buddhists, or Shintoists, or Confucianists—but of course that never entered his mind. When he said "I don't care what it is," he obviously meant "I don't care which of the three it is—Protestantism, Catholicism, or Judaism." And why didn't he care which it was? Because, in his view, as in the view of all normal Americans, they "all say the same thing." And what is the "same thing" which they all say? The answer is given to us from the current vocabulary: "the moral and spiritual values of democracy." These, for the typical American, are in a real sense final and ultimate; the three conventional religions are approved of and validated primarily because they embody and express these "moral and spiritual values of democracy."

Let me drive this home with the second text from President Eisenhower. In 1948, four years before his election, just before he became president of Columbia, Mr. Eisenhower made another important pronouncement on religion. "I am the most intensely religious man I know," he declared. "Nobody goes through six years of war without faith. That does not mean that I adhere to any sect. (Incidentally, following the way of all flesh, he was soon to join a "sect," the Presbyterian.) A democracy cannot exist without a religious base. I believe in democracy."[11] Here we have the entire story in a single phrase: I believe in religion because I believe in democracy! Precisely the same conviction, though expressed in a rather more sophisticated manner, was affirmed by an eminent New York rabbi not long ago. "The spiritual meaning of American democracy," he declared, "is realized

10 *New York Times,* December 23, 1952.
11 *New York Times,* May 4, 1948.

in its three great faiths."[12] Similar statements, I assure you, could be found in the pronouncements of spokesmen of the other two religious groups.

What I am describing is essentially the "Americanization" of religion in America, and therefore also its thorough-going secularization. This process is not a recent one. It began for Protestantism some time after the Civil War and proceeded apace in the latter decades of the nineteenth century. Sidney Mead's brilliant description of this trend is particularly relevant.

What was not so obvious at the time (he writes) was that the United States, in effect, had two religions, or at least two different forms of the same religion, and that the prevailing Protestant ideology represented a syncretistic mingling of the two. The first was the religion of the (Protestant) denominations which was commonly articulated in terms of scholastic Protestant orthodoxy and almost universally practised in terms of the experimental religion of pietistic revivalism. . . . The second was the religion of the democratic society and nation. This . . . was articulated in terms of the destiny of America, under God, to be fulfilled by perfecting the democratic way of life for the example and betterment of mankind.[13]

With remarkably little change—something would have to be said about the waning of scholastic orthodoxy and the new forms of pietistic revivalism—these words could stand as a description of the current situation. What is new, what is crucially new, is that this is no longer true merely of Protestantism; it is becoming more and more true of Catholicism and Judaism as well, precisely because Catholicism and Judaism have become American, integral parts of the three-religion America. In this, as in so many other respects, their Americanization has meant their "Protestantization," using this term to describe the American Protestant ethos, so at variance

[12] Rabbi David J. Seligson, quoted in *New York Times,* March 25, 1956.

[13] Sidney E. Mead, "American Protestantism Since the Civil War. I. From Denominationalism to Americanism," *The Journal of Religion,* vol. xxxvi, No. 1, January, 1956, p. 2.

with classical Protestant Christian faith. With the loss of their
foreignness, of their immigrant marginality, these two religious groups seem to be losing their capacity to resist dissolution in the culture. In becoming American, they have apparently become American all the way.

We are now, I think, in a position to penetrate the apparent paradox with which we initiated this discussion, the paradox of the religiousness of a secularist society. How can
Americans be so religious and so secularistic at the same time?
The answer is that for increasing numbers of Americans religion serves a function largely unrelated to the content of
faith, the function of defining their identity and providing
them with a context of belonging in the great wilderness of
a mobile American society. Indeed, for such a purpose, the
authentic content of faith may even prove a serious handicap, for if it is Jewish or Christian faith, it carries a prophetic
impact which serves rather to unadjust than to adjust, to
emphasize the ambiguity of every earthly form of belonging
rather than to let the individual rest secure in his "sociability."
For this reason, the typical American has developed a remarkable capacity for being serious about religion without
taking religion seriously—in which respect he is not unlike
sinful human beings of all ages. His ideas, values, and standards he takes from what is so often really his ultimate commitment, the American Way of Life. He combines the two—
his religion and his culture—by making the former an expression of the latter, his religion an expression of the "moral and
spiritual values of democracy." Hence his puzzling pro-
religious secularism, his secularistic religionism, which, looked
at more closely, does not seem so puzzling after all.

IV

From the standpoint of the man of faith, of the man who
takes his religious tradition seriously, what does the picture
of religion in contemporary America add up to? No simple or
unequivocal answer can be given.

On the one hand, the emergence of religion as a vehicle
of American belonging has made for a breakdown of anti-

religious prejudice. One of the most striking features of present-day American culture is the complete absence of an Ingersoll or a Darrow, of the "village atheist" on a national scale, or for that matter, except here and there, even on a village scale. Contemporary Americans, especially the younger generation, simply cannot understand the militant atheist of yesterday; he is so remote from their mentality as to be hardly credible. The breakdown of anti-religion has contributed toward the new openness to religion that is so obvious today. Yet the religion that emerges is only too often a religiousness, or perhaps a pro-religiousness, without religion, without serious religious content, conviction, or commitment. There is great danger, as one Jewish leader recently put it, that our church or synagogue cards may hide from us the basically secularistic character of our religion. There is even danger that with the rapid spread of a contentless religiousness, the very meaning of religion in its authentic sense may be lost for increasing numbers.

There is also a positive side to the "Americanization" of religion, which sees in Protestantism, Catholicism, and Judaism three forms of being religious in the American way. To the degree that this is felt to be true, the stigma of foreignness is lifted from Catholicism and Judaism, and from such ethnic forms of Protestantism as the Lutheran. There is a new freedom and tolerance, and at least the public equality of the "three great faiths" in American life. No one who remembers what misery the taint of foreignness once brought, and what a formidable obstacle it constituted to the preservation and communication of the "non-American" faiths, will fail to be grateful for this development. But it has been purchased at a heavy price, the price of embracing an idolatrous civic religion of Americanism.

I want to express myself here very clearly, and I will do so by speaking to you as Catholics. I recently lectured to the entire student body of a well-known Catholic girls' college. In the course of my remarks, I confronted them—not in such a way as to put them on their guard, of course—with Christopher Dawson's celebrated questions: "Are you Americans who happen to be Catholics, or Catholics who happen to be Americans?" Almost with one voice the girls answered, "Americans who happen to be Catholics . . ." You appreciate the significance of the question and the answer. The question really means: "Is your ultimate allegiance and your ultimate community the Universal Church, or is it the American nation?" The answer of the girls indicated that they normally thought of themselves as primarily Americans, but of course as Americans of the "Catholic kind," just as some of their friends were Americans of the "Protestant kind," and still others Americans of the "Jewish kind." Let me assure you that I have received the same kind of response from other Catholic groups—lay groups, that is—and from Protestant and Jewish audiences as well, when the question was put to them in their own terms.

What does that mean? It means that we have in America an invisible, formally unacknowledged, but very potent religion—the religion of democracy, the religion of the American Way of Life—of which the conventional religions are felt to be more or less adequate expressions. Americans do not put it that way, in just so many words, but that is how they feel and behave. In effect, this means that they participate in an actual civic religion, very much like the civic religion of the Roman Empire in early Christian times. The authentic relation between religion and culture is subverted, of which the civic religion is the sanctification, is idolatrized by being made ultimate, which means divine. Judaism, and Christianity in its two forms, become subordinated to the culture and tend to lose all sense of uniqueness, universality, and special vocation. To the man of Jewish or Christian faith, this divinization of the American Way—even if he acknowledges, as I do, the American Way to be one of the best ways of life yet devised for a mass society—must appear as abhorrent as the ancient civic religions appeared to the Jew or Christian of those days, in spite of the fact that our own civic religion is not officially established, overtly promulgated, or enforced through persecution.

It is not without significance that this conversion of democracy, or the American Way of Life, into the "common religion" of Americans has been given explicit formulation by a number of secularist-minded philosophers, such as Horace M. Kallen, who proclaims the "democratic faith" to be, for its "communicants"—the words are Kallen's—"the religion *of* and *for* religions, . . . all may freely come together in it."[14] What Kallen here states explicitly—the title of his article is "Democracy's True Religion"—is implicit in the ethos of American life and finds expression in many of its social and cultural, as well as religious, patterns. No wonder that Dean Sperry introduced his survey of religion in America with the words. "The honest critic of American affairs must therefore face the possibility that the true religion of his is not that of Protestant, Catholic, or Jew, but is rather a secular idolatry."[15]

The American conviction that "religion is a very good thing"—this may be taken as the second article in the American religious creed; the first is belief in God, and the third, and last, is that all really American religion is either Protestant, Catholic, or Jewish—the American conviction that religion is a very good thing, I say, means that religion is taken seriously and is endowed with a vigor and vitality that amazes foreign observers. But it also means that religion is thoroughly "functionalized," that is, converted into a tool for secular purposes. It is made to serve the sociological function of providing a form of identification and a context of belonging in a world of other-directed "sociability"; of this we have already spoken. But it is also made to serve the psychological function of conferring, on the one side, reassurance and "peace of mind," and on the other, a sense of power and achievement through "positive thinking." It is not our purpose to examine this aspect in any detail, but one thing should be noted. Just as religion on its sociological side seems to function best if it is unembarrassed with content, so religion on its psychological side easily comes to mean a contentless faith. In the one case, it may be said that Americans are religious about religion; in the other, that they have faith

[14] Horace M. Kallen, "Democracy's True Religion," *Saturday Review,* July 28, 1951.

[15] W. S. Sperry, *Religion in America* (Macmillan, 1946), p. 19.

in faith. I appeal to you to take this description with the utmost seriousness. So eminent a religious leader as Daniel Poling quite simply describes his own conviction about faith in these words: "It was back in those days that I formed a habit which I have never broken. I began saying in the morning two words, 'I believe.' Those two words, with nothing added, . . . give me a running start for my day, for every day."[16] Another religious leader, not a Protestant, puts it this way: "The storehouse of dynamic power on which you may draw, is *Faith*. Not religion, . . . not God, but *FAITH*."[17] And an advertisement in a New York paper of three eminently respectable churches is headed: "When Faith Alone Protects." In the entire ad neither God nor Christ is so much as mentioned. Church-going is recommended with the argument: "There are times in your life when faith alone protects. We all reach these times in hours of crisis which dot life's span. Regular church attendance helps you build your own personal reserve of faith."[18] What is this but picturing God as a great cosmic public utility, and religion or church-going as a way of charging one's storage battery of faith for use in emergencies? It is hardly necessary to point out that this faith in faith, this religion of religion, is just as idolatrous as faith in a stock or stone or the religion of magical self-salvation.

Americans crave security; they are bewildered and uneasy even in their prosperity. Americans crave personal power and achievement; they are frightened at the great heteronomous forces of a mass society which threaten to grind them into nothingness. Americans crave sociability; they are terrified at the prospect of being lost in the crowd. But most of all they crave reassurance about their goals and values, which they feel called into question and threatened on every side. And so they have fashioned their religion to serve these purposes

[16] Daniel Poling, "A Running Start for Every Day," *Parade: The Sunday Picture Magazine*, September 19, 1954.

[17] Louis Binstock, *The Power of Faith* (Prentice-Hall, 1952), p. 4.

[18] Advertisement of three Episcopal churches, *New York Herald-Tribune*, April 15, 1955.

by turning it into a man-centered cult of "peace of mind," "positive thinking," and American belonging. The religion that has emerged was bitingly described by Richard Niebuhr, speaking of latter-day Protestantism, two decades ago: "A God without wrath (brings) men without sin into a kingdom without judgment through the ministrations of a Christ without a cross."[19]

v

This is a picture of the religious situation in the United States today, but it is only a partial picture. There are other and more authentic stirrings of faith abroad, especially among the younger people on the campuses and their somewhat elder contemporaries in the suburban communities. These stirrings, fed from deeper sources, express themselves in different degrees on the various levels of interest, concern, and commitment, but everywhere the signs are unmistakable. Recent surveys have documented it,[20] and the report of the Student Council of Harvard University issued in February 1956 under the title of "Religion at Harvard," along with like expressions of student opinion on other campuses, may be taken as significant manifestations. This type of religious revival is very different, in its origins and in its expressions, from the religiousness we have been describing; it looks to religion not for "peace of mind," the "power of positive thinking," or the comfort of adjustment and belonging, but for some outlook, perhaps even commitment, that will illumine the meaning of existence and give one the resources to preserve authenticity of being in a world poised at the brink of nothingness and trying to save itself by an increasingly rigid

[19] H. Richard Niebuhr, *The Kingdom of God in America* (Willett Clark, 1937), p. 193.

[20] See esp. the report of the study of campus attitudes toward religion conducted by the Rev. James L. Stoner, director of the University Christian Mission of the National Council of Churches of Christ in the U.S.A., *New York Times*, October 22 and 24, 1956; cp. also Will Herberg, "The Religious Stirring on the Campus," *Commentary*, March, 1952.

conformism. This deeper kind of faith combines with the mass religiousness of the American people in various ways, but the distinctive thing about it is that it fights shy of institutional embodiment and involvement. This constitutes a very real problem, for a religiousness without a firm institutional framework of tradition and doctrine is bound to degenerate into eccentricity, sentimentalism, or intellectual dilettantism. And in fact something of the sort seems to be occurring here and there, although usually what happens is that the stirrings of faith aroused in the "open" period of campus and immediate post-campus life are overwhelmed and dissipated by the overpowering force of American mass religiousness. What the final outcome will be, as these two very different types of religious revival meet and confront each other, it is still too soon to say. Only the future can tell what the deeper stirrings of faith, wherever they may arise, will amount to and what consequences they will hold for the American religion of tomorrow.

But even the more dubious forms of American religion should not be written off entirely. Even in this ambiguous structure, there may be elements and aspects—not always those, incidentally, that seem most promising to us today—which could in the longer view transform the character of American religion and bring it closer to the traditions of faith it claims to represent. Nothing is too unpromising or refractory to serve the divine will. After all, the God who is able to make the "wrath of men" to praise Him, is surely capable of turning even the superficialities, inadequacies, and perversities of contemporary religion into an instrument of His redemptive purpose.

[33]

Sidney Mead
The Post-Protestant Concept and America's Two Religions*

The phrase "post Protestant" has slipped into common usage
to describe the present situation in the United States. This
development is to be seen in the context of the current popularity of describing aspects of the present scene as "post"
something—post-Christian, post-Constantinian, post-Protestant, postliberal, postmodern, postsectarian, postcommunist,
not to mention the almost sacred posts of the biblical scholars.
At least a brief flutter of recognition is almost certain to come
to anyone who can describe another element of the culture
as "post" this or that. "Postmanship" has taken its place beside gamesmanship and oneupmanship. Probably we shall
have to wait for minds and pens akin to those of Veblen and
Riesman for a profound analysis of the current fascination
with the idea that any aspect of the present is best understood in its relationship to something that, like the unfortunate
Clementine, is "lost and gone forever." Perhaps it signifies the
somber mood of those identity-conscious people who are sure
there was a past but who can find little basis for assurance
that there will be a future.

In this paper my first concern is to examine the concept
of post-Protestant America with its corollary that America
was once Protestant and suggest how, when it is accepted
as descriptive of the existing situation, it may obstruct clear
understanding of Protestantism's present predicament and of
how it got that way. My second concern is to suggest an alter-

* From *Religion in Life*, Vol. xxxiii, Spring, 1964, pp. 191–204.
Copyright 1964 by Abingdon Press. Used with the permission of
Abingdon Press and Professor Mead.

native view; namely, that the bedrock assumptions on which the legal structure of the United States rests never were Protestant in any particularistic sense, and therefore there always has been an unresolved tension between the theology of the republic and that professed in the denominations. This does not mean that the post-Protestant concept, when carefully defined, is without foundation or merit. But when it conveys the impression that the United States was once Protestant in every respect, it can eclipse the theological issue that ought to be recognized, distort the picture of Protestantism's present situation, and confuse the judgment of what is to be done next.

I

The view that the present is a post-Protestant era, with its implied premise that the United States was once a Protestant nation, has been applied in the interpretation of the present religious situation by Winthrop S. Hudson,[1] Martin E. Marty,[2] and Will Herberg.[3] A summary of their respective positions will enable us to see the general tenor of the argument as well as several of its implications.

Hudson entitles the third section of his book "Protestantism in Post-Protestant America 1914–." His definition of what he means is clear enough:

To say that the United States had entered a post-Protestant era is not to deny that much of American culture continued to be informed by a distinctly Protestant ethos, nor is it to contend that Protestantism was no longer a factor shaping

[1] *American Protestantism* (Chicago: University of Chicago Press, 1961). Page references are to this book.

[2] *The New Shape of American Religion* (New York: Harper, 1958).

[3] "Religion and Culture in Present-Day America," in Thomas T. McAvoy, editor, *Roman Catholicism and the American Way of Life* (University of Notre Dame Press, 1960), pp. 4–9. This article is an excellent brief summary of the thesis Mr. Herberg developed extensively in his book *Protestant-Catholic-Jew* (Garden City: Doubleday, 1955). The page references in the text are to the article as printed in this volume on pp. 339 ff.

American life. It is simply to affirm that the United States had become a pluralistic society in which Protestantism had ceased to enjoy its old predominance and near monopoly of the religious life of the nation (p. 129).

In answer to the question of when and how the United States became a pluralistic society, Hudson points to the "new immigration" and to how, following World War I, "Roman Catholicism became an increasingly important factor in the life of the nation, and Protestantism was confronted by the difficult problem of adjusting itself to a status of coexistence with another major religious tradition" (p. 130). Meanwhile Protestantism had been so identified with the American way of life that it had become a "culture religion" and lost its peculiar identity. The so-called "new theology," developed during the years of the late nineteenth and early twentieth centuries, tended to invest "the cultural or social process itself with intrinsic redemptive tendencies" and hence to wash out "any real distinction between the church and the world" (p. 141). This, in turn, "cut the nerve of the evangelistic impulse" in the churches, presumably insofar as it had been an impulse to save men out of the world and to stand in judgment over the culture.

In summary, it would seem that to Hudson "post-Protestant" means two things: (1) the loss in the churches of distinctiveness and identity as *Protestant,* and (2) confrontation with pluralism—specifically with "another major religious tradition" —in the society. This situation is definitely pictured as something new—the United States *became* a pluralistic society.

The remedy Hudson finds implied in the "confession of 1935" of Harry Emerson Fosdick, the archliberal of the 1920's and '30's:

"We have been all things to all men long enough. We have adapted and adjusted and accommodated and conceded long enough. We have at times gotten so low down that we talked as though the highest compliment that could be paid to Almighty God was that a few scientists believed in him. Yet all the time, by right, we had an independent standing-ground and a message of our own in which alone there is hope for mankind" (p. 172).

In brief, Hudson seems to pin his hope for the future of Protestantism on the recovery of particularity, which alone can bring a sense of structured identity to stand in judgment against the prevailing "culture religion." This in turn will require the revival of discipline in the churches. As he had argued in a previous book, "An indispensable prerequisite to the renewal of the churches as a dynamic force in American life is the recovery of discipline. The recovery of discipline, in turn, is dependent upon the recovery of the distinctive note of the Christian faith."[4]

He notes that the outstanding place where "vigor and vitality" as well as discipline and distinctiveness have been preserved is in "third force" Protestantism, that is, among "the miscellaneous threefold grouping of Adventist, Fundamentalist, and Holiness churches," and to some extent among Southern Baptists. Within the mainstream denominations hope for renewal is vested in a few isolated groups, especially among the Presbyterians and Episcopalians and, perhaps, the Lutherans (p. 174).

I do not think Hudson makes clear just how the recovery of discipline and distinctiveness in the Protestant churches would enable or even help them to adjust "to a status of coexistence with another major religious tradition." Historically it would seem that disciplined particularity in the several religious groups was precisely what stood in the way of peaceful coexistence and had to be toned down before religious pluralism was possible in a commonwealth.

The post-Protestant concept in Marty's *The New Shape of American Religion* is somewhat tangential to the main argument of the book, and in subsequent publications he has greatly qualified his use of it. But in *The New Shape* he held that it is "strict historical accuracy to call these post-Protestant times" (p. 32). At least, he added, "one could certainly not describe these as post-Catholic, post-Jewish, or post-secular times"—which may be true enough, granted one feels compelled to describe them as "post" something. Even

[4] *The Great Tradition of the American Churches* (New York: Harper, 1953), p. 252.

so, it might well be argued that if America was once Protestant, it must have been post-Catholic.

Like Hudson, Marty begins with the premise that "America was once largely Protestant" (p. 2). By this he means that "insofar as organized religion was represented in the great central events that shaped America and have become part of its mystic core, Protestantism dominated" (p. 4). But today, he continues, we see "the maturing of several processes"— "the erosion of particularity . . . by a blurry, generalizing religion"; the "smoothing of the edges of witness" by an "amiable syncretism"; and the "loss of religious content." This "process of erosion" in Protestantism "has been long and gradual" (p. 2).

What happened in the decade of the 1950's was not a revival of religion but "a revival of *interest* in religion" (p. 10), and what came to prevail was "religion-in-general." Marty equates this "religion-in-general" with the "national religion." The revival of the 1950's, then, was "the first great awakening not of mainstream Protestant Christianity as such but *of a maturing national religion*" (p. 10). This was *"The New American Religion"* (p. 14), and "no term better describes America's new religious constellation than . . . 'religion-in-general'" (p. 32). It is to be noted that Marty stresses that this "American Religion" is something *new*.

While Herberg does not use the phrase "post-Protestant," a chief concern of his article is to explain "the transformation of America from a *Protestant* country into a *three-religion* country" (p. 343). He recognizes that because Americans are all immigrants in origin, American society has always been fluid and pluralistic. How then, he asks, does an individual gain and define his peculiar identity and sense of belonging in such a mobile and pluralistic society? His answer is that the United States was once Protestant in the sense that the only acceptable way to be 100 per cent American was to be Protestant—something that Americans of other religious groups recognized. America was a one-religion country, and that religion was Protestantism. Today this situation has changed. A "three-religion America has emerged"—Protestant,

Catholic, and Jew—"these are three alternative ways of being an American" (pp. 346–347).

In this context Herberg develops his view of the washout of religious particularity. For if religion serves the function of identifying oneself as "American," this function may be "largely unrelated to the content of faith." "Indeed for such a purpose, the *authentic content of faith* may even prove a serious handicap, for . . . it carries a prophetic impact which serves rather to unadjust than to adjust, to emphasize the ambiguity of every earthly form of belonging rather than to let the individual rest secure in his 'sociability'" (p. 351). This would seem to suggest that "the *authentic content of faith*" is incompatible with willing acceptance of religious pluralism in the society; and, conversely, that if an individual seems to rest secure with such pluralism, this is reason for doubting the authenticity of his faith.

Herberg's argument continues that, having lost their exclusiveness and particularity, the three traditional faiths lend themselves to a vaguer faith that seems to include them all. Americans

are coming to regard . . . the "three great faiths," as three alternative (though not necessarily equal) expressions of a great overarching commitment which they all share by virtue of being Americans. This commitment is, of course, to democracy or the American Way of Life. It is the common allegiance which . . . provides Americans with the "common set of ideas, rituals, and symbols" through which an "overarching sense of unity" is achieved amidst diversity and conflict. It is, in a sense far more real than John Dewey ever dreamed of, the "common religion" of Americans (p. 348).

After reading that paragraph one would expect Herberg to speak next of the theological issues between the "three great faiths" on the one hand and "the 'common religion' of Americans" on the other. Instead, by unequivocally identifying "Americanization" with "secularization"—the process is "essentially the 'Americanization' of religion in America, and therefore its thorough-going secularization" (p. 349)—he seems in effect to deny that the "common religion" is a religion at all and to side-step the possibility that there is a theological issue between them to be discussed.[5] Often the American's "ultimate commitment" is to "the American Way of Life," which is secular. But, Herberg continues, the American "combines the two—his [Jewish-Christian?] religion and his culture [the common religion?]—by making the former an expression of the latter, his religion an expression of the 'moral and spiritual values of democracy'" (p. 351). Herberg's conclusion is that "we have in America an invisible, formally unacknowledged, but very potent religion—the religion of democracy, the religion of the American Way of Life—of which the conventional religions are felt to be more or less adequate expressions" (p. 353). Thus Herberg does appear to give more tangible content to Hudson's concept of "culture religion" and Marty's concept of "religion-in-general." But he does not seem to notice that what he has described with fair accuracy is the religious stance of the founding fathers, and it is hard to understand why he insists that the "religion of democracy" is invisible and formally unacknowledged—a point to which we shall return.

In summary, the concept of post-Protestant America as delineated by these men contains the following premises: that

[5] "Secularization" is so important in Herberg's thesis that it is necessary to note how he uses this most ambiguous word. In *Protestant-Catholic-Jew* he defines "explicit secularism" as "hostility or demonstrative indifference to religion" and notes that it "is a minor and diminishing force" in the United States (p. 287). In that definition the word "religion" is ambiguous. Apparently Herberg means by it the Jewish-Christian religion. Hence when he says secularism "is thinking and living in terms of a framework of reality and value remote from the religious beliefs simultaneously professed" (p. 14), the implication is that a framework provided by any religion other than Jewish-Christian would be a form of secularism. In brief, it would seem that to Herberg all that is not distinctively Jewish-Christian as he defines it is "secularism." Therefore, while in another connection recognizing that Americanism "has its religious creed, evoking the appropriate religious emotions" and "may, in fact, be taken as the civic religion of the American people" (p. 279), presumably because it is "secularism" one does not have to take its theology seriously.

the United States was once Protestant; that it is no longer so; that Protestantism, Catholicism, and Judaism because, or as, they lost their particularity and relinquished discipline were overshadowed by the religion of democracy (or culture religion, or religion-in-general) which concurrently emerged. At least to Herberg the religion of democracy is thorough-going secularism. All three employ this complex concept to interpret the present religious situation in the United States. And they come to essentially the same conclusion regarding the nature of Protestantism's present sickness; namely, it is a loss of particularity, a religious anemia, so to speak. Hence they point to essentially the same remedy—the recovery of particularity and discipline in the churches.

This entire view rests primarily on the first premise—that the United States was once a Protestant nation. No doubt this is sound enough if one means only that the Protestant churches apparently exerted more influence in shaping the mores than did other religious groups. But it is patently false when applied to what may be called the theology of the republic, upon which rests the thinking behind the Dec-laration of Independence, the Constitution, and the long line of court decisions on matters pertaining to religious freedom. Henry Steel Commager seems to me to have had the right distinction in mind when he wrote that "in everything but law, America, at the opening of the twentieth century, was a Christian nation."[6] The exception "in everything but law" is very important, for the legal structure is the skeleton that holds up the meat of the body politic. The United States was never Protestant in the sense that its constitutional and legal structure was rooted in particularistic Protestant theol-ogy. To overlook this is to confuse or completely to bypass unresolved theological issues between the denominations and the state. The issue is between the theology of the republic's legal structure, which defines even the nature and limits of religious freedom, and the theology of the denominations, which defines their self-identity and correlative reasons for

[6] *The American Mind* (New Haven: Yale University Press, 1950), p. 163.

separate existence. The question is, Are the two theologies reconcilable; and if so, how; and if not, which is to be chosen?

This question is not of recent origin but began to take shape at the beginning of colonization. The problem has not arisen because the United States was once Protestant, or even Christian in a particularistic sense, and has *become* pluralistic. Hudson, I think, is wrong in supposing that only in the twentieth century was Protestantism "confronted by the difficult problem of adjusting itself to a status of coexistence with another major religious tradition." As Marty notes, "America knew a nascent pluralism from the time two men of different faiths set foot on its shore with intention to remain" (p. 68). The question was built into the structure of the United States with the Constitution, for obviously the theological assumptions underlying its provisions for religious freedom could not be distinctively Protestant or even Christian.[7] Therefore, while the recovery of Protestant particularity and discipline in the churches is important enough for other reasons, it would not necessarily help to resolve the tension between America's two religions—and might indeed accentuate it. A great deal would depend, for example, on whose particularity was recovered from the pluralistic grabbag—whether that of John Cotton or of Roger Williams, of Isaac Backus or of

[7] Cf. George S. Hendry, "Knowing the Time," in *Theology Today*, July, 1962, pp. 157–64: "There is a curious blindness to the fact that the Christian 'assumptions' were from the first superimposed on another set of assumptions which are derived from the Enlightenment of the eighteenth century. It would have surprised the founding fathers—or the most influential among them at all events—to know that almost two centuries after their time the question would be seriously asked whether this is the post-Christian era; for they thought they were inaugurating it. . . . But since the ideology of the Enlightenment was strictly 'post-Christian' in the same sense, though in a less disguised manner than that of Communism, the Christian frame of reference could be superimposed on it without great difficulty, and the American way of life, as it is called, is the offspring of this union, exhibiting features which derive from each of its parents."

Regarding the last sentence, see my *The Lively Experiment* (New York: Harper, 1963), p. 38.

Timothy Dwight, of C. F. W. Walther or of Samuel S.
Schmucker, of Reinhold Niebuhr or of Carl McIntire.[8]

II

G. K. Chesterton, somewhat irked and then amused by
the questions he was asked when he applied for a passport
to the United States, was led to ask what it is that "makes
America peculiar."[9] He concluded that it was the fact that

America is the only nation in the world that is founded on a
creed. That creed is set forth with dogmatic and even theological lucidity in the Declaration of Independence. . . . It
enunciates that all men are equal in their claim to justice,
and that governments exist to give them that justice, and that
their authority is for that reason just. It certainly does condemn anarchism, and it does also by inference condemn
atheism, since it clearly names the Creator as the ultimate
authority from whom these equal rights are derived (pp.
125–26).

Therefore, Chesterton argued, the conception of the United
States is that of "a nation with the soul of a church, protected
by religious and not racial selection" (p. 128). His explanation of why this is so is, briefly, that when the United States

[8] By and large the theological revival since around 1930 has
sought for historical roots primarily in the right-wing tradition
which never, or never as completely, digested religious freedom
and pluralism as did the left-wing groups. Thomas Jefferson spoke
from experience both when he commended the Baptists for their
consistent advocacy of religious freedom and when he said of the
right-wing New England clergy that "the advocate of religious
freedom is to expect neither peace nor forgiveness from them."
In this connection see my review of R. Freeman Butts, *The
American Tradition in Religion and Education*, in *The Journal of
Religion*, April, 1952, p. 143.

[9] He lists the following: "Are you an anarchist? . . . Are you
in favour of subverting the government of the United States by
force? . . . Are you a polygamist?" All the quotations from Chesterton are taken from Raymond T. Bond, editor, *The Man Who Was
Chesterton* (Garden City: Doubleday Image Books, 1960). Page
references are in the text.

was born it was already made up of a great variety of people, and the new nation was projected as an asylum—"a home for the homeless"—of all the world (p. 131). It is this "idea of making a new nation literally out of [the people of] any old nation that comes along" that makes this country different.

How do these diverse people become "American"? The process could not be one of slow assimilation to blood and soil. One might say that they have been accepted upon profession of faith in the American democratic way of life and belief in America's creed. That one was practicing it was evidence of Americanization. This is what Chesterton had in mind when he said that "what is unique is not America but what is called Americanization." And "the point is not that nothing exists in America except this idea; it is that nothing like this idea exists anywhere except in America" (p. 131). Chesterton, then, concluded that "citizenship is the American ideal, . . . [the] vision of moulding many peoples into the visible image of the citizen" (p. 133), based on "the theory of equality, . . . the pure classic conception that no man must aspire to be anything more than a citizen, and that no man shall endure to be anything less" (p. 132). And this ideal rests on the dogmatic assertion that they were all "created equal and endowed by their Creator with certain unalienable rights."

The crucial question for those who use the post-Protestant concept is, What is the theology of this American creed? Assuredly it is not Protestant in any particularistic sense. Leading Protestants around the close of the eighteenth century dubbed it "infidelity," the precise meaning of which was the denial of a special revelation in the Bible; and men like Timothy Dwight of Connecticut went to great lengths to prove that from a Christian point of view it was "vain and deceitful"—a slippery path to eternal damnation.[10] It was rationalism, or deism, or natural religion—to give it a name —the theology of most of the men who had a hand in framing

[10] The literature on this point is very extensive. Reference to much of it will be found in chapter 3 of *The Lively Experiment*.

the Declaration and the Constitution and in launching the new government. It is for this reason that Marty can say:

The spokesmen of the "Religion of Democracy" school [to-day] are . . . appropriating an authentic parcel of the American past. They are more accurate in their reading of the founding fathers than are the unthinking Christians who try to make Protestants out of them and who try to theologize all the basic documents of our national history on Christian lines (p. 84).[11]

On the other hand, those who try to make secularists—in the classical sense[12]—out of them are just as wrong.

It was this theology that made theoretically acceptable the scandal of Christendom at the time—acceptance by a nation of religious pluralism and the consequent multiplicity of independent religious groups. One might say that the provisions

[11] In an article in the December, 1962, issue of *This Day* Marty noted one who "upheld the viewpoint that America never was Protestant; it was rationalist (as were Franklin, Jefferson, Washington, and many other Founding Fathers)," and acknowledged that "America may have been officially born under those auspices. But the nineteenth century, I believe, produced a new setting. The United States became Protestant." The statement illustrates the confusion of referents that is built into the discussion of "post-Protestant" America. When it is said that "America never was Protestant; it was rationalist," the referent must be the substratum of assumptions underlying the Declaration, etc., for non-Protestant groups were negligible. But when Marty says the United States "became Protestant" in the nineteenth century, I think the referent must be the prevailing influence of Protestantism, not the substratum of assumptions. Surely Marty does not mean that the Declaration was converted and baptized by Protestants so that its theology ceased to be!

[12] By "classical sense" I mean the sense in which "secularism" was used by G. J. Holyoake and others around the middle of the nineteenth century—"the doctrine that morality should be based solely in regard to the well-being of mankind in the present life, to the exclusion of all considerations drawn from belief in God or in future life." See Leroy E. Loemker, "The Nature of Secularism," in J. Richard Spann, ed., *The Christian Faith and Secularism* (Nashville: Abingdon-Cokesbury Press, 1948), p. 12.

in the Constitution and First Amendment for national religious freedom and separation of church and state were conceived in actual religious pluralism and were dedicated to the proposition that all religions are equal. They are, as Jefferson said, "of various kinds, indeed, but all good enough; [because] all sufficient to preserve peace and order." This it is that is scandalous to all Christian particularity.

The theology back of this view, and the religious stance of those who held it, is delightfully delineated by Benjamin Franklin in his *Autobiography:*

I had been religiously educated as a Presbyterian; and tho' some of the dogmas of that persuasion, such as the *eternal decrees of God, election, reprobation, etc.,* appeared to me unintelligible, others doubtful, and I early absented myself from the public assemblies of the sect, Sunday being my studying day, I never was without some religious principles. I never doubted, for instance, the existence of the Deity; that he made the world, and govern'd it by his Providence; that the most acceptable service of God was the doing of good to man; that our souls are immortal; and that all crime will be punished, and virtues rewarded, either here or hereafter. These I esteem'd the essentials of every religion; and, being to be found in all the religions we had in our country, I respected them all, tho' with different degrees of respect, as I found them more or less mix'd with other articles, which, without any tendency to inspire, promote, or confirm morality, serv'd principally to divide us, and make us unfriendly to one another. This respect to all, with an opinion that the worst had some good effects, induc'd me to avoid all discourse that might tend to lessen the good opinion another might have of his own religion; and as . . . new places of worship were continually wanted, and generally erected by voluntary contribution, my mite for such purpose, whatever might be the sect, was never refused.

Recognition that this outlook was widely prevalent among the founding fathers is enough to undermine the supposition that "religion-in-general," or the "religion of democracy . . . of which the conventional religions are felt to be more or less adequate expressions," emerged only in the twentieth century. This theology is not only *not* particularistic; it is designedly antiparticularistic, in this respect reflecting the whole intellectual slant of the eighteenth century. These thinkers held that only what is common to all religions and all sects—Franklin's "essentials of every religion"—is relevant to the being and well-being of the *common*wealth. This is the theology behind the legal structure of America, the theology on which the practice of religious freedom is based and its meaning interpreted. Under it, one might say, it is religious particularity, Protestant or otherwise, that is heretical and schismatic—even unamerican!

When the churches accepted religious freedom on these terms, they put themselves into a bind. For under such freedom each group was thrown into competition with all the others, and in this situation must base its claim for allegiance and support on its distinctivensss. At the same time, to become "American" has always meant, implicitly at least, to accept the theology of America's creed and to renounce traditional particularity along with the devil of sectarianism and all his works. The issue with which religious freedom confronted the churches was an issue between two religions—theirs and that of the Declaration.

Nor has the religion of democracy been "invisible [and] formally unacknowledged," as apparently Herberg would have it. It has been celebrated on its holy days—notably the Fourth of July, Memorial and Thanksgiving days—in proclamations and in speeches. One has but to visit a service club to see with what seriousness its cult practices are observed and its hymn sung; or visit the Lincoln Memorial in Washington to see with what devotion its shrines are visited and attended.[13] Recently it has developed its ardent particularists

[13] It is to be noted that at the time when the United States, from the post-Protestant perspective, was, or was becoming, wholly "Protestant," European visitors were commonly struck by the observance of the national religion. For example, Francis J. Grund in his *The Americans In Their Moral, Social and Political Relations* (1837): "It is with the solemnities of religion that the Declaration of Independence is yet annually read to the people from the pulpit, or that Americans celebrate the anniversaries of the most important events in their history. It is to religion they

—its fundamentalist sects—in the so-called far, or radical, or reactionary "right."

Church members in America have always been faced with the necessity to choose, implicitly at least, between the inclusive religion of democracy and the particularistic Christianity of their sect. Few have been as articulate about this as Thomas Sugrue, a New England Roman Catholic of Irish descent.[14] His church, he complained, did "not introduce him to God, or to the deep gregariousness of the spiritual life," but rather acquainted him "with religious sectarianism, and with the dismal fact that in his relation to God he must through all his life be separated from the majority of his fellow men, whom God has informed him are his brothers, and commanded him to love" (p. 19). Confronted with the conflict of religions, he choose the religion of democracy:

All religious roads lead in the end to God, just as all rivers eventually, reach the sea; pilgrims on these highways know that this is so, and realize that many roads are necessary for the many kinds of people, who begin their spiritual journeys from a multitude of points of view. It is the commanders of the highways who will not have it so; each wants preferential rating for his thoroughfare, and longs to reduce all other turnpikes to the status of tributary (p. 20).

Similar was the conclusion of the Congregationalist Josiah Strong, who, in his very popular book *Our Country*, first published in 1885, also echoed Franklin's sentiments:

The teaching of the three great fundamental doctrines which are common to all monotheistic religions is essential to the perpetuity of free institutions, while the inculcation of sectarian dogmas is not. These three doctrines are that of *the existence of God*, the *immortality of man*, and *man's account-*

---

have recourse whenever they wish to impress the popular feeling with anything relative to their country; and it is religion which assists them in all their national undertakings."

[14] *A Catholic Speaks His Mind on America's Religious Conflict* (New York: Harper, 1951). Sugrue's point here bears out Herberg's observation that "the authentic content of faith may even prove a serious handicap" to assimilation as "American."

ability. These doctrines are held in common by all Protestants, Catholics, and Jews.

Strong and Sugrue found the particularistic theology of their sects in conflict with the inclusive theology of the republic in which they lived, and, in effect, they chose the latter. And I suspect there are many clergymen and lay people in the churches in America who occupy a similar position without being aware of the theological gulf they are straddling. They participate in the activities of their churches, including all the observances, but their real theology is that of the republic. It was this phenomenon that intrigued Herberg. He seems to me correctly to have noted that America "has its underlying culture-religion . . . of which the three conventional religions [Protestant, Catholic, Jewish] are somehow felt to be appropriate manifestations and expressions. Religion is integral to Americanism as currently understood."[15] My only question about this view is the implication that the condition noted is something new. It seems to me a fair description of the position of the founding fathers as exemplified in the above quotation from Franklin.

In this context the prevalence of Hudson's "culture religion," Marty's "religion-in-general," and Herberg's "religion of democracy" is seen not as a new emergent, but as the popular triumph of the theology of the Declaration over the theology of the competing denominations. Marty noted this but did not develop its import when he quoted Oscar Handlin: "The Enlightenment prevailed over 'the forms American religion took in its development from Calvinism'" (p. 72). So Marty saw that during the period of growth and expansion

while Protestants pointed with pride to their achievements they hardly realized that the typically rationalist view of the irrelevancy of theological distinction in a pluralist society was pulling the rug out from under them. For a long time a Protestant majority gloried in its bluff, not noticing the winds which were eroding its position and its distinctiveness (pp. 71–72).

[15] *Protestant-Catholic-Jew*, p. 274.

Seen in this perspective Mr. Eisenhower's statements which have often been cited to illustrate the *new* American religious stance take on quite a different significance. In 1948 the general said, "I am the most intensely religious man I know. Nobody goes through six years of war without a faith. That does not mean that I adhere to any sect." In 1952, shortly after his election, the President said, "Our government makes no sense unless it is founded in a deeply felt religious faith, and I don't care what it is." In 1955 he declared that "recognition of the Supreme Being is the first, the most basic expression of Americanism. Without God, there could be no American form of government, nor an American way of life." Eisenhower's position in this respect, far from being "new," seems directly in the tradition of the founding fathers. Indeed, a century before their day, in 1675, the then Lord Baltimore spoke with approval of Maryland's toleration for "all sorts who professed Christianity in general." Thus early he seems to have suggested the question whether the traditional religious particularity was compatible with religious toleration—a question Protestants have not unequivocally answered. Benjamin Franklin stopped going to hear the minister whose sermons seemed designed "rather to make us Presbyterians than good citizens"—suggesting no minister could do both.

Our common concern is for the future. And, as Chesterton said, "We can be almost certain of being wrong about the future, if we are wrong about the past." If one begins with a concept of the present situation as "post-Protestant," it is natural to make the suppositional deduction that the United States was once wholly Protestant. This in turn stands in the way of seeing the true nature of the theological substratum of the Declaration, the Constitution, and the court decisions. Hence "religion-in-general" appears to signify a *new* attitude toward religion, or to be a "new national religion" rather than the popular triumph of the old inclusive theology of the republic over the particularistic theology of the denominations. Ignoring the tension between the two religions which has existed from the beginning enables one to diagnose Protestantism's present anemia as due primarily to the loss of particularity and discipline and to prescribe their recovery as the remedy. Slighting the Creator-centered theology of the American creed (in Chesterton's sense) enables one to identify Americanization with "thoroughgoing secularization" to which, it is implied, Protestant, Catholic, and Jew in order to be true to the authentic content of their faiths must be opposed.

But not only does entertainment of the concept tend to back one into this box, it tends also to confuse the issues of the present in a way reminiscent of the battle with "infidelity" during the late eighteenth and early nineteenth centuries. No doubt secularization in the classical sense of practical atheism is a common enemy before which the lines between the three faiths—Protestant, Catholic, Jewish—fade into relative insignificance. But, I would add, so do the lines between them and the religion of the republic. This is what men like Timothy Dwight did not recognize in their day, so they spurned the potential help of such "infidels" as Thomas Paine, who directed his *Age of Reason* and later writings against the common enemy, atheism. Marty has suggested that in doing so they "were fighting what amounted to 'the wrong war at the wrong place, at the wrong time and with the wrong enemy.'" And insofar as we permit "secularism" to become an "all-purpose concept" similar to what "infidelity" became in Dwight's time, we court the tragic irony of re-enacting the entire struggle "in our time in relation to this newer catch-all term."[16]

On the other hand, recognition that the theology undergirding the practice of religious freedom has always been in conflict with the distinctive theology of right-wing Protestantism enables one to diagnose Protestantism's present sickness as a psychosomatic indigestion, resulting from an inability either to digest the theology on which the practice of religious freedom rests or to regurgitate the practice. I am told that an animal that cannot regurgitate can be killed by getting it to accept as food something it cannot digest. I do not think

[16] Marty, *The Infidel* (New York: Meridian Books, 1961), pp. 21, 16.

Protestantism can give up the practice of religious freedom which it has accepted. Therefore, I conclude, if it cannot learn to digest the theory on which such freedom rests, the prognosis cannot be a happy one.

There is a largely neglected strand in the Protestant tradition representing the attempt to come to terms theologically with religious pluralism and, indeed, to see it as a positive good. Hudson wrote a most perceptive article delineating its emergence among some of the Independent divines of seventeenth-century England.[17] From thence I think it might be traced historically through eighteenth-century pietistic and evangelical movements to its flowering in the formation of the Evangelical Alliance in 1846. By that time its leaders had adumbrated a doctrine of the church (denominationalism as over against sectarianism) consistent with the practice of religious freedom. But, for whatever reasons, their work has become an almost forgotten chapter in American church history. Perhaps one reason is that any group in order to move in the direction suggested by the evangelicals would have to risk losing its life of particularistic distinctiveness. How very difficult this possibility is to entertain is illustrated by the stance assumed by those who hold the post-Protestant concept we have been examining. Perhaps if leading churchmen were more willing to risk the loss of their understanding and practice of the faith—of its particularity—instead of clinging to its denominational swaddling clothes of distinctiveness, there would be more hope for a renewal of life.

Possibly there is merit in what appears just now to be a very minor refrain:

What we are beginning to realize is that God in his providence has permitted a common type of faith and life to emerge from the freedom and the denominational variegation of American Christianity. Out of separate historical traditions which find it increasingly difficult to maintain their relevance we find ourselves meeting one another with common convic-

17 "Denominationalism as a Basis for Ecumenicity," *Church History*, March, 1955.

tions, a common sense of mission, and common methods of doing our work. Many of us would like to join in a large-scale union.[18]

[34]

H. Richard Niebuhr
Reformation: Continuing Imperative*

In a rash or vain moment I accepted The Christian Century's invitation to describe the course of my theological pilgrimage in the recent past. Now that I have made various notes on my recollections of the past and my interests at present I have become more aware than I was of the dubious nature of this enterprise in self-analysis. I am tempted to defensiveness and self-justification by writing an *Apologia pro Vita Sua;* to take myself too seriously as though my theological ideas were representative of more than my own mind; to present myself as more logically consistent than is likely; to present feelings as ideas. To write a wholly honest account of my ways of thinking would require a more personal confession than is fitting in public discourse. For I suppose that no matter how much all of us work out our thoughts about God and man, life and death, sorrow and joy, in response to common and public events, it is in every case the highly personal, not to say private, experiences that most immediately affect the basic form and formulations of our faith. About such things I neither ought nor want to write. Yet I must redeem my promise and give an account of what I think and how I have come so to think. While, then, I shall attempt to write nothing but

[18] Ronald E. Osborn, *The Spirit of American Christianity* (New York: Harper, 1958), pp. 137–38.

* Copyright 1960 by Christian Century Foundation. Reprinted by permission from the March 2, 1960 issue of *The Christian Century.*

the truth, it is clear to me that I shall not tell the whole truth; partly because I do not know it; partly because I owe the whole truth about myself, so far as I know it, only to God. With such warnings to myself and to the reader in mind I begin.

I

The history of my convictions and concerns over the last 30 years—not to go back farther—seems to me to be not only continuous but also consistent. Yet I suppose that a purely objective critic of my activities in theological teaching would find reason to believe that I had changed my mind in fairly radical fashion not once but twice during that period. He might say—and I would agree that in the early 1930s I had given up my connection with that ethics- and religion-centered way of thinking about God and man which is roughly called liberal and that I had affiliated myself with the movement variously called dialectical theology, theology of crisis, neo-orthodoxy and Barthianism. He would, I think, also say—and again I would agree—that in the 1950s I had turned against that movement in its later forms and the tendencies associated with it and had given indications of resuming contact with the earlier modes of theological thought. In support of the latter judgment this objective critic could call attention to the fact that whereas in the 1930s I had written and spoken in support of the separation of the church from the world, in the later period I deplored the kind of separation that had taken place; that whereas I had been called a Barthian (though I never accepted the label) I now dissociated myself from Karl Barth's theology; that while once my interest had been strongly oriented toward the church-union movement, I now displayed little concern for that enterprise and looked elsewhere for the reformation of the church. So far as external, rough facts go I would agree with such a critic, but I would disagree with his implied interpretation for I would want to rejoin that nothing in history is fixed—neither liberalism nor orthodoxy, neither church-union nor churchly relevance to the world—and further, that these things have never been causes for me to the extent that loyalty to them was for me a measure of intellectual or personal integrity.

So far as I see it my history has been about as follows: The '30s were for me as for many of my generation in the church the decisive period in the formation of basic personal convictions and in the establishment of theological formulations of those then (sad to say, not in such a way that my unconscious as well as conscious mind has been wholly permeated by it) was that of God's sovereignty. My fundamental break with the so-called liberal or empirical theology was not due to the fact that it emphasized human sovereignty; to interpret it in that way is to falsify it in unjustifiable fashion. It was rather due to the fact that it defined God primarily in value-terms, as the good, believing that good could be defined apart from God. And now I came to understand that unless being itself, the constitution of things, the One beyond all the many, the ground of my being and of all being, the ground of its "that-ness" and its "so-ness," was trustworthy— could be counted on by what had proceeded from it—I had no God at all. The change was not a change of definition of God but of personal relations to my world and the ground of the world, to the givenness of life, history, myself. Since I came to that conviction or since it came to me, I have worked considerably at the problem of the nature and meaning of "value" and at efforts to understand the basic relation of the self to that on which it is absolutely dependent. But the old theological phrase, "the sovereignty of God," indicates what is for me fundamental.

Two other convictions were associated for me in those years, as they are now, with divine sovereignty: the one was the recognition of our human lostness, sinfulness and idolatrousness; the other was the understanding that trust in the ground of being is a miraculous gift. How it is possible to rely on God as inconquerably loving and redeeming, to have confidence in him as purposive person working towards the glorification of his creation and of himself in his works, to say to the great "It": "Our Father who are in heaven"—this remains the miraculous gift. It is the human impossibility which has been made possible, as has also the enlistment of

these unlikely beings, these human animals, ourselves, in his
cause, the cause of universal creation and universal redemption. So far as I could see and can now see that miracle has
been wrought among us by and through Jesus Christ. I do not
have the evidence which allows me to say that the miracle
of faith in God is worked only by Jesus Christ and that it is
never given to men outside the sphere of his working, though
I may say that where I note its presence I posit the presence
also of something like Jesus Christ.

II

When I write about the nature of faith I am made aware
that I brought over into my reorientation of the '30s a kind
of methodological conviction that had been formed in me
long before, whether in the school of the liberals or simply
in modern existence as such: a conviction of the radically
historical character of human existence. I am certain that I
can only see, understand, think, believe, as a self that is in
time. I can understand that, because I live after Christ, I can
realize the possibility of a pre-existent, eternal Christ or a
second person of the Trinity. But all of this remains theoreti-
cal theology for me and I do not see that faith comes to me
or to my fellowmen through any doctrines about what lies
back of the historical event. It comes to me in history, not
in doctrines about history.

Some of my critics—and, alas, I myself—have called this
position one of historical relativism, which for some people
at once means subjectivism. Historical relationism is probably a better term, since it does not involve subjectivism.
However that may be, if taking our own historicity very
seriously means being a liberal then I remained a liberal
even in the '30s though religiously speaking I was, as I hope
I remain, closer to Calvin and Jonathan Edwards than to the
theologians who thought they were taking history seriously
by speaking about progressive revelation or the development
of religion and thus taking themselves out of history as though
they could regard it from a vantage point above it—an error
which in other forms is present among the orthodox and neo-
orthodox as well.

So much for the coming of fundamental religious convictions and theological orientations that make me think of the
years between 1930 and 1935 as the time in which I began to
think the way I do now. Of course I brought along with me
into that period what I had previously learned through experience and study. I did not abandon religious empiricism
any more than I abandoned historism or neo-Kantian
epistemology. As we all do I had to rework my past and not
leave it behind. But there was another than the personal past
to be reworked and reappropriated. As for other men of my
theological generation reaction against liberalism meant reaction against its rejection of the social past; its suspicion of
tradition; its super-Protestantism in not only passing over the
whole medieval period but also the period of the Reformation
itself. With the aid of my colleagues and students I turned
back to the "Great Tradition." Edwards, Pascal, Luther, Calvin, Thomas and Augustine became important. But that is
the familiar story of the whole generation.

So far as practical churchmanship was concerned it seemed
clear to me that whereas the reform of culture (the great
concern of the social gospel) remained one of the church's
never-ending responsibilities—to which certain theologians
were especially called (and I tended to regard my brother,
to whom I was indebted for many things, as belonging to
that group)—the time called particularly for the reformation
of the church, and I was among those for whom this was the
special task. As a convinced Protestant (not an anti-Catholic)
who saw the sovereignty of God usurped by the spirit of
capitalism and of nationalism I felt strongly that the times
called for the rejection of "Culture Protestantism" and for the
return of the Church to the confession of its own peculiar
faith and ethos.

In that movement of church reformation—dramatized in the
struggle of the German Confessing Church with National
Socialism—Karl Barth was the decisive spokesman for the
primacy of faith, for the independence of the church, for
God's transcendence. Barth functioned as the prophet of the
movement though he disclaimed the role. The struggle of the
Confessing Church in Germany with German Christianity and

National Socialism formed the dramatic center of the movement toward church reformation and it is apparent that the consequences of that struggle remain effective in much modern theology, especially on the continent.

III

Now 25 years have come and gone since that formative period of the '30s. Much has happened during that time in public and in private spheres—wars and peace, prosperity and adversity, sickness and health, death and life. Student generations have come and gone with their various climates of theological opinion and their changing needs. But what has happened to me and the events in which I have participated have not changed my fundamental convictions about the sovereignty of God, the lostness of men (though lost in a physically enlarging cosmos) and the gift of forgiveness through faith. Experience and study both have led to some changes in the theological formulation of those convictions. The complex, dynamic, interhuman as well as human-divine interaction of trust and loyalty has excited my wonder and challenged my efforts to understand faith more than ever. Perhaps it is this concentration on faith as trust and loyalty which has led me farther away from the road that many other postliberals—particularly Karl Barth—have taken. So many of them seem to me to have gone back to orthodoxy as right teaching, right doctrine, and to faith as *fides*, as assent; they tend, it seems to me, toward the definition of Christian life in terms of right believing, of Christianity as the true religion, and otherwise toward the assertion of the primacy of ideas over personal relations. When I think about this I have to say to myself that important as theological formulations are for me they are not the basis of faith but only one of its expressions and that not the primary one. I discover further a greater kinship with all theologians of Christian experience than with the theologians of Christian doctrine. So I find myself, though with many hesitations, closer to Edwards and Schleiermacher, to Coleridge, Bushnell and Maurice than to Barth and the dogmatic biblical theology current today in wide circles. To state my understanding of our theological

situation briefly: I believe that the Barthian correction of
the line of march begun in Schleiermacher's day was absolutely essential, but that it has become an overcorrection and
that Protestant theology can minister to the church's life more
effectively if it resumes the general line of march represented
by the evangelical, empirical and critical movement. Some
new studies in modern theology have convinced me that the
movement from Schleiermacher to Troeltsch was by no means
so humanistic as its critics have asserted. Existentialism also
has served to reinforce my concern for the personal, for the
religiously experienced, for I-Thou relations between God and
man and between men. Among contemporary theologians it
is Bultmann who above all seems to me to represent this
empirical and ethical strain in theology. I feel great kinship
with him in his intentions.

IV

Reflections on the sovereignty of God and the forms of
faith have led me to see that the problem of the church—
at least as it appears today—is not the problem of separating
itself only from the idolatries and henotheisms of the world
but from its own idolatries and henotheisms. (By "henotheism"
I mean the worship of one god who is however the god of
an ingroup rather than the ground of all being.) I see our
human religion now, whether non-Christian or Christian, as
one part of our human culture which like other parts is subject to a constant process of reformation and deformation, of
metanoia (repentance) and fall. And in that process the
deification of the principles of religious society is no less dangerous to men, no less misleading to their faith, than the
deification of national or economic principles. If my Protestantism led me in the past to protest against the spirit of
capitalism and of nationalism, of communism and technological civilization, it now leads me to protest against the deification of Scriptures and of the church. In many circles today
we have substituted for the religion-centered faith of the 19th
century a church-centered faith, as though the historical and
visible church were the representative of God on earth, as
though the Bible were the only word that God is speaking.

I do not see how we can witness to the divine sovereignty without being in the church nor how we can understand what God is doing and declaring to us in our public and private experience without the dictionary of the Scriptures, but it seems to me that in our new orthodox movements we are moving dangerously near to the untenable positions against which the Reformation and the 18th-century revival had to protest.

While I am speaking of my protests I must include my rejection of the tendency in much postliberal theology to equate theology with Christology and to base on a few passages of the New Testament a new unitarianism of the second person of the Trinity. In my confession of faith, as in that of many men I know, the expression of trust in God and the vow of loyalty to him comes before the acknowledgment of Christ's lordship. I realize that it is not so for all Christians but I protest against a dogmatic formulation that reads me and my companions out of the church.

My primary concern today, however, is not to protest. It is still that of the reformation of the church. I still believe that reformation is a permanent movement, that *metanoia* is the continuous demand made on us in historical life. The immediate reformation of the church that I pray for, look for and want to work for in the time that may remain to me is its reformation not now by separation from the world but by a new entrance into it without conformity to it. I believe our separation has gone far enough and that now we must find new ways of doing what we were created to do. One side of the situation is that represented by the "world" today, at least the Western world. It seems to me that in that world men have become deeply disillusioned about themselves and are becoming disillusioned about their idols—the nations, the spirit of technological civilization and so on. They no longer expect the powers in them or around them to save them from destruction (whether through holocaust or boredom) or from the trivialization of an existence that might as well not have been. The so-called underdeveloped nations—including Russia—do not yet know that there is no hope and no glory and no joy in the multiplication of our powers over nature, and we have no way of saving them from going through the experience through which we have passed or are passing. But in the West the most sensitive, if not yet most, men are living in a great religious void; their half-gods have gone and the gods have not arrived. The religious revival we are said to have had in recent years has been, so far as I can see, less a revival of faith in God and of the hope of glory that a revival of desire for faith and of a hope for hope. And it further seems to me that our churches have been filled (our seminaries too) with men and women who are experiencing that emptiness; further, that there is in the society at large a host of similarly minded persons who have not even considered the church as possibly ministering to their need. I am haunted in the presence of that situation by the phrase: "the hungry sheep look up and are not fed."

I do not believe that we can meet in our day the need which the church was founded to meet by becoming more orthodox or more liberal, more biblical or more liturgical. I look for a resymbolization of the message and the life of faith in the One God. Our old phrases are worn out; they have become clichés by means of which we can neither grasp nor communicate the reality of our existence before God. Retranslation is not enough; more precisely, retranslation of traditional terms—"Word of God," "redemption," "incarnation," "justification," "grace," "eternal life"—is not possible unless one has direct relations in the immediacy of personal life to the actualities to which people in another time referred to with the aid of such symbols. I do not know how this resymbolization in pregnant words and in symbolic deeds (like the new words of the Reformation and the Puritan movement and the Great Awakening, like the symbolic deeds of the Franciscans and the social gospelers) will come about. I do count on the Holy Spirit and believe that the words and the deeds will come about. I also believe, with both the prophets and, of all men, Karl Marx, that the reformation of religion is the fundamental reformation of society. And I believe that nothing very important for mankind will happen

as a result of our "conquest" of space or as a result of the
cessation of the cold war unless the human spirit is revived
within itself.

[35]

Daniel Day Williams
The New Theological Situation*

*"It is in the mode of thought known as process theology
where I find the most significant movement toward a social
theology. . . . I do not propose to try to prove that this mode
of thought has the answers to all theological questions. I
believe it is on the right track, but my concern is to try to
identify the problem which this theology must solve. What
we need to do is to carry through to a new theological con
struction on the conviction that the relation between God and
his creatures is through and through social. All the traditional
doctrines must be reconsidered."*

Theology is in trouble. Perhaps it always is, but we are
conscious of a sharp new turn in the theological situation
since 1960. We are all making our attempts to assess what
has been happening, and I offer here one such attempt.

The present situation includes the widespread upset in theological thought and the loss of authority of modes of theological work which have dominated the scene for two generations. Whitehead says that climates of thought last about
thirty years. If we measure roughly from the first years of
the 1930's (when Reinhold Niebuhr published *Moral Man
and Immoral Society* and the theology of Karl Barth first
became known in America) to 1960 (the year of the Second
Vatican Council and the sharp increase of interest in the writ-

* From *Theology Today*, Vol. xxiv, No. 4, January, 1968, pp.
444–463.

ings of Dietrich Bonhoeffer), we have a remarkable demonstration of Whitehead's point on the American scene.

I

Today it is widely stated that Christian theology is in "disarray." One of my wise colleagues always speaks of "theological chaos" when he refers to the present situation. One hears from many quarters of the "collapse" of theology. It is said there should be a moratorium on the use of the word "God." Indeed for some "God is dead," and the newest theology is not about God at all but about man, and, curiously, about Christ without God. Protestants, one critic writes, are "filled with self-loathing." A reflective American who has been away from this country for two years, Warren Ashby, caught up on what has been happening by reading the last two years of theological journals, and he entitles his report, "Theological Existence Among the Ruins."[1] The disruption in the Roman Catholic Church seems far deeper than we have yet comprehended. Leslie Dewart, a Canadian Catholic theologian, has written a provocative essay entitled *The Future of Belief* on the thesis that Christianity "suffers from absolute theism." He declares against all the scholastics that God has no essence. With Paul Tillich, Dewart wants to get rid of the phrase "the existence of God." This is not to deny God's reality but to declare that God's presence to man is possible only within radical freedom on both sides. "God is made visible by our realization, indeed, by our creation of him in us, for, morally speaking, God is made to exist or not to exist by man's freely chosen existence."[2] In the spirit of these startling paradoxes many of us find an echo of our own state of mind in these sober words of another Roman Catholic, Daniel Callahan: "At a time in my life when I should be solidifying and developing positive convictions—any kind—I see in my mind more of chaos than of order, more blind alleys, than clear paths."[3]

[1] *The Christian Century*, March 22, 1967.

[2] Leslie Dewart, *The Future of Belief* (New York: 1966), p. 126.

[3] Daniel Callahan, "The Relational Nature of Theology," *The Christian Century*, Feb. 2, 1966.

Undeniably there is a new turn in the theological situation. The question is, "What does it mean?" I disagree with the view that the present situation is chaotic and formless, and that theology is in extreme disarray. There is a central issue in this eruption of new modes of theological thought, an issue which is really not new, though it has taken on some new features. There are some common concerns among the so-called "death of God" theologians, the searchers for a new hermeneutic, the process theologians, and between them and the giant theological systems of Barth and Tillich and Brunner whose authority appears so drastically shaken. My thesis is: theology is distinguished today almost universally by the search for a genuinely social conception of man, of God, and of reality.

Theology is in search of such understanding partly because the pressing problems of human existence in our time demand it, and partly because traditional theology has always had an unresolved tension between a genuinely social and a monarchial conception of God and his relationship to man. This thesis applies to the question of theological authority, to theological method, and to the content of theological assertions. In using the word theology I have in view its meaning as the interpretation of the faith of the believing community, the church, but one of the clear features of the present situation is the re-assertion that theological work involves reflection on all aspects of human experience. Karl Barth's attempt to keep theology clear of all entanglement with philosophy has simply collapsed.

II

An obvious feature of the present situation, but the one that is most difficult to explain, is the sudden disappearance of the authority of the great theological systems which until recently bore the major weight in articulating the faith of the church. The dogmatic expositions of Christian doctrine (and when have there been three more powerful ones than those of Karl Barth, Emil Brunner, and Paul Tillich?) have suddenly lost the center of attention, and are not the major subject of theological inquiry, nor are they invoked in that inquiry. It is as if this systematic language about God has suddenly been drained of its power to communicate the meaning of God. I am not referring primarily to the "death of God" thinkers. They are not unimportant indicators, but by themselves they do not give us the key to the theological situation. I point rather to the widespread concern of the new generation of theologians with questions about meaning, truth, and language which have been pressed by the philosophers. Barth and Brunner tried to by-pass the philosophical analysis of meaning.[4] Tillich accepted its necessity, but while, I think, he met the positivists' questions at the right point, the discussion is far from over, and his own metaphysical language quite clearly does not carry conviction even to many disposed to accept some ontology.

Beyond this particular philosophic challenge, however, there is the issue about the nature of revelation and its expression within the structure of Scripture and dogma. Appeals to revelation once were clearly authenticated by reference to the biblical witness, or to Jesus Christ as witnessed to in the Scripture. H. Richard Niebuhr's *The Meaning of Revelation* is now a classic of this movement.

But now the appeal to Scripture, as the bearer of revelation, produces as much resistance as conviction. It is not that scriptural authority is ultimately rejected, but the *meaning* of Scripture, the mode of its interpretation, the diversity of views of its historical development are more prominent issues than any unity of outlook. Barth formally appealed to the Scripture as the "supreme norm of Church dogmatics"; but what questions are settled thereby? If this rather sudden movement away from the implicit authority of the formal norm of dogmatics is a fact, what does it mean?

An important and unusual answer is being given to that question today. The answer lies, in part at least, *in sociology*. When we ask what the new theological situation revolves around, the first answer is clear; it is the theme of social existence, of secularity, of the radical reconstruction of the

---

[4] Daniel D. Williams, "Brunner and Barth on Philosophy," *The Journal of Religion*, Vol. XXVII, No. 4 (1947).

church's relation to society. Further, there is at the present time a "moralizing" of theology. Dr. A. Th. van Leeuwen declared in a recent lecture that "all theology is ethics," a statement which might have delighted Albrecht Ritschl but would have caused its author, in most theological circles between 1930 and 1960, to be regarded as a hopelessly quaint sort of theologian.

Ethical concerns are so put to the fore today that the meaning of all theological assertions and the meaning of God for life are sought in relation to ethical decision. This ethical dimension is bound up with the sociological situation of man today, in which political action becomes the primary sphere of the discovery of significant meanings. Paul Lehmann's *Ethics in a Christian Context* represents the new theological mode with the use of the category of the "politics of God" to describe the messianic structure of history and human society. I may add that I think Professor Lehmann keeps a finely balanced relation between the freedom of the now social situational context and the givens of Christian faith, a balance which other contextualists do not always preserve.

Some have said that the sociological disturbance is itself the explanation of the disappearance of God, but this seems to me a superficial analysis which requires further interpretation.[5] What has happened is that people at grips with human problems have discovered that there are issues of human justice and survival which cannot be handled within the exclusiveness of some traditional theological positions. There are problems which demand human intelligence, technique, and political action in concert with people of many faiths and sometimes of no faith or only of implicit faith. Suddenly a theological ethic which tries to arrive at solutions on the basis of well defined traditions of grace and law seems irrelevant.

It is not that the questions about God, or religion, or metaphysical reality are no longer asked. The secularity of the "secular city" seems to me largely a myth. But it is true that

[5] For example, G. Vahanian, *The Death of God* (New York: 1961).

in the pluralism of our culture, and amid the anguish of
human problems on the mass scale in the great cities, and
especially where churches which preserve the traditional language of faith have become irrevelant to human issues, the
forms in which the question about the meaning of life is
asked become drastically altered. What has happened is that
a new sense of what is real, of what human action can effect,
of the boundaries of human existence, has been born, and it
has yet to receive an expression in language which gives
shape to ultimate concerns as they appear in this new context.

The turn to sociological analysis in the search for meaning is a reiteration of an ancient theme: man's search for the
meaning of life through the discovery of the justice which
orders his social existence. Consider Plato's *Republic*, for
example. But now the religious communities and their traditions appear as part of the problem rather than the source
of the solution. Contrast this situation with that of the confessional church in Germany and, in a different way, the
Social Gospel in America. These church movements set themselves against the prevailing cultural gods and found in the
gospel a judgment upon that society. In contrast, the new
ethics has turned from the theme of the divine judgment as
the ground of Christian action to a search for the basis of
moral decision in the concrete human situation, met in terms
which are open to human inspection.

Underlying the new theological situation there is a drive
toward a new conception of man in society. If this be true,
then the question of the ground of the human *sodalitas*, the
"Republic," becomes the critical issue for theology. In what
forms of social existence can man avoid self-destruction and
find the way to the fulfillment of human possibilities? If theology cannot show what meaning faith in God has for this
task, it has little chance of being heard today.

There is a further effect of the new sociological situation.
The question of the exclusiveness of the Christian revelation
was sharply raised by the Barthian theology. The claim to
absolute and exclusive possession of faith about life is simply
impossible today, sociologically speaking. The engagement
with the problem of human society simply does not allow

for action with others on the basis of a parochial claim to absolute possession of truth. If one points to the Marxists as exceptions, one must realize how skillful the Marxists in Asia and Africa have been in adapting forms of language, symbol, and meaning to the indigenous religions. They have not radically displaced them, but have accommodated themselves to them. (China is a particular problem here. Perhaps part of the present struggle arises from a conflict over the kind of cultural totalitarianism which Mao has imposed, but we do not know.)

III

The claim to an exclusive knowledge of God, the kind of claim put forward by Barth, Brunner, and Hendrick Kraemer, simply seems irrelevant to the meeting of men in present society as they wrestle with their problems. Sociologically, the "death of God" is closely related to the death of this kind of parochialism. But belief in God is supposed to redeem us from parochialism. Why does not the present need for a basis of human sociality lead to the strongest possible affirmation that God alone makes the one universal claim and all others are relativized?

The reason this has not happened is I think related to the way in which the Barthian theologies and those akin to it went about this problem. They tried to avoid parochialism by the assertion that Christianity was not religion, or a religion, but that the revelation in Christ "sets a question mark against all religions." So far we were set free from claims to the absoluteness of Christianity *as a religion*. This was one sign of the secularization of theology in our time, and there is real continuity between this radical strand in Barth's theology and the present situation. Barth was seeking for a universal category of humanity, set free from all special claims for a group or tradition except the claim that in the one man, Jesus, every man has been given his real history.

The difficulty is that this claim was still made on the basis of one single locus of authority. Barth's position on the other religions and with slight modifications, both Brunner's and Kraemer's not only separated Christian faith from religion but declared all religion to be nothing but idolatry. They sought the universal truth in Christian faith, but in doing so restricted this truth solely to the one tradition, the one Scripture, the one form of faith in which they stood.

Certainly this sociological awkwardness does not settle the question of truth. It is indeed possible that all religion outside the Christian revelation is idolatry. But when you seek a universal basis of faith and insist that your understanding of faith is the only valid understanding, you have erected an impassable barrier to any discussion. Everything is relativized to be sure, the forms of religious expression, the particular traditions; but one thing is not relativized, and that is your understanding of what faith is.

Gerhard Ebeling has put what I see as an untenable position so neatly as to make the issue transparently clear: "Christian faith is not a special faith, but simply faith. . . . The history of the word 'faith' indicates that we are not dealing with a religious word of universal occurrence, but that the concept of faith comes from the Old Testament, and obtained in Christianity its central and decisive significance."[6] Which is to say that only Christianity knows what faith is, so that any discussion of the meaning of faith in any other context is futile. This is my conclusion, not Ebeling's, but my point is that this is the logic of his position and that in the present human struggle for sociality, for some kind of common humanity, this position simply does not meet the crying need of man seeking community in our history. Of course there are issues about the nature of faith. The question is whether they are discussable, and by whom.

What I am arguing receives its practical documentation in the fact that the Kraemer-Barth approach has broken down so far as the World Council of Churches is concerned. The Mexico City meeting and the subsequent discussion at New Delhi make it plain that the churches feel it necessary to adopt some new kind of perspective in the discussion with other religions.

[6] Gerhard Ebeling, *The Nature of Faith* (Philadelphia: 1961), pp. 20–21.

Is there a basis upon which men can meet one another in freedom beyond the parochialisms of exclusive claims? This is the real issue posed for Christianity today. Must men be freed of faith in God in order to find one another as men?

We come here to the heart of the present theological situation, and we meet one of the oldest issues in Christian thought, the relation of the divine sovereignty to human freedom. Is there a more threadbare and stale discussion in the whole theological tradition? But old and stale or not, it is that issue which more than any other determines the present theological situation.

Most men today do not feel absolutely dependent on anything. Begin here with this challenge to Schleiermacher's definition of religion. The recovery of the reformation doctrine of justification by faith in the neo-orthodox movement was a reiteration of the theme of man's sin and his utter dependence upon God's grace. Without God's mercy, life is nothing but death. And faith itself is a gift of grace. Theologies have always been uneasy about the doctrine of predestination, but none of them has known how to get rid of it and still hold to the classical view of God as the disposer of destiny. Tillich's theology comes out no differently from Barth's on this point.

But there is a perennial result of the doctrine of predestination. It produces a resistance, and finally rejection. Modern man has experienced a creativity which was unimaginable in previous eras. Does man add nothing to the process of life and history? To be sure, this creativity is shot through with demonic destructiveness. One can argue that there is much ground for fatalism in the present culture. But regardless of this argument, a considerable and articulate part of the cultural leadership does not feel fatalistic. The reason is not that men are so optimistic about solving all human problems. The reason is that some human problems can be solved, and they are often problems of technology, political strategy, and a reconstruction of the conditions of human existence which reaches from rebuilding the human body and control of the genetic code to the establishment of colonies on other planets. I do not see how a theology of absolute predetermination can survive in this situation. Man has work to do and power to do it with, and his resources are in large part in his intelligence, will, and cooperation with the "forces of nature."

If the relation between man and God is to be interpreted in this situation, that relation must in a fundamental sense be social with freedom on both sides. Man before God cannot be less than man at grips with his world and his problems. Something like this surely is what Dietrich Bonhoeffer meant when he spoke of man coming of age. The childish reliance on God alone to solve problems which require human effort must be put aside.

It is curious that some "death of God" theologians who quote Bonhoeffer on this point do not go on to quote what he further says, that we should find God not in what we don't know but in what we do know. This opens the way to reconsideration of the doctrine of God. God's power must be involved with man's freedom, and man's freedom must not be compromised by arbitrary assertions about the way in which God exercises his power.

IV

If we examine the development of two major contemporary theologies, those of Karl Barth and the school of the new hermeneutics, we find confirmation of the thesis that the relation of the divine sovereignty to human freedom is a critical point.

One cannot read Karl Barth's great *Church Dogmatics* without being conscious of the creative movement of his thought away from the traditional view of God as static being to a full rendering of God's free personal activity implied in his revelation in Jesus Christ. God's being is the freedom to act in love. With this key Barth develops the doctrines of the perfections of God in what is surely one of the major theological accomplishments in this century.[7] After reading this section, one may well wonder at those who say language cannot be used meaningfully about God today.

Barth believes he gets rid of all traces of the impersonal

[7] Karl Barth, *Church Dogmatics* (London, 1957), Vol. II/1, Chap. 6.

absolute lurking behind traditional doctrines of the attributes. He eliminates all doctrines of timelessness and spacelessness. God is living, acting, outgoing, and he is thus in his free decision. He has acted as he creates the world and takes our humanity upon himself in Jesus Christ. Barth develops the doctrines of God's holiness and grace, mercy and righteousness, patience and wisdom, unity and omnipresence, constancy and omnipotence, eternity and glory. Yet when it is all done, I believe Barth remains caught in the presuppositions of traditional theology with all the special doctrines which have made Augustinianism and Calvinism problematic in their view of human freedom. For while Barth's view is that God acts in freedom, he never fully faces the implications of the question as to whether the world's life adds anything to God, and that is the test question. At some points Barth explicitly denies that the world does add anything to God's glory or life or joy. Barth is still committed to the view that God must be absolutely the monarch of all things, in no way dependent upon anything which happens in the world. Barth strives mightily to see time in God; God is pre-temporal, temporal, and post-temporal. But Barth finally lets God's absoluteness swallow up all real temporality in a simultaneity which seems to be no different from Augustine's *totum simul.* In discussing God's response to the world, a question which is raised sharply by the reality of prayer, Barth bases his case on God's command that we pray, but what there is ontologically in God that could be affected in any way by prayer is not stated.

Barth brilliantly treats omnipotence and omniscience in relation to God's freedom to act in love. These attributes are not to be understood in abstraction from that freedom. But when we ask what difference this makes to traditional theological determinism, Barth does not open the way at all to a genuinely social relation between God's power and human response. Barth says: "If we ask why creation or each of us or everything has to be as it is, the only answer is that it must be so by God's free will."[8]

8 *Ibid.,* p. 561.

It must be remembered, and it supports our thesis that the social concern lies at the base of theology today, that Barth's exposition of the doctrine of man is one of the powerful statements of a social anthropology. The image of God in man is his creation for life in community, his being with the neighbor, seeing, speaking, hearing, sharing in creative life. But Barth will not allow that this image of God gives us any knowledge of God himself. The image of human sociality gives us no clue as to its source.

It is well known that in 1956, Karl Barth gave a lecture to the Swiss Reformed Ministers Association (Arrau) on *The Humanity of God,* in which he reviewed the stark position of his early theology and tried, as he says, to speak another word to correct the balance. That lecture confirms our thesis that theology is really seeking a genuinely social doctrine of God and man. Barth pleads that God's deity does not exclude but *includes* his humanity. "God is human, His free affirmation of man, His free concern for him, His free substitution for him—this is God's humanity." These are illuminating words. Yet they bear in themselves the block of which I speak, for nothing in Barth suggests that God's humanity means he is enriched, added to, or fulfilled in any way by man. God sacrifices himself for the human race. And "it remains true that God, as Creator and Lord of man, is always free to produce even in human activity and its results, in spite of the problems involved, parables of his own eternal good will and actions."[9] Yet Barth does not seem to see that this reduces human life to an illustration of something else; it has nothing of its own import, it merely reflects what God has put into it. What God has put into it is very good indeed; Barth seems close to universalism. He wants no private Christianity, but he cannot say a positive word about man "outside," except that the outsiders are really only insiders who have not understood and apprehended themselves as such. With that paradox I will leave Barth. His theology is a *half way stage* toward the theology which can satisfy the

[9] Karl Barth, *The Humanity of God* (Richmond, Virginia: 1960), pp. 49–51; 54–55.

inner directive of our situation to find some positive worth in human existence.

v

The new hermeneutical school, with its sources in Bultmann and in Heidegger's later philosophy, has proposed a corrective to the rigid biblicism of the Barthian method. Its central thesis is that theology has to do with the communication in word-event of the meaning of God. All "objectivating" thought of God or indeed of man is a violation of the personal reality with which theology deals. This position also illustrates our claim that theology is today searching for a social doctrine in a context of respect for social relatedness in all theological meaning.

We must not make God or other persons into "objects." We must not freeze doctrine into objective structures. All this offers welcome freedom to theology. But this new "personism" has not carried through a radical questioning of the concept of the divine monarch, and indeed it is hard to see how it can produce any doctrine of God at all. Everything is reduced to "word-events." Ebeling says, "If the word 'God' means the basic situation of man as word situation, then by speaking of God one perceives man at the point of his linguisticality."[10] But then we must ask, "What are the criteria for speech about God?" Language requires a context in something which is more than language. But that context is never given, it cannot be, when this Heideggerian exclusiveness of meaning-as-speech is affirmed. There is no way to get beyond endless speaking, and it is speaking about what?

Ebeling does say that the word "God" shows that man is not master of himself. He lives from the power of a word that is not his own, and at the same time thirsts after the power of a word that likewise cannot be his own. In so far as a doctrine of God is here implied, Ebeling slips into the old monarchianism, and the passivism with respect to man that goes with it. "Man needs language more for hearing than for speaking, for believing than for acting . . . because he lives

[10] Gerhard Ebeling, *God and Word* (Philadelphia: 1967), p. 28.

by the word, man is ultimately not a doer but a receiver."[11] There is much in Ebeling's view of faith and of language as the "body of our spirit" which moves toward a genuinely social theology. But what he has so far said seems ambiguous at best when it comes to a reconstruction of the traditional doctrine of God.

It would be appropriate here to refer to some theologies which have moved toward a reconstructed theism which sees man before God in creative freedom. Outstanding American theologies have moved far in the direction we are pointing, notably those of Reinhold Niebuhr and H. Richard Niebuhr. Robert L. Calhoun's *God and the Common Life* stands as a landmark of the new theism. I have less acquaintance with the current continental scene, but the theologies of Moltmann and Pannenberg, and the thought of Hans Schmidt, seem to incorporate an historical conception of reality, and, at least in the case of Pannenberg, show a new interest in metaphysics.

It is in the mode of thought known as process theology where I find the most significant movement toward a social theology, and the appraisal just offered of the theological situation is obviously influenced by the point of view which takes the metaphysics of process thought to be of especial significance for Christian theological reconstruction. This theological movement is represented not only by Protestants, such as Norman Pittenger, Schubert Ogden, Bernard Meland, and Charles Hartshorne, but also by Roman Catholics such as Teilhard de Chardin, Peter Schoonenberg, and now in a radical form by Leslie Dewart.

I do not propose to try to prove that this mode of thought has the answers to all theological questions. I believe it is on the right track, but my concern is to try to identify the problem which this theology must solve. What we need to do is to carry through to a new theological construction on the conviction that the relation between God and his creatures is through and through social. All the traditional doctrines must be reconsidered: creation, freedom, election, community,

[11] *Ibid.*, pp. 30–31.

the nature of love, sin, grace, incarnation, and eschatology. Nothing can be left out. Nothing is unaffected.

VI

The trend of contemporary theology is toward a social doctrine of God and reality. But what is meant by social? It is just this concept which theology needs to examine and to which it can bring real illumination out of the biblical faith through the implicit understanding in the Christian tradition of what the relation is between God and his world. In seeking to make this relation explicit there are many modes of attack. There is the new metaphysics with its social doctrine of being. That has been widely discussed. I wish here to suggest a somewhat different method of interpreting the meaning of sociality. Without substituting logic for ontology can we lift out the logic of social relationship for analysis? So much traditional theological language has rested on the logic which denies social relationship. This is one way of purifying our theological discourse.

The development of modern logic moves in realms where it is difficult to follow without elaborate technical preparation. Yet if theology seeks the *logos* of *theos* then surely the quest for an adequate logical exposition of our discourse about God is part of our vocation. And when we have difficulties, we may take some comfort in the fact that the logic of informal languages seems to be far from a systematized science, and that fundamental problems of logical structure may be, like the structure of the atom, windows upon infinite horizons of meaning.

There have been hints that there can be an analysis of the structure of social relatedness. There is Josiah Royce's essay, *The Principles of Logic,* first written for Windelband's *Encyclopedia of the Philosophical Sciences,* in which Royce defines logic as the science of types of order and suggests that a logic of modes of action could set forth the necessary structure of all possible action and, we may conclude, therefore, of interaction.[12] I am not concerned with Royce's par-

[12] Josiah Royce, *The Principles of Logic* (New York: 1961).

ticular argument. It still appears as an idealist's search for the *a priori* deduction of the nature of the empirical world. But Royce's suggestion that we need to extract the logical order implied in the world as living, moving, and becoming is one which theology might profitably follow.

The most suggestive essay is that cryptic lecture of Whitehead's, *Mathematics and the Good,* which he delivered toward the end of his life and in which he brought together his two fundamental interests, mathematical logic and the theory of value. In a thoroughly platonic spirit he declares that the concerns of mathematics are incomprehensible without the distinction of good and evil and that good and evil can only be understood in relation to the mathematical structures of finitude and infinity. Whitehead's argument revolves around his view that all value implies limitation. It exhibits the concreteness in one determinate experience of possibilities and actions which participate in an infinite potentiality. The argument is evocative, and, as it stands, surely inconclusive. Yet it may be of first importance for a logic of social reality.

Charles Hartshorne has developed his major themes in an analysis of the logic of perfection as it applies to God and the world. I am obviously indebted in a special way to his thought.

What are the logical requirements for the intelligibility of the process of becoming in which valuable beings are present, increase, and pass away, clash with one another, and receive mutual support? What are the logical requirements for such a process when it has a supreme member whose potentiality of value is infinite and which is related as its necessary partner to every finite good?

Some requirements would be: (1) The logical structure exemplified by anything would include the interaction of each occasion of experience with others in such a way that each comes to be and has its worth not only within itself but in what it draws from and gives to other things. That is, in its definition what a thing is involves patterns and consequences which include its origin and its destiny in relation to other things. If one says this is nothing but the search for the logic of organism, I can agree except that we should not beg the question of what we mean by *organism*. What things *are* involves the patterns or relationships, the fields in which they exist. (2) Our logical structure must involve judgments of value, of the meaning and worth of things for each other, in which judgments of better and worse are possible. Experience is through and through value experience, for each is something for the other in a social universe. "The good of things" is not a generic term for private experiences but refers to qualities of relationship, of things which interact. The value of anything involves its value for other things as well as for itself.

We are trying to describe the society of being, not only of finite entities, but the society of all things with God who is the ultimate structure-giving reality, and who is related to all finite things in a way which is peculiar to his deity. In a discussion of the ontological argument, Professor Findlay says that it becomes clear the idea of God has unique logical properties. This is a critical point for theology. Can these properties be identified and related to other logical requirements? If so, our language about God can be subjected to some kind of intelligible patterning.

We can state some aspects of the requirement of a language about God in a social structure. (1) The relationship we have to describe which holds between God and the creatures must be one in which there is a necessary determination from the side of God which does not hold from the side of the creatures. We are describing a society in which one "member" is necessary to every other member without exception, but of no other member of the society can this be said. We are members one of another, but we are all members of a society which has one member necessary to the whole. This raises all the questions about freedom. We are not free to alter the structure of this society. To reject God we have to plunge toward nothingness, as St. Augustine saw long before the existentialists. But it means that God's qualification on our freedom is not an absolute one. (2) The significance of this special structure is made clear when we raise the value question. We have to describe the goods of existing things in such a way that their real good, their destiny, is bound up not only with other creatures but with their contribution to that continuing eternal reality which participates in all becoming.

What we have to describe then is a society in which each finite member has value for itself, for every other finite member, and each has a value for the supreme member of the society. Every particular value judgment has as its true subject the whole society seen from a perspective. It is the very essence of theism to hold that to love another in God is something more than loving another in himself. Yet we need not devalue the love for the other as he is. This neighbor is to be loved as a unique member of the society, but each neighbor not only has a value for every other neighbor, he is made in the image of God and has a value for God which is unique and which enhances the life of God himself through whatever of positive value this member contributes.

God then has a value for every member of the society, and this is his value as the Lord and Father of all. What God lends to the creatures is himself as the homeland of all, and as the supreme valuer of every individual. Hence we are valued by God for himself as increasing the joy and the suffering of his being. He must wrestle with our defection and rebellion. Valuing is a concrete personal process, and it has its tragic side.

There is nothing more revealing in the logic of the traditional theology than its conclusion that the world adds nothing to God. We have seen that Karl Barth does not escape from this position. Man adds nothing to the divine glory. I think there is no answer to the "death of God" position on this basis.

VII

Every theological program either looks toward some reform of doctrine or reinterpretation of doctrine. Doctrines are not infallible. They are the expression of meanings which lie forever beyond complete rationalization. The new theological situation calls for a forthright review of traditional doctrines. Its motive is not to refute criticisms made from another

standpoint or to make traditional doctrines more palatable but
to recognize that there is unfinished business within the
Christian faith which theology must examine.

I select two doctrines for brief mention, two which seem
most problematic to many of our contemporaries, creation
and the trinity. Does the logic of the society of being throw
light on the problems here and point toward reconstruction?

The doctrine of creation is not only religiously important
but it brings Christianity into discussion with every cosmology.
Since Hume, a central question has been, "Do we need the
category of a creator of the world?" The universe moves on in
its evolution and dynamism, its powers and structures. If
the doctrine of creation out of nothing seems essential to
theology, it appears meaningless to science. We seem to be
holding theologically to a doctrine which has no function in
man's self-understanding or his science.

Meanings can be assigned to the assertion of "creation out
of nothing," meanings related to the sovereignty of God, the
essential goodness of the world, the limits of all our explanations of existence. The traditional doctrine of creation may
have such theological significance. But if the assertion that
God is creator is to have any relation to man's experience of
this world, then creation must be interpreted so that God's
participation in the world's becoming is intelligible in relation to the world's ongoing life. Creation as actual creativity
can be understood, first, as the participation of the creatures
in the structure of possibility of the universe, the structure
which is the primordial dimension of God's own being. Second, creation is sharing with the other the power to be.
Creation as social act involves the willing of the other's being as creative agent. Causation, in a social structure of
creation, becomes a two-way process. What God brings into
being he accepts as introducing a new cause in the universe,
a cause which affects the experience of God himself. Surely
there are hints of this in Genesis as God sees that the creation
is good, and discovers that there are eccentricities in the behavior of the creatures made in his image.

A social doctrine of creation is not confused by problems
of the before and after of the society of creatures, for there is

no creation except in time. Without God as the structure of possibility and the power of being, nothing can be; but the creatures participate in a creative process which involves the interaction of God and the creatures. Thus the logic of sociality leads to a development, not an abandonment, of the doctrine of creation.

Such a logical clarification might purify our language about God, even the language of prayer. On the whole, the liturgical and devotional tradition has had a better language of social interaction than the theological tradition. But there is much to be desired in the correction of both. Consider the prayer for fair weather in *The Book of Common Prayer:*

> Almighty and Most merciful Father, we
> humbly beseech thee of thy great goodness,
> to restrain those immoderate rains
> wherewith thou hast afflicted us. And
> we pray thee to send us such seasonable
> weather, that the earth may, in due
> time, yield her increase for our use
> and benefit, through Jesus Christ our Lord.

Do we dare propose an alternative?

> O God who in thy loving relation to all
> things sharest with us the unfinished
> struggle and the accidents of natural
> processes, sustain us in our search for a
> more humane and fruitful life in our natural
> environment; encourage our search for new
> resources for the control of floods and
> drought, lead us always to acknowledge that
> we belong in the one great society of being, and
> give us grace to share our goods and our hopes
> with all thy creation, through Jesus Christ our Lord.

If we are to press a social doctrine of reality, the temptation to put the doctrine of the trinity in the center of the theological task is almost irresistible. I shall not resist it!

The doctrine of the trinity is the outgrowth of the biblical experience of the action of God in and through a life which was in perfect social communion with him, the life of a real man, in communion with the real and living God. The pattern of Father, Son, and Spirit in one substance was an attempt to protect this fundamental assertion of the church and to find a speech which would embrace the logic of the divine creation, self-giving, self-revelation, and the exhibition of the divine life as love. What the doctrine of the trinity became is a long story; but from the beginning it offered some resistance to the too simple identification of God with the absolute monarch. At least it had this implicit meaning.

In our time from Hegel and Schelling and the mediating theologians to Barth and Tillich there has been an important development to the doctrine of the trinity in which arithmetical puzzles have been set aside. It has been seen as the church's expression of the character, the quality, the essential nature of the divine life as creative self-giving spirit.

Some doctrines of the trinity have indeed seemed to move toward a fully social doctrine of reality. If God is love, he must be more than "one," he must exemplify the communion of love in his own being. So trinitarianisms which have stressed the divine society would seem to be akin to the theology we are calling for. Unfortunately the monarchial tradition has been so strong that the concept of the divine society has been precisely the way in which God is protected from any real involvement with the world. Since he is complete love in himself, it is said that he needs nothing. The divine society becomes the alluring pattern of what the world would like to be but cannot, and God's communion with the world really adds nothing to the completeness and blessedness of the circumincession of the Father, Son, and Spirit.

Once we break the spell of this "apotheosis of the self-contained" and see that love means commitment to the adventure of life with the other in freedom, the doctrine of the trinity may be interpreted so as to do justice to its biblical roots. God has created the world and has given his own Son to live and die there, and thus has revealed himself as self-giving love. He really does go out of himself to participate in, to suffer with, and to move through the world's history to a fulfillment even he does not fully know or control.

What the world offers God is little enough in one sense.

Our social view fully asserts the possibility of the perversion of freedom, the reality of the plunge into nothingness. Man's freedom is the freedom for self-destruction as well as self-affirmation. All of this is in the potentiality of a genuine society. No order without chaos, no freedom without the possibility of distortion, no love without unlove as its threat and its shadow.

But God loves just this world, with its risk and its chaos, and us as we are. The trinity should not be used for a periodization of history, with separation into the ages of the Father, the Son, and the Spirit. That has always led to fanaticism. All the life of God is present in every age within the creative adventure, the one God who shares with the world in its life.

VIII

In trying to state the line upon which theology might advance today to meet the problems which underlie the present situation with its apparent confusion, I might seem to be claiming that all that is needed is some adjustment in the traditional doctrines in order to stem the polemics of the new humanism, to overcome the radical disbelief bred in the secular city, and to mitigate the destructive aspects of the clash of faiths. I intend to say nothing so foolish. What man's life is to be with God and without him in this century no one can see. It will be filled with anguish, tragedy, and great hope no matter what our theologies say. But theology is as necessary to man as breathing. It deals with the questions which are at the center of every human life in whatever language they may be put. It can interpret the anguish, and purge and support the hopes. In this new and difficult situation we can ask what has happened in the theological tradition, why it has happened, and then begin to see what we have to do.